DOGS AND LAMPPOSTS

Richard Stott

DOGS AND LAMPPOSTS

8th July, 2008

To Giles,

Happy reading!

Signed on behalf of my beloved husband

Penny Stott

Published by Metro Publishing
an imprint of John Blake Publishing Ltd
3 Bramber Court, 2 Bramber Road,
London W14 9PB, England

www.blake.co.uk

First published in paperback in 2007

ISBN: 978 1 84454 555 1

All rights reserved. No part of this publication may be reproduced, stored in a retrieval system, or in any form or by any means, without the prior permission in writing of the publisher, nor be otherwise circulated in any form of binding or cover other than that in which it is published and without a similar condition including this condition being imposed on the subsequent publisher.

British Library Cataloguing-in-Publication Data:

A catalogue record for this book is available from the British Library.

Design by www.envydesign.co.uk

Printed and bound by CPI Antony Rowe, Eastbourne

1 3 5 7 9 10 8 6 4 2

© Text copyright Richard Stott 2007

Papers used by John Blake Publishing are natural, recyclable products made from wood grown in sustainable forests. The manufacturing processes conform to the environmental regulations of the country of origin.

Every attempt has been made to contact the relevant copyright-holders, but some were unobtainable. We would be grateful if the appropriate people could contact us.

All profit from the sale of this book will be donated to the Pancreatic Cancer Research Fund.

*For Penny, without whom ...
And for Emily, Hannah,
Christopher and their cousins,
because of...*

RICHARD STOTT was an award-winning journalist who held five national newspaper editorships – a Fleet Street record. During his twelve years as an editor he was in charge of the *Daily Mirror* twice for a total of six years, the *People* twice and was the last editor of *Today*. He was the editor of the *Mirror* under Robert Maxwell and kept the paper going when scandal engulfed the Mirror Group after Maxwell's death and the subsequent revelation of his wholesale fraud and theft.

He was the British Press Awards Reporter of the Year in 1977 for his investigation of the Don Revie corruption and match-fixing scandal, and was shortlisted for three other awards in the Press 'Oscars', once for his investigation into the disappearance of Labour MP John Stonehouse and twice for his weekly column in the *News of the World*. During his three year editorship of *Today* he received the What the Papers Say Award for Editor of the Year in 1993.

Richard Stott died on 30 July 2007. He was 63.

CONTENTS

PREFACE	ix
CHAPTER 1	15
CHAPTER 2	33
CHAPTER 3	57
CHAPTER 4	87
CHAPTER 5	105
CHAPTER 6	117
CHAPTER 7	141
CHAPTER 8	173
CHAPTER 9	183
CHAPTER 10	203
CHAPTER 11	213
CHAPTER 12	229
CHAPTER 13	261
CHAPTER 14	277
CHAPTER 15	299
CHAPTER 16	321
CHAPTER 17	337
CHAPTER 18	357
EPILOGUE	369
APPENDIX	373
INDEX	379

PREFACE

When I started writing this book, I had no idea where it would lead me. I knew, of course, what had happened during four decades in journalism, an achievement not granted to everyone who spends more than 30 years in the Street of Shame in the shadow of El Vino, the enticing arms of the The Stab in the Back, or succumbing to the lethal Irish charm of John Mullally's Vagabonds. No, I wasn't sure what emotions, stirred by all the yellowing cuttings, acres of circulation figures, board minutes and diaries, would surface after so many years lying dormant in desk drawers, attic bin bags and cellar cardboard boxes, the accumulation of my three decades on the *Daily Mirror* as reporter, features editor and editor. Some of my *Mirror* documents hadn't seen the light of day since they were bundled up and dumped on my doorstep back in the winter of 1992. The Montgomery years were not rich in sensitive human relations.

In the end, I went through them all, anger, frustration and a painful self-examination as to what could have been done to avoid the twin horrors of Robert Maxwell and David Montgomery, two men who ruled the Mirror Group as their personal fiefdom with a mixture of fear and loathing. They had in common an unalterable belief that they were right and had godlike instincts and insights that would solve the problems of the Mirror Group. Then there were the mornings rocking with laughter at some remembered anecdote, some lunacy that lit up the day, often to do with Maxwell, so hopelessly demonised now that it is almost impossible to retrieve him as flesh and blood, even though he possessed an enormous amount of both. His corrosive influence is well known, but there was more to him than that. He was certainly a monster, but I have tried to recreate him, good bits and all, to show what positive things he did for an ageing and complacent newspaper group that had been neglected by successive managements and cowed by all-powerful trades unions. While I was writing this book, the Department of Trade and Industry finally published its investigation into the flotation of the Mirror Group, ten years after it was set up. As so often happens with DTI reports, it had been rendered irrelevant by time and the watering down of its findings by the consistent picking over of it by expensive lawyers representing powerful financial institutions. In spite of its marathon examination of the flotation, the inspectors' report fails to address the internal problems of the *Mirror*, the quality of Maxwell's board and why he managed to take over such a high-profile group. It remains true to this day that the biggest corporate fraud in British financial history did not produce one criminal conviction. Maxwell should never have been in a position to buy the Mirror Group in the first place. He survived the first DTI report in 1971 because he took on the trades unions at the British Printing Corporation and saved the NatWest bank £17 million when all seemed lost. After that, the die was cast, and with Reed International's management in despair over trade union avarice, it was only a matter of time before the *Mirror* was his.

For decades, the paper had been without a proprietor, although laymen may be forgiven for thinking Cecil King was one; he certainly did. The corporate approach was no match for an explosive industry where lost production could not be redeemed. Maxwell struck it lucky on two fronts. He bought the group for a song – £113 million, and the value of the Holborn Circus building alone accounted for most of that – and he entered Fleet Street at a time when computerisation and direct input by journalists had at last become a reality, spelling the end of the craft unions.

I have also tried to express the sense of betrayal felt by members of the staff towards the board of directors both under Maxwell and Montgomery, a betrayal felt even more keenly under the latter by journalists, because three of those directors were former newspaper editors. The extraordinary and senseless brutality of Montgomery's régime was outside the terms of reference of the Department of Trade investigation, and the pusillanimous actions of the Maxwell board went largely unremarked because the inspectors felt they had bigger fish to fry, although the biggest fish of all never got anywhere near the batter. The story of the last days of Maxwell and the months after his death is drawn not just from my own recollections and those of others, but from minutes of the then just publicly quoted Mirror plc, company documents and, after Maxwell's death, confidential reports to the board on what went wrong, where and why. They make startlingly different reading from the eventual DTI report and have the advantage of being compiled immediately after it was realised that not only had the pension fund been raided, but almost £100 million of company money had been removed in less than six months from right under the noses of the Mirror board.

This is not intended to be solely a story of what happened to the *Mirror* after Maxwell took over, although there is a lot of that. It is a trip through newspapers in the second half of the twentieth century as the electronic revolution first threatened and then overwhelmed the traditional methods of gathering news. Once again newspapers had to adapt, as they did to the advent of television. At the same time, there was a major cultural and political change with the arrival of Mrs Thatcher and her middle-class army. Shortly before her installation at Number Ten the *Sun* overtook the *Mirror* as Britain's largest-selling daily paper. This was not just because Rupert Murdoch startled and eventually subdued the *Mirror* with a bright, brash newspaper with a page-three topless girl, but also because he embraced the spirit of Thatcherism, as did many blue-collar workers in despair over what appeared to be an irrevocable split in the Labour Party, the right and left wings of which seemed to act as two separate parties.

Thatcher also took on the trades unions, initially reluctantly, after they used their enormous power in the late '70s to challenge the right of government to rule while ignoring the long-term wellbeing of their members. Labour was helpless in the face of such an assault and paid the penalty with 18 years in the wilderness. New Labour was born out of that turmoil – first Neil Kinnock of the soft left saved the party; in the short time available to him, John Smith consolidated it; and, finally, Tony Blair seized the centre ground. The consensus politics of pragmatism was upon us.

But consensus is no good for a paper like the *Daily Mirror*; it thrives on controversy, commitment, passion and strong opinions vehemently held. For much of its near 100 years of life, it has been in a minority, the voice of the small man against the monolith of government and the excesses of granite-faced bosses. In the 1960s and early '70s, under the increasingly uncertain and bibulous leadership of Hugh Cudlipp, it became the helpmate and, at times, co-conspirator, of a Labour Government, a role not conducive to red-blooded tabloid journalism, but by the 1980s it was able to revert to its role as a thorn in the side of the otherwise all-conquering Mrs Thatcher. However she also ushered in a new affluent, car-owning, council house-buying, working-class. In its wake, inevitably, came the 'me first, sod you' society. A swaggering new generation which, together with older blue-collar workers who felt betrayed by the trades unions, formed an enormous alternative market to the *Mirror* for Rupert Murdoch's *Sun*, which perfectly reflected their mood under the editorships of Larry Lamb and Kelvin MacKenzie. Although outsold by the *Sun*, the '80s were still good days for the *Mirror* because we were the opposition. By the '90s, the mood had changed again as the country tired of Thatcherism and realised that the tyranny of the Great God Market was as divisive as any other kind of tyranny.

The 1970s, however, ushered in a new era of reporting, more investigative, querulous, iconoclastic. I took full advantage of it, investigating the affairs of ministers such as Reggie Maudling, Ernie Marples and John Stonehouse, the MP who faked his death and hot-footed it to Australia. It brought me up against the wrath of the law, the Establishment and the Prime Minister, and at times it could be lonely and intimidating. But the overriding sense was one of exhilaration. Whenever you were told, leave it alone, you're playing with fire, print that and you're dead (as in career, not life – at least I think it was), you knew you were on course. On all three investigations I was warned off by a selection of the above. It was to be a good training ground for editing.

Tabloid newspapers are all vying for the middle ground now, and the vast masses of the middle class – Worcester man, Mondeo man, Richard and Judy woman, what used to be Marks and Spencer woman. But the trouble with everyone standing in the middle of the road is that someone is going to get knocked over. The newspaper which has been consistently the most successful is the *Daily Mail*, and it has adopted an increasingly right-wing isolationist stance. Much of the *Mail*'s success is down to the enormous investment sunk into it and its sister paper, the *Mail on Sunday*. But it is also iconoclastic, a voice of ranting protest in a world increasingly dominated by public relations, sound-bite, and presentational glib and glitz: one where the untouchables of modern tabloid journalism are Mark Bolland, Prince Charles's spin doctor and Max Clifford, fixer to the stars. Even editors bow down before them in the hope of scraps from their clients' tables where truth is not always on the menu but image manipulation is. You do not have to agree with much of its strident right-wing campaigns to admire its flavour, commitment and readiness to plough its own furrow.

It is an easier task to do that on the right than it is on the left, but on the left is where the heart and home of the *Mirror* should be and, when you are staring a circulation of less than two million in the face, at home is a good place to be. There is a genuine debate to be had over the New Labour pragmatic approach to politics. There are serious questions to be asked about Tony Blair's consensus, his achievements and ideals, and it is not surprising that the *Mirror* over the past traumatic decade has found itself sometimes floundering in the same debate.

New Labour's first term in office was tentative and vague, in spite of genuine progress made on child poverty, unemployment and welfare reform, however timid. It is the *Mirror*'s historic job – done with varying degrees of certainty over the years – to articulate where Labour governments waffle, to demand action where ministers dither, to present fearless and muscular argument and campaigns for those too weak or poor to speak for themselves in a world dominated increasingly by presentation, self-interest and the influence of big money. The *Sun* now supports Tony Blair, unsurely and often without conviction, and it has managed to change since the wild days of MacKenzie without losing too much circulation, but it is a paler version of the paper it once was.

The *Mirror* is frequently a superior package, but it has to be more than that; it must remain the conscience of the best of Old Labour while embracing the best of the New. Like Tony Blair, its record on that has been a little wobbly. It needs to fight privilege, injustice, poverty, unemployment and the iniquities of an unfair society which sees the rich getting richer and the poor poorer at a faster rate than anywhere else in first-world Europe. The *Sun* will not do that, it is an altogether different animal, and will go where the interests of Rupert Murdoch's News Corporation takes it. News Corp is its own focus group, the *Sun* is its own consensus.

The *Mirror*'s owners Trinity Mirror have an unenviable job. Not only do they have to deal with the bruising legacy of Maxwell and Montgomery, they also have has to take on the baggage of a once great newspaper, the best days of which were almost half-a-century ago. Media commentators – those 'sad anoraks' as Brian MacArthur of the *Times* so aptly described them – are notoriously inaccurate and badly informed when discussing the 'great days of Cudlipp's *Mirror*'.

Few commentators have ever looked at those issues which are, for the most part, parochial, thin, unexciting and cosy. Not wonderful journalism perhaps, but the paper of the '50s did speak for simpler people in a simpler time. By the time the *Mirror* hit a circulation of five million in 1964, the people were beginning to speak for themselves, and Hugh Cudlipp – whose interventions in the paper he never edited were intermittent and often capricious – had lost the plot. This book begins as the *Mirror*'s star is beginning to wane, taking over where Maurice Edelman's *The Mirror: A Political History*, left off. In almost a century of existence, no paper has been so roundly abused, envied, hated, derided, ridiculed and, occasionally, praised and admired. In its time, the *Mirror* has probably deserved it all.

I have taken the title of this book from H.L. Mencken's famous observation that the relationship between the journalist and the politician is the same as that between a dog and a lamppost. Yes, but both want to be the dog and occasionally both are prepared to put up with being the lamppost. The two professions are quite capable of spells in the gutter, and for journalists it is not a bad place from which to observe the stars. 'Journalists belong in the gutter,' said Gerald Priestland in an *Observer* article in 1988, 'because that is where the ruling classes throw their guilty secrets.' Quite so. I reckon that my career can be neatly divided between Dog and Lamppost. As a reporter I was the dog, and quite a few politicians finished up with wet trousers, but editors can often be both and, with Maxwell as proprietor, the lamppost was often drenched. At least as a columnist I got to do the watering again. So here is the life of one journalist with at least one foot where it should be – in the gutter.

There are many people who have assisted me with this book, but Fleet Street can be a spiteful place so they all remain anonymous. They know who they are. I hope when they have read it they think their help worthwhile. To them, my grateful thanks.

Moreover, no editor's life would be bearable without a brilliant personal assistant, personal traffic warden and secretary. For 15 years, from my appointment as *Mirror* features editor, Gill Hemburrow was about as perfect as it is possible to be. She coped with Maxwell at his most unpleasant, and *Mirror* staff at all times, with good humour and was more than a match for those who thought they could take her on. She even coped with life under Montgomery, although she despised everything his régime stood for, before making the cultural leap and moving to Wapping to join me at *Today*. To her, my heartfelt thanks.

None of this adventure would have been possible without my family, as the dedication shows, and the constant support of Penny, my wife for 32 years, still here with her feet firmly on the pavement. Whatever happened to me in the Street of Shame, she has remained on the sidewalk when all about her were slipping and sliding. We have three great children all of whom have decided to take the rocky road – Emily as an actress; Hannah as a Sky TV presenter; and behind-the-scenes writer and sub-editor, Christopher, heading off towards the media and film world after obtaining his degree at Goldsmith's.

My thanks, too, to the carnival of fools, conmen, comedians and knaves who people our newspapers. And to the circus of clowns, lion-tamers, high-wire acts, jugglers, ring-masters, contortionists, tumblers, geniuses and drunks of whom I have been a part for so long. It may not be a proper job but, by God, forty years of trying to read between the lines has certainly been a bit of fun. And, after all, what else can we do?

1

It's not every day you have the chance to bring down the British monarchy. But there was no doubt about it, the rather elderly coffee-stained cassette in my hand might well do just that . Not only was Prince Charles clearly caught indulging in an affair he swore blind existed only in the mind of his demented wife and a few tabloid newspaper journalists, but there was the heir to the throne quite clearly explaining in his strange, strangled voice that it was just his luck to turn into a Tampax. 'My luck to be chucked down the lavatory, and go on and on for ever, swirling round on the top, never going down.'

Now what the hell do you do with that? Publish and be damned? You probably would be. He certainly would. But a Privacy Bill would have been the price for running what became known as the Camilla Tape and, given the febrile state of the monarchy on that summer day in 1992, only a few weeks after Diana had launched her sabotage attempt through the medium of Andrew Morton's book, Charles could quite easily have taken the monarchy down the pan with him.

Here was the Prince of Wales – according to his staff, a paragon of virtue, a diligent husband trying to save his mentally disturbed wife from herself and her wild delusions that he was having an affair with his old flame, Camilla Parker Bowles – talking dirty to the woman he had always claimed was nothing more than a dear, loyal friend. This dear friend, he said, he needed several times a week. He wanted to live inside her trousers ... he yearned for her ... he wanted to feel his way along her ... all over, up and down ... in and out. Good God, what had we been given?

The tape sounded like a particularly far-fetched episode of *Spitting Image*. It was funny, but it was too embarrassing to laugh. If true, the *Daily Mirror* had been handed the proof that not only was Charles having an affair with Camilla, but that he had consistently lied about it, and so had his detectives, Scotland Yard and his advisers. For it was inconceivable that his bodyguards had not passed on the true state of his marriage, but his affair, too. We knew the bodyguards turned a blind eye to a bit of extra-marital philandering because there was pictorial proof of Fergie's poolside dallying with John Bryan while the Yard's finest lolled around nursing their suntans. Yet the official position was that Charles and Diana needed time to repair their marriage in the wake of the Morton book, that the Prince was showing the utmost patience in dealing with a wife on the threshold of madness and that they needed space and time together to prepare for a royal tour of South Korea.

By the back end of 1992, Buckingham Palace was into desperate damage limitation and courtiers were compromising themselves with increasingly desperate abandon. Penny Junor, a Charles journalistic groupie, published an 'authorised' version of the Charles and Diana story in a vain effort to repair some of the damage done by Morton's book and the Princess's co-operation and undisguised hostility towards her husband and his family. The Junor series, published in the *Today* newspaper, was submitted to Charles's office for a view and the word came back – publish. In this version, Diana was painted as secretive, neurotic and obsessed with Charles's 'wholly innocent' relationship with Camilla. HE WILL NOT DENOUNCE DIANA, HE KNOWS SHE'S UNWELL, read the headline.

At the same time, James Whitaker, the redoubtable *Mirror* royal correspondent, talked to Charles's right-hand man, Commander Richard Aylard, about Junor's report, although at the time he did not know the Palace had approved it.

'No, the Prince didn't want to do anything,' said Aylard. 'He is worried about the Princess's volatile and emotional state and thinks it is unfair to attack her.' It was obvious, said Whitaker, that Aylard intended the briefing to be used, and it was.

Aylard was by no means the only person in the Prince's côterie to stoke the fires against the Princess. Nicholas Soames, then a junior minister and once an equerry to Charles, never let an opportunity go by to knock her in private, often to the *Mirror*'s political editor Alastair Campbell, himself no Diana fan and no great enthusiast for the Royal Family. It was no wonder she was in a distressed mental state; she had real and justified fears that the Palace was trying to turn her into a basket case in order to save the reputation of the heir to the throne. The more she protested about his relationship with Camilla, the more the courtiers whispered against her. Buckingham Palace was desperate to keep the lid on a scandal threatening to blow away the monarchy and the royal tour of South Korea was seen as vital in bringing a new stability to the Royal Family and, more specifically, the royal marriage. In order to stop any more damaging revelations editors and royal correspondents were told to give Charles and Diana space to rebuild their relationship – an old stand-by, that was used in the dying days of the relationship between Fergie and Prince Andrew.

In this climate there was no way we could run the Charles and Camilla tape, although by the time the royal tour had started Harry Arnold, a first-rate veteran royal reporter, had established beyond doubt that it was genuine. There were sufficient clues in the conversation – one of Camilla's children's birthdays; the strike of late 1989 by ambulance drivers in which Andrew Parker Bowles was playing a part in keeping emergency ambulances on the road – to convince us that it was indeed Charles and Camilla. We also had it technically checked to make sure it wasn't spliced-together excerpts – just as well, as the Palace whisperers, including Charles himself, were to claim it had been cobbled together by clever forgers from scraps of several conversations.

The truth, as usual in such sensational disclosures, was altogether more prosaic. In the early hours of Monday, 18 December 1989, only 13 days before Diana's own taped conversation with James Gilbey – 'Squidgygate' – Charles was on a mobile and speaking from Eaton Hall, Cheshire, the stately home of his great friend the Duke of Westminster, Britain's richest man, where he was staying overnight at Eaton Lodge, one of the cottages on the estate. Camilla was at her home in Corsham, Wiltshire.

The alternative Charles scenario about the tape – again articulated by the devoted Junor – was that somehow the security services arranged it for reasons that remain unclear or, alternatively, the Junor preference, that Diana did it herself because she had sophisticated bugging equipment available at Kensington Palace. In fact, the tape was made by a Scouser who had had a few pints of lager and a curry and decided he would test out his latest gadget, an electronic homing device that picks up cellnet signals. As the time was around 2.00am there weren't too many about, so he homed straight into Charles and Camilla.

'This bloke was reading a speech and I didn't pay too much attention,' he said, 'until I realised it sounded very like Prince Charles. That's when I decided to record it and straight away he started out with all this stuff. I couldn't believe it.'

The tape remained a party piece until the *Sun* ran the Squidygate chat with Gilbey. Our man then decided to sell his hot potato to the *Mirror* and walked into our Manchester office with it. No spies, no conspiracy, like most of history's eye-openers, straightforward bad luck.

All the royal tapes – Diana, Charles, Fergie, the Duke of Edinburgh –

were made within a comparatively short time, in between this particular search scanner becoming available and the royal minders' realisation that mobile phone conversations could be picked up by them.

As the Prince and Princess flew off to South Korea, the Camilla tape remained firmly under lock and key. We certainly could not run it with Buckingham Palace telling the world this was the comeback tour, the time when the couple would try and put their battered marriage back together again, with Charles naturally in the lead role of wise counsellor and adviser to his wife, calling on all the reserves of forbearance, compassion and understanding with which his staff was so keen to invest him. Now we knew different. The Prince, Scotland Yard and therefore Buckingham Palace's senior advisers knew he was living a lie, that the Princess, however neurotic, ill and disturbed, was right about the central fault-line of their marriage. Charles had been having an affair with Camilla and continued to do so whenever he could. The lengths to which he would go in order to spend a night with her were exhaustive, as the tape revealed. Both were prepared to dupe their partners in order to be together. To this end they engaged the connivance and demanded the deceit of friends, some of whom professed to be close to both the Prince and the Princess. All this was revealed by the tape which I finally took to an eminent QC; it was worth it to see the look of shock and alarm on his face as he confirmed the obvious. It was proof of adultery by the Prince of Wales with Camilla Parker Bowles, the wife of a fellow Army officer. So Charles could be court-martialled as well!

The royal tour of South Korea was a disaster from start to finish, played out in front of a fascinated and appalled world. It was clear that Charles and Diana loathed each other and were seriously unhappy; the pictures were so grotesque they became known as 'The Glums'. The Palace gamble had failed disastrously and the royals were once again the laughing stock of the world. It was time to put the record straight, but how to do the story without bringing a Privacy Bill in its wake?

MPs and press watchdogs were already yapping over publication of previous tapes, encouraged by an ill-judged outburst against Andrew Neil's *Sunday Times* by the Chairman of the Press Complaints Commission, Lord McGregor, over the paper's serialisation of the Morton book. It was, he said, 'journalists dabbling their fingers in the stuff of other people's souls'.

We were about to dabble with parts more private and ticklish than their souls. The nature of our tape was bound to make matters worse because it was so intimate that anyone who listened to or read about it felt like a voyeur. On the other hand, it was final proof of Charles's giant and audacious confidence trick on his wife and the British people; he was living a secret life while using some of his most intimate friends to keep it so. At the same time, the Royal Family still maintained it set the standards of family life for the country. We had to publish. But how, if we were to avoid the traditional fate of messengers bearing unwelcome tidings.

At this time – the winter of 1992 – little was known about Camilla Parker Bowles, so I decided to run a series on her called *Camilla Confidential* in which we described her as Charles's lover and quoted selectively from the tape without admitting we had one. Both Charles and Camilla would be quoted directly. For example, 'Your great achievement is to love me,' appeared just like that with no explanation of how we had obtained the quote. Harry Arnold put the series together and it made one hell of a read, but it wasn't until the third day that anyone realised we must have a tape in order to publish the confidential – not to mention scandalous – matters we were revealing. From Buckingham and St James's Palaces there was a stony silence. The full tape was gradually revealed as details leaked from the *Mirror* and the whole of it was run from the United States to Australia. There wasn't a whisper about a Privacy Bill but the contents of the conversation not only vindicated Diana's suspicions of Charles's behaviour, but provided the evidence she needed to leave him. Six weeks later I saw her on a plane to Antigua where she – much to the consternation of Fleet Street's royal watchers – was travelling economy class in a seat next to the lavatories. By this time her separation had been announced.

'How are you?' I asked.

'Fine,' she said. 'And you?'

'Not bad,' I replied, although I was still feeling a bit sore because I had been sacked as editor of the *Daily Mirror*, one of the early victims of the ethnic cleansing of David Montgomery's post-Maxwell reign as Chief Executive.

'Oh, and by the way,' she said as I turned to leave, 'Thanks.'

During the Golden Jubilee celebrations the royals went to great lengths to airbrush Diana and her memory from the picture whilst Mrs Parker Bowles was subtly insinuated into the big events. This was coupled with strategically-placed old friends of the Queen who popped up on documentary tributes making sure they missed no opportunity to stress how difficult Diana was. The public relations offensive to smooth Mrs Parker Bowles' progress – and paper over the extent of Charles's double-life a decade and more earlier – worked as well as the prince's image machine could have wished, so in order to understand the depths of Charles's mendacity and his willingness to risk his own reputation and family, as well as that of Mrs Parker Bowles, the tape should be read as a whole (see Appendix). It is not only a fascinating insight into this self-pitying, petulant and self-absorbed man, but a salutary lesson in how the Royal Family is capable of claiming to be one thing and exhorting us all to follow their example – remember the Queen's millennium Christmas message in which we were told that she had brought up her family to adhere strictly to the teachings and values of Christianity – while going to the most elaborate lengths to behave in quite another. It is a failing that remains with us.

The received wisdom in Buckingham Palace is that the mystique surrounding the Royal Family began to fall apart with the making of the 1960s film about their family life, a project enthusiastically supported by the Duke of Edinburgh in a laudable effort to show that the family was a real one. By today's standards it was harmless enough and attracted a bumper audience of people marvelling that the royals actually did things like organise their own barbecues. It was uncontroversial, good fun television and did the image nothing but good. The problem went much deeper. Britain changed for ever in the 1960s with the arrival of a young generation that discovered its own power economically and culturally. Its voice was raucous, persuasive, selfish, decadent and at once both supremely sure and unsure of itself. No longer would that uncomfortable time between childhood and emerging from National Service as obedient adults be the space occupied by carping school teachers, furtive teenage fumblings and bullying drill corporals. The Rock Revolution was upon us; so were Peter Cook, *That Was the Week That Was*, David Frost, mini-skirts, the Pill, Twiggy, teenagers commanding a million pounds and the football genius of George Best. In the next decade the Royal Family was going to become increasingly irrelevant and, slowly, newspapers began to recognise the fact. However, the power of the Windsors was still awesome.

In the mid 1970s, Princess Anne went on a trip to East Africa with the *Blue Peter* presenter Valerie Singleton. The *Mirror*'s Paula James, an excellent, if acerbic, reporter, went with them. It was not a happy time, particularly when Paula described the proceedings as Princess Anne attending Valerie Singleton's royal tour of Africa. A good joke, but the Palace was not amused. Complaints were made to the editor and, to the *Mirror*'s shame, Paula was withdrawn from the tour. It was not the last time the might of Fleet Street's pen was to be blunted by sabre-rattling from the big house at the end of The Mall, but the high water mark of excessive fealty to the throne had been reached.

By the end of the 1970s interest in the royals had fallen to an all-time low, to such an extent that a visit by the Queen to Scandinavia was not attended by one single news organisation. Newspapers, like the country, were bored with a family that was becoming increasingly old, crotchety and bald. Mass TV was giving us *Morecambe and Wise*, *The Two Ronnies*, *Monty Python*, punk rock and *Starsky and Hutch*, a clutch of dowdy men and women in pearls and garters came well down the bill. Then Diana happened and in the next decade the Royal Family was thrust once again to the centre of the stage. The trouble was, it hadn't changed and had no idea of the nature or the ferocity of the force that was now with them. Diana brought with her *Dynasty* and *Dallas*, from padded shoulders to improbable plot lines. Old jealousies resurfaced, new ones were forged and the cast was augmented by the arrival of Fergie, the oversexed, wicked sister-in-law, a must for any successful long-running soap. The country was hooked, but the old stars carried on as if nothing had happened to the old music hall act. Indeed they still believed, in spite of all the evidence to the contrary, that the Royal Family was the star when in fact they were all bit-part players to the one truly great international TV superstar who had been brought into the storyline because Charles's role was fading and they needed to sort him out. Instead the bit-part player took over the show.

It was this failure to understand the power of Diana that brought about the royals' disasters. Charles at first became irritated and then sullen as he heard the groans of crowds when they realised they had drawn the short straw of walkabouts and had chosen his side of the road. He, like the rest of the family, had never had to play second fiddle to anyone, never mind a mentally fragile girl. Their reaction was frosty, and as she grew more unhappy and ill, an air of haughty disdain took over. The Queen and Prince Philip ignored her increasingly eccentric and desperate behaviour, while Charles, forever looking for someone else to take the blame for his own shortcomings, blamed his parents for not being more supportive.

The sub-plot was developing nicely. The royals were now attended by the Rat Pack, Fleet Street reporters whose job it was to monitor and report their every move for a voracious public and demanding editors. This group was both despised and underestimated by the Palace and the broadsheet newspapers. In fact, they were top-rate, hard-working reporters and photographers with long and keen noses for a story. The

Palace stored up trouble for itself by consistently denying reports which later turned out to be true. This in turn led to some stories being printed, usually speculation about a royal pregnancy, which weren't true because nobody would trust a Palace denial.

When Robin Janvrin – now Sir Robin and the Queen's private secretary – was appointed her press secretary, I took him to lunch with James Whitaker in an attempt to resolve this. I said I would read him any big story we wrote before publication and accept his guidance as to whether it was right or wrong. If he denied the story, I would accept his denial without question, but if it subsequently emerged he had lied, I would publish the details of our conversation. He accepted the rules and, several months later, Whitaker wrote that Princess Anne and Mark Phillips were to separate and an announcement was to be made at the end of the week. I called Janvrin, reminded him of our agreement and read him the story.

'Give me half-an-hour,' he said.

Twenty minutes later he was back. 'Can you change "the end of the week" to "imminent"?' he asked.

If only relations between Palace and press had remained so simple.

Meanwhile, the juvenile leads were warming up. The relationship between Fergie and Prince Andrew was too hot not to cool down. She was an impulsive, physical, essentially warm human being, all the things that make Buckingham Palace deeply suspicious. Prince Andrew, who had discovered the delights of the actress Koo Stark – when the *Mirror* first revealed this romance we had to hold up publication for a day because we couldn't find any suitable pictures in our library of her clothed – was a good-time boy, constantly in search of a leg-over, which suited Fergie fine. But she found the rest of the family, apart from the Queen who was attracted to her uncomplicated outdoor jollity as a refreshing change to the difficult Diana, pretty tough going. The Duke of Edinburgh was particularly scathing, as were the senior courtiers whose natural Upstairs snobbery recognised a gal from Downstairs when they saw one. She was not to disappoint them, revealing her affair with John Bryan, an American spiv and man on the make, in the most spectacular yet totally Fergie way with the topless swimming pool pictures, more than 100 of which found their way into the pages of the *Mirror*, providing us with the most extraordinary public feeding frenzy in newspaper history.

John Bryan masqueraded as Fergie's 'financial adviser', but he was clearly a conman type with an eye on the main chance. And Fergie was certainly that. He told anyone who cared to listen that he was working on getting Andrew and Fergie back together again and pleaded with the royal rat pack to give them space, that well-tried royal ploy. He even went to the lengths of turning up at James Whitaker's home to give him an 'in-depth background briefing' about the situation. What he was really doing was trying to make sure Fergie's upcoming holiday in France wasn't monitored. The couple needed privacy to mend some fences, time to get to know each other again, he said. Yes, he was speaking on behalf of the Duchess, but very unofficially, you understand.

His timing was immaculate, as both Fleet Street and the Palace were still reeling from the effects of the Morton book and similar signals were being sent out about the attempts to sort out Charles and Diana. Newspapers were on the twin horns of a dilemma – we could face the backlash of blame for the destruction of two royal marriages, so Bryan and Fergie got their way. Or they would have done if it hadn't have been for the assiduous attention to detail of the French paparazzi who discovered her arrival at a minor French airport and tracked her down, following her to the remote French farmhouse where her affair with Bryan was about to become news around the world.

To begin with the French photographic team didn't realise what they had snapped. The first call went to Whitaker who was told that they had topless pictures of Fergie by a swimming pool. On the face of it this was a problem for us. The *Mirror* had dropped glamour pictures – there were no readers' complaints – and was very iffy about gratuitous topless beach pictures. Nonetheless, if Fergie was sporting herself topless in front of her Scotland Yard minders, the pictures were certainly worth checking out. When he saw what they were, Whitaker, excitable at the best of times, was beside himself. He didn't want to tell me over the phone, but they were dynamite. Two days later, 117 photographs were spread over my kitchen table and James had already eaten a breakfast intended for five.

He was right, they were sensational. There was Bryan snogging Fergie, giving her no peace and certainly no space and proving what a natural born liar he was. But there was a problem. The pictures had been sold to *Paris Match* and we had to wait for four days; waiting meant leaks and leaks meant Bryan and other newspapers would get to hear about what we had. Which is exactly what happened. The *Sun* tried to rip us off by paying printers in Spain to hand over copies and Bryan attempted to have the pictures banned by a court order, a plan that worked in France where a draconian privacy law is ruthlessly exploited.

In England, he lost, but from the court hearing it was clear he had no idea how damning the pictures were and we had no intention of disabusing him. He thought they were purely topless shots of Fergie. It wasn't until midnight, when Bryan saw the first edition of the next day's paper that he realised the full horror. 'Oh my God,' he exploded when he realised, and phoned the bad news through to the Duchess who was staying with the Queen at Balmoral. The breakfast up there the next morning must have been a corker.

The reaction to what became known as the 'toe sucking' pictures – in fact, he never did suck her toes – was extraordinary. Bryan's dash to the High Court had ensured maximum TV exposure, something that would have cost millions to buy, and the *Mirror* sold out of its print run which had already been extended to cope with the expected rush. But we had hopelessly underestimated and had to start reprinting the paper at 8.00am in order to produce another 400,000 copies, something that hadn't happened since the end of the Second World War. Papers were changing hands at £5 a go, which was a damn sight more than the company shares in that immediately post-Maxwell era. In the course of three days, we sold an extra 1,500,000 copies. The *Mirror* had bought not only a sensation but a bargain; we paid a rock-bottom price for the exclusive British rights.

In France, the story was quite different. The photographer was fined and the pictures banned in yet another Gallic triumph over the public's right to know. If there is anyone left in Britain who thinks the French have the right idea then they should look at the mess they got themselves in over the scandal of President Mitterrand's illegitimate daughter. Many in the French press knew of his second family but conspired to cover it up until Mitterrand himself decided to stage manage the revelation of her existence shortly before he died. France was convulsed, and an embarrassed media had a lot of explaining to do. Meanwhile, the daughter, 22-year-old Mazarine Pingeot, cashed in by publishing a thinly-disguised autobiographical novel.

There are two approaches available to those who wish to protect their privacy. The first is by claiming straightforward invasion of privacy under the European Human Rights Act; the other is claiming breach of confidence, usually by a disaffected employee. It was by this route that Prince Charles tried to send me to jail for publishing part of one of the best and most revealing books on the royals by a former member of their household. Mrs Wendy Berry was housekeeper at Highgrove and saw the fights between Diana and Charles at first hand. The book is full of insights and anecdotes and remains the only truly independent account of the disintegration of the Wales's marriage. But it is much more, presenting a below-stairs view of them upstairs which would warm the cockles of republicans' hearts. Charles had the book banned in Britain, preventing

Mrs Berry revealing anything she found out while working in his employment at Highgrove. It sounds fair enough, except that what Mrs Berry had to say was not only pertinent to the truth of the Wales's marriage – which both of them had talked about at length publicly for their own purposes – but had been published throughout the world. Much of her book dealt with material already printed in Britain, but it was the anecdotal evidence of everyday life which was so damning.

In the United States, the book sold more than 100,000 copies and extracts were printed all over Europe, Australia and Japan, as well as on the Internet. Only the people who foot the bill for the royals were not allowed to know what they got up to behind the iron railings. I believed, quite wrongly as it turned out, that because Peter Wright's *Spycatcher* had been published here on the grounds that it was already available to the rest of the world, the same would be true of Mrs Berry. Wrong, and the Attorney General on behalf of the Prince set out to stick me in the slammer.

Mrs Berry was prevented from publishing in Britain on the grounds of confidentiality, something that, as we have seen earlier, Charles is quite prepared to waive when he thinks it is in his interest to do so. Nor were the Palace panjandrums worried about the book written by Diana's private secretary Patrick Jephson, who was given tacit approval by the Queen's private secretary Sir Robert Fellowes to write a 'well balanced' book which the Palace would 'vet for accuracy'. In other words a book that showed Sir Robert, his mates and employers in a good light. No problem with confidentiality there, old boy. One rule for Upstairs, quite another for Downstairs.

Mrs Berry's book is considerably better than Jephson's, so if you can find a copy in the United States snap it up, it's a great read. It is a sobering thought that while Jephson was free to do the chat show circuit to help flog his book, Mrs Berry was forced to live as a fugitive, condemned to be sent to jail if she returned to Britain, and was liable to have all her money and possessions taken away if the law so ordained.

In my case, the judge told me I was lucky to avoid the slammer and fined me £25,000, a bill mercifully picked up by *Today*, the newspaper I was editing at the time. Yet it remains ludicrous and against all natural justice that a couple who, over a prolonged period of time, quite deliberately set about destroying their own and each other's privacy and confidentiality and who encouraged their employees to do the same for their own narrow and selfish advantage, should be given such blanket protection by law. It is the far-reaching consequences of this that have always made politicians shrink from introducing privacy legislation, for however it is framed they will always be open to the criticism that they are protecting themselves and the rich and powerful from the gaze of us lesser beings. The right to sleep soundly in someone else's bed and to cajole people to do what you say while preserving the right to do quite the opposite yourself is a privilege fiercely protected by rulers and royals alike, and we forfeit the right to expose it at our communal peril.

Politicians can at least be held accountable for legislation they seek to introduce; judges cannot. And it is through the judicial back door that privacy legislation is being introduced by stealth. The European Human Rights Act enshrines two principles among others; the right to freedom of speech and the right to privacy, principles that are often mutually exclusive. So far, privacy is winning and the right to know is being steadily whittled away by an unelected, often unrepresentative and largely unaccountable judiciary. Judges are not noted for the protection of freedom of speech or the right of newspapers to know, and the European Human Rights Act has given them the chance to introduce privacy legislation that has neither been publicly discussed nor approved.

Under rulings made by the judges, it was decided that the rights of Michael Douglas and Catherine Zeta Jones to sell their wedding outweighed the right of anyone to take an 'unauthorised' picture of it. That right was even extended to include Douglas's right to doctor pictures he didn't consider portrayed a satisfactory image of himself. This ruling is so perverse that it is at odds with Lord Denning's decision in 1977 when he allowed Chris Hutchins, the then public relations man of Tom Jones and Englebert Humperdinck, to publish his account of their antics and sexual exploits specifically because what he had to say exploded their carefully cultivated image. It is difficult enough for newspapers nowadays to penetrate the artifice of the PR man and spin doctor without having to cope with the courts weighing in, too.

By the end of the first year of the Human Rights Act, we had reached the stage where a picture taken of a surviving Siamese twin on public ground from a public place was banned because the family had done an expensive financial deal with another set of newspapers. But this was taken much further by Mr Justice Jack, who ruled that sexual affairs were bound by a pact of confidentiality, even though the footballer in question Blackburn Rovers' Garry Flitcroft, was about to be exposed for conducting two flagrantly public affairs. It is hardly surprising the appeal court jibbed at that one and reversed the decision

A story of one more randy footballer may be neither here nor there.

But this is not how stealth legislation works. The law is remade gradually by a succession of decisions, and what newspapers were given back by the Flitcroft ruling was chipped away again by the decision to back Naomi Campbell in her breach of confidence action against the *Daily Mirror*, even though the model resorted to perjury in order the attain it. The rule now seems to be that you can reveal a celebrity's drug addiction, but not the details of it. The signals are confusing, but the rash of rulings under European law mean that it is, at the very least, now arguable whether the Camilla tape or the Fergie pictures could have been published in Britain, although you could publish the fact of Charles's adultery or Fergie's affair. This is pedantic nonsense, as the details of both the tape and the pictures respectively reveal so much about the nature of the liaisons and the cavernous gap between public face and private conduct. It isn't just the royals who would rush for judgment. Adulterous ministers like David Mellor, a keen supporter of John Major's Back to Basics campaign, would have almost certainly tried to ban the story of his dalliance with an actress. Of course, newspapers could argue a public interest defence, but if their past record is anything to go by the judges would be much more likely to lean towards the Royal Family than a mass circulation newspaper. The judges might claim they are doing only what the politicians should have the guts to do themselves, that the people want it. But there is actually no evidence they do. When we published the John Bryan and Fergie pictures the Queen's first public reaction was to accuse the *Mirror* of a gross invasion of privacy in the hope, presumably, of shooting the messenger. It didn't work – there were no public complaints and the overwhelming reaction was that readers were delighted we had seen through the lies and pretence.

The same was true when we exposed Charles's lies over Camilla. The tape was an invasion of their privacy, but that was trumped by the astonishing catalogue of deceit, hypocrisy, conspiracy, humbug and contemptuous misleading of the British public that had been conducted for years by the Royal Family and their willing conspirators among Buckingham Palace's senior courtiers. Such scandal is unlikely to be uncovered by a cosy off-the-record chat with the Queen's private secretary or the Archbishop of Canterbury.

In the years following the death of Diana – in which the royals had a hand by removing her HRH and therefore the protection of the British Embassy in Paris – Buckingham Palace, and particularly Charles, has discovered a new rapier to supplement the blunderbuss of suppression. The spin doctor reached the St James's Palace, headquarters of the Prince of Wales, in the silken shape of Mark Bolland, a former director of the Press Complaints Commission who, however, continued to maintain his links by living with his successor, the equally feline Guy Black. Bolland learnt his black art at the knee – figuratively of course – of Peter Mandelson, and he mirrors many of his attributes, acting both subtly and invisibly to influence editors. He rarely stoops lower; royal reporters are for the press officers. Bolland is a man who lunches, who lets drop the little indiscretion, answers questions with the barely perceptible raising of an eyebrow, expresses distaste and disapproval with the glint of stiletto. It is Bolland's job to rehabilitate Prince Charles and make Camilla acceptable as consort initially and then, if he can, as Charles's wife. The ultimate goal is to see her crowned Queen although all accept this is, for the moment, reaching for the moon. But that is the game plan and Bolland plays it the hilt. He is skilled, witty and holds selected editors in the palm of his hand. Stroke him and you will get a story; displease him and you are out of the loop. Needless to say, few are prepared to write that Bolland is behind Charles's leaks, whether it be that the Queen has met Camilla or that the heir to the throne is mightily displeased with brother Edward over the attempts to film Prince William. Much is known of Charles's attitude to Edward thanks to Bolland. His strategy is working, too; Charles is gradually being rehabilitated in the public mind as time begins to fade Diana's memory. Even the potentially disastrous scandal involving Prince Harry's drug taking and heavy drinking was turned to Charles's advantage. The *News of the World*, which had painstakingly investigated the problem for months, clearly had more information than it eventually divulged. The paper's editor, Rebekah Wade, was criticised for doing a deal with the Palace, but this criticism is misplaced, she was right to settle for publishing in part rather than being prevented from publishing anything by legal constraints or threats of injunctions. Where she went wrong was to run with the story a toe-curlingly cringing leader praising Charles as a father, when it was apparent from her own report that he had been anything but.

Less than a decade after the *Sun* and the *Mirror* exposed the decadence and greed of the royals which nearly brought them down, Bolland and Black managed to arrange that the tenth anniversary party of the Press Complaints Commission was attended by Charles, Camilla and Prince William. Editors vied for a quiet confidential word with each of them, forgetting that their job was to be on the outside looking in at the party, not wrestling each other for invitations to Highgrove while the royals and the PCC congratulated them on how well behaved they had been since

Diana's death. All nonsense, of course; the truth is that the royals don't sell papers as they did when Diana was alive. If they did, the guest list for that PCC party might have been rather different. Diana's death has changed very little; all the fine talk about not using paparazzi pictures is humbug. The *Daily Mail*, which took the lead in pledging not to use them, now uses more than anyone else.

The royals haven't changed either, in spite of all the weasel words. Charles blames his bad times on the press, complaining that most of the proprietors are based abroad – true when the old Rothermere was alive and Conrad Black maintained his Canadian citizenship – but not so much now. Anyway, his real target was Rupert Murdoch, the one newspaper baron who has continued to view the royals with a mixture of cynicism and contempt they have done much to deserve.

The heir to the throne continues to lecture us about the quality of life in Britain today, he lectures his brother about not mixing business with royalty and demands that the House of Windsor faces up to the challenges of life in the twenty-first century. Yet this is a man who inherited the £346 million Duchy of Cornwall at the age of 21, is prepared to adopt eccentric business practices and sell Duchy trees to himself for a cool £2.3 million and take freebie holidays for two dozen of his friends on the yacht of an ancient Greek multi-millionaire who used to support the all-torturing Greek fascist regime of the 1960s.

Neither has there ever been any public discussion about the Prince's consistent championing of organic foods while selling a huge range of Duchy organic products; is this not mixing business and royalty? Today the monarchy and its hangers-on are more like the Royal Family of the Windsors' German forebears of the eighteenth century. Even Edward who pleads poverty is reckoned to be worth around £9 million. Yet few voices are raised in anger.

The royals remain in a time capsule at the end of The Mall, as I found out one chill November evening in November 1991 when the Duke of Edinburgh invited me to dinner.

He had decided relations between the press and Palace had reached one of its periodic 'all-time lows' and he wanted to know how matters could be improved. What he actually intended was to find out what the Palace could do to shut us up and, as with every other initiative of this kind, it was doomed to failure. Charles and Diana tried it by inviting editors to lunch *à trois*. The Queen tried it by inviting senior hacks to a palace party where the only tangible result was the loss of a few BP ashtrays. And the Duke tried it by organising a working dinner which was attended by, among others, Sir Bernard Ingham, Mrs Thatcher's Downing Street press secretary, Conrad Black, owner of the Telegraph Group, Andreas Whittam Smith, the founder and editor of the *Independent*, Sir Angus Ogilvy and various assorted lords who looked and sounded as if they belonged in the cast list of a Shakespeare history play. I was the token tabloid editor, suggested by the Earl of Carnarvon, the Queen's racehorse manager, who had taken a shine to me because, when editor of the *People*, we had sponsored a series of races at Newbury, his home turf.

In case you are invited to dinner at the Palace, be warned. You don't just sit down and start chattering away. You sit where you are told and for the first part of the meal – in this case a staggeringly large hare which looked like a side of beef – you talk only to the man (they were all men) on your left. Then for the second half you turn and talk only to the bloke on your right. Obviously, somewhere along the line the reverse happens, because otherwise we would all have been talking to the backs of each others' heads, but I was far too confused to notice the borderline. If you are still with me you will no doubt be wondering how you know when it's all change and you turn the other way. The answer is you watch the Duke, who half-way through the hare did an exaggerated turn of his head and talked at the top of his voice to the chap who had been on tenterhooks not eating anything, waiting for just such a move. You then do the same. General discussion isn't allowed until the Duke talks to the guest sitting opposite him. I say general discussion, but in reality it isn't because everything had to go through Philip. So when I was asked to sing for my supper by explaining what tabloid newspapers thought of the Royal Family, I set about telling him that everything revolved around Diana because she was by far the most fascinating member of the family, hardly a dissertation calculated to make the Duke's heart grow fonder of me, the *Daily Mirror* or Diana. At the end, with the assorted dukes and belted earls who made up the remainder of the dinner guests wheezing in apoplexy, the Duke exploded, 'You mean we are some sort of soap opera?'

'Well yes,' I replied, 'you are.'

I was never invited back. It was, I suspect, the first and last time reality had been allowed to invade Buckingham Palace. The barricades went up and didn't come down again until they were torn away by the public relations disaster that followed Diana's death. And even then, in spite of all the fine words and pledges, they went back up again as soon as they thought nobody was looking. True to form, the Royal Family learnt nothing from peering into the abyss. Both as individuals and as an institution they are teetering on the edge of irrelevance, playing to an increasingly indifferent audience.

And that, as we all know, is the kiss of death to even the most long-running of soap operas.

2

The 2001 general election wasn't notable for much – John Prescott's left jab, the only time the Left managed to land a punch; the low turnout; the lukewarm return of Tony Blair endorsed by only one quarter of the country... and the early morning primal 'I am not a quitter' scream of Peter Mandelson as he was re-elected in Hartlepool. It was at once a screech of survival, pain, anger, hate, love, frustration and neglect. The howl of a politician in exile aimed right at the man he had been instrumental in placing in Downing Street. Peter Mandelson reckoned he had been betrayed because Tony Blair had not only sacked him over the Hinduja passport affair but, in that final confrontation in Blair's study, the Prime Minister told him his political career was over and that he should resign, not just as a minister, but as an MP as well. For the Northern Ireland Secretary at that moment it was the ultimate betrayal. Peter Mandelson had made Tony Blair Prime Minister, and the Prime Minister had broken him.

A few months earlier, the searing video grab of Tony Blair and Peter Mandelson sitting next to each other, shattered and drained, on the Government front bench after Mandelson's second enforced resignation in 2001 had been a seminal moment for New Labour. This was raw emotion, the end of a political career for one, the butchery of a friend for the other, and all over something that shouldn't have mattered at all. It was a human tragedy played out for the highest stakes of all, a prime minister's trust and a minister's honesty. The events leading up to Mandelson's resignation showed three of New Labour's big four beasts in none too flattering a light, struggling in a morass of misjudgement, half-truths, exaggerations and attempts to paper over cracks that led to an unprecedented second Cabinet resignation for Mandelson, brought about finally by a Prime Ministerial misjudgement when Tony Blair felt his old friend and Northern Ireland Minister would be found to have lied by the inquiry into the passport affair. It remains the deepest cut yet inflicted on New Labour's self-belief and the scars remain.

One of Tony Blair's favourite quotes about himself is from an Australian magazine in which he is described as 'a nice kind of bastard'. He had certainly been both that fateful Wednesday in January and it was a grim irony that Labour's famed presentational skills were much to blame for the scandal that never was and a resignation that should never have been. It goes to the heart of Tony Blair's administration and New Labour's modern jazz quartet – Blair in charge of strategy, Brown on tactics, Mandelson and Campbell on presentation and delivery. That is how they set out to change the Labour Party and had succeeded in spectacular style.

It was a quartet that began to harmonise as far back as 1992 when, as editor of the *Daily Mirror*, I can remember Peter sitting in the back of my car going through a speech line by line on the phone with the young Tony Blair, then Opposition Spokesman on Employment. Peter had marked him out already as a future leader and he was nurturing him. Labour failed that time under Neil Kinnock, but five years later all four finished up in Downing Street.

Yet there was dissatisfaction. Brown brooded; he wanted Tony's job. All his political life had been geared to it, and he blamed Mandelson for the humiliation of not getting it, although it was obvious to any neutral that Blair was a better front-of-house man than Brown. Mandelson didn't want to be in the Cabinet Office and outside the Cabinet, he had been too close to Tony for too long to swallow that. He wanted a real job and he was prepared to tell anyone who would listen. Instead, he got the poisoned chalice – the Dome.

In government Peter changed. He found new glitzy friends, even going for weekends with Charles and Camilla; he didn't see his old friends and some of them were hurt. It got worse when he eventually made the Cabinet as the Trade and Industry Secretary. Mandelson is easy to demonise, the Prince of Darkness, Labour's Machiavelli – and his skills are admired more by Tories than by Labour traditionalists. Yet to the surprise of many he was an extremely good minister at the DTI and well regarded by top officials there. But the Robinson loan affair exposed a difficult and politically dangerous side to him. He suppressed the truth. He didn't lie, but he didn't tell the whole truth. It is inconceivable that he did not understand the potential dynamite of his £373,000 loan from Robinson when, as Secretary of State, he was political head of the department investigating the minister's business affairs. Yet as the time-bomb ticked away, he was more exercised about whether he should come out of the closet and declare that he was gay, which he intended to do in a controlled interview with the *Independent*. The Robinson affair is fundamental to understanding Mandelson's behaviour over the Hinduja passport crisis, for although the crises were different in content, they show some remarkable similarities as far as Peter's behaviour pattern is concerned. He professed hurt and concern over one aspect of his life while ignoring a potentially more damaging part.

Why didn't he tell Blair about the loan from Robinson? Such an acute political brain must have recognised the fatal damage non-declaration could cause and it was that, rather than the loan itself, which brought about his resignation. I believe a substantial part of the problem was that although he was an excellent minister, Peter failed to adapt to life at the sharp end of government. In spite of his reputation, he is a solitary, emotional and easily hurt man. The revelation by the *News of the World* about his homosexuality in the 1980s caused him so much pain that he remained celibate for years. The rift with Gordon Brown hurt him deeply and both men are petulantly obsessed with the other. In opposition, Peter felt he was much more on a par with Brown, although this was not necessarily a view shared by Blair. In government, both were very hot on the Cabinet acting as a team and clearing any major pronouncements through the Prime Minister's office, but neither was much good at doing so themselves.

Blair took a big risk bringing Mandelson back into the Government and received a lot of flak for doing so. It wasn't just because he was an excellent and close adviser, but he was a consistently good minister, as he proved once again in the Northern Ireland office where he mended some fences with the Unionists who had fallen out with Mo Mowlam. They felt she had instinctively sided with the Catholics; a tempting proposition, as they are considerably less dour than the Unionists. However Mo may try to rewrite history now, she was a busted flush in Ulster. David Trimble had given up on her. Northern Ireland would try the patience of anyone, and all the leaders there know they have a straight through-line to the Prime Minister if they want it. That means too often the Ulster Secretary is little more than a cipher, good for long, boring, piddling detail, but not necessary for the big headline-grabbing initiatives. Mandelson recognised that and was beginning to feel that old sense of frustration and lack of fulfilment. That is what Campbell meant by him being 'semi-detached', a belief Campbell had held for some time and an important insight into understanding Mandelson's state of mind at the time the Hinduja affair blew up.

It started innocuously enough with a parliamentary question from the

Liberal Democrat MP Norman Baker to Jack Straw asking 'what representations he has received' on the applications for British citizenship for two of the four Hinduja brothers from Mandelson and Keith Vaz, then the Minister for Europe. Innocuous, but dangerous. The Hindujas had put £1 million into the Dome's Faith Zone; Peter Mandelson was Dome Minister and the Hindujas had received their passports from Labour after being turned down by the Tories. There were also persistent stories about their involvement in India over arms dealing. Put that witches' brew together and there is potential trouble.

The question took some time to answer, Mandelson pointing out that he did not make 'representations'; this suggests active support for their case. In fact, he asked only if conditions for acceptance had changed. Nothing wrong in that, the question was eventually answered and nobody paid any attention to it until the *Observer* ran a report – largely inaccurate – about Mandelson 'helping' Srichand Hinduja to obtain his passport. Mandelson insisted that the matter was dealt with properly through his private office.

On the Sunday afternoon, with little interest being shown in the report, Alastair Campbell spoke to Mandelson. Campbell had the news reporter's nose for trouble and could see there was the potential for it here. His version is that he questioned Peter very carefully about what had happened, on at least two occasions asking him if he was 'absolutely sure' that his explanation to the *Observer* was correct. Absolutely, replied Mandelson. It then became the official explanation from the Prime Minister's office. Mandelson's account is that he was more angry about a story in the *Sunday Times* alleging a bust up between him and Brown over election planning and paid scant attention to the *Observer* story, and certainly not to whether his private office had dealt with the call or not. What was unfortunate and accepted by both sides is that in the briefing of those papers interested in following up the story Downing Street said that Mandelson had been asked to involve himself, which 'he had refused to do'. This was clearly inaccurate and not a fair reflection of Mandelson's stated position. Knickers were beginning to twist.

The position was complicated by Culture Secretary Chris Smith in the Commons the next day, who further refined Mandelson's original statement by claiming that his 'sole involvement' was through his private secretary. At this stage, nobody at Number Ten knew of a conversation shortly before the Commons question was answered between Peter and Jack Straw. That soon changed. Straw, who had been away for the weekend with his wife, phoned Campbell saying there was 'a real problem' here because his junior Mike O'Brien remembered speaking with Mandelson and that Straw had personally told Mandelson of the call only days earlier. He could not have forgotten that, even if he had forgotten the original call. Knickers were not only twisting, they were becoming damp.

Peter's defence is that the phonecall, whether he made it or not, is of no importance as he didn't push the Hinduja case. He had other things on his mind as the Northern Ireland peace process was in one of its periodic crises. All this is true, but the problem of the Jack Straw conversation remained. The next day, Campbell and Mandelson concocted a statement in which the truth played little part, claiming 'Mr Mandelson's office has now been able to look at the records in full … [they] had discovered that he had a very brief telephone conversation …' In fact, nothing of the sort had happened. The idea was to try and show that Mandelson had taken charge of the situation when he clearly had not. By the evening, there was a full-blown crisis with both Downing Street and Mandelson now compromised by this phoney statement. It was made worse by Mandelson insisting on TV that he had forgotten nothing, a clear contradiction of the official line, which in itself wasn't true anyway. This was now a rolling cock-up with every attempt to seize the initative making matters worse with a media that scented rich blood – Peter Mandelson's.

By the next morning, with the papers awash with *Government in Mandelson Crisis* stories yet again, Blair decided his long-term ally and faithful Pancho had to go. When he arrived at Number Ten Peter was still unaware of the extent of the crisis; he thought he could weather the storm. He was soon to be disabused. As the two men sat opposite each other in Blair's study, the Prime Minister came straight to the point.

'There is no doubt about it, you have lied,' he said.

'I haven't lied, I deny it,' replied Mandelson.

'Very well then, it's a fib.'

Blair wasn't for turning, the decision had already been made. There was no doubt in the Prime Minister's view that there had been a phone call, that Jack Straw had reminded him of it and that Peter had needlessly plunged the Government into crisis.

'You will have to resign,' he said.

'What, now?' exclaimed an astonished Mandelson.

'Yes,' said Blair.

'From everything? Politics is my life, you are telling me to end my life,' he replied.

Blair, it appeared, wanted him out of his Hartlepool constituency as well. There was no going back. 'I'm afraid that is right,' said Blair. 'Your political life is over. It is because of who you are, if you were anyone else this would not be happening.'

Mandelson made one last desperate attempt to save his career. 'But there is an inquiry into this. If an inquiry finds against me I can resign then, why can't I do that?' he asked.

But Blair wouldn't have it. 'That would be worse,' he replied. 'Hammond will find that you lied and it will be much worse if you were forced to resign that way, it is better to go now.'

So Mandelson was catapulted out of office. The 'nice kind of bastard' made sure his landing was as soft as possible. He paid a fulsome tribute to him and suggested he take Northern Ireland questions in the House. But one of the principal architects of New Labour was out, not for a high crime but for blowing his presentational skills. If his statement to the *Observer* had read: 'Although I cannot remember doing so, I am told I had a brief phonecall with the appropriate Home Office minister, but at no time did I support or endorse this application for citizenship,' he would still be in the Northern Ireland office. Why he did not do so remains a mystery; even he can't really explain it. The most likely explanation is that he could see the worst-case scenario presented by the implication of the question and couldn't face more headlines about sleaze and the Dome, even though he had behaved with careful propriety. He was media-weary, battle-fatigued. Peter Mandelson is not fire-proof and when you cut him, he bleeds.

The Prime Minister was wrong about Hammond branding Mandelson a liar. That is why Blair was so quick to underline Mandelson's honesty when he succeeded in having the inquiry reopened, even though there was no substantial extra evidence. No doubt, if Blair could push the rewind button, he would have waited for the result of Hammond's inquiry and Mandelson would have survived. But the point was he believed he did not come clean over the O'Brien phonecall, and Jack Straw's reminder. As a result, he created a needless and damaging crisis for the Government. The man who for years had gone through Tony Blair's speeches looking for elephant traps had finally fallen into one himself, and this time there would be no return. For a politician so punctillious and sharp about the precise image and presentation of others, it was an extraordinary and eventually fatal flaw that he was so careless with his own.

Blair had no compunction about sacking Mandelson and ending his ministerial career, the Prime Minister's view remains that he repaid his debt to his friend and adviser by taking the hits when he brought him back so quickly after the Robinson affair and had been repaid by a thoughtless and silly risk.

The saga was to have one more twist. When the Hammond report was eventually published, Blair was presented with a prickly problem. Why did Mandelson have to go, his political career in ruins, if he had done nothing wrong? This was just the sort of thing the Prime Minister used to refer to Peter Mandelson, and this occasion was no exception. He told Mandelson he was going to say that the former minister had been 'unwittingly misleading'; what did he think of that? Not a lot was the answer. 'If you say that I will not take it lying down,' Mandleson retorted. 'You will have me to contend with.'

'So what should I say?' said an increasingly desperate Blair.

'Say the past is the past, time to move on and draw a line underneath it,' said Mandelson, reverting to his old role and helping the Prime Minister out of this latest and most bizarre crisis. It was a blackly ironic way for the Prince of Darkness to end his ministerial career, although after the election he was once again to be whispering in Blair's ear and it was he who recommended that the Prime Minister visited President Assad of Syria during the early days of the Afghan war, a visit that was not a success even though Mandelson had smoothed the way with a three-hour visit.

The Mandelson affair presents a bleak picture of the way modern British politics conducts itself, forever driven by a voracious 24-hour-a-day demand for news and a political party that is both obsessed with and repelled by Britain's media. There were lots of niggling little untruths, misrepresentations and a fair bit of trimming designed to counterbalance what Downing Street sees as an enormous right-wing agenda set by newspapers wholly hostile to Labour. It is not only governments who are guilty of ruling by soundbites – newspapers and television are too. This is a worldwide problem; for example, in the United States during the 1988 election campaign, the average length of uninterrupted speech by a presidential candidate on TV news bulletins was 9.8 seconds. By 1992 this was down to 8.2, yet this was in a battle for the most important political post in the world. No wonder politicians are tempted to believe that the only effective way to win the headline battle is to fight fire with fire. Hence the fixation with presentation and delivery and why both the Northern Ireland Secretary and Downing Street finished up misrepresenting the truth. Mandelson feels he was let down by Jack Straw who, he reckons, overstated the case against him, branding him as a liar. He also blames Campbell for misleading briefings. Campbell, on the other hand, is very positive that he too was not told the whole truth by Mandelson in the vital early days when the crisis could have been avoided.

It is an extraordinary aspect of Peter's character that three days after he was sacked he turned up unannounced at Campbell's home where he was holding a party for his partner Fiona's mother. There were many old friends of Peter's there and the majority were moaning about him, claiming they hadn't seen him since he started dining with the A-list. He behaved as if nothing out of the ordinary had happened and greeted his old friends as if he had seen them only the week before. Now that really is semi-detached.

For a man with such an array of enemies, many of them in his own party, it is remarkable that Peter Mandelson turned out to be his own worst enemy. But then he is full of surprises. He turned out to be an excellent minister; many thought he would be terrible. He failed to keep the team disciplines he thought so necessary for the smooth running of the Labour Party. When it was elected with such a thumping majority, his first concern was that there were so many new Labour MPs – a significant number of whom nobody had expected to reach Westminster – that the calibre would be poor and create problems for the Prime Minister. In fact, the vast army behaved remarkably well and kept the faith; it is the founding brothers who have fallen out – Mandelson with Brown and Brown on and off with everybody. The relationship between Premier and Chancellor is close but testy and often sullen on the Chancellor's side.

In the first two years the party was bound by its pledge to stick to Tory spending plans, a promise thought necessary in order to convince the electorate that Labour really was New. This led to a dog-in-the-manger attitude by Brown, who barely disguised his contempt for Health Secretary Frank Dobson and didn't have much time for David Blunkett at Education, either. The consequence was that in Health, particularly, there was no serious strategic thinking for the time when money could be invested.

The result was a fearful backlash against the Government, which trumpeted just before the 1997 election that 'Britain had 24 hours to save the NHS'. Five years and 43,800 hours later, Blair and Brown were forced to lay their political lives on the line with a massive injection of cash. Why had they waited so long? Because Gordon Brown had consistently rubbished initiatives by ministers and refused to fund their ideas. That is why he commissioned the report by Derek Wanless, the former Chief

Executive of NatWest, whose own record of success was patchy to put it kindly, but at least Gordon was pulling the strings. He may not run the theatre, but he could still be the puppet master.

Labour still sticks to its commitment to a totally free health service, something that is becoming an impossibility. It is quite a different service to that introduced by Nye Bevan back in 1948 and, if we are to preserve its general excellence there has to be some form of rationalisation, otherwise it will collapse under the weight of its own commitments. Only Labour can undertake this because few will trust the Conservatives to do so, particularly after the way they laid waste our public services during the Thatcher and Major eras.

Yet Brown held the purse strings so tight that Blair, even though he recognised the groundswell of dissatisfaction from the grass roots, was unable to prise the money out of the Chancellor's hand. The only way he could do it was by making a unilateral announcement on TV, government by *Breakfast with Frost,* and even then Brown fought a rearguard action to try and reduce the commitment. Part of the problem is that Brown really is eaten up with jealousy over Blair's position and harbours a scarcely concealed contempt for Cabinet colleagues, something that is not helped by his lack of outside interests which marriage has failed to change.

It is a curious fact of political life that the Prime Minister may be accused of behaving like a president but in fact he has no departmental clout. The Prime Minister's office relies on other minsters' departments to do his policy bidding, and as any viewer of *Yes, Minister* will know, it is easy to frustrate even the most determined of premiers. He has tried to counteract that by introducing his own advisers like the much derided John Birt, and it is why he finds it easier to take the initiative in foreign affairs when he can deal one to one with presidents and other prime ministers.

Politicians can be remarkably naïve about real life, confirming Rupert Murdoch's view that they know nothing about the ways of the world and should be treated accordingly. Such otherworldliness led to the débâcle of Geoffrey Robinson, the fury over Bernie Ecclestone and the charge that New Labour enjoys the patronage and social whirl of the rich and powerful. Robinson was a rare bird, a Labour multi-millionaire who was therefore on constant call to chip into the pot. He funded Gordon Brown's office and baled out the *New Statesman* when it was in danger of folding. Blair took a holiday in Robinson's Tuscan villa and Brown visited his flat in Cannes, but nobody was ever quite sure where the cash came from.

Sure, they knew he had been something to do with Jaguar and the MP had an engineering company, but that was about it because that was all Robinson ever let anyone know. Therefore it came as a shock to discover that Robinson's millions came from his elderly lover, a Belgian widow with the splendidly apt name of Madame Joska Bourgeois. The tubby MP for Coventry North West was a toy-boy, and the Labour Party was being supported by the rewards of being a rich woman's sexual plaything. It was an even bigger shock to find out that Robinson had a rival for the cash, which he kept firmly offshore – the Belgian taxman. When he finally read Tom Bower's book on Robinson, Peter Mandelson, who had used him as his own private building society, said it made him feel sick. Apparently, he had no idea what he had been up to, although he had known him for 20 years.

Shortly before he bought the *New Statesman*, I went to see Robinson about editing it, on the recommendation of both Campbell and Mandelson, but there was something that wasn't quite right about him. For a man who was so wealthy, he was extremely difficult to contact and there was no obvious way he had earned all his cash. Warning bells started to clang and I warned the Labour leadership that, to misquote Mrs Thatcher, here was a man with whom we should not do business. Nobody listened, of course. They never do.

Both the Bernie Ecclestone affair and the never-ending saga of whether to ban fox-hunting stem from the same root cause. How do you deal with those who have poured money into your election coffers once you are in power? The Ecclestone £1 million is notorious, but less well known is that Labour received £1.1 million from the Political Animal Lobby, a pressure group dedicated to the abolition of hunting. The attempts to ban hunting took up an inordinate amount of parliamentary time and it is clear Blair wished it would go away, but he couldn't let it go because of the donation to the fighting fund. Yet fox-hunting is like the abolition of the House of Lords, something that obsesses Westminster but does not rank at the top of ordinary people's priorities when they are struggling to cope with the complexities of everyday life. Bernie Ecclestone was canny in his £1 million investment, a punt that has repaid him handsomely. He got his way because, although the Department of Health is determined to ban all smoking advertising for obvious departmental reasons, Blair is nothing like as evangelical, and if pressed, would admit privately that he is not in favour of banning cigarette advertising, taking the pragmatic view that all this would achieve is the cigarette companies moving the industry out of this country and into Asia.

Without his £1 million donation Ecclestone would not have got off the starting grid as far as access to Number Ten was concerned. No Prime Minister is going to refuse a hearing to someone who has injected £1 million into his campaign and he would no doubt make the point that Ecclestone should not be penalised for doing so by being prevented from putting his case to the Prime Minister just because he was a donor. The treasure chests of both parties would soon be empty if that was the case.

The Conservatives have a much greater problem with the massive single donations they have received. At one stage, they appeared to be bankrolled almost entirely by Michael Ashcroft, the businessman whom Hague levered into the new improved House of Lords where cronyism and cash have become the necessary pedigree for admission. In the old days, slave trading used to be the means by which to grace the ermine. This is the same Michael Ashcroft who was the subject of a report to the Foreign Office by our man in Belize. He suggested he was responsible for masterminding new financial laws in the country which, though not Ashcroft's intention, had, attracted men with lumpy jackets, squashed noses and funny money. Ashcroft has now been helped out by a further £5 million promised if the Tories stoke up their anti-Euro campaign; you can guarantee this money will not finish there, it will want to talk up the argument for getting out of Europe entirely.

Newspapers are not immune from this either. The *Sun*'s support is considered vital to New Labour, so vital that when the election date had to be changed from May to June, one of the main concerns was how to extricate the *Sun* from Downing Street's earlier tasty dropped morsel, the 3 May polling date which the paper had supported enthusiastically. No wonder the *Mirror* despairs occasionally. Actually, although the *Sun* is considered important as a supporter for obvious reasons, the main aim is to stop it reverting to the Conservatives because, together with the *Daily Mail*, Downing Street believes it can drive a right-wing agenda, but individually they cannot do so. Divide and rule works in newspapers as well as politics.

Number Ten's close focus on its simmering relationship with Fleet Street, bordering on the obsessional, boiled over in the Lilliputian row about Tony Blair and the Queen Mother's funeral. The *Spectator* magazine ran an article by Peter Oborne, a political journalist and none-too-admiring biographer of Campbell, under the headline HOW TONY BLAIR TRIED TO MUSCLE IN ON THE MOURNING, claiming the Prime Minister was 'forced to accept his role... was going to be modest,' after, it was claimed, Downing Street had communicated that the Prime Minister was unhappy with arrangements which did not recognise his importance. This was followed up a couple of days later by a rather more guarded article in the *Mail on Sunday*, by its political editor Simon Walters, headlined, HOW BLAIR TRIED TO HIJACK ROYAL FUNERAL. Blair went potty. He was furious that it presented his character as one of such overweening ego that he was prepared to thrust himself into the centre stage of a spectacular set-piece state funeral for one of Britain's great twentieth-century personalities.

Campbell, on Blair's behalf, complained to the Press Complaints Commission in virulent terms, branding the *Mail on Sunday*'s report as 'malicious invention' and blanket-denied both stories. But the stories were not without foundation in as much as they had come from the office of Black Rod, quite probably from the man himself, General Sir Michael Willcocks, who was charged with organising the parliamentary end of the funeral pomp and circumstance. After an initial denial of the story Willcocks confirmed some of the essentials: that there had been a series of Downing Street phone calls to his office, and he felt, rightly or wrongly, that he was being put under undue pressure. The Downing Street reference to the PCC was a mistake for it is essentially a compromise and resolve body and with two totally opposing accounts – Downing Street accepted there had been phone calls but denied absolutely that any pressure had been brought to bear – there was no way Campbell was going to secure a grovelling apology. Worse, any compromise would be used by the newspapers to claim victory. This indeed was what happened and a small, but significant, head of steam was built up demanding Campbell's removal. This was a 'crisis' almost entirely manufactured by Conservative newspapers, especially the Mail group and the *Telegraph*, owners of the *Spectator*. Their spin was that Downing Street had been humiliated, that it was yet another big blow to Blair's credibility. He had been caught out, they said, by spin and lies, the hallmark of this Labour administration. It was, they trumpeted, a triumph for accurate reporting and fearless newspapers in the face of a ruthless government machine determined to suppress the truth. But the reality was a long way from that as the letter of resolution from the PCC deputy director Tim Toulman made clear. In it, he pointed out that the two accounts were so different the commission would never be in a position fully to ascertain the facts and that the issue would remain largely a matter of interpretation. But, crucially, he went on: 'None of the three publications concerned [the *Evening Standard* had also run a version of the story] has produced evidence in their defence that the prime minister himself was involved in any way in any of this, or that he at any stage did anything wrong or sought for himself a greater role in the proceedings. And during our investigation so far, nothing new has been provided to suggest otherwise.' In other words, the thrust of the stories' projection was untrue. Yet the Tory papers' campaign to remove Campbell and demonise Blair made no mention of this. You can see why Labour's obsession with the Press, inherited from the grotesque caricaturing of Neil Kinnock, is so deep-seated. Most people now will have a vague memory of Blair trying to grab the limelight at the Queen Mother's funeral, although there is absolutely no evidence to support that contention. It isn't only Downing Street that uses spin and presentation and in this case the Prime Minister was more spinned against than spinning. The Tory press had targeted Campbell in much the same way as they had, successfully, gone for Mandelson in an attempt to pick off the Prime Minister's closest supporters. They succeeded with Mandelson because Blair misjudged the situation. There was no way it was going to happen again.

For two such old friends and political allies, Mandelson and Campbell were like chalk and cheese. Mandelson loved the showbusiness glitterati, the rich and the famous. He enjoyed joining Charles and Camilla for a weekend at Highgrove and he was welcomed with open arms in the salons of Armani London. Campbell, on the other hand, is abrasive to the point of being rude and has no time for the perfumes of Kensington. He prefers his home life in Hampstead and is more reliant than one might at first expect on Fiona Millar, his partner and mother of his three children. He jogs an impossible amount of miles each weekend – he finds it helps with his asthma – and watches Burnley trying to play football when he can. If Mandelson is the butterfly, Campbell is the wheel.

Campbell is no royal fan; he had scant regard for Diana, although he dubbed her the 'People's Princess', a line taken from a *Today* leader, and was less than enthralled on his first visit to Highgrove when he was told to use the tradesmen's entrance and refused permission to use the swimming pool until Charles intervened. This did not increase Campbell's attraction to the Royal Family.

The two presentation and delivery men, so close in opposition, drifted apart under the pressure of government. As illustration, Campbell points out that his first child knew Mandelson well, his second only slightly and his daughter not at all. Campbell remains openly contemptuous of most of Mandelson's friends, particularly the Conservative ones. The rift between the two widened over the Hinduja affair. Both are adamant that the other is to blame, although Mandelson's public enemy number one remains Jack Straw, who, he is convinced, did for him, partially because he reckoned, rightly, that Straw wanted to be Foreign Secretary in a second-term Labour Government. It was a job Mandelson himself coveted. Campbell's view is suitably robust on this. It's bollocks, he says.

There is quite a lot nowadays that Campbell considers bollocks, and top of the list is the parliamentary lobby, that semi-secret society of political editors and reporters who receive twice-daily briefings from the Prime Minister's press secretary and then weave their own web of words around them. Campbell opened up the briefings, making them much more accountable than they used to be. But over the four years of the first Blair Government he became increasingly disenchanted by his former profession, regarding it now with unmitigated contempt. He hardly even reads the newspapers, relying instead on a media digest. Although he loathes the print journalists and what he sees as their endless ability to make up stories from little or no facts, his finest invective is reserved for the television media which he dismisses as the 'babble factory'. His view is that the lobby is obsessed with gossip and its own agenda and is driven by a deep laziness. It is certainly true that any group of journalists who rely on briefings for their daily fodder tend to become lazy and substitute conjecture for hard fact; football reporters and City journalists spring to mind. With this mindset, it was not surprising that Alastair was determined to move out of the briefing front line and into the more strategic role of Director of Communications, leaving the lobby to be briefed by an apolitical civil servant. But if it is true that lobby journalism leaves a lot to be desired, it also true that Alastair does not take kindly to criticism and sees it as a personal affront to himself and his boss. In that he is like Blair. All prime ministers live in time capsules: pushed, cosseted, guided from plane to train to car. They are constantly ruled by schedules, digests, briefings and advisors. In spite of their protestations, they rarely have time to listen to ordinary people with ordinary everyday grouses. Blair truly cannot understand why people are so impatient with the progress of New Labour reforms. He told me 'I feel like that Monty Python sketch. You know, the one where the guy complains "What have the Romans ever done for me?". We have done a lot.' He pays lip service to the fact that people are entitled to want more than Labour has so far delivered, but his real view is that Labour has achieved much – House of Lords reform, minimum wage, a sustained attack on child poverty, education, devolution. He blames a hostile, deeply-conservative, media for this, as does Campbell, who finds it hard to believe any of the hacks are up to his exacting standards, explaining it to me once by saying that life is a series of glass ceilings and, as you go through them, you realise the man above really is not very good.

I assume we have all failed his test as he rose effortlessly to the top of the skyscraper, waving goodbye not only to me, but Peter Mandelson and Neil Kinnock on the way. It is often said that he has attached himself to older men at every stage of his career, although his critics who point to a close relationship with Robert Maxwell while at the *Mirror* are wrong. He was never close, self-preservation kept him at arm's length. Any decent reporter used his wiles to keep out of Maxwell's way if they had any sense, and Campbell had plenty of that. He is criticised for using myself, Neil Kinnock and Alex Ferguson of Manchester United, and so he may. But what else are ambitious young men meant to do? In the 1997 election campaign both Blair and Campbell leaned heavily on Ferguson, whose football strategist's brain was much in evidence. You are so far ahead, he told them, don't take any unnecessary risks. Keep the defence tight, don't make silly mistakes, take your chances but don't endanger your lead to do so. It was advice followed to the letter. Campbell attached himself to older men because it was the quickest way to attain the experience of age without having to learn the hard way. There is surely nothing wrong in that. It also brought him closer to seats of power. But, apart from the relationship with his partner, Fiona Millar, the two strongest and most emotional friendships of his life have been with contemporaries, Tony Blair and a reporter called John Merritt, who was to die tragically young. Campbell and Merritt, who met on the *Mirror*'s training scheme in Plymouth, were the opposite sides of the same coin. Alastair, a shrewd politician of a reporter, always looking for the opportunity of advancement but never in a crawling way, indeed his approach was rather the opposite. His instincts were to get close to power and then use it – he rarely challenged it. Merritt was a natural iconoclast, the better reporter for it, and a man whose natural game was to challenge authority and the status quo and expose their shortcomings. These two opposites forged a close and lasting bond, broken only by Merritt's early death after a long and courageous battle against leukaemia. Alastair made a tearful and moving address at his memorial service, recalling how Merritt had brought him back to sanity after his final spectacular drinking spree.

Alastair is now effectively the Deputy Prime Minister with Cabinet Ministers phoning him for steers on how the Prime Minister feels on any given subject. But as Tony's original cronies drop off the perch, the enemies begin to muster as they do in any government. This will be the real testing time of Tony and Alastair as Cabinet Government is now virtually non-existent and the Downing Street warlord's rule is presidential rather that first among equals. Only Brown's fiefdom next door presents anything like an equal force. Fine if all is going well, but very high risk when the tide turns against you, as Mrs Thatcher found.

The much despised lobby, the elite of political journalists, is waiting for the whiff of blood and it is more a question of *when* they scent it than *if*. Alastair can expect no mercy then and, however justified he may have been in his complaints about lobby spin, presentation and misrepresentation, the happy band of brothers and sisters will get him in the same way as they harried Tony Blair into panicky mistakes over the second Mandelson resignation. This system, designed to protect unaccountability on both sides, is capable of being manipulated and deeply corrupt, victory going more often than not to the politician who is the cleverest and deadliest leaker. The problem will not be solved until all meetings are fully and accountably on the record. That way the public can judge who is leading whom by the nose. And it can lead to some pretty strange places.

In the spring of 1989, the Transport Minister Paul Channon briefed a few favoured journalists off the record at the Garrick Club about the progress the Scottish police had made in the investigation of the Lockerbie disaster. He said they knew everything about the bombing, that the bomb came from the Middle East and that it was put on board the Pan Am jumbo at Frankfurt. He told them the police would know very soon who planted the bomb and where he was. However, two days later he gave an on-the-record interview claiming that he was 'not yet clear' on any of these matters. Two days after that, he was asked specifically if he or his department leaked the fact that the security services would soon know who was responsible for Lockerbie. He replied; 'That report was total news to me ... I know nothing about the details of the enquiries.' Channon wisely refused to repeat his denials in the House of Commons and, in a front page piece in the *Daily Mirror* I accused him of being a liar. This bizarre situation was made even worse because all the journalists he briefed were bound by lobby *omerta* and would not write about his double-dealing, citing not only lobby rules but rules of the Garrick Club which insisted that nothing said there could be reported! Now that really is élitist. There is nothing new in this; Neville Chamberlain did it six months before the start of the Second World War when, in an unattributable briefing to the Lobby, he announced that the European situation looked promising.

Blair shares Campbell's concern over the system of lobby briefings. Once when I had finished interviewing him on his RAF jet he leant over the table and said in a fierce whisper: 'What am I to do about the lobby? These twice daily briefings are the equivalent of two House of Commons prime ministerial question times. They are grillings for three quarters of an hour, often bringing up apparent contradictions in policy or speeches sometimes years old. It is impossible for a press spokesman to deal with questions like that. And if we can't we are accused of muddle and drift,' he said. 'What do we do?' I told him it was easy. Get rid of the lobby and introduce televised press conferences. That way the public can make up its own mind and decide whether the spin attached to Government briefings is justified or not. Blair said he wasn't sure he could do that, but six weeks later Alastair announced that this was indeed what was going to happen. I don't think I had suddenly produced a shining light, I reckon the two of them had been planning something of the sort for some time, and my reaction stiffened their resolve. However even if the Campbell plan succeeds the lobby will continue to exist in some form or another, the addiction to intrigue and mischief of both politicians and journalists will see to that.

Campbell is Blair's most trusted adviser; they are more like old university mates than prime minister and press secretary, but this brings extra pressure as ministers and senior civil servants use Campbell constantly as a sounding board. I think it unlikely he will complete a second term with Blair and even more unlikely that he will return to newspapers, he is too irritated by them. Watch out, though, for life at the top of the Premier League. If he was offered the chief executive's job at the right time, he would take it, even though Blair would vigorously try to stop it. At least there would be no problem with access to Number Ten.

It's all a long way from Turf Moor, home of Campbell's kings in claret and blue where, as unknowns, he, Blair and Mandelson once went to a needle game between Burnley and Hartlepool United. Peter turned up in a fetching, flowing blue-and-white Hartlepool scarf, specially knitted for him by an elderly lady admirer in the constituency. In spite of it being a New Labour obsession, Mandelson's knowledge of football is what could charitably be called rudimentary, and when he arrived for the game he tagged along with Blair and Campbell who went to stand behind the Burnley goal with the others festooned in claret and blue. Campbell told him he had to go up the other end with Hartlepool's travelling army – all right, platoon – which he did with ill-disguised bad grace and a toss of his blue-and-white scarf. At the end of the game, Blair and Campbell were moving off the Burnley terrace when a chant suddenly started up. At first they couldn't quite catch it, but eventually it became clear as

Peter threaded his way through the departing fans to meet up with his friends. With one voice, the Burnley army was singing; 'Who's the wanker in the scarf?'

New Labour arose from the ashes of a party that had been riven by dissent caused by two opposing and irreconcilable factions, personified on the left by Tony Benn and on the right by Roy Jenkins. In the middle, Harold Wilson tried to hold them together and it is a tribute to his peculiar genius that he managed to do so until it all became too much and he decided it was time to go. The old Labour Party had achieved much of what it set out to do, but its founding fathers at the Farringdon Street Memorial Hall back in 1900 would have been mightily disappointed in their trades union descendants of the 1970s. The Labour Party was all but destroyed by the men whose turn-of-the-century leaders had given birth to a party because of a profound sense of injustice and a determination to destroy the indignity of poverty, the humiliation of illiteracy, the wretchedness of slave wages and inhuman working hours and the degradation of the workhouse. But by the late 1970s, the Labour Party was frightened of trade union power and failed to protect the country against the winter of discontent. Its failure was to deprive them of office for almost 20 years. Labour was to return, rebranded, reborn, revitalised as the party of consensus and social democracy, triumphant and electable, pragmatic, middle-class, even bland, the greatest rebirth of any political party in British parliamentary history. And much of it was down to the wanker in the scarf.

* * *

It is said of Neil Kinnock that Labour MPs could see him making a top-rate Prime Minister, they just couldn't see how he was going to get there. His speech to the party faithful in Bournemouth where he laid into the cancer of Militant is the finest conference speech I have ever heard and it destroyed Derek Hatton's army, something even Degsy now reluctantly admits. He did a prodigious job in saving the party, but his fate was to be John the Baptist to Tony Blair's Messiah. The country pulled back from the brink in 1992 when, with less than two weeks to go, Kinnock looked set for Number Ten. What went wrong? Was it the over-triumphant Sheffield rally, over-confidence, some damaging own goals, or was it the personality of Kinnock himself, or even that of Glenys?

Probably a bit of everything, but glowering over the political scene was a general, if vague, belief that Labour had not thrown off its commitment to the trades unions and that, when confronted with the ballot box, many people just did not trust Kinnock enough to break with the ties of the past. He had been the saviour of the party, but when it came to the last knockings, the country wasn't yet ready to be saved from what was an ailing Conservative Party desperately in need of a retread after 13 years in office. Over-confidence also set in during the last ten days. There were far too many in Kinnock's close circle openly discussing what jobs they were going to take when the call eventually came. It even affected Kinnock himself, and his remark to me at the party to celebrate his twenty-fifth wedding anniversary was revealing: 'What do you want then, Stotty boy ... a knighthood or the Lords?' A joke no doubt, but not the sort of joke you make in semi-public ten days away from a general election. Kinnock was a naturally warm and outgoing man, his exuberance could be taken for over-confidence and that is probably what happened at the now notorious Sheffield rally. Certainly it is an experience that should go into the campaign book as something not to try again.

John Smith's boob on national insurance must have done some collateral damage, too. He made the mistake of suggesting that increasing it was not the same as increasing income tax, which strictly speaking it isn't, but few people care enough to bother about the difference. What it did was to allow the Tories to play the Labour tax and spend card, the double whammy which certainly struck home. Ironic since Brown and Blair were to use the same money-raising device ten years later to inject unprecedented funds into the National Health Service. The reaction this time was markedly different. Even Conservative supporters accepted that it was necessary, much to the chagrin of Iain Duncan Smith. For Kinnock, the 1992 defeat was a terrible blow. I think he really did believe he was home and hosed, although in the last few days from my office in the *Mirror* I did notice a falling off of Labour drive; so did Peter Mandelson. The momentum was halted after the party's health campaign came unstuck – an issue they should have won hands down – but they chose to focus on an individual case, always dangerous because you leave yourself open for the other side to pick holes in your example. Labour was warned of this by the *Daily Mirror*'s superb medical correspondent Jill Palmer, a reporter with an immense amount of experience in that field. The party researchers chose not to take her advice, and suffered the consequences.

The 1992 campaign was not as brilliant as the one in 1987 when Thatcher was worried that the Tory performance under Norman Tebbit was seriously underperforming against Labour's under Mandelson.

Certainly, the Labour campaign was slick and startlingly different to anything that had been seen in Britain before, but the policies weren't there and, in the end, neither were the voters. Thatcher needn't have bothered, she cantered home.

Mrs T herself was remarkably good company in private and she liked the *Mirror* team. Paul Foot had even taken her to a *Private Eye* lunch. She used to invite me to Number Ten receptions, most of which I didn't go to, but when I did our conversation was always the same.

> Thatcher: 'Well Mr Stott, we are doing well for you, aren't we? You must be paying a lot less tax.'
> Me: 'You are doing a marvellous job for us, Prime Minister. Your policies mean the readers turn to the *Mirror* because it is the only paper they trust to tell the truth.'
> Thatcher: 'Come on, Mr Stott, we have done so much for you personally.'
> Me: 'You've kept me in a job Prime Minister.'

On one occasion, I had to pick up an award for Paul Foot who had refused to attend because she was presenting them. Mrs T was noted for being extremely tactile, and held on to my hand when she passed over the prize.

> Mrs T: 'Where is he then, Mr Stott?'
> Me: 'Er, he won't come because you are handing out the prizes Prime Minister.'
> Mrs T: 'Oh, do tell him not to be such a silly boy.'
> Me: 'I did Prime Minister, I told him you were looking forward to seeing him and discussing trade union reform.'
> Mrs T: 'Oh, he's in favour of it is he?'
> Me (trying to beat a retreat but held firmly by the hand): 'Not exactly, Prime Minister.'
> Mrs T: 'Well, tell him to come round and we must have a chat.'

* * *

It is a fair rule of thumb for editors that avoiding politicians and lawyers makes for a much more fun-packed life. It isn't possible all the time, but it is particularly horrible when the two come together. This happened to me when David Mellor, then a minister in Mrs Thatcher's Government, went on a freebie holiday to Spain with his family and a friend, Mona Bauwens, daughter of the treasurer of the Palestine Liberation Organisation. I ran the story in *The People* as the holiday was shortly before the Gulf war, when British hostages were being held by Saddam Hussein as human shields. The PLO supported Saddam.

The import of the story in my view was simple: Mellor, as a member of the Thatcher Government, should not have been taking a free holiday worth £10,000 from Mrs Bauwens at a time when Britain was preparing for war with Saddam. Mellor didn't sue *The People*, although he threatened to do so in a phonecall, which, as a mixture of patronising claptrap, threats and conceit is hard to beat. Reporter Mark Thomas asked Mellor if he thought it wise to take the holiday in the political climate at the time, a perfectly reasonable question to a government minister, I thought.

Mellor thought otherwise. 'Oh dear, oh dear. I should be very careful in writing any of that,' he said. 'This is a monitored call. Bearing in mind all this is being recorded, I am making no substantive comment on anything you are saying. If you think this is a matter of public interest, you may well go ahead, publish and be damned.' But the then Chief Secretary to the Treasury wasn't finished, far from it. He warned Thomas 'as an old soldier' that he was 'dealing with people who are conscious of their reputations and have the wherewithal to defend them ... I am not in the least bit embarrassed about my holiday arrangements. If there is an innuendo I don't like, that Mrs Bauwens doesn't like, or her father does not like, then you are dealing with people who won't hesitate to take action. I hope your penmanship is experienced enough to steer around what strikes me as being potentially sharp corners in this story.'

Yuk. Not the sort of guy you would want to have a drink with in the Last Chance Saloon, or indeed anywhere else.

We published, Mrs Bauwens sued, Mellor did not. But it was clear that the story was about Mellor and not Mona Bauwens, as I told the jury when the case eventually finished up at the High Court with *The People* accused of libel. No editor in his or her right senses would fight a libel action in court unless they really believed in their case, it is too dreadful an experience for that. If you are to be cross-examined by a big money QC, you have to be sure of your ground in your own mind and have an absolute belief in the rectitude of your arguments. For tabloid newspapers, libel actions are the equivalent of summary execution. They rarely win even when they are clearly in the right, as with the *Sun* and Bruce Grobbelaar.

Luckily, I had a good time in the witness box and actually enjoyed the cross-examination of Richard Hartley QC, who helped by dropping a couple of clangers. First, he asked me if Maxwell 'still' interfered with leaders in the paper. I pointed out that it would be a little difficult as he was dead, unless, of course, Hartley had a direct line to him. Then he wanted to know if I had the original of the letter of support sent to Saddam by the PLO, a ludicrous request because, as I pointed out, Saddam had it, and if he wanted it he should go and demand it from him – I wasn't going to. Juries like a bit of knockabout and there was plenty of it and, for once, the QC was at the receiving end; it made a pleasant change. Mellor got it in the mush, too, from our QC, the incomparable George Carman. George not only represented us, he believed in the case and thought Mellor wrong to take the holiday. He made this quite obvious with his memorable description of him as an ostrich with his head in the sand exposing his thinking parts.

As the case wore on, it became clear the holiday was in breach of the ministerial rulebook which states, 'It is a well-established and recognised rule that no minister or public servant should accept gifts, hospitality or services from anyone which would, or might appear to, place him or her under an obligation. The same principle applies if gifts etc. are offered to a member of their family.' If Mellor had had any doubts he should have asked Mrs Thatcher, and we know what she would have said. No, No, No.

John Major, with his propensity for doing the wrong thing at the wrong time, supported Mellor and said there was no pressure on him to resign when the jury came back with a split verdict, 6–6. In effect, it was a vote of no confidence in Mellor. Indeed, if the judge, Mr Justice Drake, had been allowed the casting vote, which is permissible with a split verdict, he said later he would have come down on our side. 'It was a fair comment on a matter of public interest,' he told George Carman's son Dominic. 'When a high ranking politician accepts hospitality from someone who is connected with terrorism, it doesn't look right.' Mellor tried to hang on and Major tried to save him, but the final straw came when Downing Street had to admit that Mellor had not consulted the Prime Minister about the holiday. The Minister for Fun who had warned the press we were drinking in the Last Chance Saloon, was told to finish his glass and get out. It was a rare victory for a tabloid newspaper on a major issue of public importance, the accountability of a minister taking gifts in kind who was prepared to threaten and bully the paper in an effort to keep it quiet. He nearly succeeded, too.

The day after the *People* published its story, there were no follow-ups in the dailies, largely because Mellor had poured cold water on the story and hinted that it was not only untrue but would be the subject of legal action. At the trial, Mr Justice Drake, who appeared initially to be against us, asked me why, if the story was of such major public interest, there had been no further coverage from other papers. I told him it was because of the threat of legal action, but the real answer is that reporters were too lazy to follow the story properly and all too happy to accept Mellor's blanket rebuttal without further enquiry. It is a particular Achilles heel of political reporters. In the end he was brought down by his own arrogance as much as a fatal lack of judgement. It was a satisfying moment, even though most people still think Mellor was forced to resign because of his affair with a bit-part actress in which it was alleged he was into toe-sucking while wearing the Chelsea strip – two inventions used to justify the size of the cheque that was being paid by Kelvin MacKenzie to the actress and Max Clifford for her 'revelations'. It was not the only time a politician was brought down by the truth but remembered for the lie.

Just in case you think I am getting carried away by all this, the *People* under my editorship managed to lose spectacularly to Esther Rantzen in another case in which I was convinced we were in the right, but we ended up shelling out a fortune, although the damages were reduced on appeal. The only consolation was that her solicitors, the very respectable pin-stripe firm of Herbert Smith, tried to saddle us with £370,000 costs, which a judge eventually reduced to £190,000, an overcharge of nearly 50 per cent. No wonder the Lord Chancellor is constantly going on about legal fees.

The judge in the Rantzen case was Mr Justice Otton, now Lord Justice. The action revolved around a paedophile who had been employed at a boys' school and the *People* took Esther Rantzen and Childline to task for knowing about him but not doing anything about it. In the end, we were proved expensively wrong.

At one stage the judge asked if I had any children at school. I told him I had; Christopher was more or less the same age as the boys in question. After we lost, I retired to lick my wounds and one evening went to a fiftieth birthday party for Christopher's sports master at the school. Martin Alden was a Peter Pan, an eternal schoolboy with some surprisingly influential friends. When Wimbledon, our adopted team, reached the Cup Final against Liverpool in 1988, I managed to get four tickets and carried them off in triumph to tell Christopher, then nine, and a member of Martin's crack Under-Tens football team. He was less than impressed. 'Four, is that all?' he asked. I assumed he was having life too cushy and told him we were extremely lucky to get any, never mind four.

'It's virtually impossible to get four,' I said, hoping for some gratitude.

'No it isn't,' he said, 'Mr Alden's got more than that.'

'Oh yeah,' I sneered, 'and how many has he got then clever clogs?'

'One hundred and eighty-six. He's keeping them in his fridge.'

As I said, Martin had some influential friends, and the school did share a training ground with the Crazy Gang, the sometime affectionate name given to the Wimbledon team. This influence extended to the guest speaker at his birthday party, and who should it be but Mr Justice Otton, who proceeded to tell an extremely dirty travelling salesman-type joke, to the clear embarrassment of a number of the ladies present. Realising who he was – judges look almost normal without their wigs – I started a rumble of *sotto voce* protests, 'disgraceful' ... 'who does he think he is?' ... 'never been so disgusted in my life' ... that kind of thing.

Afterwards on the dance floor, I manoeuvred Penny and myself close to him and his wife and started complaining in a loud voice and looking directly at him. There was a look of utter horror on his face as he recognised me. He was out of the door in less than a minute. It made me feel happier, anyway; it's rare you get the last word in a libel action.

Politicians and judges are the twin *bêtes noirs* of journalists. Our interests rarely coincide and there is a deep and hearty dislike on both sides. I have spent much of my life in newspapers exposing the one and trying to defy the other, with varying degrees of success. I also became embroiled in investigating that third shadowy profession, the Secret Service, the incompetence and self-regard of which even outshines that of Westminster and the judiciary. Yet somehow, one summer morning, I found myself being grilled by MI5 about the fitness of the Prime Minister's right-hand man to hold office. Why did Alastair drink? Has he had any extra-marital affairs – as far as I know, no, but actually he isn't married – do I know any reason why he shouldn't be allowed to see sensitive Government documents?, and so on. I was one of the referees Alastair had put down to dissect his past. MI5 seemed only vaguely interested. 'Actually, I've drawn the short straw,' explained the little Welshman in shiny shoes. 'I could have gone to Brussels and interviewed Neil Kinnock ... he's the other referee, you know. I could have done with a trip.'

Normally I was on the other side, moaning about MI5's poor vetting procedures. Now I was part of it, grassing up the Prime Minister's right-hand man to a bored spook. It had been a long, sometimes rocky, journey.

3

I was conceived over an ironing board during an air-raid alert shortly before Christmas 1942. The air-raid was a false alarm, I wasn't, and life has been precarious ever since. To the best of anyone's knowledge, this was the last time my father touched my mother in anything resembling an affectionate way. It was unsurprising really, if the result was to be so drastic. A constant reminder of what he had left behind when he packed his yellowing leather suitcase (it had once been a rather fetching 1920s cream) and headed for the delights of Wolverhampton and the galvanised charms of Willenhall Motor Radiators. He was to spend the rest of his life there, interrupted only by short weekend trips back to our home in Oxford where he spent most of his time in the Lamb and Flag or the Randolph Hotel, wondering why he had bothered to come back. From the moment he left Oxford and his job as chief jig and tool designer at the Pressed Steel Company – 'makers of difficult shapes in sheet steel', and suppliers of all steel bodies to the rapidly-expanding motor industry – Fred Brooks Stott was a lost man. He lived the life of a barfly bachelor, making his home in a series of bedsits in Wolverhampton's smoky villas or in the upstairs spare rooms of pubs which always smelt of stale beer and last night's Senior Service. He inhabited a middle-aged, single man's world of the 1950s, which was limited enough in those dank, depressing, nothing years immediately after the war, but in Wolverhampton there was little to offer but the fortnightly relief of a top-class football team which provided the glamour this grimy but surprisingly park-laden and prim town lacked.

Freddie in the bar was everybody's friend, but outside it there was nothing except a damp, cheerless room in which to hang his two suits and the pub overcoat which never came off between October and March. It constantly covered his body either in the street or on his bed, having the smell of a million cigarettes, countless spilled pints, the dregs of a thousand meaningless conversations and a fractured web of long-discarded dreams. That coat hung on him like his life – shapeless, threadbare and heavy with the whiff of tedium and a life unfulfilled. It hadn't always been like that.

Freddie was the only son of John and Amelia Stott, born on 17 April 1894, putting him in his fiftieth year when I arrived, another powerful incentive to wanderlust. John Stott was a wool spinner who made his home in Andrew Street, Bury. He clearly had ambitions though, because by the time Freddie married, John was describing himself as 'gentleman'. Freddie was doted on, the birthright and downfall of many an only child. He was undeniably bright, a talented piano player, a formidable mathematician. His talents lay in engineering design and draughtsmanship and, after technical school in Bury, he started work at the beginning of the First World War as a draughtsman with the Coventry Chain Company Ltd, 'contractors to Admiralty, Civil Service, War Office, India Office and the Crown agents for the colonies'. No shortage of work there then. This was followed by a move to Derby as a jig and tool draughtsman at Rolls-Royce making aero engines.

By the end of the war, he was a member of the Royal Flying Corps stationed, for reasons nobody can fathom, in Egypt, where curled and faded pictures show him relaxing in the shade of an oasis looking at flimsy bi-planes. For this he received several medals but saw no action. His war service was rarely referred to, largely because no one – including, I suspect, Freddie himself – could remember what he did apart from getting sunburnt. That made such a deep impression on him that for the rest of his life when he was forced to sit on a beach, he did so wearing a handkerchief on his head and rarely removing his jacket and trousers.

After the war, he returned to Bury and then was off to Cork working for Fordson's in its pattern and tool department. It was here that Freddie Stott became Brother Stott and joined the Masons' Royal Arch chapter, Lodge 209, where, according to the little red book of rules, 'no discussion of a religious or political nature shall, under any pretence whatever, be permitted in this Chapter'. As this was 1922 and Ireland was in ferment, most of the meetings must have either been conducted in silence or resounded only to the sound of members scratching each others' backs. Brother Stott, I guess, was more interested in the bar. Neither politics nor religion were his forte.

It must have been an odd place to take a bride, particularly a young slip of a girl from a large family, the apple of her father's eye, whose whole knowledge of life up to this point was obtained working behind the bar of her father's small hotel, the Norfolk Arms in Glossop. Freddie was a regular and he became entranced by the auburn hair and pencil waist of Bertha Pickford, the second daughter of John Joseph Pickford's five children. John Joseph had crossed the Pennines from his home in Sheffield where his father had eked out a living as a timber salesman. But John Joseph preferred the rugged beauty of north Derbyshire to the suffocating hymn to Victorian heavy industry that locked his Brightside home in a grip of smoke, grime and steel.

There is something perverse but heroic about the Pickfords' decision to become timber salesmen in Sheffield but, heroic or not, John Joseph decided to tap the wood rather than sell it and become a publican, or licensed victualler, as the gentility of Victorian manners and marriage certificates preferred. He began his lifelong profession at the Plough Inn, Dinting, where he met and married Ellen Eliza Holgate. They were inseparable for the next 52 years and died within six months of each other. John Joseph remained a committed Liberal throughout his life and one of my very few memories of him remains a splendid rant against Winston Churchill, which coming as it did only three or four years after the Second World War, deserves ten out of ten for balls.

John Joseph and Ellen Eliza – they were both referred to by both names – had four daughters and a son. Bertha – how she hated that name – was the practical and sharp-tongued one; Harriet the eldest, studious; Alice, mousy and shy, who, in later life, was to make a career out of writing letters to the *Sunday Express* after she married Charlie Simpson, the man who invented the hovercraft. Yes, I know the world says it was Sir Christopher Cockerell, but it wasn't. Uncle Charlie invented a full working model in 1929 and sent it off to the Air Ministry, which replied that it had 'no practical utility for the RAF'. He tried again at the beginning of the Second World War, describing his invention as 'a heavier-than-air machine with propellers on horizontal shafts which could be made to hover over any given area.' Again, the thumbs down.

In the 1950s, he ran a post office at Hillmorton near Rugby and I happened to be staying with him and Aunt Alice when the news of Cockerell's 'invention' broke. Uncle Charlie contacted the Ministry of Defence, which, fearing a major scandal, hot-footed it down to the post office with his file. But, by now, Uncle Charlie was old and ill and he couldn't make his experiment work, much to the obvious relief of the man from the ministry. Uncle Charlie was heartbroken, embarrassed and humiliated. It was the first time I saw a grown man cry.

After Alice there was mother's brother Joe, quiet, nervy and overwhelmed by his sisters and Nellie, Aunt Jill, the youngest, explosive, fun. She was to join the Land Army and make her life with a pretty woman called Mae. Aunt Jill's lesbianism was never spoken of, but they were a wonderful, carefree couple with a passion for horse racing, cricket and strong drink. For years, they kept a massive house in Sefton Drive, Liverpool, where they looked after their lodgers as if they were kings. The baths in this rambling old Victorian house were so large they needed big rubber balls as bath plugs. The drug den fate of Liverpool 8 was a long way off when Aunt Jill lived there. Mae always maintained the myth of being a 'Mrs' whose husband had been killed in the war; it wasn't until shortly before she died I realised she was, and always had been, a 'Miss'.

But Bertha was the one for Freddie, probably the most unsuited of the four in temperament to complement his own laid-back, devil-may-care lifestyle. He was seven years older than his intended, but in spite of her no-nonsense practicality and sharp tongue, her horizons didn't stretch much beyond Glossop and she was swept off her feet by what was really not much more than a charming, talented, impecunious wanderer who, even at this stage, didn't tend to stay in one job for long. They married at Dinting Vale in August 1924 and returned to Freddie's bachelor home in Cork's Park Villas where he assumed life would continue much the same as before, but now there was somebody else to cook his supper.

Bertha was heady with excitement, yet her knowledge of the world was naïve even for a rural Derbyshire lass of 23. The world wasn't long in waking her up. She was propositioned on the night-ferry over to Ireland, while Freddie was propping up the bar, by a man who, ambitiously, tried to test the new bride's honour by offering her a Double Corona cigar. A furious Bertha told her new husband about it; he was interested, but only in exactly how big a Double Corona was. She should have known then that married life, like the crossing, was going to be stormy.

If she didn't, her first major event as Mrs Fred B Stott left her with no illusions. Cork's Victoria Hotel was glittering for the annual Christmas bash and Freddie and Bertha were dressed up to the nines. But he was no great consort and, as soon as they arrived, he disappeared. For the next hour, Bertha was shaking off the men in a way that only happens at Christmas parties or to a new bride with an 18-inch waist and auburn hair, but there was still no Freddie. Suddenly, there was a great commotion from the other side of the room; all Bertha could hear was a few garbled words floating across a sea of dinner jackets, whispering silk and mothballed fox fur.

'Give him air, let him have air ... Loosen his collar ... smelling salts ... quick.' Clearly, something had happened and, even at this early stage, Bertha had learnt enough about her new husband to know that he would be involved somewhere. Her worst fears were realised as a phalanx of Fordson's brillianteened young men, preceded by one of those self-important, middle-ranking executives fanning the crowds apart with imperious shouts of, 'Make way, make way,' and followed by a prostrate Freddie, comatose and soundly beaten by the best gin Cork had to offer. It was the end of her first big do, a humbling disaster which was to be repeated in varying degrees over the next 40 years. Freddie so loved his drink, but it treated him with contempt. It was to be a lifelong companion and it remained unfaithful to the end, a partner that turned a clever man into a fool, a caring if flawed one into a maudlin, rambling embarrassment, an occasional nuisance to be endured or humoured but never loved as he might have been.

The marriage was already set on its grim path when their first child, Patricia, was stillborn. It is difficult to guess the effect it had on either of them as they never spoke of it, but it is fair to assume it didn't do the marriage much good. Within a year, Judith arrived and, three years later, John, named after both parents' fathers, a rare moment of unity. Snapshots of those early family years show a distance already beginning to develop between husband and wife. Freddie must have been bemused at becoming a father, it was not his style. He remained uncomfortable with children throughout his life and, to his own, he was distant and awkward, reciprocated in varying degrees by all of us – my sister always called him The Prune. He and I had a shared love of football, and the nearest we ever came was on my visits to Wolverhampton where we spent our time happily in cinema restaurants eating egg and chips and talking about the great Wolves team he had just taken me to see at Molineux. The ability to name the whole of that world-beating Wolverhampton Wanderers side of the middle 1950s is one of the few legacies I have from him. Don't believe me? Williams, Short, Shorthouse, Slater, Wright (capt), Flowers, Hancocks, Broadbent, Swinbourne, Wilshaw, Mullen.

By the end of the 1920s, the Stotts were living in Oxford where Freddie had started work at Pressed Steel before moving on to Morris Motors, already home of what was to become the heart of the British motor industry. Homes in Headington and Walton Street were eventually followed by a move across town to Museum Road where my mother, fed up with no job or money of her own, would begin what was to be an extraordinary career as an Oxford landlady or, in her words, 'hostess to the university'.

It was at this stage that yet another of my father's natural characteristics began to assert itself. By the mid 1930s, he was well established at Morris Motors as an engineer and a well-regarded one at that. William Morris, soon to be Lord Nuffield, and the father of the British car industry, was loyal and generous to those who had been with him from the start and Freddie, if not in at the basement, was certainly milling about on the ground floor. His friends all hit the heights, going on to be directors of Morris Motors, with comfortable and respectable lives on Boar's Hill or installed in North Oxford's Victorian splendour. They became commercial successes, almost, but not quite, accepted as equals by the dons and *savants* who lived in big houses courtesy of the University and, while doing as little as possible for as much as possible, treated the whole of Oxford's most beautiful but privileged district as their own personal fiefdom. The University was everything that made Oxford beautiful, unique and exquisite, but it was also everything that was shabby, corrupt, indolent, selfish and snobbish, both intellectually and socially. This is the side of Oxford the students don't see, or don't wish to. It's the part the dons and the city's famous undergraduate sons never write about; the town is only there to serve the gown. The gown rustles, and the town buckles.

My father only buckled after too many pints. He never did take to management, trades unions or Morris himself. While his contemporaries vied with each other for Morris's favours, Freddie became king of the Morris Motors Athletic Club's snooker club, winning its championship twice and taking on the great Fred Davies in an exhibition match, a sign, as far as my disapproving mother was concerned, of a misspent middle age. She just could not understand why he was throwing away the chance of becoming a director at Morris's. For better or worse, frequently the latter, he was his own man and it was that, as much as the horror of a new and definitely unplanned baby, and my mother's by now ill-concealed contempt, that drove him out of the house to a world of pints and pork pies in Wolverhampton. He never again lived for more than a day or two at a time in Museum Road, but spent his holidays – two weeks a year – in a converted railway carriage on the Thames five miles outside the city at Bablockhythe. This was to be his haven, mowing the lawn, fishing and spending marathon sessions at the Chequers pub before tumbling into his iron bedstead in what used to be first-class. He lived almost entirely on egg and chips, augmented by the occasional soggy pie perked up by lashings of Lea and Perrins Worcestershire sauce. That red-and-cream carriage, courtesy of the Great Western Railway and one of ten that would bring palpitations to any modern planning authority, was the nearest he came to heaven. The carriages and their outside, corrugated-iron earth lavatories were an eyesore and, in summer, a smelly, flyblown one at that, bordering the most magnificent stretch of the Thames's upper reaches. He was no reader and never learned a line of poetry in his life, but he would have agreed with Matthew Arnold's *Scholar Gypsy* about the joys of returning home on summer nights and 'crossing the stripling Thames at

Bablockhythe', his own personal Rubicon which put distance between his failed marriage and remoteness from his children, his humdrum job and single-room life in Wolverhampton.

To reach our carriage it was necessary to cross the stripling Thames by ferry which could take two or three cars. My mother didn't pass her driving test until she was 50 and, when she did, her ambition far outstripped her driving talent. She bought a grey Rover Roadster. It had one serious disadvantage – at 4ft 11in she couldn't reach the pedals, so she had to wear especially built-up shoes. These, too, were less than perfect as the thick crêpe soles gave her little control of the pedals, something which became painfully clear when she overshot the ferry and the car's nose ended up in the river, much to the merriment of everyone in the Chequers, my father particularly, who took the view, rightly as it turned out, that this would deter his wife from regular visits to Bablockhythe.

It remains a mystery to me how this ill-assorted couple managed to come together in such a remarkable physical union over the ironing board in the basement sitting room of 4 Museum Road that December night in 1942. They barely tolerated each other and my father was already spending much of his time away from home working on the development of the Hurricane fighter. It was a life that suited him well, weeks on end away from home in the men-only club atmosphere, occupied with no-questions-asked top-security work in an all-out war effort. His efforts that strange night were no doubt encouraged by several pints of Morell's Oxford Ale, but my mother ... well, the very best to be said was that it was against the run of play. Loneliness, insecurity, a mid-life crisis and war may all have played their part, and at 42 she may well have felt that whatever happened that night there would be no unforeseen consequences. As, indeed, there were not for the first six months, since she had no idea she was pregnant, putting her lack of periods down to the menopause.

The truth, when it dawned in the mid-summer of 1943, was harsh and unforgiving. My father jacked in his job and went to Wolverhampton, my imminent arrival clearly being the last straw. When I arrived in the early hours of 17 August 1943, the Allies were breaking through into the toe of Italy, Sicily was ours and the RAF attacked the factory producing rockets and flying bombs at Peenemunde in the Baltic. An altogether good day for the war effort, but not much of one for Freddie. He was nowhere to be found and remained incommunicado for the next six days. A new child was the last thing he wanted, and no amount of hefty wallops for the Axis powers was going to make it any better.

I returned from the nursing home to Museum Road and the doting ministrations of my new godmother, a splendid Edith Evans lookalike and a formidable ex-landlady of the King's Arms Hotel next to Oxford's Bodleian Library who, legend claimed, had managed to quell the excesses of successive hearties from Brasenose, Trinity, New College and Wadham, with one withering look and a wobble of heavily-powdered jowls. The King's Arms was safe in the ample hands of Lilian Mary Peacock (Miss), from hereon known as Lily P.

August 1943 was not the best time to have a baby, but for the new inhabitant of Museum Road it could not have been better. The house was full of uniforms, two of whom, Major Judge and Colonel Kiker, were proud and beribboned representatives of Uncle Sam's US Marine Corps. More important, they had access to the PX, and suddenly the larder of No 4 began to fill with strange tins of stuff nobody had ever heard of. Tins of sweetcorn jostled for shelf room with jars of instant coffee and mayo. The gentle art, practised by all good university landladies, of ripping off students' ration books could be temporarily abandoned. My mother, while welcoming the goodwill of our US allies and mildly flirting with Major Judge, was nonetheless scathing about American military prowess. 'By the time they have got all their jewellery and necklaces off, the war will be over,' was her contribution to the reaching out of hands across the sea. It didn't stop her stockpiling the instant coffee, though.

Bertha – or Berthe, or Bee, or Bebe as she liked to be called depending on her mood – was a formidable woman by anyone's standards. She developed a cruiser-like carriage in middle age, largely due to her diminutive height. This in no way inhibited her. She was a robust landlady, keeping a knowing eye on both the undergraduates' drinking and their attempts to organise a sex life, usually in her rooms. She was no prude, but neither did she want to fall foul of the prim University Delegacy of Lodgings, which licensed landladies and therefore held thrall over our homes, because the houses were rented on the understanding that the rooms were let to undergrads. In the days after the war, the University was in constant combat with the students, many of whom had served in the war and had witnessed events which left them older and wiser than many of their professors, and who did not take kindly to being told they had to be tucked up in bed – on their own, of course – by midnight. My mother's way of dealing with this was to employ her sixth sense, a must for all landladies, that 'something was going on'. Once she was sure, she would knock on the student's door with the immortal words, 'Come on, Mr Smith, I know you've got a girl in there.' This would be enough to shrivel the desire of even the most ardent lover.

In a losing battle to control its students, Oxford did not even allow them to leave the city without permission, so you can imagine the consternation one Friday afternoon when my mother returned home from shopping to find a scrawled note on the hall table from a splendid chap called Geoffrey Cox who lived in the first-floor back room. It said simply; 'Gone to Paris for a haircut.' This was living. She said nothing. It may be coincidence, but on his return there was a whiff of exotic perfume in the kitchen for the next few weeks.

It was around this time that my mother began the fantasy of writing her book, which was to be called, for no reason anyone could fathom, '*All Change at Dinting*'. Years later, sitting round my sister's kitchen table, when she was still no further on than discussing her opus, she mentioned her plan to Lady Antonia Fraser. Lady Antonia was a famous Oxonian and was reputed to be a rather better rugby player in her youth than most of her male contemporaries at the Dragon School. She was also very beautiful and famous for sex, presumably among those who aspired to her favours but who had no chance of making the team.

Lady Antonia was rightly dismissive of my mother's title and suggested '*I Know You've Got A Girl in There*'. Much better, but how did she know it was my mother's catchphrase? Simple, she explained. On more than one occasion, she had been the girl.

It was a book never to be written and the early days and indiscretions of the likes of future Cabinet minister George Younger and Charles Guinness, who shared the two-bedroom top flat in an unlikely early twinning of the Beerage, would remain forever locked in the memory of my mother's petty cash book. Once, when the postman delivered a telegram for George Younger, she told him he was out but Mr Guinness could take delivery. The postman was most offended – 'If you think I've come all this way just for your sport then you've got another think coming,' and refused to believe my mother's explanation that she wasn't taking the mickey and the two men really did share a flat. A Bhutto arrived to attend Christ Church via the first-floor front and Thomas Hetherington, later to become a Director of Public Prosecutions, was installed in the second-floor front. By this time, my mother was looking after No 2 next door for a Swedish divorcée who was meant to be on site but rarely was.

Into No 2 came the redoubtable Mrs Lydia Jones of Ximeno Avenue, Long Beach, California, blue hair and fly-away glasses glinting in the late Oxford summer sunshine. Mrs Jones was at Oxford as chaperone to her son and the apple of her American eye. Vince was a giant, crew-cut football and ice hockey player who had come to Oxford to study for a year. He did little of that but he did take up stock-car racing and, such was his prowess on the football field, that he made the Oxford University rugby side even though his knowledge of the rules was sketchy.

Vince Jones was a small boy's dream. My first American sandwich – enormous and filled with layers of pastrami, lashings of mayo and all sorts of unimaginable delights – was eaten in the back seat of his car returning to Oxford from Harringay dog track, where Vince and his green-devil stock-car had been competing. He smashed it up but not before taking out many rather more flimsy British machines. Life was never quite the same after Vince and Lydia returned to California although we received long letters from her for years to come. Lydia had acted as an unofficial landlady at No 2, which, considering she was paying rent and my mother shouldn't have been running the place anyway, was pretty decent of her. But when she left, my mother took over to such an extent that the family was made to go next door for a bath, thus saving on our heating bill and staying clean at the expense of the unfortunate Swedish divorcée. If, when presented with her gas bill, she thought she had managed to corner the market in obsessively clean undergraduates, she didn't say anything. We were never caught during her infrequent visits, although there were a number of close shaves when my mother double-rented rooms, only for the original and legitimate tenant to return from vacation unexpectedly to find his room occupied and, on occasions, his gramophone and wireless in full unauthorised use.

Museum Road ran adjacent to the Pitt Rivers museum, a Gothic tribute to the Victorian explorers and, at right angles to St Giles, a dead end culminating in the Lamb and Flag, a haven for serious Oxford drinkers who turned their backs on the literary Eagle and Child on the other side of St Giles's great highway. It straddled the twin memorials to the Oxford Anglo-Catholic movement, a Victorian and Oxford enthusiasm led by Edward Pusey, whose memorial, Pusey House, stood on the west side of St Giles, and John Keble, whose red brick memorial, Keble College, towered over our back garden. Together with John Newman, who later changed teams and became a Cardinal, these three fired up Oxford with a muscular High Church Anglicanism called the Oxford Movement, the aim of which was to keep the church at the head of all national affairs. It split the Church of England and it split Oxford, but Pusey and Keble were popular enough to be immortalised when the University, which, in Oxford, considered itself to be well above both Church and State, decided to develop its enormous acreage in North Oxford with plenty of smells and bells provided by the Catholic church of St Aloysius.

Museum Road, as befits a street sandwiched between such religious heavyweights, was heavily hierarchical. At the far end, closest to the cobbled Lamb and Flag alley, presided over by the massive presence of its conker tree, are two unattractive 1938 houses thrown up by St John's college – at that time monarch of all it surveyed – to house dons with families, something that was forbidden until half-way through the nineteenth century. These houses are surrounded by a high brick wall and cut off from the rest of Museum Road, presumably to stop university folk being contaminated by any contact with the townspeople in the remainder of the street. The road's higher numbers were classic North Oxford semi-detached, four floors and a basement designed by John Dorn, one of the most influential architects in the explosion of styles which are now probably the finest concentrated example of late-Victorian residential building to be found anywhere in Britain. Museum Road was split by Blackhall Road and the lower numbers made available to the lower orders. Our house was one of the first built – in 1864 – and leased to a hairdresser called Frederick Irwin. Six years later, Keble College was built, hemming in our suburban red brick with its own and presenting our back garden with a wall of brick, relieved only by the zig-zag white patterns that are Keble's trademark. It was the first red-brick college and the critics hated it, although, to me, it has always had a perverse charm. No better example of epic red-brick Victorian religious building can be found than Keble chapel, although architectural sensitivity was not one of Keble's strong points, a fact underlined a century later when half of Museum Road, including our house, was knocked down to provide student accommodation in what was a monstrously ill-proportioned and ugly piece of vandalism. It would have been laughed out of any council planning department outside a university city. Of all the appalling architecture Oxford has erected to provide for its staff and students' comforts, the Museum and Blackhall Roads developments must rank as one of the most cynical. No. 4 became a dons' car park, a monument to the triumph of privilege over people and proof that, in Oxford, the University rules whether it's OK or not.

But in the 1950s, the street hierarchy was still alive and we all knew our place. At the far end then, in the crabby little white stone dons' houses, were Professor Harold 'Tommy' Thompson, chemistry don, a pioneer of studies into infrared and one of the finest teachers the University had on its books. He was also founder of Pegasus Football Club, a short-lived but remarkably successful football team made up of former Oxford and Cambridge blues which in the early Fifties won the Amateur Cup twice in three years, before disappearing as quickly as it arrived. Professor Thompson was to become Sir Harold and go on to be chairman of the

Football Association where he became famous for loathing Don Revie and fondling the bottoms of air stewardesses.

In the second of the dons' houses lived the Sherwin-Whites. These families had two sons, the blond, curly-haired Richard Thompson and the smouldering, brooding David Sherwin-White. You could tell he was clever because he always wore the blue sweater and corduroy shorts of the Dragon School, the élite uniform of Oxford's budding intellectuals.

The boys at the end of the road were pleasant but distant and rarely descended from Olympus to play in the street with the likes of Kay Merrick, the very Welsh daughter of Reading's stationmaster who unaccountably lived in Oxford, the splendid Davies girls who lived opposite us at No. 3, and the tubby and shambolic Cyril, funny, none too bright but my blood brother.

In our early years, Cyril and I and our battered pedal cars were inseparable, until he left the road when his mother lost her job. After that, life dealt him off the bottom of the pack. In trouble with girls, in trouble with the law and finally committed to a mental hospital before he was out of his teens. Word used to come back about him every few years, like a missionary in Africa, but I never saw him again.

The Davies girls were the daughters of a don who had not yet become senior enough to have his own walled garden. Alas, when he eventually managed a move to Norham Road, a class address without a doubt even though it was only a quarter of a mile away, all contact ceased with Susan, Jane and Virginia; they were my first experience of girls and, between them, had all the delight and danger which must have made them wonderful young ladies. All I have of them now is a dog-eared book called *Cricket, Do It This Way*, given to me on my ninth birthday when I still harboured ambitions to play for England by dislodging Denis Compton. Together, in the summer we trekked down South Parks Road, passed the pathology labs with their pickled organs – where did they get those? – glinting in the window and the smell of formaldehyde a constant reminder of mortality; through the University Parks, across the punt rollers which separated Parson's Pleasure, the dons' nude bathing area of the Cherwell, from the rest of the world and into our own Dame's Delight. Dame's Delight was carved out of a curve in the river next to Parson's Pleasure and was open to the families of university members, those of us who could con our way in, and young men who didn't fancy being touched up by scrawny, oversexed dons at Parson's Pleasure. It was at Dame's Delight that I learned to dive from a high board, the area where most of the girls congregated as they could see across the tatty green corrugated iron partitions into Parson's Pleasure. In Oxford, the first sight of a full-frontal male nude was invariably classical, but at least 70, wispy haired, blue-veined, long and dangling and steeped in Latin verse.

At the other end of Museum Road lies Keble College's Warden's Lodgings, not as well appointed as many college masters' homes because the austere founding principles meant Keble wasn't built for grandees or rowers. Today, the high-minded and saintly John must look down from his incense cloud and wonder what has happened to this legacy, the red-brick warrens around the quad plastered with the graffiti of years of late-twentieth-century boating success. Keble was built as a memorial to high-church Anglicanism and, in the 1950s, was presided over by the Rt Rev Harry Carpenter whose son Humphrey, being the youngest in the road, was invariably picked on. On the rare occasions he ventured out, he was forced to retrieve a pavilionful of footballs, tennis balls and cricket balls, which had been kicked, thrown or hit over Keeble's walls.

The two sets of children divided equally between those born to continue the rule of an intellectual élite and the rest of us. If you had any doubt where your future lay, the Pitt Rivers Christmas Lectures test would resolve it. They cost sixpence and were children's lectures on anything from dinosaurs to the evolution of Man. Humphrey Carpenter, David Sherwin-White, Richard Thompson and their sisters all went. The Davies girls, Kay Merrick, Cyril and I took the sixpence but didn't go, preferring instead the delights of football and a rather more exciting if rudimentary explanation of Man, relying on the Davies' girls superior knowledge of the nursery slopes. Nonetheless, both David and Humphrey survived the tedium of the museum lectures and developed into terrific writers. David dropped the White and wrote the script's for the films *If ...* and *O Lucky Man* two seminal pieces of cinema work of the 1960s and '70s. These spectacular early successes, where he took a machine-gun to everything that had helped to form him, were to be the high points of his career. His enormous talent was squandered by Hollywood and he suffered a severe nervous breakdown. Yet his 1990s book *Going Mad in Hollywood* is sad, brilliant and funny. Anyone who can order David Owen out of his house because he said he didn't like David Storey's play *The Contractor* cannot be either bad or mad. David Sherwin was – and perhaps still is – a talent the British cinema needs, and it is extraordinary that he has been left for so long to do little but fly his model planes in the Malvern Hills.

Humphrey went on to become a famous biographer, weighing and judging facts, figures, opinions, character, relationships, actions and reactions with an easy flair and style which must owe something at least to those Christmas lectures and his scrutiny of the motives of those who persecuted him when he ventured out into the street. The rest of us – me, certainly – did not have that easy intelligence born of true academic blue blood, and it was made painfully obvious from an early age. This was nobody's fault, that was the way it was if you were Oxford town living cheek-by-jowl with Oxford gown. But you felt your inferiority early.

The Stott family was a jumble of conflicting passions. Freddie was clever, skilful, selfish – a man to avoid direct confrontation with his responsibilities if he could. A man's man, at home in pubs and the snooker hall, harbouring a healthy distrust of bosses. He was content with the limited horizons provided by Willenhall Motor Radiators and the Bablockhythe railway carriage.

My mother, though, was restless, desperate that her children should have the chances she didn't, and furious at the twist of her life which had given her a talented but unambitious husband and a role which confined her to providing for university students instead of providing them. She could have been, and, in some of her more purple moments, was, an actress. Her ambitions there were fulfilled by Judith – intelligent, bright, a stunning, unorthodox beauty and sparkling on stage – an effervescent and seemingly eternal girl, whose charms were going to captivate a stream of actors from John Gielgud to Albert Finney. Her stage career started like a dream, playing Wendy in *Peter Pan* where she learnt the first rule of the stage – if something can go wrong, it will. One of her earliest theatrical experiences was to be fitted up with the flying harness the wrong way, so that when the magical moment arrived and Wendy flew in her nightdress, she did so upside down, desperately trying to protect her modesty in front of a houseful of shocked mothers, nannies and bemused children. My mother was never happier than when preparing for one of Judith's first nights; for her, it was the fulfilment of her own destiny and justified, as she perceived it, the sacrifice of her own ambitions.

My father, on the other hand, was dismissive about a world he neither cared for nor understood. He was deeply suspicious of the arts and when he first heard that Judith planned a stage career he suggested she would be good only for scrubbing the boards, not treading them. His rare expeditions to the theatre, however, were spectacular. When *Peter Pan* arrived on tour in Birmingham, Freddie decided he would go and see it. Unfortunately, he had several pints before arriving and somehow managed to con his way through the stage door. All theatres are mazes backstage so he quickly got lost while looking for Judith's dressing room. She was on stage and the play had reached that crucial point where Captain Hook is about to make the Lost Boys walk the plank of his pirate ship. Wendy is tied to the mast and as the boys prepare to meet their doom and the little audience weeps, she has to turn her eyes from this appalling scene and say, 'These are my last words. Dear boys, I feel that I have a message from your real mothers and it is this; "We hope our boys will die like English gentlemen." The audience sobs ... except it didn't that night, for peering in through the wrong side of the ship's porthole, like a sea monster from the deep, was Wendy's true father's face, blinking and glistening in the spotlights and repeating in a sentimental and slurred voice, 'That's my daughter there ... that's my daughter.' At this moment, Wendy's thoughts of what she would like to do to her father went far beyond Barrie's plans for Hook as she watched him being rugby tackled by stagehands and chucked out into the street.

It would have been reasonable to suppose that this incident might have curtailed his trips to the theatre via the stage door, rather than the more orthodox method of the foyer, but it did not. A few years later, Judith was playing Hero in John Gielgud's celebrated Shakespeare Memorial Theatre's production of *Much Ado About Nothing* with Peggy Ashcroft, and they were installed at the Palace Theatre in Shaftesbury Avenue. Freddie had been at the Motor Show where refuelling was not confined to the cars. Once again, he managed to ghost his way past the stage door man but, with a day's supply of Watney's inside him, his immediate destination was not my sister's dressing room but the lavatory. Now one of the most rigid of theatre rules is that backstage lavatories are kept open and unoccupied during a performance, especially costume dramas, so that principles can unloose doublets and hoist crinolines, do the business of mere mortals, and return to the stage on cue. Freddie's knowledge of the theatre was rudimentary in the extreme, so there was no chance he knew this convention. And even if he did, he would have considered his need to remove a small river's worth of Red Barrel rather more pressing than any claims of Sir John or Dame Peggy, which is how he came to be locked into the lavatory nearest the stage just as Sir John dashed off, codpiece flying, for a quick pee before re-entering, stage left, much relieved.

There is nothing worse than being desperate for a slash, assuming release is at hand, only to find the door locked. After much pounding and muttered oaths, there was still no reply from the other side where my father had entered that bourn from which no traveller readily returns, a drunken sleep. The pounding woke him, however, but Sir John was already back on stage, with relief still the best part of an Act away.

Apparently, the last scenes of *Much Ado* have never been despatched so quickly. Neither had my father, who once again was dragged out and thrown into the street. The only comfort for Judith was that nobody ever found out who the mystery pisser was, and in 45 years she never plucked up the courage to tell Sir John the identity of the man who had caused so much ado at *Much Ado*.

My mother was scandalised by such goings on and it hardened her even more against the man she had married. She was as great a respecter of reputations and position as he was not, and her anger kept him in Wolverhampton for several weeks before he considered it safe to return to Oxford for a weekend. On these enforced exiles, he used to build up an assorted rag bag of stuff which he picked up in various late-night pub exchanges. So when he returned home at Christmas on the (shaky) basis that my mother wouldn't start a full-scale screaming match over the turkey, all sorts of strange wonders made their appearance, much of which I still have. So an extended-play, signed copy of Anne Shelton singing 'My Yiddishe Momme', 'With love from Anne Shelton', jostles for attention next to a sheet of writing paper from the Victoria Hotel, Wolverhampton, containing all the signatures of the 1952 Springbok ice-hockey team.

The same year, this supremely unreligious man, who had introduced me to the delights of Wolverhampton Wanderers, gave me a Bible which he bought cheap from a man in a pub. My mother gave me a football; no wonder we were a jumbly sort of family. Freddie, however, redeemed himself by yet another pub meeting with a man who had a friend who knew the husband of Billy Wright's landlady. In those pre-Posh and Becks days, before Billy had met Joy Beverley, the Posh of her time, even the England captain, with more than 100 caps to his name, lived in club digs. My prize was a visit to meet the great man who occupied the back bedroom in the house. The only concession to his prodigious achievements was that the front room was given over to his caps and trophies. Billy's match-day breakfast was a plate of runny tinned tomatoes, and the team's after-match perfumery confined to a foot-long bar of industrial pink carbolic soap, cut into 11 slices.

My mother was a complex, boiling mixture of insecurities, frustration, laughter, fury, wit and ambition. She deferred to rank and privilege and was a sucker for 'breeding', which was just as well as you couldn't move in Oxford for all three. But she was nobody's fool, had a shrewd eye for antiques and was remembered with vivid affection by her students as a most formidable woman. You messed with Mrs Stott at your peril. In a character study by an unknown hand I discovered in her papers there was this description headed simply 'B'. If it wasn't about her, it should have been: 'Possessing a strong dogmatic character. Unselfish yet thrifty, excitable, clever yet sometimes falling short of generous. A loyal, sparkling friend, bubbling over with mirth and yet sometimes, possibly quite morose. Loves power and likes to rule, gives one the impression sometimes of hardly possessing a human heart and yet can be most sympathetic. Too easily thrilled by anything sensational.'

Where this assessment came from I have no idea, but the fact that she kept it must mean she recognised the thumbnail portrait. There is no doubt that for all of us she was the driving force and most formidable influence in our lives. She was too much for Freddie and he knew it, so he did what he always did when he couldn't hack it. He walked away and didn't return to live in the family home until he was dying, when, once again, he needed my mother, and, in a curious way by then she needed him. She nursed him until he died, riddled with TB and in great pain from prostate cancer, at the age of 70. All he left was £4 and 800 Embassy coupons. I finished up with the coupons, and I've still got them – my mother didn't even get a pension. For the last 20 years of their marriage, the part of a man in her life was played by an old mac, Wellington boots and a felt hat she hung on the ground floor banisters to convince burglars she didn't live alone.

By the time my education began in earnest, I was a confused conflict of influences which were made even more liquorice allsort-like by my being packed off to Christ Church Cathedral Choir School. This was tucked away in tiny Brewer Street, by the side of Pembroke College, off St Aldate's, close to the grand Tom Tower and the cathedral which the school served by educating its choir. The school sounds as if it should have been at the top of the Oxford prep school tree, but it was very much the poor relation to the Dragon, Magdalen College School and New College choir school. The idea was that I should make the choir – with the radically reduced fees that went with it – but luckily for its reputation the attempt failed, and I was one of those confined to the strictly sectarian part of the school, thus avoiding the tantrums and tongue-lashings reserved for the choir by the great Tommy Armstrong, Cathedral choirmaster and organist until he went to take over the Royal College of Music. This freed me to make eyes over the English Hymnal at the girls of Headington School, across the aisle at Evensong – 'Immortal, invisible, God only wise', wink, wink, snigger, smirk, blush.

My time at Christ Church taught me how to play football in cowpats – we weren't wealthy enough to have a proper pitch and had to make do with the cow field in the meadows – a lifelong fascination for Charles Dickens' *Tale of Two Cities* which was read to us by the French mistress before lights out, an equally lengthy obsession with cricket and a love of church music, thanks to being forced to listen to my schoolfellows in the cathedral choir every Sunday. It was at Christ Church, too, where I met my first delightful set of loonies, from the gin-drinking, stick insect Maths mistress, Miss Rachel Crothers, to the Welsh beer-swilling rugby fanatic Jimmy Humphries, who took us for every game except rugby which we never played. He hated soccer and, on the occasion when he could be bothered to get involved, he used to amuse himself by picking up the ball and running with it before hoofing it over the bar and claiming three points. We weren't terribly good at football, although our home record wasn't bad because finicky opposition teams, for some reason, didn't like falling head-first into cowpats.

Miss Crothers excelled herself in the horse-racing field and tended to bet in the afternoon after a couple of large ones in the pub. On Derby Day 1953, she reeled into afternoon assembly, announced that Gordon Richards had won the race for the first time, tried to close the door and collapsed in a heap. Miss Crothers did not stay the course. Ann M'Carogher was an altogether different sort. A refined, aloof, prudish and frustrated Irish spinster, she taught us French and held a candle for the headmaster, the Rev David Dendy, whose gentle wife was an oasis for the young boarders when life became too Spartan, harsh or unfair. Sadly she died in her thirties and Mr Dendy married the school matron in what a few – certainly Miss M'Carogher – saw as unnecessary haste.

Miss M'Carogher, for some reason nobody could fathom, carried an influence with the college authorities which was probably the result of her ability to network mercilessly among parents. And although Christ Church was a school you only went to if you didn't have the ability or the clout to get into the Dragon, there were enough university parents to see poor old Dendy off to a rural parsonage where he could indulge his passion for speaking Latin as if it was a living modern language with the horses and cows of North Oxfordshire. A comedown from a conversation with the Dean of Christ Church, but perhaps more inspirational. The trouble with trying to speak Latin as if it was still in use was that there was, all too often, no word for modern objects. Part of the fun for Dean and Dendy was the challenge presented by such obstacles, thus a football would become, in Latin, a round leather ball made up of 12 parts and used by the people for games with the feet. Not side-splitting, I agree, yet how the Dean laughed. But when it came to scandal, and sexual scandal at that, however mild, Latin or no Latin, Dendy was out; not sacked, of course, it was just that he might prefer a living somewhere else. Immediately.

With a Common Entrance pass scraped, it was off to Clifton College in Bristol as a boarder. Why? Because my brother had been there and because I was not wanted at home during the term time filling a bed which could be rented out. But why both John and I were sent there remains a mystery; it is quite likely that one of my mother's student favourites went there – it would have been enough for her. Whatever the reason, it was a foolhardy decision because she didn't have the money to pay for it and my father was no help. He paid nothing except the rent on the house and his own lodgings in Wolverhampton. It was Lily P who lived at No 22 down the road who coughed up when my mother got into difficulties, which she did almost immediately.

Lily P and Ma Stott were two landladies with big reputations in the days when undergraduates expected not only a fully cleaned room every day, but also prodigious breakfasts, served on trays with individual teapots, cereal, eggs, bacon, toast and marmalade, all taken up to them in their rooms by me before I went to school. First of all I did the trays for Number four before running down the road to stagger up the endles flights of stairs at Number 22. Never once did I discover an undergrad anything but alone in his bed.

My early holidays were a week alone with Lily P in genteel hotels on the south coast: Eastbourne, Worthing, Bognor, hardly the most exciting of prospects for a young boy. But she had a suprisingly relaxed attitude to youth, no doubt forged from years of policing the King's Arms where she brooked no argument. In her old age she came to live with us after my mother moved to the Oxfordshire countryside. Lily P died sitting in front of the fire in one of our chairs at home, my mother chattering to her for ten minutes before she realised she was dead. I was sent to find the local district nurse who did the laying out, which I did as she was downing her third pint of Guinness in the pub. I was detailed to help with the laying out – because I was the one likely to benefit from the will, explained my mother – but by the time I returned with the district nurse, rigor mortis had well and truly set in. 'You'll have to sit on her legs while I pull down the top so we can get her nice and straight,' she explained through waves of Guinness breath. This we managed to do but by now it was dark and we were working in front of the French windows with the lights off, it wasn't a sight for the neighbours. All seemed to be going to plan when suddenly there was a squeak and Lily P sat bolt upright, silhouetted against the dusk filtering throught the windows. 'Don't be silly dear,' said the district nurse, 'you just lie back,' and gave her a huge push, bending her back to the more orthodox pose of the dead. It was an unusual introduction to mortality.

My mother was no fool about money, but Clifton was expensive and she still had the occasional expense with brother John who was learning the hotel business, not one of commerce's natural high-payers. She managed to outwit the taxman for most of her life and was sharp enough to make Lily P, a spinster with no dependents, my godmother, an inspired choice as I was quickly adopted as the child she never had. She was less lucky with my godfather, an Oxford property developer called Eddie Lougher who was both extremely Welsh and extremely fat. Once again he was chosen because of his wealth and lack of dependents, but she had not anticipated the natural stinginess of the Welsh, and when he died he left me two cufflinks, both silver, but unfortunately not a pair. I still wear them; Uncle Eddie wasn't the only one who could be perverse.

My time at Clifton was, unknown to me, frequently interrupted by letters asking for the fees to be paid as my mother struggled within a limited budget to give me the education she never had. It was a vain attempt to shape me into the kind of young man she had so often seen take up residence at Museum Road. These were cultured, assured, financially secure young men, fresh from public schools or national service in a smart regiment, who, even after the war, made up the vast majority of Oxford's student population. By the early 1950s, times were changing and the grammar schools were beginning to break through, but Ma Stott had seen too many examples of 'what the university wants' to think for a moment that the son of a landlady could make it back as a student, without a 'proper' education. Clifton provided that, but it couldn't change the boy who remained stubborn, class-conscious, a hotch-potch of conflicting and incomplete ideas and, above all, solitary and reticent. The only assets were a sharp tongue and ready wit, not always an advantage.

In the late 1950s, Clifton and the public schools were on the cusp of revolutionary change, but they were still run in much the same way as they were in the days when they turned out boys tailored to run the Indian civil service. I did not take readily to school discipline, partly through arrogance and partly through a 'sod you' approach to authority inherited from my father. None of this made for a successful public school career and I was memorable for one reason only – I was the first boy to get out of the Combined Cadet Force purely on the grounds of being unwilling to submit to its discipline. By the time I was at the top of the school and in the middle bench of the sixth form, I was still a cadet, I had passed no corps exams and was remarkable only for marching a troop of my giggling fellows up the chapel steps instead of around the parade ground. I could take a .303 (Boer war vintage) to pieces like an expert, but I never bothered to learn how to put it back together again.

Field craft was an excuse for a smoke and Field Day for a glass or two at the pub after using what passed for field craft skills to lose our company commander. The Corps was run by Regimental Sergeant Major Graham, Royal Marines, a caricature of an RSM but a lovely man. When I was eventually allowed by the headmaster to bin the Corps in favour of, allegedly, working on my History and English courses, I took my uniform back to the Armoury, the subterranean headquarters of the RSM smelling of oily four-by-two, blanco and Brasso. I was met by RSM Graham in uncharacteristically reflective mood. 'You have beaten us, Stott,' he said without a hint of malice. 'The headmaster has let you do something which will eventually destroy the Corps. You have been able to get out of it because you hate it and for no other reason apart from the fact that you made a bloody nuisance of yourself. Nothing will be the same again, others will do it and the discipline will be finished.'

He was right. Others did, and by end of the 1960s the CCF was seen for what it was, a hopelessly hierarchical and bone-headed way of training boys for a world that no longer existed and few cared for anyway. RSM Graham was a good man, a great deal better than many of those he had to train and, like the ace shot he was, intuitive and accurate enough to know that by 1961 he was presiding over a doomed tradition.

It was the only impression I was to make on Clifton – apart, that is, from the scandal of the Housemaster's Ward which overshadowed my last term. By the age of 16, I had many prejudices and half-formed opinions but was unable to sustain anything remotely like a cogent argument. I was immature, even for 16, difficult and resentful of authority. Teachers were there to be borne and dispensed with as quickly as possible. Then, after taking my O-levels and doing rather worse than even I expected, I found myself in the Upper Fifth English and History set lorded over by a man who was to become a legend. John Thorn, wavy black hair falling over his eyes, expansive, masculine but with a strong feminine side, prodigiously clever, unorthodox and compelling, took over my life. At least, that's how I saw it. He was not everyone's cup of tea and both at Repton and Winchester where he was to become headmaster he had his enemies. But in late 1959, this man was a mixture of God and Jean Brodie to those of us lucky enough to be his chosen ones. We weren't necessarily the *crème de la crème*, although some of his eight or so 'specials' clearly were; we were just the ones who interested him, and we were those singled out for special play readings, discussions on ethics, current affairs and anything else that took his fancy. He taught us to think, to abandon the sweeping generalisations we considered so impressive, to examine what we really felt, and not be ashamed or afraid to do so. In a phrase which many years later he decried when I reminded him of it, he told me, 'Remember Richard' – he always called us by our Christian names in private, unheard of then – 'the truth is neither black nor white, it is a dirty shade of grey.'

Yes, of course, I have heard it many times since, but that first time, in Johnny Thorn's Clifton flat, with the assorted noises and snorts coming from Bristol zoo next door, those words to dogmatic 16 year-olds not only gave us that bolt of encouragement, to mould our principles, but also the confidence to stand by them when all around were abandoning theirs.

In the space of one glorious year, John Thorn gave a handful of raw teenage boys the power to reason without fear, and the clarity of sight to be ourselves. We still continued to grope around, bumping into furniture in the darkness of confused adolescent minds, but at least we were beginning to find out that we had furniture and where some of it was. This was, I think, the year that defined what I was to become, because he made me see clearly what I was. And what I saw was not adequate. There were many flaws – there still are – but the foundations were laid and the guiding principles would never be seriously challenged again: honesty in your dealings with others and with yourself; clear and, if necessary, merciless examination of your own motives; the courage to speak the truth as you see it; defence of the rights of those who, for whatever reason, are in no position to defend themselves, because you are lucky enough to possess gifts that make it a moral imperative for you to do so.

I don't suggest I was paragon enough always to live up to such high ideals, but they provided the certainties against which all things were judged, and at least when I didn't live up to them, I knew I had been found wanting. They look silly and twee when you write them down, but there's nothing I can do about that. I have seen clever people founder and powerful people fall because they have not instinctively reached for their founding principles when the pressure is on, probably because they didn't have any.

The year fled by and, by the middle of 1960, I was away from John Thorn and into the sixth form, but his teaching was never to leave me; for that alone, my mother's odd choice of Clifton College was more than justified.

In the school soccer team – not a difficult 11 to make as it was scorned at Clifton – I played left-half, servicing a swift outside-left called Clive Thompson who was to find fame and great fortune as the chief executive of Rentokil and President of the Confederation of British Industry, where his major claim to industrial immortality was his ability to increase profits by vast amounts, earning him the nickname of Mr 20 Per Cent. This, however, came to an abrupt halt when he found that in order to pay his lowest paid workers the new Labour Government's minimum wage, he would have to increase the pay packets of 10,000 of his employees. His appearance in the Clifton football team was the last recorded instance of the Thatcherite Sir Clive being comfortable on the left wing.

My only other sporting foray was into the boxing ring; where the school team was under the command of the wonderful Gordon Hazell, a former British middleweight contender with a body to match. Not only was he so well developed that he could make those golf ball muscles come up on his arms, he could manage it on his calves. Gordon was a magnificent man, Bristol born and bred with an accent to match and a homespun philosophy that revolved around the solar plexus, 'centre of the nervous system, Stott,' and English literature. 'Health is wealth – who said that, Stott?'

'Shakespeare, sir.'

'Quite right, don't forget it and you'll be all right.'

This kind of inquisition usually took place on the boxing squad's five-mile boot runs across the Downs, and once you had sussed out that Gordon expected Shakespeare to be the answer to everything, the questions weren't overtaxing. He had a cleanliness fetish, always wore a pristine white tracksuit – 'Next to Godliness, Stott' – he was a fitness fanatic and turned the Clifton squad into a mini professional unit. He had one or two fine fighters – I was handy with a decent right hand but not one of Gordon's greats – and he turned us into a real force with a mixture of training and sheer professionalism. He was well versed in the black arts of boxing; he himself had had to retire, unable to come out for the sixth round of a fight in Rome with the European middleweight champion, after ether mysteriously got into the sponge in his corner. As a result he couldn't see or breathe. We didn't quite go to those lengths before a fight, but we were encouraged not to shave for a week – older boys only – and became well versed in the art of rubbing your stubble along an opponent's face when in a clinch, turning your man into the ropes while pinioning his arms. Gum shields were introduced, making even the most angelic boy look ferocious; boxing boots, ditto; and proper slinky shorts. Add this to Gordon's ability to talk down the opposition within their hearing – not done at all in public schools – and our results far outweighed our talents. The headmaster was so appalled by this Ali-like professionalism that Gordon was told to tone it down.

'Winners in mind, winners in body, Stott ...?'

'Shakespeare, sir.'

Gordon was also an expert on the boxer's curse, at least in public schools. 'I know what you lot do when you're in bed, can't keep your hands off yourselves. Well it's no good, masturbation is the same as a five-mile walk, and so's a wet dream ... Stott?'

'Shakespeare, sir.'

Gordon had an answer to this perennial boarding school problem. The answer to wet dreams was to wear a cotton reel tied to your back at night. The reason for this, he explained, was that boys only had wet dreams when lying on their backs, although, as far as I know, Shakespeare had nothing to say on the subject. With the thought of a cotton reel being infinitely preferable to a five-mile walk on the night before a fight, the more impressionable of us tried it out with the unsurprising result that we were all knackered in the morning because we were constantly woken by the cotton reel.

Gordon Hazell inspired great loyalty and was a natural teacher as well as one of the finest post-war middleweight boxers this country produced, but his cause can hardly have been helped when *Harpers and Queen* published a *Good Schools Guide* in 1988, the year he retired. The school was 'slightly wild and undisciplined', reported the guide, the headmaster an enigma and the teaching staff was 'of very mixed ability', except for Gordon Hazell who was a 'first-rate physical training instructor'. The governors must have loved that.

What is more of a tribute to Gordon is that Clifton was the last public school to bow to the political correctness of abandoning boxing, which culminated with a major colour supplement feature on the man who had been its inspiration for 30 years, something no other Clifton master had achieved. He inspired such Boy's Own loyalty that one Cliftonian who went on to box for Oxford against Cambridge was inspired in his corner before the last round of a particularly gruelling and close-run fight by the university's coach whispering in his ear, 'Do it for Gordon, do it for Gordon.' Of course he did.

The end of boxing at Clifton in 1988 was the final bell for Gordon Hazell. His life had been his boys and the school boxing. In his retirement, he cut a lonely figure as he walked the school playing fields at Beggar's Bush reliving the 33 years of boys – from the fleaweight under 6st 8lb to the over 12st heavies – who had worn the blue-edged vest of the Clifton boxing colours. He was probably remembered more than any other master of his generation, yet he died alone, at the age of 72 in 2001. A boxer's death.

The painful warrior famoused for fight,
After a thousand victories once foil'd,
Is from the book of honour razed quite,
And all the rest forgot for which he toil'd ...

The lines could have been written for Gordon Hazell, and this time they really are Shakespeare.

By the beginning of the 1960s, I decided I wanted to be an actor, although with precious little evidence that I was any good. Clifton had a fine tradition of those who had strutted their stuff on the school stage: Michael Redgrave, Trevor Howard, John Cleese and my contemporary Braham Murray, who went on to have a distinguished career as director of the Royal Exchange in Manchester. The tradition continues with the magnificent Simon Russell Beale.

I was not up to this heady standard, and the only reason I decided on the stage was because of the success of sister Judith who was rightly horrified I should consider such a career with so little evidence of talent. I have always adored the theatre and have been lucky enough to meet and know many of its finest exponents, but I was strictly audience and critics' side of the footlights and Judith knew it. She had a plan to protect the theatre from such foolhardiness and detailed her great friend, the director Peter Wood, to dissuade me from this suicide mission, and his campaign was as short as it was brilliant.

Peter: 'A great friend of mine is one of the best actors I know, he was wonderful as a drama student and has a tremendous voice. He's now on television every day.'

Me: 'That's terrific. What does he do?'

Peter: 'He's the speaking clock.'

My defences were breached in one go and, confidence drained, that was the end of my theatrical ambitions. At the age of 18, I started to look towards another trade where the pursuit of the egocentric and obsession with self is paramount – journalism beckoned. But as I prepared to leave school and do battle with the world, there was one more twist that in those gentler days could have graced the pages of the *News of the World*. It was the Scandal of the Housemaster's Ward.

Michael 'Willy' Lane was a sympathetic, humane schoolmaster, a family man with a sense of humour who enjoyed a drink and smoked like a chimney. He had iron-grey, crinkly hair, a smile to match and a gravelly voice which could turn in anger to an alarming bark. His wife Patricia was approachable, funny and easy-going. Apart from their own children, during term time they also looked after the daughter of a friend who ran a hotel in Dartmouth. Her name was Caroline, she was only 15, and all the boys who took a remote interest in girls – which, in spite of the general reputation of public schools as training grounds for lifelong homosexuals, was most of them – adored her from afar. But afar was as near as you got; in spite of the Lanes' modern approach to house mastering, it did not include being able to sample the nubile delights of the private side of the house ... until, for some unfathomable reason, the young Caroline took a shine to me – 17, spotty and up to my neck in A-levels.

This friendship gradually grew by the properly English public school method of playing croquet on the lawn in front of School House where you could be seen by everyone – boys and masters. By the autumn, there was no doubting the mutual attraction and Willy Lane took the, in retrospect, extraordinarily brave step of allowing me to take her out, on the flimsy and untried grounds that I was a responsible senior member of his hierarchy. It worked well to start with, but school responsibility was no match for teenage ardour and eventually we stayed out far longer than was permissible, actually in the cinema watching a terrible film called *The Queen's Guards* which, of all people, starred Jess Conrad but also featured my sister Judith, the only defence for admitting to actually paying to see it.

Willy Lane, fearing the worst as we arrived back hours late, went nuclear. Gross breach of trust ... let him down ... severely embarrassed as he was meant to be *in loco parentis*, and ending with a thundering, 'This is the last night you spend under my roof.' Disaster. Disgrace. Humiliation. And a terrible film to boot.

This was in the days before being expelled became a fashion accessory and, in the end Willy Lane and the headmaster pulled back from the brink, partially, I think, because he thought he was a little to blame himself, but also because of some nifty footwork by brother John Stott, an old Cliftonian and 11 years older than me, who showed commendable quick thinking and imagination by claiming my mother had recently suffered a heart-attack and this news would probably kill her. This was not strictly the truth – she had had a heart murmur – but John was not to be denied his moment of high drama centre stage. Anyway, it worked, I was demoted from house prefect to nothing, banned from contacting Caroline and warned that one false step would see me out. That should have been the end of the matter but it wasn't, thanks to Mrs Armstrong, our splendid house matron, a Scots widow with a romantic turn of mind who started running notes between the star-crossed lovers which, if discovered, would not only have seen me on my way but her, too. This was too close to

Romeo and Juliet for comfort, right down to the nurse as intermediary.

Luckily the pressure was relieved by John who had rediscovered the taste for Clifton life, coming down every weekend to throw drink down the throats of myself and my closest friend Henry Acland. Henry was Deputy Head of House and had been told to keep me out of trouble by Willy Lane, a vain hope for either of us. As the end of our last term and real life approached, Henry and I began to take drinks in the evening, inspired by the weekend trips to fine Somerset restaurants courtesy of brother John. I was getting used to life in disgrace and had become something of an icon for the Bolshies, so it was a bit of a downer when I was suddenly reinstated. We celebrated in Henry's study with a bottle of gin diluted with orange squash, drank far more than we should and, as a result, had difficulty in speaking. Normally, this wouldn't have mattered too much, but Henry hazily remembered he had to take house prayers which both entailed a reading and leading the boys and masters in prayer. As he couldn't see the page, never mind get the words out, disaster and disgrace loomed once again. I wasn't in a brilliant state but could still speak in a Reggie Bosanquet fashion, so offered to take prayers. When we assembled, I told Willy Lane that I had taken over from Henry as a symbolic gesture of my rehabilitation and return to respectability. Luckily, by 9.00pm Willy had usually had a convivial dinner himself so he was unable, or possibly unwilling, to detect the reek of Gordon's. I dispensed with the reading and went straight into the prayers – 'Sometimes we need to change the format to understand more fully the import of what we are doing here', I explained with only the hint of a slur. As we knelt down, me with rather a thud, nobody was praying harder than I was.

By the end of term and an entrance exam to Christ Church in the offing, I was once again allowed to see Caroline. Willy Lane must have been a glutton for punishment. But by now I was too under the influence of Britain's new wave of angry young men to care much about university. I went for my exam at Christ Church wearing a corduroy cap, sloppy sweater and jeans and looking – I now realise – rather foolish. You need to be immensely clever or rich to get away with that at The House and, as I was clearly neither, the whiff of a cloth cap was enough for Christ Church to slam the gates under Tom Towe,, there was no chance of Chips With Everything at a college where Wesker was assumed to be a tin of cat food. So it was on to Keble, my mother's landlords and my next-door neighbours for as long as I could remember.

My interview was a disaster. It was with one of those prissy English dons who delight in making young people feel even more uncomfortable and insecure than they do already. He did it by talking about *Beowulf*, something I had neither read nor knew anything about beyond the fact that it was earlier and even more impenetrable than the densest of Chaucer and the *Faerie Queene* rolled into one. He knew perfectly well what he was doing as he turned the screw further and further until I had had enough and hit back, telling him exactly what I thought of him in Anglo Saxon not available to the saintlike Beowulf, the monster Grendel or even his water hag mother. How sad can you get – I read it later to find out what I had missed. It would be warming to report that this bruising encounter, made even worse because it took place in such familiar surroundings, resulted in the scales falling from the eyes of Keble's English department as it collectively realised there was a no-nonsense young man of real if raw talent come amongst them. No such luck, I was told to get out and a report on my behaviour was sent to Clifton.

That year saw the school chalk up record entries into Oxbridge, but Stott RK was not among them. It was the end of my attempts to embark on a university career and I left school to the traditional hymn 'The Day Thou Gavest Lord is Ended' ringing out in the bleak December darkness from Sir Henry Newbolt's famous chapel, all prepared to strike down the foe that comes with fearless eyes if only I could identify who he was. I had not the faintest idea what I wanted to do beyond the catch-all of 'journalism'. Write a blockbuster play, certainly. Be the next Director General of the BBC, without a doubt, but beyond that, nothing. Which was just as well, because apart from working as a waiter for the next year, that is exactly what I did.

In my nineteenth year I was launched into the world. Six O-levels, two As and a bottom-of-the-bill scandal to my name, but the rest was unformed, unpromising and rather lumpy clay. The verdict from fading reports for 1961 – English: 'A very alert individual, alive to the problems of his subject, but a little unconventional in some of his ideas. Should do well.' I could put up with more of that, even if at the time it seemed unduly optimistic.

Sixth form essays – 'His essay on censorship contained some good ideas which were very loosely joined together to form an argument which he expressed far more cogently in the discussion we had later. I found his poem interesting though a little surprising. He had undoubtedly tried to express sincere feelings which were far more introverted than I would have expected.' Luckily the poem is long lost.

From Willy Lane – 'Interested in ideas and original thinking. This is a valuable step forward, providing it remains within the limits of his own character and intelligence. He must be sure that those ideas are really from him and are not part of a show he is staging for the world.' Written before the Caroline crisis, of course, but pretty accurate I think.

The theatrical influences on me were fierce. My sister was currently an item with Albert Finney and she had previously had an affair with Robert Stephens; I had known Maggie Smith since I was a boy: Peter Wood I regarded as a friend and someone I could talk to about myself; through Judith, I had met John Gielgud and Peggy Ashcroft, and run errands for Edith Evans (who looked disconcertingly like my godmother Lily P and often behaved like her. Both had the ability to fart loudly and totally ignore it.) From each of these remarkable people, I grafted something onto my own personality, except that my own, such as it was, was confused, occasionally angry and intolerant, helped along, no doubt, by having no idea about what to do next.

I went to ground in the basement of Lily P's house at 22 Museum Road and started writing theatrical reviews of Oxford University Dramatic Society's and the Experimental Theatre Club's productions. It was an especially vibrant time with my old school contemporary Braham Murray and the young American Michael Rudman about to make waves far beyond Oxford. I didn't make a ripple and when I tried my reviews on the University editors I was airily dismissed because I wasn't a member of the university and would I kindly get lost. At least I had been given a taste of that most bitter of journalism's fruits – rejection.

So my immediate future was behind the bar of my brother's catering company, where every weekend I tried unsuccessfully to seduce female wedding guests, fortified by stolen glasses of champagne paid for, unknowingly, by the bride's father. Caroline had dumped me once I left school; she had fallen for the next generation, an Elvis Presley lookalike who did not make the same mistake as me. She went on to marry an art master at Canford School, which had its 15 minutes of fame when what the massed brains of generations of staff thought was a whitewashed scrawl in the school tuckshop turned out to be an art master's nightmare, a £7 million bas-relief from the walls of King Ashurnasirpal II and dating from the ninth century BC.

Then Henry took me home to his beautiful house and gardens at Killerton in Devon, a county the Aclands had graced since the twelfth century. Independent, proud, free-thinking, the family was one of the oldest in the country which could trace a direct descent through the male line. Henry was the youngest of three sons and his father embodied all of the Acland traits. Sir Richard was the fifteenth holder of his title; he became a Liberal MP in 1935, but soon converted to socialism. Unlike many, he practised what he preached. He formed the Common Wealth Party during the war and he crusaded for common ownership on moral as well as wealth grounds. The party was spectacularly successful in a series of by-elections, probably because the wartime coalition meant there was virtually no opposition, foreshadowing Labour's landslide general election victory of 1945, which ironically buried Acland's party. He himself joined Labour in 1947 as MP for Gravesend, but his highly developed sense of morality and conscience was too much for post-war politics, and in 1955 he resigned from the party in protest against Britain's manufacture of the hydrogen bomb. In the general election the same year he stood as an independent and suffered the inevitable fate of independents. His political career dead, Sir Richard became a teacher at Wandsworth Comprehensive and then a lecturer at St Luke's College, Exeter. In 1944, he put his own home where his mouth was and gave all his land, including Killerton, to the National Trust where, to this day, its gardens remain one of Devon's most delightful attractions.

If John Thorn triggered the confidence to think and the principles on which to base those thoughts, then Richard Acland introduced me to the cause. Labour politics were treated with scant regard at Clifton, and in mock general elections anyone brave enough to stand as its candidate usually came in for some pelting and jeering. Clifton might have encouraged free thinking but it didn't advocate treason and it remained liberal with a small 'l' and Conservative with a big 'C'. So, in the evenings around Killerton's kitchen table, with Sir Richard at the head expounding his beliefs, hopelessly but heroically impractical and idealistic, ideas gradually began to take shape. I started to fill in the gaps that the astute Willy Lane had noticed. The Conservatives were the party of power and privilege, based on the making and retention of money at the expense of the vast majority of people. Labour, for all its faults, was the party which represented those people and was the only organisation big enough to fight the Tories' voracious appetite for power. Life, however the Tories might try and dress it up, was a matter of Them and Us.

Throughout their long history the Aclands of Devon could so easily have been Them, yet they weren't; they were big landowners, but they were also educationalists and public benefactors. Not exactly Us, but not Them either. Sir Richard died, I guess, a disappointed man, but whatever else he did, he provided the foundation of my ideas. For better or worse, the overture and beginners were ready, and Willy Lane's parting words notwithstanding, I was ready to stage my show for the world. There was one drawback – there was no audience.

4

So now I was left to the tender mercies of brother John. Restless, dynamic, inspirational, daredevil, he was all of these things. But he was also undisciplined, impulsive, extravagant and eventually self-destructive. His mind was original and bright but it fluttered like a butterfly from flower to flower. He had trained in the hotel business and taken his fair share of knocks, from crashing in Italy's Mille Miglia sports car race when he was meant to be on duty at the Excelsior hotel in Rome, to diving off the wooden bridge at the Trout Inn near Oxford into what turned out to be 4ft of water. John and cars didn't mix; he loved them but he kept on crashing them, and the more he crashed them the bigger and faster was the replacement. After one particularly bad smash, I bought him a Scalextric set; at least he could catapult himself off the road without too much damage.

John was the kind of guy who was always in the soup. When working at the Savoy he was the one who was lumbered with queries from aides to the old Aga Khan about a £30 item on his bill. It was because he wet the bed, said John. Impossible, His Highness, the spiritual leader and Imam, does not wet the bed, it is an insult to Muslims, was the outraged retort. Nonsense, replied John, he always wets the bed and he is always charged £30. This was getting out of hand and an international incident of incalculable proportions was looming. It was only averted by the reception manager grovelling, pointing out that the bill had, of course, been wrongly made up and the £30 was for room service. Naturally, said the Aga's men, and paid up.

The old man did, in fact, wet the bed all the time, but nobody had told John that it always went down as room service. For that he was punished by being sent to clean up after Roy Rogers' horse which had used the ballroom as if it were the wide open spaces of Wyoming. That was the problem with John, things happened to him.

By the time I left school, he had started his own outside catering business near Aylesbury, called Black Boy – after the pub where it was based – and featured a big round face of a black boy on the side of its trucks. Such things didn't matter in the 1950s. By 1959 he had opened Aylesbury's first supermarket, one of the first of any size anywhere in Britain and well before its time. The local paper was ecstatic: 'One-stop shopping is coming to town. Aylesbury housewives will be able to do the whole of their week's shopping under one roof.'

'This is not going to be a copy of a multiple store, this is going to be our impression of what a supermarket should be,' Mr Stott told the *Bucks Herald*. And it most certainly was. There were separate meat, deli and cheese counters to match any of Waitrose's finest today and the layout was spectacular. It was John Stott at his inventive best, but he failed to capitalise on it, lost interest and eventually sold out to Tesco after falling out with his partner who was the moneybags. These were probably his happiest times but, as his marriage fell apart, he started drinking too much and gradually fell into a despair all too familiar to those who are ruled by the bottle. For 30 years his life was to cannon from one crisis to another. Much of it was spent drunk, but right up to the end he retained his remarkable flair for big-event catering. In some ways his marriage to Kate, a major's daughter and general's grand-daughter, was an image of our parents', two people hopelessly mismatched and destructive of each other. Its failure was the ruling passion of his life and it was eventually to destroy him. But at his best he was full of bounce and life with the ability to spark those around him, a mixture of both the best and the worst of our mother and father, and his early death at 59, beaten at last by drink, loneliness and despair, left me angry and bereft; angry for such ability wasted, and bereft, because in death you only remember the good times. He hated the University because of its élitist closed shop and its never-ending ability to take as much as it could from him for free and give nothing back. It is a satisfying irony that he is buried in Iffley churchyard in Oxford next to John Sparrow, the much celebrated Warden of All Souls and epitome of the University's closed and precious world. John's grave is a mass of wild flowers planted by the children he adored but with whom he was never able to build a stable relationship because of his obsession with the failure of his marriage. Warden Sparrow's is barren.

Working as a waiter, driver, warehouseman and dogsbody in a catering company is about as hard a graft as you will find. But it does mean that I make a good cocktail, terrific hangover cures – essential if you are to be a serious journalist – and an unbeatable prawn cocktail sauce. I can tap beer barrels, an unnecessary skill nowadays, add up the price of six pints of bitter, three large gins, two whisky macs, a Dubonnet and bitter lemon, two Snowballs, a rum and black and add a couple of bob tip without anyone knowing, before you can say 'Next please'. The barman's art came disconcertingly easily. Or at least some of it did. I was not flavour of the night when, as wine waiter at a big corporation do in Buckingham town hall, it was my job to serve the red, white and rosé. Now handling two bottles is easy but three is a problem, particularly when the space is tight and you have to lean over ladies wearing big chests and chunky mayoral chains. Disaster struck when I leant over the mayoress to refresh her glass, forgetting I had the rosé tucked under my left arm. As I leaned over, the ice-cold Anjou gently poured itself right down her cleavage. This was made worse by my natural inclination to mop it up, tangling the cloth with the chain of office, pulling the top of her dress away from the community chest. I was sin-binned to wash up for the rest of the evening.

This and other mishaps – I kicked a silver tray across the marble floor of Claydon House in the middle of a quieter passage of a Mozart concerto during one of the Verney family's concerts, and forgot to load the champagne for a society wedding – hastened my search for another job. I had tried the *Coventry Evening Telegraph* – no dice – and the *Oxford Mail* turned me down, too. But then it was rather over ambitious to show the editor my poems – *I would have thought I was a prat too.*

Then, just after I had once again posted my application to become the next BBC Director General, my brother's supermarket manager John Tidmarsh rang.

'There's an advert for a junior reporter on the *Bucks Herald*. If you shift your arse, you could get an interview,' he said.

My mother decided there should be no mistake this time. Wary of my interview technique, she was going to take charge. No poems, no rows, no swearing. This was going to be a regular orthodox interview where the candidate wore a suit, spoke politely and, if necessary, grovelled, lied and exaggerated himself into the job. Welcome to journalism and the *Bucks Herald*, largest sale in Mid and North Bucks, proprietor Brian de Fraine, editor Gareth Harry, professional Welshman and mainstay of the Aylesbury and District Rotary Club. The big time was just around the corner and Ma Stott was not going to miss out. Clean your shoes, cut your hair and put on a tie. And for God's sake, *be pleasant.*

Gareth Harry was like a Welsh corgi – short, fat, red-haired, snappy and with a great waddling sense of his own importance. Public school boys don't impress us here at the *Bucks Herald*, he said, when he asked where I went to school. Ma Stott wasn't having that after paying so much for it and let Harry have it with both barrels, quite forgetting her earlier strictures to me. The school taught people how to behave (not entirely true), gave the boys good contacts for later life and, to prove it, my other son John is a very good friend of your proprietor (almost true). This was enough for Harry, not the bravest of men. I was hired at £5 15s a week, to start on 14 January 1963, which turned out to be freezing cold and blowing a blizzard.

In those days Aylesbury was still the market town it had always been, little houses and shops clustered round the market square, huddling together, it seemed on that icy Monday morning, to keep warm. The editorial offices consisted of not much more than a dilapidated small house in Great Western Street leading down to the station, with a composing room and press hall at the back, the domain of Taff Roberts, another Welshman, with a skimpy roll-up constantly hanging off his lower lip. There was one gleaming flatbed press which could print 3,000 newspapers an hour, just enough for the run of 20,000. Taff Roberts ruled 'downstairs' and the editor ventured in there only on Wednesdays and Thursdays. We published on Friday.

Harry's office was on the left as you negotiated your way from the front door across ripped and dog-eared lino. As a mark of office, he was allowed a faded rug and behind him were the dusty volumes chronicling Aylesbury's past. The advertising department – one thin room – was on the right and the manager, Mr Adams, held the editor in contempt. His space salesman, Vic Brooks, was as flash and well-appointed as you would expect a young man to be at the beginning of his sales career. But it was upstairs where the editorial was ground out, in three tiny as well as smoke-filled rooms looking down towards the station. There were seven reporters and Steve Cox, a Geordie deputy editor who also loathed Harry and didn't miss an opportunity to do him down, in a rather prissy way. 'That's bloody silly, y'know, we should never do that,' he used to tell him once he knew we were all listening, forever the disloyal deputy. The reporters were led by Phil Fountain, a local newspapermen to his fingertips, who could have made Fleet Street without any bother. But he loved Aylesbury and he knew it inside out. Local councils and courts were meat and drink to him. Immaculate shorthand note, all the councillors and the cops at his beck and call, the holder of a 1,000 borough secrets. He didn't drive – he went everywhere on his bike – and smoked roll-up Old Holborns. His number two was Wendy Groves, the women's editor, who lived with her mother and was constantly the subject of speculation about her sex life. She had a 'gentleman friend' but, wisely, he was never allowed anywhere near us. That was the senior room. The foot soldiers were crammed between the senior room and the sports department run by Jimmy Attryde who doubled up as the Tring district reporter. Jim's main job was finding new headlines to describe Aylesbury United's latest defeat. His best came after United had once again been thrashed, but this time by nine goals to nil. That Friday, Jim revealed the next day's game would see Aylesbury's brand-new and top-secret defensive plan in operation. The following week he announced the plan had worked well, but there were some teething problems. There must have been, because this time the lads went down 6–1.

Our room was presided over by John Batson – clipped moustache, glasses, brown-check pork pie hat. He had seen better days and there was a crushed sadness to him, always sitting down with a sigh, a man who had seen too many stories and hopes go down the pan. He had previously worked on the *Daily Express*, the only one of the *Herald* staff with national newspaper experience, and his conversation, wheezed through untipped Senior Service, was invariably about The Beaver (Lord Beaverbrook) and Chris (Arthur Christiansen) the legendary *Express* editor. 'Reporters were always being fired,' he explained. 'The only reason I lasted was because I sat behind the door.' As a gesture to Batson's seniority, he was allowed to do a weekly column, 'Meet Mine Host', necessitating a trip every Friday to a pub – often way out in the country – to write about the landlord and his wife. He must have been very conscientious about his column, because he never returned to the office.

The engine room of the reporting staff were Jeff Hockey and Roger Duckworth who had both worked on evening papers – in South Wales and Lancashire respectively – and were therefore men of enormous gravitas. Roger constantly moaned about the lack of Boddington's in the south; he hated southern beer because 'it makes me rift'. Which it certainly did, and to great effect, in a steamy, smoke-ridden, little room with no ventilation. This would set off Roger's odd little tee-hee laugh which was invariably followed by his explanation; 'I'm sorry, lady and gentlemen, but I thought I heard mice.'

Jeff was a Liverpudlian who smoked his cigarette clamped between his teeth. This didn't stop him talking, but it did make him look impressively fierce, particularly when a gritted, 'Bloody hell, Duckworth,' was allowed to escape as Roger dropped yet another Aylesbury Brewery flame-thrower. The juniors were myself and Julie Lunn: lovely, cuddly, giggly, blonde-haired Julie, who was engaged to the son of the local baker. Julie was delighted by my arrival because it meant she didn't have to pick up the *Telegraph* and *Times* from the local newsagent and sweep it for any local society weddings. More important, she was off Deathin'. That was now my job.

Deathin', as Phil Fountain called it, was writing up obituaries of local people who'd croaked during the week. It was grisly, often boring, but an unbeatable way of training a new reporter to deal with those in distress. My first solo effort made the national press. I had gone to the home of a recently deceased local dignitary and was all prepared for the usual scintillating prose: 'He was a well-known member of the Aylesbury and District Royal Antediluvian Society of Buffaloes and for many years a leading light of the Bifurcated and Tubular Rivet Company's sports and social club,' when his widow cut me short and said there was no need for any questions. 'He did everything before he died,' she explained. 'All you have to do is to fill in the date he passed on … he couldn't do that you see. He never trusted newspapers, always getting things wrong, so he wrote his own notice. He doesn't want it cut or anything and he doesn't want you messing about with it.'

I wasn't sure whether this was normal practice and asked Duckworth for advice. Clearly, it wasn't all that normal because the next day it was a page lead in the *Daily Mail* and Duckworth and I shared £2.

Deathin' was a ruthless business and the two undertakers, Mr FH Sheffield and Mr KY Green were locked in mortal remains combat for the right to ferry customers across the Styx. Mr Sheffield was swish with a proper chapel of rest and humming music, while Mr Green worked from the back of his DIY shop. They were the first port of call on Monday morning, but you were in serious trouble if you left off what Mr Sheffield called his 'trade plates', the last line of the obit: 'Funeral arrangements were by Mr FH Sheffield of Great Western Street, Aylesbury.' Sheffield always used to complain that Green knocked the coffins up in his lunch hour and that the worms would be through them in less time than it took the old man to eat his ham and pickle sandwich. Green prided himself on his workmanship, done 'here on the premises'. Their clients' relatives, however, were invariably patient with a hesitant young reporter and frequently invited me to stay for lunch, sometimes with alarming results.

Together with the bereaved family, I had just finished a tasty dish of fish and chips when the paper was swept off the table to reveal we had been eating off one of Mr Green's finest coffins. 'Grandad always loved his chips, now he's had 'em,' his daughter in law pointed out as she screwed up last week's *Herald* and cleared the remains of the vinegar stains from the coffin lid. Often the bereaved would want you to be at one with the subject you were immortalising and insist that you view the body, 'so you can get a feel of what Mam was like'.

At least with Deathin' you couldn't put your write-up in on the wrong week. You could with weddings, because they came in on forms and you – or more correctly, Julie – had to be careful she got the dates right. As she churned these out on Friday afternoons, following a session in the Railway Tavern paying off one slate and building the foundations of another, she wasn't always as careful as she might be. The explosion on Saturday morning was a joy to behold as Harry went ballistic after taking an earful from a weeping bride-to-be who Julie had married off a week early. The wedding forms were minefields, not just because of the tongue twisters – 'the bride looked radiant in grey-green Gros grain' – but because of the misprints, not always Julie's fault. The forms are filled out by the bride and groom and sent in to the paper, and one of the questions to answer was: 'What was the bride's gift to the groom?' Answer: 'An eight-day travelling clock.' Very nice, too, except that it appeared in the *Herald* as 'an eight-day travelling cock'. Another happy day ruined.

Everyone loved Julie, but she was the bane of Gareth Harry's life. He liked everything in order, neat, tidy, in its place. And Julie was never in her place at 9.00am when Harry arrived, on the dot, in his gleaming black Morris Traveller estate. Around about 9.25, she would turn up on her scooter, half-dressed, hair all over the place, helmet askew, Aylesburys very own Goldie Hawn. There was no escaping the Welsh inquisition, as she had to pass his door. Poor old Harry had the habit of stamping his foot when he went balistic and this, in turn, had an unsettling effect on photographic reproduction. Deep in the bowels of Great Western Street was the picture department run by Maurice Cousins and his sidekick Barry Keen. Maurice was one of those Go–Ahead photographers who not only had his own van, but was the star of a series of Horlicks strip cartoon adverts. This showed Maurice too tired to get up in the middle of the night to cover a fire, which actually wasn't too far from the truth. In the strip cartoon this was put down to 'night starvation', miraculously solved by Maurice drinking Horlicks every night. The result, at least in the advert, was that Maurice leapt around covering everything and winning no end of awards to the general acclaim of his colleagues. The truth was a little different. Maurice's biggest problem was the picture department's enlarger which was too big for the cramped cellar. In order to fit it in, the joists of the floor above had to be removed, and this was the floor of Gareth Harry's office. So every time he put his foot down over Julie's timekeeping, the enlarger shook and another set of pictures bit the dust. The inevitable result of Julie being late for work was that the best of the previous day's pictures went up the creek as well.

There were other occupational hazards. Roger Duckworth was bollocked by Harry because Aylesbury's Methodist minister smelt beer on his breath while he was taking down the list of stallholders at the church fête on Saturday afternoon. It is certainly true that we used to retire to the Railway Tavern on Friday and Saturday lunchtimes for a game of darts, a pie and a pint or two. It is also true that after some hard practice, Roger had overcome his aversion to southern beer and was resigned to the fact that he would just have to rift a lot, something else that may not have played too well with the Methodists. But we were hardly on big money for a six-day week, and most of the wage packet was paid straight over to Ernie Blake, licensee of the Railway, who ran our slate, for which he had to be repaid with our custom. I lived on beer and pork pies, luckily, my constitution was less unstable than Roger's.

After this, the Methodists went to the top of our hate list, along with the local MP Sir Spencer Summers, a typical Tory shires backbencher and time-server who every week without fail sent us stuff about his interventions in parliament. If Sir Spencer had a brain then he had mislaid it long ago in the cause of Tory loyalty and his own career. The axing of railways by Lord Beeching, a 'campaign that has produced a great scheme for transport in Britain', was one of his better ones, but by late 1963 what was really worrying him was the fact that the Conservatives were about to lose power for the first time in 13 years. Time and again, he returned to his theme that 'time for a change' was 'one of the most dangerous things we can encounter. This is not like a game of cricket when you change the bowler to give the other chap a chance. There are more important things at stake,' he said. The *Bucks Herald* was, of course, true blue and the Labour Party was always referred to as 'The Socialists'. The editor was a member of the local Rotary Club, but that is as far as his political thought went; he knew what the owner wanted, and all the local politics were left firmly to Steve Cox and Phil Fountain.

Phil was a Labour man to his fingertips so his column, an excellent example of local journalism, provided some balance to the solidly Conservative bias. At least 20 miles up the road we had a prospective Labour member with a bit of colour who, legend had it, had already upset the editor of the backwoods *Buckingham Advertiser* by suggesting he should have a phone installed and even offering to pay for it. It was the first time I had come across Captain Ian Robert Maxwell, MC. A year later, he was back in the news not only as a new MP but because he had been fined for shaving while driving his Rolls Royce at 60mph. He had managed to upset everyone by failing to turn up in court, bringing a stinging rebuke from the magistrates because he was 'quite indifferent to the summons', even though he had been swerving across the road and almost forcing other motorists off it while scraping off his five o'clock shadow.

Once I had passed my three-month test, I was taken into the courts by Phil and Wendy, both to be taught the basics of reporting magistrates' hearings and to be grounded in the legal knowledge all reporters need to find their way around covering them. There is no better way to learn and there were no better teachers – patient, interested, experienced and wise. Their guidance was worth 100 college journalism courses, as well as blooding me in the murky end of human nature. Occasionally there would be a tasty scandal, like the arrest of 13 men for cottaging at public lavatories in the aptly named Back Street, Wendover – inevitably rechristened Bendover.

The Bendover 13 came from all sorts of different professions and it was a story that held the market town in thrall. The evidence was detailed and didn't pull any punches as the police had kept watch on the 13 from a skylight. 'Defendant A went into the cubicle, Your Honour,' intoned the police witness. 'I kept observation and noticed Defendant B enter the cubicle next door. I then noticed a hole in the partition and observed Defendant A pushing his erect member through it. Defendant B looked at it and then said …' But what did he say? The policeman had forgotten and asked to look at his notes which he then leafed through for what seemed an age, as the court sat there agog. The tension was unbearable until he suddenly found it.

'Defendant B replied, Your Honour, "No thank you, I don't smoke Woodbines."'

It was a privilege to be there, as it was when a young PC became flustered explaining that a well-known local (female) drunk had been caught urinating in the street. She was 60 and ravaged by too many bottles of Extra Strength, but she sat in the dock just grinning at him and saying he was a nice-looking boy and what she would like to do to him if only she could get him outside. It was enough to put him off. 'I kept watch on the defendant, Your Worships, and saw her squat down and remove her clothing. It was then that I recognised the accused.' Even the magistrates snorted.

The Back Street public lavs featured once again in my journalistic career at the *Herald* before mercifully passing out of my life for good. I was on the way back from a job with photographer Barry Keen when I spotted Rudolf Nureyev. We decided to follow him and he went into the Back Street gents. The intrepid seeker after truth did likewise and asked him what he was doing there – a daft question, you might think. Actually, he explained, he had been visiting Margot Fonteyn's husband Roberto Arias in Stoke Mandeville Hospital a couple of miles away, where he had been taken after being paralysed during an assassination attempt in his native Panama. Ah, that explains it, I said, and left him to it. I was still a long way from Fleet Street class.

That particular class descended on us a few hours after 3.08am on 8 August 1963. By 9.00am I was at Cheddington railway station trying to find out why the night mail train had been stopped on its way from Glasgow to Euston. Nobody was saying much except that about £60,000 had been stolen. I hadn't a clue what to do, the station was almost deserted and the area around the raid, at Bridego Bridge a couple of miles from the station, was cordoned off. I was due to file a report to the Press Association on behalf of the editor, who was the local stringer.

Then, that bit of luck all reporters pray for. There was an engine in the station and the driver leaned out and spoke to me. 'You from the local?' he asked, clearly noticing that I was 19 and green. 'Jump up here, what do you want to know?'

So there I was in the cab and this bloke telling me everything, how the train was stopped, how driver Mills had been cracked over the head and what had disappeared. 'They reckon it could be £60,000,' I said. 'Nah, no chance, it's at least a million in cash and there were jewels on board, too,' he replied. So I filed everything to the PA including the £1 million line and Fleet Street went bananas. I was oblivious to this as I was still out on the road. Back in the office, Harry was doing his pieces, too, because the PA was accusing him of invention as the Yard would confirm nothing about this astonishing claim. Of course, he couldn't admit that he had sent his most junior reporter to cover the story and that junior wasn't due to write his stuff for his own paper for another hour. Harry was tap-dancing and the enlarger in the cellar picture department was jigging away to such an extent that poor old Maurice couldn't get a sharp shot of the Royal Mail carriages out of it. When I eventually did surface, the Yard was confirming my figure – it was to go to £2,631,684, more than £25 million at today's value – and Harry was busy taking the plaudits from the PA news desk which hadn't had a beat like it for years. One thing, however, still puzzles me about that day. My driver friend got everything right, he knew so much because he was the man brought in to drive the locomotive off the main line. So what about the jewellery? There have been consistent rumours through the decades that there was a priceless haul on board, but it has been equally consistently denied. Yet would a man who was so correct about everything else be wrong about that? I doubt it.

The Great Train Robbery put Aylesbury on the map and became the centre of a massive Fleet Street operation. For me, it was the first chance to see the top operators at first hand, and what operators they were. When Leatherslade Farm, the robbers' hideout, was found in the village of Oakley, Fleet Street's finest drunk the village dry within an hour. Aylesbury's venerable old hotels – the Bell, King's Head and White Swan – never had it so good either, and the train robbers themselves took on the role of heroes. It was like market day every day. The Government didn't like it one bit. The gang weren't that clever, though; all their names were known within 48 hours of the heist and the Yard heavies, Gerald McArthur and Tommy Butler, were sitting pretty.

By the time of the trial, moved to the Rural District Council Chamber because of its size, the train robbers had become the equivalent of film stars. Women who wouldn't dream of committing an illegal act cheered them on their way; there was no doubt on whose side the residents of Aylesbury were. Of course it was disgraceful that train driver Jack Mills should have been hurt, but the sheer daring and glamour of the job outweighed the sympathy for his injuries and neither the politicians nor the law liked it. The 30 year sentences shocked the town and most of us thought they were vindictive and unjust, a vicious reaction by an Establishment which had been made a laughing stock once too often; the Profumo affair was still riding high in the public consciousness. The train robbers had shown how absurd and lackadaisical Post Office security was and the feeling in Aylesbury was good luck to them. It was my first experience of the wrath of an Establishment scorned and it was an unpleasant sight. The sheer inhumanity of the 30 year sentences is still a pockmark on the face of British justice, particularly when the Libyan found guilty of the Lockerbie bombing received ten years less. The judiciary used the fig leaf of driver Mills's injury as the excuse for such lengthy terms, but a battered train driver is hardly the equivalent of a man guilty of the murders of 270 people.

The star of the Great Train Robbery trial was Gordon Goody, one of the leaders and a man with a pretty dreadful record but considerable magnetism. In the dock he stood, head and shoulders above the rest, impeccably dressed, sharp and angular, yet with a face that spelled danger and cruelty. He was the housewives' choice as they waited patiently in the queues outside the RDC offices for a seat at the best show in this or any other town. There is no doubt that Goody was guilty of the robbery, but there is considerable doubt about the methods used by the police to obtain his conviction. The most damning piece of evidence was traces of yellow paint found on the soles of a pair of his shoes taken from the pub where he was living at the time, they matched the paint from a tin found at Leatherslade Farm. Goody always claimed the shoes had been nowhere near the farm, and it is strange that the paint tin was not removed from it until some considerable time after the rest of the evidence. Goody has no doubt the paint was planted on his footwear and I have little doubt he is right.

I once asked Tommy Butler about it during an Old Bailey trial I was covering when I ran into him outside the court. By this time I knew Butler quite well – he was a taciturn man, a bachelor living with his mother and a long-time girlfriend who worked in a pub. He always wore the same suit – blue serge – and lived, breathed, ate and drank police work. He was a formidable and impressive man with a Roman nose and deep-set, piercing eyes, but a policeman of his time, not above fighting fire with fire. I asked him straight out whether the evidence against Goody was planted and waited for the explosion, but it never came. 'Gordon Goody was guilty of that job,' he said. 'There is no doubt it was a true bill.' But no denial. Butler was a detective who chose his words carefully and I am sure this occasion was no exception. He believed the ends justified the means, although I do not believe he would stitch up someone for a crime he didn't think he had committed. The trouble is, once you become judge and jury as well as policeman, the temptation to play God as well is strong. Much of the evidence against several of the train robbers came from the discovery of finger and palm prints at the farm – even though Bruce Reynolds has always insisted the farm was wiped clean under his supervision. Perhaps they did become slapdash in the aftermath of the robbery, although it would be surprising in the case of Goody who was fanatical about leaving no trace of his involvement.

Three years after the train robbery I was given a fascinating insight into the working of Tommy Butler's mind when I was investigating the empire of Charlie Richardson and his associates. One of Richardson's men had been brought back from Gibraltar and was appearing in court at Greenwich. Butler had arrested him as he stepped from the plane and was due to give evidence in court. Meanwhile, the man, along with several others, had been brought independently to Greenwich. Now the

Richardsons were not daft and, with the help of their solicitors, had perfected a standard reply when they were arrested or charged. This was always a variant of, 'I am completely innocent of the charge as will no doubt be proved in the courts in due course.' Because he hadn't been in court, Butler did not know this and when he came to give evidence of arrest he startled the court with claiming the reply was, 'Come on, Tom, I had it away on my toes, who grassed?' Not surprisingly, this was followed by an immediate outburst from the dock claiming the most pernicious 'verbal'. Even some of Butler's sidekicks had the grace to bury their heads in their hands. Maybe Bruce Reynolds got it right when he observed wrily, 'Tommy Butler was doing the job society expected of him.' Whatever the truth, he was the most remarkably dedicated policeman and his unrelenting pursuit and eventual capture of Reynolds was an example of extraordinary and tireless police work.

The Great Train Robbery introduced me to the rough and tumble world of Fleet Street on the road, a splendid circus of loonies, piss artists, wonderful reporters and great photographers, whose ratlike cunning and ability to do each other over was more than a match for cops and robbers combined. Wherever this pack turned up, there was mayhem and magic, broken windows and heartbroken girls, empty bars and rich cab drivers, legends were made overnight and so were Aylesbury's maidens. The show ran continuously for almost nine months and nothing was going to be quite the same again. It wasn't just Tommy Butler who was doing the job society expected.

By now, I had become 'A Columnist'. RICHARD STOTT MARSHALS THE TEEN AND TWENTY PARADE was my byline and they didn't come much better than that. The column had been written by Jeff Hockey, but he had had enough of Aylesbury; the train robbery had rekindled his interest in daily journalism so he went back to South Wales. It was a time when youth culture and youth cash was beginning to make an impression on a post-war Britain that up until then had neither. In 1960, young men disappeared into the armed services for two years and girls went to the cinema or danced around their handbags at the local palais. Now the young were taking over with a vengeance. National service had been abolished and eyes were being lifted over the limited horizon of an apprenticeship, courtship, marriage and settling down in a nice semi. Rock 'n' roll was in, fashion was blossoming and the bloom of youth was king. I pontificated about everything, from Aylesbury's lack of facilities for the young to the danger of Purple Hearts – this after my first ever investigation into the town's pill-popping youth: 'Two young people who openly admitted that they are taking the tablets said as many as 25 per cent of the teenagers who go to Saturday night dances have taken them at one time or another.' But like virtually everyone else, I was on the cusp of the excitement of the new and the traditionalism of the old. With all the certainty of the spectacularly ignorant, I lectured the shocked mass of Aylesbury parents about the dangers of drugs: 'Now we must ask ... how has it happened, who is ultimately responsible?' OK, clever clogs, who? The font of youth culture was in no doubt: 'We come now to the parents. And, in my opinion, this is where the blame lies. Any grown man or woman who allows a daughter to go to the Assembly Hall unaccompanied needs his or her head tested. It would be interesting to know how many parents of 14- or 15-year-old girls have ever been to a dance there.' Rereading it with that terrible blush of embarrassment, the interesting question that needs answering is why anyone keeps cuttings like that. Every week I was on about anything from the dangers of drinking – all right for me, no good for young girls – to the shortcomings of pop groups. There was nothing like the certainty of uncertainty, it was that sort of time.

It was this last phenomenon which brought me down to earth, and not before time. The Saturday night dances – they weren't yet gigs – were held at the Borough Assembly Hall and were run by a part-time impresario called Eddie Friday whose day job was public health inspector. Eddie was a brilliant man, immaculate cream evening jacket and crisp bow-tie week in, week out, he came from a generation that preferred the quick step and excuse me's to the rowdy sweats of electric guitar and pill-popping. But, every Saturday, Eddie had got someone from somewhere: Johnny, Mike and the Shadows; Russ and the Sabres; Dave Lakaz and the G Men; The Kubas – all names that died the death off the Market Square before scurrying back to their jobs as accountants and catering managers. Occasionally, he got lucky and I got the interviews. Gene Vincent could hardly move because he had fallen off so many motorbikes, girls and Jack Daniel's bottles. He smelled terrible because he wore top-to-bottom leather and never washed. Eddie's greatest coup was the Swinging Blue Jeans, riding high at number two in the charts with 'Hippy, Hippy, Shake'. He had booked them months before this hit and had got lucky. They tried to buy themselves out of the contract – Aylesbury's Borough Assembly Hall was never destined to be one of the great venues – but Eddie wasn't having it, nothing was too good for Aylesbury was his view, and quite right, too. I got the interview for my third column and, after the mandatory riot, I asked Norman, Ralph, Ray and Les about what they felt the future held and how long they could keep going. The implication of this was when would they settle down and do a proper job? Now these four were tough Scousers who had been the resident group at The Cavern and, in their time, had taken some hard knocks, so this little prick was easy meat. 'How much do you earn then, mate,' asked Norman, Ralph, Ray or Les. '£6 5s a week,' I replied.

'Good education, too, we can tell,' they pondered, chewing on their ciggies. 'We didn't have much schooling so perhaps you can explain it to us. We are pulling £1500 a week and we can't move for work. Now tell me, which of us is the cunt?'

The question was not intended to open a debate. They are still working.

The rough edges were beginning to be knocked off, but as 1965 dawned I wanted a wider stage. The *Bucks Herald* had been fun and I was lucky in my first year to have been involved in one of the biggest stories of what is still the greatest news year of the last 50: The Duchess of Argyle's divorce; the Profumo scandal; the Great Train robbery; the Kennedy assassination; Beatlemania; the exposure of Peter Rachman; and the resignation of Harold Macmillan. I was impatient to be part of such a gaudy cavalcade and I wasn't going to join the parade in Aylesbury. National newspapers were still unattainable but a news agency serving them wasn't. London was calling and my mind was finally made up in two whirlwind weeks over the new year.

First, I met my new brother-in-law. Sister Judith had been starring in Peter Shaffer's double-bill *The Private Ear* and *The Public Eye* in Australia after ending her relationship with Albert Finney. She was probably on the rebound, but she couldn't have bounced into a nicer bloke and his TV show was currently the toast of Sydney. But the first I heard of Dave Allen was when he took the suicide slot on *Sunday Night at the London Palladium*. The Beatles were scheduled to appear and no British-based entertainer was daft enough to take the spot before them. Davy took the gamble – at least he had known them when he was compère of the Granada travelling shows, starring Helen Shapiro. The Beatles opened the second act, or at least they did until they suddenly hit the jackpot half-way through the tour. Davy has always claimed that John Lennon was the worst poker player he knew and when the Beatles pulled out was in hock for at least £1 million in the non-stop, three-month school. Not bad when nobody was earning more than £25 a week.

He was flown over to Britain specially to do the show and he was superb. In spite of the hysteria from the audience, he made no reference to the act to follow, relying on his own talent to see him through and reckoning that at least he was appearing before one of the biggest audiences in recent years. I had no idea he was already an item with Judith in Sydney and didn't know until after they married. He decided to gamble, throw up his Beatle-like following in Australia and try to break through here.

I met him for the first time when Judith organised a dinner party; the other guests were Paul McCartney and Jane Asher. She reckoned it would soften the blow! The Beatles had just completed an epic tour of the United States and McCartney's face was grey, he hadn't seen the daylight for almost a month because during the day the four were told to keep their hotel curtains drawn, the cops fearing a riot if they were spotted. McCartney and Asher were an interesting pairing, she the acme of middle-class respectability and a stage actress through and through, him a working-class Scouser with a world-class talent. I reckon they split up because she insisted she wanted a life of her own and that she wasn't prepared to spend her life as arm candy, even to a Beatle. McCartney couldn't hack that.

Davy was a refreshing antidote to the luvvie world of the theatre which can become suffocating, and in me he recognised a fellow soul. In spite of some bad family times, we have remained firm friends, he is a delight and a comic genius but, like many comedians, a deeply serious, even solitary man. He is the true standard-bearer for the TV comedy that followed him, smoothing the path and pointing the way for acts like French and Saunders and Eddie Izzard.

Davy wasn't the only lifelong attachment I was to make in that fortnight. I went to a party in one of the tiny doll's houses which used to be dotted around the tiny streets of Chalk Farm. There I met Penny, a stunning blue-eyed blonde, and one of five beautiful girls sharing the place. Her father, I found out, was an Air Vice-Marshal. 'Good, I've got a Spitfire outside,' I said, which was true, a Triumph Spitfire. I took her for a drive and gave her my impression of Elvis Presley singing 'Are You Lonesome Tonight?' something which could be done with safety in those pre-breathtest days. By the end of the evening, neither the Spitfire nor I were likely to be flying anywhere so I retired to bed, one of the five in the two dolls' bedrooms. I had a good idea I had chosen that of the younger daughter of Air Vice-Marshal Sir Colin Scragg, KBE, CB, AFC and bar, but wasn't sure until she arrived to find her bed occupied. For more time than was strictly necessary, she hesitated and then climbed in, with most of her clothes on. With a sigh, she turned the picture of her father on the bedside table to the wall.

My ambition turned unalterably to London. I had finished with Sir Spencer Summers telling me that it was indeed now time for a change – 'The Conservatives should harness that phrase for the next election,' was his new line, after the country had decided it was time for a change whether he liked it or not. Neither was I interested in the thoughts of the new member for Buckingham who was bombarding us with them from the Commons after bouncing back from Razorgate. 'The plan for a big new town in North Bucks is a pipe dream,' boomed Captain Maxwell, going on to produce nine lengthy points as to why this should be obvious to anyone with an ounce of intelligence. He was talking about Milton Keynes, population today 187,000.

But, as always, there was still one more hard lesson in journalism to learn before I left the *Herald*. Julie, Roger and I went on a crawl around the country pubs. Roger by this stage had become so southernised that his stomach could take even the roughest of the rough produced by the Aylesbury Brewery Company. I, however, could not, and was caught short in the wilds of the Chilterns at Dunsmore. I made it to the lav, but only just. Then, horrors. Not only was there only one slice of newspaper on the hook, but it was my column, with my face staring out from it. What a comment on the transience and standing of newspapers and their hacks. I bowed to the inevitable, cursing the irony. I turned the page over and used Victor Tattersall's column, 'Bringing farming down to earth for you'. It certainly did, but at least muck spreading seemed more in keeping there.

It was time to go. Phil and Wendy had given me the best possible grounding in the journalist's trade. They were a great tribute to the craft of the local paper, neither wanted to go anywhere else, they had a great love for their town which even then was beginning to change with new office blocks, shopping centres, walkways, car parks and cinema complexes in the offing. They were the guardians of its future as well as custodians of its past. The *Bucks Herald* passed out of the ownership of GT de Fraine and Co and into the arms of a big combine. It is now an excellent package, a great deal better than those old flat-bed days of the 1960s – crisp, clearly laid out and sectioned. It just misses the Phil Fountain column.

My last task was to tell the Welsh wizard that I was off. I was already in his bad books because I had been asked to the re–opening of the local finishing school at Hartwell House, a fine eighteenth-century building accommodating the House of Citizenship, a college for high-class and wealthy girls, run by Miss Dorothy Neville-Rolfe. Hartwell had been badly damaged by fire and Miss Neville-Rolfe had got her old mate the

Queen Mother to come down and re-open it. When the invitation, suitably embossed, arrived in the office, Harry assumed it was for him. He was not happy when he found out it was for me. I had covered the fire and its rebuilding progress assiduously, largely because the girls were serious crumpet.

He took the news of my going quietly, much to the relief of Maurice Cousins's enlarger. It was some time before he spoke. 'I think, Richard,' he was choosing his words carefully, 'you will make it to Fleet Street ... But if you do, don't ever think you can come back here.' And with that ringing endorsement, I packed up the Spitfire with all my worldy goods and headed for the Big City and the Bright Lights. Except the city was north Kent and the shabbier suburbs of south-east London, and the bright lights were confined to a one-bedroom flat in Sidcup.

5

If Dan Ferrari had not existed, Fleet Street would have invented him. He was born of Italian Swiss parents and his real name was Lino, hence Dan Leno after the great music hall star. He had big round glasses, large soulful eyes and an enormous Terry Thomas moustache which he was constantly wiping. He had a booming, baritone voice, combined with an infectious chuckle, and he was the legendary night news editor of the *Daily Mirror*. Ferrari could spot a hole in a story from 20 paces, a bullshitter from 40 and a conman a week before he tried the scam. He had joined the *Mirror*, reluctantly, when his long-suffering wife Joyce decided she had had enough of his freelancing capers, the final straw being when he was convicted of using the police radio to get a beat on stories. In those days it wasn't simply a matter of tuning into the VHF, you had to have equipment, which was so enormous it looked as if it belonged to a platoon from the Royal Corps of Signals and had to be packed into a van. For this reason Ferrari often arrived before the police at anything happening on his patch – the whole of north Kent and south-east London – so the police decided to set him up with a fake major incident and catch him red-handed, which they duly did.

Dan was the boss and founder of the Ferrari Press Agency of Parkhill Road, Bexley, known to every national newspaper as Ferrari of Dartford, the nearest major town newsdesks – notoriously hazy about geography – would recognise. When he joined the *Mirror*, the agency remained in the back room of his house, the office connected by an antiquated switchboard to both house and the outside world and so unreliable it frequently cut off both. When I joined, the agency was run by an old friend of Dan's, Frank Dunkley, who had fallen on difficult times, the collapse of his first marriage had brought relentless pursuit by his ex-wife. This is why Frank often used to go missing, usually around maintenance cheque time. He drove an enormous and extremely battered Ford Consul which once, a long time ago, had been whitish. He was a disconcerting driver because he used to lie along the front bench seat and drive from the middle, giving the impression that there was no driver at all. The reason for this, he said, was in case his ex had put detectives on to him, they would not be able to see him and therefore any writ they wished to deliver would remain unserved. When it was pointed out to him that not even a very thick private detective would believe the car was driving itself, he shrugged and said they hadn't caught him yet.

As you will have gathered by now, the choice of Ferrari was a gamble. The money wasn't good – how could it be, with the boss having such financial problems? – and the agency survived on its wits. It was under siege from the big London guns of the Fleet Street News Agency, run by Tommy Bryant, and the one in North London run by John Rogers. The Ferraris had to be paid their rent, and after that there wasn't a great deal left, even when the stories were making the papers. On the plus side was the *Daily Mirror* connection. If Ferrari reckoned I was OK, I could get shift work and then ... who knew? News agency work was not for faint hearts, it was the brute end of journalism, no frills, plenty of dirty tricks and no quarter asked or given. No room for poncy columnists here, this was hard news reporting – ruthless, constantly teetering on the edge of respectability and accuracy, and strewn with the carcasses of those who couldn't hack it. At Ferrari's, there was an added frisson of danger. The Old Man ran the night news desk of the paper which ruled Fleet Street at that time and he saw your copy. He saw the quality, the speed, the accuracy and how you fared against the opposition. There was no hiding place.

The job of the news agency was to provide stories, either on spec or ordered by a paper, for all the dailies, Sundays and the London evenings, the *Standard* and *News*. The good money came when a big story broke on your patch and you pumped the copy up the road in great quantity and as fast as you could make it. At the same time, you provided back-up and local knowledge for the staff men who graced you with their presence, normally in the pub, where they waited for their 'contacts' – of which they rarely had any, apart from you. The rest of the time was spent trawling local papers for stories to follow up and sell to the evenings where they would be swallowed up in a strange world of overnights, slips and flongs – flong was the material used to mould a page made up the day before for early edition printing next day. These stories were not meant to last and were gradually replaced by live news and, therefore, in a bid to catch the eye, were not always quite as accurate as they might have been.

Part of Ferrari's patch was the A2 from Bexley, no M2 in those days, through to the Medway towns, and the verges had become home to an ever-increasing gypsy community. When their champion, a Labour MP called Norman Dodds, died, there was a clamour for picturesque quotes from the gypsies, which I duly went and collected. Their leader was an old man called Eef Smith who could neither read nor write. Frank's eyes lit up when he heard this, as it meant copious quotes from the gypsies could be supplied in future without the inconvenience of traipsing out to the A2. It wasn't quite as bad as it sounds as we knew them all, and when we did go out there Eef told us to say what we wanted anyway. So we did, and the gypsies received rapturous coverage. All went well until the *Sun* – old broadsheet *Sun*, not the Murdoch version – decided they wanted to do a feature on this scholar gypsy. I went out to let him know, only to find out that he had gone to the great caravan in the sky. Worse, he had appeared to have given his last set of quotes to us a couple of days after he went on his celestial travels. Not good news, not good news at all. Frank was quick on his toes. Eef had sadly died he told the *Sun*, and the whole camp had gone into mourning. They were incommunicado until after the funeral which would be held secretly as, he said, was the gypsy custom. It wasn't at all; I think it was held at Eltham Crematorium. By fudging the day of the funeral, he fudged the day of his death, too.

He wasn't always so lucky. Norman Dodds's demise meant a by-election in Erith and Crayford and, if the Tories won it, Harold Wilson would lose his overall Commons majority. As a result a whole load of frontbench big-hitters went down to this charmless, windy bend in the Thames to speak on behalf of the new Labour man, Jim Wellbeloved. Housing minister Richard Crossman was targeted by anarchists and Trots, booed and jeered and forced to shut up. All this I duly reported, dictating my copy to Frank, who was at home so the two of us could get it over quicker, thus beating the opposition. The next day I was appalled. Several newspapers appeared to carry a ludicrously exaggerated version of what happened, my copy had been discarded and instead they had used that of some demented reporter I hadn't spotted. Thoroughly despondent, I went into the office where I found Frank a happy man.

'Great show today,' he said. 'Wonderful stuff.'

'What do you mean, it's not mine,' I said. 'God knows how they got that.'

'Ah yes, well, I tightened it up a bit, added some oomph.'

He certainly did. Hardly had he finished when the phone went. The Labour Party was going berserk at the papers; Frank had happened to dictate copy to the more right-leaning ones, and they were being accused of exaggerating for political purposes. Luckily, Labour over-egged its complaint and one or two of its own porkies could be disproved, which meant that Frank could fling enough dust to get us out of it, but I had been taught a valuable lesson – you can lose your credibility only once, so don't lose it.

On the other hand, you must be published or die. So all freelances have to develop a good nose for a story, its follow up, and a network of local contacts who work exclusively for you. It is hard, unremitting work, lonely, often tedious – you are frequently put on doorsteps for hours on end by newsdesks watching their own backs – but once in a while that old black magic covers you with fairy dust.

The circumstances surrounding the death of Brian Epstein have been the subject of endless speculation and conspiracy theories. Was he murdered? How did reporters get to the scene before the ambulance? Somebody else must have known what was going on. At the time Epstein's butler discovered his body, someone else appeared to know what was happening far too quickly. Therefore, somebody else must have known he was dead. Fascinating, but alas no conspiracy, no mystery killer.

It is true that somebody did know of his death even as the first of The Beatles was being told by the butler. It was me. As part of our listening system we had a number of GPO telephone operators on our books who used to tip us off about news items, usually so small they didn't make anything. Nonetheless, they received a retainer, so when the phone went and it was one of our usual tipsters, I didn't pay too much attention until he asked if I knew Brian Epstein was dead. I didn't, but assumed I was late hearing the news. 'Well, he is, found dead from an overdose just now, in his bed in London. I'll ring you back in five minutes.' Meanwhile, I got on to the *Daily Express*, as they were the best payers in those days. The *Express* had heard nothing but took the tip exclusive for £50. A few minutes later, my operator was back on explaining how he knew. One of The Beatles was down in Sussex and, in order to make the connection, the butler's call had to go through our man's Kent exchange. He listened to the first few words as he always did to make sure the connection was properly made, so he overheard the conversation. He telephoned me as the butler was still speaking. Meanwhile, in London, the *Express* was so fast in getting to Epstein's flat – it was still a newspaper in those days – that the reporter arrived before the ambulance. Hence the story about the tip-off to the press before anyone else knew. True, but no murder conspiracy.

Plenty of murder and conspiracy, though, with the Richardson brothers. The Great Train Robbers had provided the glamour; the Richardsons now provided the menace. Charlie and Eddie ran South London, with a little help from Frank Fraser, alias Mad Frankie or Razor Fraser. The river separated them from the Krays who ruled the East End and ran protection in the west. As a few *quid pro quo* the Richardsons took their protection rent from the car-parks at Heathrow. Both gangs made plenty, but the Richardsons, Charlie anyway, was brighter. They started out as 'fancy goods salesmen' or 'wholesale chemists', both fronts for a particularly 1960s scam called long firm fraud. What happened was this: Richardson set up a company with stooge directors. They traded normally for a couple of months, selling goods cheap to market traders. They then upped their orders to manufacturers and asked for credit which they were given because they have a good record of paying on the nail. They continued to do this for another couple of months until they asked for more credit which again they were given because of an exemplary record. It was then they hit hard. In went the mega orders to every supplier. After three months the suppliers started demanding payment but got nothing. By the time they checked the company out it was long gone, disappeared just like the directors. The warehouse full of goods was flogged off cheap to the markets, Eddie and Charlie were left with a stash of cash to set up the next, even bigger, scam and by the time the suppliers sent round the door-knockers the warehouses were empty. But Charlie was cleverer. He decided to launder his money through South Africa and it was here he eventually became unstuck when one of his sidekicks was charged with murder.

Eddie, meanwhile, had been rather silly. He didn't have his brother's brains but he did have Mad Frank. Eddie decided he wanted a slice of the action at a club called Mr Smith's in Catford. A chubby Thames lighterman called Billy Haward, not a gangster in the Richardson league but jealous of what he saw as his patch, decided there was no room for both of them. And at 3.00am one March morning in 1967 the war exploded, leaving one man dead and several strewn around the front gardens of genteel Catford. One of them was Frankie Fraser who was recognised as soon as police discovered him. He had been badly hurt, shot in the legs, and was losing a lot of blood. It took police a long time to find him and call an ambulance; strange, because they are usually so thorough on occasions like this.

Meanwhile Eddie, who had also been shot in the leg, had made his way to Chislehurst Hospital where he admitted himself under the name of George Ward. This was Sod's Law at work for Eddie, because few policemen knew what he looked like; he had been careful to keep himself out of the limelight. One of the very few who did was John Cummings, a former head of Criminal Intelligence, and now the top policeman based at Catford. When he confronted him in his hospital bed, the conversation went something like this:

Cummings: 'What is your name?'
Richardson: 'Ward, George Ward.'
Cummings: 'Really … what is wrong with your leg.'
Richardson: 'I've injured it.'
Cummings, sitting down on the bed: 'I think you are Eddie Richardson.'
Richardson: 'You're wrong there, my name is George Ward.'
Cummings, sitting on Richardson's leg: 'No, you are definitely Eddie Richardson, aren't you?'
Richardson: 'Aaarghh … Yeeeeees.'

Not in the manual of police interrogation techniques, but it saved a lot of paper work. My fascination with the Richardsons and their methods led me down some interesting alleys, one of them threateningly blind, when I received a phonecall from a theatrically villainous voice: 'Lay off, Stott, or you better start learning Braille,' was the message.

Unnerving enough to report to the police and for me to be given protection for a few days. Not that it would have done much good, my minder loved the idea of spending some time in the pub, so we could have been sitting targets for any potential assassin.

The Richardsons, rather than Krays, showed how far organised crime had been allowed to take root in London. It was astonishing that even Tommy Butler did not recognise Eddie Richardson, and it was astonishing, too, that when the Richardsons came up for trial there was only a cursory guard over the jury. Their sidekicks managed to get hold of the jury list and at least one was approached. It was the Mr Smith's club shooting case which ushered in majority verdicts. Up until that time, the Home Office had been blissfully unaware that anyone would try to do something so un-British as nobble a jury. But Eddie Richardson was going to get his come-uppance in jail, suffering a fate few even of his greatest enemies would have wished upon him. He was to become one of Lord Longford's favourite prisoners.

Anyone who has seen a premier division gangster close-up will not take kindly to the cuddly image of the old lags now. Frankie Fraser tries to con us that really he is a bloke with a heart of gold and, like the Kray brothers, he only harmed others in the same business. This isn't so. Fraser oozed hatred and violence. I was once backstage at Greenwich Court, reading some charge sheets in the gaoler's office, when suddenly Fraser loomed over me in the doorway. His face was contorted with cruelty, the kind of face you get when you have spent decades inside perfecting your favourite hobby, smashing up prison officers. For one irrational moment I thought he was going to attack me with one of his chosen weapons, an iron bar, perhaps a razor or knife. Then I saw the handcuffs. It was ten seconds of instinctive, primeval fear of a psychopath. Now he does adverts for Campari.

News agency reporting was a solitary job. We did not have a newspaper office teeming with life, just a room stacked high with old copies of the *Kentish Times*, *Kent Messenger* and *South East London Mercury*. My beat, particularly as I dug further into the Richardson empire, tended to revolve around Greenwich, Lewisham, Deptford and Catford. I made Greenwich court my headquarters, where an understanding trio of gaoler, chief clerk and stipendiary magistrate made for a tolerable life. The Magistrate was Mr St John Harmsworth who looked like a diminutive version of Robert Morley. He was a big racing man and enjoyed the ebb and flow of the flotsam and jetsam that drifted past him every morning at 10.00am. He was a natural candidate for those little items from the courts the *Evening News* used to love so much, such as this:

> The last thing David McLoughlin can remember was putting on a half-crown bet at the bookies. Then he went down the pub and one thing led to another and, well, that's how he finished up in the cells on a charge of being drunk and disorderly. As is the way with these things, Mr McLoughlin was skint and when Mr Harmsworth asked him how much he had on him this time – as you can see he had more than a nodding acquaintance with the Irishman's cycle of life – he replied, 'Very little sir, I had 2s 6d [12.5p] on Lester Piggott in the Cup yesterday, but I don't know what has happened to it.'
>
> 'Good Heavens,' replied the magistrate, almost jumping from his seat. '2s. 6d. in the Chester Cup on Aegean Blue? It won at 22–1, Mr McLoughlin. Away with you, you've got an awful lot to collect.'
>
> 'Oh, thank you, sir,' replied a somewhat bemused winner.
>
> 'And, Mr McLoughlin, be so kind as to return here with 15s.'

On another occasion Harmsworth had been to the police Christmas party and was being given a lift to the station to catch his train home in a police car. Suddenly, a drunk rolled into the road. 'I'm sorry, sir,' said the driver. 'We can't leave him here, he'll get killed.' This evil-smelling bundle of Christmas cheer was wedged into the back-seat alongside the magistrate, from where he began a tirade against the monstrosity of a legal system that stopped him enjoying himself. This quickly turned into an attack on the local magistrate from whom this furious and drink-inflamed bundle had received many previous convictions. 'That bastard, he'll do me for a fiver. No Christmas spirit, just enjoying myself. If only he could see the way you are treating me now, a poor innocent man minding his own business …' Then he noticed he had company in the back. 'What they got you in for,' he said in the darkness. 'You're drunk. Here let me out, you've put me in the back with a drunk.'

The next morning Harmsworth was on the bench and his companion of the previous night was brought in. Usual evidence, drunk and disorderly in the street, arrested for his own safety, claimed he was only enjoying himself at Christmas. Harmsworth declared a Christmas amnesty, letting him off without a fine adding, 'We are not always bastards you know.'

By now, soberish and the night before a total blank, the drunk looked puzzled but grateful. 'I would never say that, sir. And I'll punch anyone on the nose who does.'

This was the sauce that gave flavour to the coverage of London, but we are now served up with pre-packaged and microwaved news and features which turn the *Evening Standard* into bland and unappetising fare. There is no whiff of the river, you can't hear the markets or glimpse the parade of whores, pimps and nancies through the courts of what is one of the great carnivals of the world. And while all this is going on the men and women who should be chronicling this teeming scene are sitting vacantly double-clicking, clacking and electronically searching and mailing themselves into a cybernothing.

Greenwich Court was an excellent office, the best place to meet policemen, lawyers and a few villains. It was also one of the few points of contact with other journalists and the front line between Ferrari's and Fleet Street news agencies. It was there I first met Kelvin MacKenzie and the lovely willowy Jackie Holland, who was to become his wife. Jackie was a life-saver, as we existed on nothing much. Her father worked at Smithfield and occasionally full blooded red steaks found their way to my rudimentary kitchen, enough to keep you going for a week. MacKenzie comes from a family of South London journalists, his parents divorced and he was then living with his mother Mary, a press officer with the Greater London Council's housing department. Kelvin had just started at the *South East London Mercury* as a junior reporter and, within a year, joined us at Ferrari's. He was never comfortable as a reporter, and agency work is all that and nothing else. He was also in charge of his two brothers and, on the evenings when his mother worked late, had to dash home and make their tea, not something that endeared him to Frank Dunkley. He hated agency work, and before long was off to Birmingham and a job on the *Post* and *Mail* where he would discover his great talents for newspaper production and projection.

The press benches at Greenwich were also graced by the fragrant presence of Lady Olga Maitland, who was working for Fleet Street news agency. On long boring committals, it was not unknown for hands to stray towards her aristocratic leg, advances that were quickly put down with a thwack born from years of breeding and horse management. Her father was the Master of Lauderdale, an ancient Scottish title, and with such a pedigree it was right that Olga adopted a proper hauteur with her press box colleagues. She sat right down the end, a useless place for a news agency, because it meant you couldn't make a quick getaway. Not that it worried Olga as she had that patrician calm, never hurrying anywhere, certainly not to file a story. On occasions, she used to return to Fleet Street's offices to write them up, because, she explained to Tommy Bryant, the phones outside the courts weren't working. Of course they weren't, the mouthpieces had been removed and were sitting in my pocket.

Olga was the perfect opposition, she simply could not understand all this nonsense about rushing to phones and gabbling a story to the copytakers on the *Standard* and *News*. It is not surprising as it later transpired that Tommy had taken on Olga as a favour to her dad and was paying her expenses only, £2 a week. When the National Union of Journalists found out, the brothers went potty and demanded huge sums of back wages which, of course, Tommy could not pay. As a way out, he organised a job for her on John Junor's *Sunday Express* – the old boy was always a sucker for a title and a pretty leg, and if they came together so much the better – and that is how she started as a gossip columnist. God knows how she became an MP. I always found her unionbashing a little churlish, as she might never have had a job if poor old Tommy hadn't been shamed into getting John Junor to bale him out.

There are some stories that stay with you for ever. If you are lucky they have good vibes, if not, well, you just live with it. The Hither Green train crash happened on a chill Sunday evening in November 1967. Once again, our network of spies had worked well. This time, we received a call from a phone operator who took the first 999 call, so we were on the scene very quickly. I should have guessed what I was in for when Frank said he didn't want to go; he had covered the Lewisham train disaster ten years earlier and he had no desire to repeat the experience. He was prepared to sit up all night filing copy and making calls, but he did not want to be on the scene.

Train crashes are the worst form of disaster. In plane crashes the passengers are invariably dead; ships you can't get to quickly so it is all over by the time you do; and road accidents do not tend to be on a massive scale. With train disasters the injuries are horrific but not necessarily fatal, and you can get there quickly so the reality is all too obvious and casualties can be enormous and the carnage frightful. At Hither Green, the scene was like something out of a gigantic field hospital. Limbs were being amputated on the spot, the screaming and moaning was constant, bits of people, blood, mangled carriages, mud and the stench of burning flesh were everywhere. Forty-nine people died that night and the memory does not fade. By 5.00am I decided to walk down the line to see if there was any obvious cause for the derailment that had resulted in such mayhem. After about quarter-of-a-mile I came across a huddled group of men, their enormous belted mackintoshes and hats meant only one thing, they were from the Railway Inspectorate and they had discovered something interesting. They didn't see me in the darkness as I joined their huddle, they were too intent on looking at the track. There was a broken rail. I decided to break cover. 'Is that the cause?'

No answer. Backs turned. Try again.

'If that was on my Hornby Dublo, my train would have come off,' I said.

Surprisingly, they still didn't ask who I was. Then one turned round and said simply; 'The principle's the same, but the people are real.'

I had my story for the next day. It is a pity that more than 30 years later Railtrack forgot the people were real and shoved safety to the bottom of the agenda as Gerald Corbett and his board worked out their apparent priorities – a new pay structure and bonus system for themselves. If any of those Railtrack bosses had been at Hither Green that night, they would not have been so cavalier about dismissing safety concerns as the number of broken rails and signals passed at red escalated and were ignored by men grown fat and complacent on massive pay cheques and obscene bonuses.

By now, thanks to Dan Ferrari, I was doing shiftwork at night on the *Mirror*. I had passed my first big test, he thought I had the makings of a Fleet Street reporter and was prepared to back me, although I doubt he would have if he had known that to alleviate the boredom on the way home in the early hours of the morning, along Jamaica Road, through Greenwich, across Blackheath and along the Sidcup by-pass, I used to stop at all the green traffic lights and go through all the reds.

Night-time on a paper like the *Mirror* did that sort of thing to you, it tends to bring out the nutcases, and one such was a correspondent called Jones of Pontardawe. I was standing in on the newsdesk one evening when a memo from him dropped saying that he had just met a talking dog in a pub and would like us to do a feature on it; he was offering it exclusive. The dog belonged to a Mr Evans and he would be pleased to co-operate. Now Dan Ferrari knew Jones of Pontardawe well and suggested I might like to ask him who taught the dog to speak.

'A good question that, I will give you a note on it when I have spoken to Mr Evans,' said Jones.

Ten minutes later it arrived. 'Memo to Newsdesk re talking dog exclusive. 'Mr Evans's dog was taught to speak by his horse.'

Dan was as adept at dealing with loony callers as he was with errant reporters. The man who invented the Time Machine was typical.

'I've invented a time machine,' said this rather strange, spaced-out voice.

'Oh yes,' growled Ferrari.

'Yes, I can go forwards in time, backwards in time, sideways in time. Backwards, forwards, sideways ...'

Ferrari cut him off. 'Good. I want to see it.'

Time Machine man had never had this kind of encouragement before and was rather taken aback.

'When?' he asked.

'Bring it in yesterday,' said Ferrari and banged the phone down. He wasn't always successful, however. The *Mirror* crime man, a lovely East-Ender called Ed Vale was nicked for drink-driving on his way home, an occupational hazard for a crime man. He had been taken to an East End police station and Ferrari had been informed by the station sergeant. He immediately came to the support of his man, a response made keener by his distrust of policemen.

'Mr Vale,' he proclaimed, 'is one of our finest reporters. He would not break the law in this manner. He drinks only rarely, there has clearly been a mistake. I insist on seeing him.' And with that Dan commandeered the office car and set off for the East End. Ed was certainly a fine reporter but to suggest he drank only rarely was stretching it a bit. However, there was no stopping Ferrari now.

By the time he got to the nick he was ready for a virtuoso performance. 'I have known Mr Vale for 15 years,' he said. 'And in that time I have known him to take a drink only on the most important of celebrations. There is clearly something behind this and I intend to find out what it is. I demand his release immediately. On the infrequent occasions Mr Vale does take a small drink he sings ...' Pause for dramatic effect, 'And I hear no singing,' concluded a triumphant Ferrari bringing his fist down on the station sergeant's desk. At that, the sergeant said nothing, opened the door leading to the cells, and from the depths came the loud but unmistakable sound of Ed at full tilt ... 'A Scottish soldier, a Scottish soldier ...'

And to think I was about to join all this. Bliss. Sheer bliss.

6

The day the *Daily Mirror* hit a circulation of five million, the much underestimated editor Lee Howard wondered, in the midst of all the rejoicing, why it wasn't eight million. This may seem a little greedy, but his logic was impeccable and contained a hidden siren which nobody heeded. The *Mirror* had virtually no competition; Associated Newspapers' *Daily Sketch* was lively but Conservative with a circulation hovering around the 850,000 mark; the *Daily Express*, the *Mirror*'s nearest competitor in sales terms, was complementary rather than a serious competitor, and the rest were nowhere. So why was a sizeable chunk of Britain's working-class not buying the people's paper. It was a question nobody thought important enough to answer.

Hugh Cudlipp, from his lofty home on the ninth floor of the new Holborn headquarters, was journalistic monarch of all he surveyed. It was party time again, and how the *Mirror* loved a party. Hugh Cudlipp, architect of the modern *Mirror* and its success, was a genius of tabloid journalism in the 1940s and '50s. He had produced a raucous, cheeky and sometimes rude paper prepared to take on the big guns. The stricture to Soviet leader Khruschev: 'MR K! DON'T BE SO BLOODY RUDE!'; 'COME ON, MARGARET, PLEASE MAKE UP YOUR MIND' over her on-off relationship with Peter Townsend, and others were to go down in Fleet Street folk lore. But such is Cudlipp's legend that 'WHOSE FINGER ON THE TRIGGER' is also attributed to him by many old Mirror hands, including me. It was in fact the brainchild of Sylvester Bolan, Editor of the Mirror during the 1951 General Election campaign, and more obviously famous for being sent to jail for contempt of court. Tame stuff by today's standards, but daring then, a forerunner of Kelvin MacKenzie's *Sun*, but without the invented bits, the xenophobia and barely-disguised racism.

The *Mirror* party to end all parties followed the announcement of the *Mirror* circulation passing the five million mark in May 1964, the highest daily newspaper sale ever achieved in Britain or anywhere else in the world. The Albert Hall was booked, the bash was called the Golden Ball

– not to be confused with *Private Eye*'s much later Golden Balls libel fund – and simply everyone who was anyone was invited, and quite a few who weren't. The *Mirror* always involved its readers and they swelled the crowds of celebrities from politics, stage, screen and the new explosive world of pop music where young stars were being created every day. Cudlipp was installed in the Royal Box with copious amounts of booze and friends, looking out over his loyal subjects, not just the readers but the distinguished guests as well. When the *Mirror* said jump, you jumped. Yet Cudlipp failed to heed that old gypsy warning, that the hour of your greatest success carries the seeds of your destruction.

The Beatles had been invited, their visit kept secret because of the fear of fans going berserk, but when they arrived their presence could not be kept quiet for long. They were ushered through a labyrinth of backstage corridors towards the Royal Box; nonetheless they were soon spotted and the fans were up and at 'em. Brian Epstein's minders fought their way to Cudlipp's throne room with the Beatles and Epstein struggling behind them. The *Mirror* public relations chief John Jenkinson had his coat ripped from him and the fans started swarming up the pillars of the hall in a bid to reach their heroes. Eventually the tattered four and their usually immaculate manager fought a way through the mayhem into Cudlipp's box. He, however, was less than impressed – who were these guys usurping his party? He took one look at The Beatles, mop heads even more dishevelled than usual, and shouted, 'Get those long-haired fuckers out of here.' Epstein immediately turned on his heel and led The Beatles from the Hall.

It was a defining moment, when the power in popular culture tilted permanently away from newspapers towards a new mass movement. The *Mirror* had been supplanted by The Beatles in the new television age and however much he railed against them, there was nothing Cudlipp could do about it. It was almost as if he knew, and was determined to emphasise, his own growing disenchantment with the young, rebellious, two-fingered generation, no matter that all they were doing was much the same as he had done 15 years earlier.

Cudlipp continued to loathe The Beatles. Not long after the Albert Hall débâcle, he banned them from the papers 'unless they strangled their grandmothers with piano wire'. It was the petty act of a diminishing dictator and the only harm it did was internally to Cudlipp's reputation and externally to the *Mirror's* circulation. Hugh Cudlipp was the living proof that great newspapermen should not hang on beyond their sell by date. The Beatles had toppled him from the perch of popular culture, and the *Mirror* was about to be toppled, too, by a brash young Australian who was to sweep away the remnants of the immediate post-war years and Britain's cosy newspaper paternalism. Cudlipp was to despise Rupert Murdoch as much as he did The Beatles. Murdoch, in turn, still dismisses Cudlipp with 'I always thought of him as a pamphleteer.'

I hadn't the faintest idea of any of this when I joined the reporting staff of the *Daily Mirror* in July 1968 at a salary of £32 a week. The *Mirror* was still the biggest-selling newspaper in Fleet Street by a mile and the *Sun* was the broadsheet IPC version launched by Cudlipp in 1964 with a brilliant advertising campaign – 'The newspaper born of the age we live in' – a promise not matched by the eventual product, in spite of some brave innovations, such as a floating masthead and big picture essay on the back page. The slogan was more applicable to the Murdoch version which launched in 1969 after he bought the *Sun* for a song – £50,000 and a service agreement with Odhams – because Cudlipp wanted to avoid massive redundancies and, anyway, he believed Murdoch would founder.

What is now largely forgotten is that before Murdoch stepped in, IPC had been negotiating with Maxwell to sell the paper to him. Many reasons for the sale have been put forward, pledges that the old *Daily Herald* – the *Sun* replaced it – would not be merged with the *Mirror*, the political fallout from a Labour paper being lost and the saving of jobs. But the fear of a backlash from the trades unions impacting on the *Mirror* and the belief that Murdoch would fail anyway were the driving forces; that is why the Australian interloper managed to walk away with the title at a bargain basement price.

For IPC, offloading the *Sun* was a matter of urgency. Profits had been slashed from £14 million to £9.4 million and the shareholders' dividend cut. Cudlipp's golden touch had deserted him as the *Sun* struggled, its circulation plunging below one million. Cecil King's IPC, so long the god of publishing, was found after all to have feet of clay. So was Cecil himself. For years, he had behaved like a patrician proprietor talking of 'my newspapers' and 'my magazines', but by the late '60s he had become disenchanted with Harold Wilson's Labour Government and his own lack of recognition by it. Not that old Harold hadn't tried. He offered him a life peerage, membership of the Privy Council and a junior ministerial job. But that was nothing like enough. King wanted an earldom – Earl King would certainly have been grand – but Wilson patiently pointed out that Labour was pledged to abolish hereditary peerages.

By 1968, he was beginning to show signs of the madness which destroyed his uncle Lord Northcliffe, setting off on a grandiose plan to put together a government of national unity run by public figures and businessmen and fronted by Lord Mountbatten. King naturally would be a crucial part of this government. When he talked to Mountbatten about his blueprint for Britain in front of Sir Solly Zuckerman, then an adviser to Wilson's Government, Zuckerman walked out calling it 'rank treachery' ... 'All this talk of machine-guns at street corners is appalling. I am a public servant and will have nothing to do with it. Nor should you, Dickie,' he warned.

Dickie didn't, so Cecil wrote a long front-page rant in the *Mirror* under the headline 'ENOUGH IS ENOUGH'. It certainly was; King was ousted as Chairman and Cudlipp took over, even though he had approved the King article. 'A very good first violin but not a conductor,' was King's bitter but accurate observation of his long-time number two.

King's removal meant that everyone moved up one and I came in at the bottom a couple of months after he left. I had eventually convinced the *Mirror's* news editor Roly Watkins of my worth, covering the first British heart transplant at the National Heart Hospital in London. The story belonged largely to PJ Wilson, a *Mirror* reporter of great talent with an easy if muddled charm that invariably unlocked even the most reticent of potential informants. PJ – so called after his initials because his name was Peter and Peter Wilson was 'The Man You Can't Gag' on sport – had already made inroads into the National Heart and had a telephone operator acting as his eyes and ears who would tell him the truth about the patient rather than the *Mirror* having to rely on bland hospital statements. However, PJ was a sucker for conspiracy and he developed an intricate system of codes so his man could telephone him without attracting any suspicion. This is all very well as long as you remember your own codes, which PJ sadly did not. So when his snout called him early one evening and said, 'The eagle has taken the rabbit', he knew that there had been some big development, but he had no idea what it was. He told me of his dilemma and I suggested he should tell Dan Ferrari that something was happening at the National Heart. I would go down and see if I could dig up anything, meanwhile he would try and unscramble his own code. Luckily for me – and PJ's exclusive – I approached a young doctor coming off shift and gambled by suggesting that their patient had taken a turn for the worse and was on the way out. She was so surprised she confirmed everything. PJ had his exclusive and I had my staff job.

Wilson was a great *Mirror* reporter. He instinctively knew the right stories and how to handle and project them, and he had that unteachable ability to get on with people, however distressed or reluctant to talk. He also had the priceless gift of being able to ask the idiot question that nobody else dared to for fear of being made to look daft. It was invariably the question that brought forth the most illuminating answer. But PJ was accident prone. Once, while working on a local newspaper, he was walking to work in his new brothel creepers, late as usual, when he was offered a lift by a mate on his powerful twin-exhaust motorbike. Salvation was at hand and Wilson hopped on the back, hanging on for dear life, arriving at his office with seconds to spare. Then, disaster! He tried to get off, only to find that his crêpe soles had become firmly welded to the twin exhausts and, try as he might, he couldn't unstick them. He had to abandon them there and go to work in his socks, leaving motorbike and owner to the tender mercies of Norwood High Street's housewives who were convinced that the pillion passenger had been blown off the back leaving only his shoes behind.

Mechanical matters were not PJ's forte, although he loved big cars and was the proud owner of a gleaming Austin Westminster. One Sunday morning he was due on at 10.00am but didn't appear. Ferrari – by now news editor, a job he didn't like – wanted to know where he was, convinced I was covering up for him.

'Where's your mate?' he asked, with a hint of menace.

'No idea, Dan.' Half-an-hour later, the question was repeated with growing menace. Then Wilson appeared, walking somewhat stiff-legged, but apart from that he seemed all right.

'Where have you been? Dan's growling,' I said.

PJ ignored me and sat down gingerly.

'PJ, he wants to know where you've been, you'd better tell him.'

'None of his business, old man, or yours.'

'Oh come on, PJ, you can't get out of it, he'll insist on knowing.'

With the sigh of a man who knew his pleas were hopeless, he said, 'OK, old man, as long as you don't laugh.'

'Of course not,' I replied, suppressing a smirk.

It appeared that Wilson had taken his Austin Westminster to the carwash that morning, and half-way through the cycle the whole thing ground to a halt. Now most sensible people would sit there until somebody came to sort it out, but Wilson was not sensible. He got out, and just as he did so the whole thing started again, giving him a good lathering followed by a splendid hose down.

'Dreadful,' I said, virtually weeing myself.

'But why are you walking as if you've got a candle up your bum?'

Wilson fixed me with a stare daring me to laugh. 'Because, old man, I forgot that I had asked for the hot wax finish.'

And, true enough, on close examination his suit had taken on that look beloved of market traders' wax jackets. It was cracked into thousands of little jagged bits of crazy paving as the wax began to peel off.

He had only just got over that when he was sent on the maiden voyage of the *QE2*, a disaster of heroic proportions where nothing worked and even the boat taking the press corps out to the ship caught fire. For Wilson, the crisis reached trauma point when he was on the lavatory in his cabin and tried to turn on the light. The light had been wired up to the bell push by mistake and instead of shedding light on the Wilson toilette, he was visited by an obviously gay steward who thought his luck was in. It coloured PJ's views of luxury cruising forever.

The reporting staff of the *Mirror* when I arrived was run by Roly Watkins, a former Manchester man who had worked out of New York. Roly saw himself as the conductor of an orchestra. It was a convenient way of ridding himself of unwanted job applications, of which there were many, without giving offence. 'I see my newsroom as an orchestra playing symphonies every day,' he would begin to an eager supplicant. 'I look down the room and I see my violins to the left, my cellos and violas to the right. Behind them, the oboes, flutes, trumpets and trombones with the percussion behind that. And together we make the finest music in Fleet Street. You I see as an oboe, and I am afraid at the moment I am stacked up to the hilt with oboes.'

Watkins was over-optimistic about producing the finest music in Fleet Street; indeed, some of his players weren't making any music at all. His deputy and leader of the orchestra was Len Woodliff, whose mild, courteous manner, pipe and moustache belied the fact that he had won the Military Cross and bar during the Second World War. Len was a compassionate man who listened without complaint to the moans and groans of reporters, an occupational hazard for deputy news editors. But he could take the gentle touch too far. A reporter called George Fallows had been shipped back from America after suffering what was probably a mild nervous breakdown aggravated by too much drink. Roly told Len to go easy on him, which was fair enough, but that was six years earlier and George hadn't been given a job to do in the whole of that time while he 'recuperated'. He just sat in the middle of the newsroom smoking his pipe and reading the papers. We carried passengers like that, but we also carried people like Alfred Richman who was of no practical value except that Harold Wilson liked him and used him as an errand boy. Alf took grave exception to this description, claiming he was the local government correspondent, as indeed he was, except that he never did a stroke of work unless it was going to political conferences where he looked after Wilson's bits and pieces.

John Jackson, a hardened reporter who had introduced me to the delights of Fleet Street by having my car towed away at Heathrow Airport when we covered the Aldermaston march from the front line of the press room bar, was one who ran foul of Alf. Jackson was waiting for Wilson to arrive at Euston one afternoon so he could question him about some passing political crisis, when he spotted Richman. 'What's going on, Alf?' he asked, not unnaturally expecting him to know Wilson's inner thoughts as he had just travelled down with him.

'Don't ask me anything,' replied Richman angrily. 'All you lot think I'm nothing but Wilson's bagman and I've had enough of it. It's bloody wrong and I won't have it. Bugger off, I'm saying nothing.'

At this point, Euston's station master, resplendent those days in morning coat and top hat when kings and prime ministers were around, touched Richman discreetly on the elbow.

'Excuse me, sir,' he whispered just loudly enough for Jackson to hear. 'I've put the prime minister's bags in your car.'

Roly's orchestra was a strange crew. Nick Davies was known universally as Sneaky because of his habit of talking behind his hand, which was unsurprising, really, as he ran an underwater diving equipment business from his office phone.

Ron Ricketts, undoubtedly the kettle drum who hated all executives (weasels) and features staff (wankers). Ron was the office moaner, which was quite a title given that all reporters moan. He never listened to what anyone else had to say, invariably finishing his latest diatribe with, 'Am I right? I'm always right,' and then when his unfortunate quarry was lost for words, he would cup his ear and shout, 'Pardon? Pardon?' A difficult trick, Ron, but not a bad examination for budding executives. He had the infuriating habit of often being right, but he would never have made an executive himself, he preferred to be the pub version, where it wasn't necessary to take any responsibility. However, he was a fine father of the National Union of Journalists chapel, responsible for negotiating house agreements, individual deals within newspapers rather than the industry as a whole.

The flute was Sally Moore, lovely Sally in the impossibly short skirt who had the extraordinary knack of asking the most embarrassing and personal questions on the telephone and getting away with it.

In the rest of the pit, there were plenty capable of blowing their own trumpets, chief of whom was Kenelm Jenour, the son of a Portsmouth jeweller who was not afraid to advertise the family wares on his fingers. During the *Mirror* sponsored car rally to Mexico to coincide with the 1970 World Cup – a fiasco costing a king's ransom – Jenour arranged a candlelit dinner – 'This is Acapulco baby, we dine under the trees' – for himself and Wilson and a bevy of beauties he had somehow managed to bring together. Ken Jenour knew how to dress, hair beautifully coiffeured, ruffled evening shirt immaculate, velvet DJ looking as if it had been sprayed on. Fashion was not Wilson's strong point and he turned up looking as if he had just completed the rally in one stage from Buenos Aires, which is more or less what had happened. Ken was in his element, looking and behaving more like Roger Moore than even Roger Moore would find acceptable. Sadly it was not to last. As he flashed his rings and teeth in front of his admirers a huge and immensely heavy exotic Mexican fruit fell right into his soup, throwing a generous helping of particularly glutinous gaspacho all over his ruffled shirt.

On the piano was Dan Ferrari's front-of-house man, Peter Prendergast, or Peter Posh as Ed Vale called him. Peter was Stonyhurst-educated with a cut-glass accent and a pedigree to match. His father was a spy, 'the bravest man I ever met' according to Don Wise, the *Mirror*'s legendary war correspondent, and that was some tribute. John Prendergast had gone native in the Kenyan bush during Mau-Mau, living wild and covering himself in elephant dung to convince the Mau-Mau he was a harmless loony. His intelligence reports back to base were invaluable. During the Eoka troubles in Cyprus, he had their leader, Colonel Grivas, literally in his sights but he was prevented from arresting him – or worse, killing him – by a Foreign Office fearful it would jeopardise peace talks with Archbishop Makarios. Peter was half-Irish and half-Palestinian, a wonderful mixture, and the girls loved him. One reporters' Christmas lunch saw him doing the Gay Gordons down the thronged aisles of office parties, picking up girls and dancing them up and down the restaurant. Unfortunately, he had to work that evening and it happened to be the night John Stonehouse, an MP who had faked his death in Miami, turned up under arrest in Australia. It fell to Prendergast, who was feeling no pain by this time, to contact our man in Melbourne – who happened to be the cricket reporter covering the England v Australia test series – to glean more information. Our man could not be traced, so Colin Cowdrey came to the phone. Prendergast is a fanatical cricketer and immediately stood to attention when he realised it was the great man himself on the line. Sadly, the day's wear and tear had taken its toll and Peter fell over, dragging the phone with him.

From the floor, he started to tell Cowdrey how to play the Aussie fast bowlers, Denis Lillee and Jeff Thompson. Staggering to his feet he slurred, 'Now listen, Colin, you should always go forward, play forward.' And with that he gave an example of how he himself would play the two fastest men in the world. It was an over-ambitious stroke and once again Peter fell to the ground with the phone on top of him.

A week later, I was in Melbourne and found myself next to Cowdrey at a New Year's Eve party. He started telling me of this conversation he had with Peter. 'A bad line, I think ... he was rather indistinct and there was a terrible clattering which seemed to come from the other end. He was giving me some advice on how to play Lillee and Thompson.'

'Ah yes, erm, sorry about that,' I said. 'He is a great fan of yours and sometimes he gets, er, over-enthusiastic.'

'Not at all,' replied Cowdrey. 'He was absolutely right.'

Over the water in New York were the trombones, not quite 76 of them but not far off. The staff consisted of five reporters who were meant to service both the *Daily* and *Sunday Mirrors*, but in reality were there to service the head of the bureau, Ralph Champion, a friend of Cudlipp and a prodigious old soak. Legend had it that the bureau grew to such a size because Ralph managed to work his way through reporters' livers, necessitating another fresh drinking companion to be sent out. Ralph rarely went out on jobs unless it was to somewhere he had never been before, which was unlikely, as he had been based in New York for more than 20 years. However, when train robber Ronald Biggs was discovered in Rio de Janeiro, Ralph decided to go and have a look at the place, a sightseeing tour that, sadly for the *Mirror*, only included the minimum of reporting.

A job in the States was the most assured way of winning promotion on your return to reality, although on occasions re-entry was sometimes difficult. Poor old John Smith, a most accomplished reporter and writer, went to the *People* only to be consigned to being sent endlessly round the world for years. Sounds good, until you are on your fifth orbit. The way not to get on was to catch Ralph powdering his nose, which he did around midday before taking his accustomed seat in Costello's, the New York version of the *Mirror* pub the Stab in the Back. Ralph's nose had begun to show signs of wear and tear from the enormous amount of whisky it had witnessed course down its owner's throat, and it needed mollifying before each session.

No such problem for the great Brian Hitchen, later to be editor of the *Daily Star*. Even then he looked remarkably like Mussolini, although he didn't start sounding like him until he launched his splendidly ranting right-wing column. Hitchen has extremely rare blood and whenever he ran short of a few dollars he could sell a pint for £60, enabling him to eat his favourite immensely hot goat curry, which he did with the aid of two napkins, one in the orthodox place and the other tied round his sparsely populated but profusely perspiring head.

Our orchestra toured the provinces, too, with staff men in the major cities of the UK. Syd Young in Bristol who played the system reckoned he had his patch so stitched up he was capable of covering any story from his garden. Danny Daniels in Birmingham was the opposite, a born worrier but little escaped either of them. In the Midlands, Frank Palmer played the clarinet, literally. It was Frank who ruined my overcoat, along with an elderly but extremely windy dog.

I had gone up to join forces with him on a most unlikely story, Labour's Margaret Beckett caught in a love triangle. She wasn't Margaret Beckett then, she was Margaret Jackson, the prospective candidate for Lincoln. She had fallen for the chairman of the local party, Leo Beckett, and Mrs Beckett number one was none too happy. There was what was politely known as an altercation in the local Labour club and Mrs Beckett number one threw a cup of tea at the woman who was to become Mrs Beckett number two and, eventually, Labour's deputy leader. In time, Mrs Beckett number one agreed to talk, but only after her dog had taken such a liking to me that it sat on my lap and refused to leave. It proceeded to let out a series of highly toxic farts much to Palmer's amusement and the detriment of my overcoat. The coat never recovered and had to be consigned to the bin, a victim of the eternal fearless quest for truth and, as Frank put it, 'the price you big-time operators have to pay for coming out of London to see us buggers in the sticks'.

Roly's strange orchestra was much in demand and most nights there were tours of the *Mirror* by women's institutes, schools and the like. One evening, a synod of bishops was being shown round the newsroom, an impressive 75 yard-long floor, as the first edition was going to bed. There was much activity around the backbench – the night editor's desk – putting the final touches to the page-three lead, a story about a girl with an ample bust who had been turned down for a job because it was considered too large. 'Funnies' like this are known as straight banana stories and this particular one was by a reporter called Margaret Hall. The bishops nodded their way past in a flurry of purple just when the chief sub, Vic Mayhew, decided to double-check the author with Dan Ferrari. Mayhew was a great production journalist with a turn of phrase as powerful as his love of pubs. He would, for example, express his dislike of a story he thought unworthy to lead the paper with the comment: 'If that's a splash, my prick's a bloater.' On this occasion, he was equally forthright. 'Dan,' he shouted over the heads of the bishops, 'the girl with the big tits, is that Maggie Hall?'

By the end of the 1960s, the *Mirror* had become caught up in its own success and, apart from some daring assaults on the sexual liberation front by Marje Proops and women's editor Felicity Green, the paper tended to rest on its laurels; everyone assumed the party would go on for ever. One of the problems was a party of a different kind – Labour. The party the paper supported had now been in power for six years after 13 in the wilderness of opposition – always the more comfortable place for a fiery tabloid – and Cudlipp, Sydney Jacobson, editorial director and political editor John Beavan were all part of the Labour top table and each was to go to the House of Lords as a reward. The ballsy, anti-Establishment, raucous tabloid journalist of the Forties and Fifties had made way for a newspaper baron who was now espousing leaders along the 'Work harder you bastards' line. Cudlipp also developed the idea of a mission to explain in the *Mirror*, introducing a pull-out called *Mirrorscope* which had all sorts of worthy and esoteric features in it, including, on one memorable occasion, an interview with Warden John Sparrow of All Souls college, Oxford. Not exactly *Mirror* territory. All this happened when the country was tending to go the other way, television had taken hold, and so had the pop culture of the young, in music, fashion and football. Yet the people's paper was becoming more and more worthy, admirable of course, but, well, boring.

In 1969, the *Mirror* did dare to launch a colour magazine. It came out on Wednesday and was brilliant. The editor was a 28-year-old former art student called Mike Molloy and even today, more than 30 years later, the magazine stands the test of time. The problem, as with all colour magazines, was that it cost a fortune and there was never any hope of it breaking even. Indeed, the more successful it was, the more money it lost as it was distributed free to readers, included in the cover price of the paper. Therefore, the larger the circulation the more magazines we had to print and the greater the cost, and that was before you paid the newsagent extra for handling it. The magazine brought back one of the *Mirror*'s former feature writers Keith Waterhouse as a columnist and introduced a new name in cookery – Delia Smith. In spite of its excellence, Cudlipp's nerve failed and it was canned less than a year after its first issue, another expensive failure only months after Murdoch's *Sun* first peeped over the horizon.

Reaction to the first edition of the *Sun* at Holborn Circus was one of derision. It was seen as a rip-off of the *Mirror* of the early 60s, cheap and cheerful, but no threat. Once again, when the executives crowded into the editor's office to view the new arrival, the only person to sound a note of caution was Lee Howard. Cudlipp gave it six months – 'There's nothing to worry about there then' – and opened another bottle of champagne.

Lee Howard was a massive man with a huge mane of white hair. He had been an aerial photographer in the Second World War and won the Distinguished Flying Cross. But he was an old-fashioned editor; in the three years I was on the staff under his editorship, I never once saw him on the floor of the newsroom. He remained in his office all day, most of it spent drinking, which he began at 11.00am with a crony from the advertising department. Lee was still there at 1.00am when he would call the newsdesk for his car to be brought round. That is the only time I spoke to him until after he retired, when he upped sticks from both Britain and his marriage, crammed his 20-stone-plus frame into a Mini and drove to Rome where he set up home with the *Mirror*'s reporter there, Madelon Dimont. Lee was content to let Cudlipp run the politics and the night editor, Geoff Pinnington, run the backbench. Features and sport largely ran themselves and the *Mirror* trundled on from day to day with the occasional Cudlippean blast, of which this had become typical:

WAKE UP, BRITAIN!
WE'RE LIVING IN THE PAST
WE'RE TOO SLOW
TOO SLEEPY
TOO DAMN SMUG!

Yes, maybe, but that was the readers he was talking about and the uncomfortable truth was that the criticism could equally be levelled at the *Mirror*. Cudlipp was without question the quintessential tabloid man, but tabloid journalism is about time and mood as much as anything and he, and we, were out of our time. There was nobody to tell Cudlipp, though. This man had been the inspiration of the *Mirror* off and on for more than 30 years. He was capable of producing front pages that made governments wince during the day and host parties at night for the *Mirror*'s National Pets Club where readers were encouraged to bring along their pets –

Top left: My father Fred in his Royal Flying Corps uniform – a first world war photograph for his parents.

Top right: My mother as a teenager: 'I had an eighteen-inch waist in those days, you know.'

Bottom left: Demanding even then ... on the steps of 4, Museum Road, Oxford during the war.

Bottom right: Our cream and red converted railway carriage by the side of the Thames at Bablockhythe. (*Left to right*) Godmother Lily Peacock (toughest pub landlady in Oxford), me, my mother, father and brother John. Enough to give a planner the vapours nowadays.

Top left: Me having a crafty drag for my brother with his TR2 which he was to enter in the Mille Miglia. The satisfied smile is because he pulled me out of a Greek lesson.

Top right: My mother at the gate of Number Four. Not a landlady, please – Hostess to the University.

Bottom: Gordon Hazell's 1960 Clifton College boxing team. He always wore white tracksuits and was obsessed with cleanliness – a stark contrast to the boys' dirty minds. A featherweight me is second from the right, back row.

Top: With Prime Minister Harold Wilson at Ellesborough golf club near Chequers. He wasn't pleased to have his game interrupted by a hick reporter. 'What did you go round in?' I asked. 'These trousers,' he said.

Bottom: Hamming it up again at the *Bucks Herald* in Roger Duckworth's reporter's hat and scarf. I bought the typewriter from my brother for a tenner.

Mean and lean. Doorstep reporter at the Ferrari of Dartford news agency ...

Top left: ... and the man himself – legendary night news editor Dan Ferrari, with Fleet Street's most ferocious moustache.

Top right: My sister Judith was a big hit in Peter Shaffer's *The Private Ear* and *The Public Eye* in the West End. She took over from schoolfriend Maggie Smith.

Bottom: Married to Penny – with brother-in-law and best man David outside the RAF church, St Clement Dane's in April 1970. (*Picture by Derek Hope*)

The end of an epic journey. Labour MP John Stonehouse (*left*) returns to England after faking his death in Miami and turning up with a new identity in Australia. With him is Scotland Yard's DCS Ken Etheridge who had developed a hearty disrespect for MPs during the Poulson corruption inquiry ...

... and here's why. Former Chancellor of the Exchequer Reginald Maudling doing what he did best at a 1971 Savoy hotel wine-tasting competition. Etheridge was one of many who believed Maudling should have been prosecuted for corruption.

A rogue's rogue ... former Tory transport minister Ernie Marples at the moment I confronted him with his tax evasion and breach of exchange control regulations.

(*Picture by Albert Foster*)

ranging from a baby elephant to an anaconda – letting the latter out of its cage to see if it could squeeze his marketing director to death.

The life was gradually being squeezed out of Cudlipp's *Mirror*, and the first grip of the anaconda came when, fearing a takeover of IPC, Cudlipp organised a reverse takeover by Reed, a former subsidiary and always referred to by him contemptuously as the wallpaper manufacturers. He must have had an idea that the sea was going to be choppy for he decided to quit on his sixtieth birthday; it would, he said, be an 'unpardonable vanity' for him to remain in a business that should be run by young people. He really should have taken his own advice five years earlier, for he left no natural heir; he was far too autocratic a captain for any of his lieutenants to be trusted with steering the ship. The *Mirror* was left effectively rudderless, and at a time when the ship desperately needed a guiding star.

Cudlipp's farewell was as gargantuan as expected. He had more of them than Frank Sinatra and if 'My Way' had been around then it would have been sung, or slurred, at every one. The climax was the farewell of farewells at the Painted Hall in Greenwich, reached by a flotilla of small boats from Charing Cross pier. It was the biggest armada to sail up the Thames since the evacuation of Dunkirk, and its return journey carried as many casualties. The celebration was classic Fleet Street – sentimental, drunken and bitchy with sporadic fighting. Some never made it to the dinner, wandering off into the pubs of Greenwich, some had to be carried in, mortally wounded but still bravely prepared to continue the battle through the meal. Some were so exhausted by the fight they fell asleep where they sat.

As course followed course, the wine flowed and the speeches and eulogies were rolled out, the mood began to take against Cudlipp's successor Alex Jarratt, a former civil servant with the Ministry of Agriculture and a strange choice as successor to Cudlipp as boss of IPC and later Reed International. Eventually, as he rose to speak he was roundly booed by the tattered but undefeated army still able to draw breath. The whole dinner was being tape-recorded as a gift for Cudlipp, but two young reporters infiltrated the sound system and added their own more down-to-earth commentary to the litany of praise from speaker after speaker. It was rendered unuseable.

There was one other issue to be settled – which of the two up-and-coming young Turks, one in news, one in features, was likely to be a future editor? The battle was between Mike Taylor, night editor, and Mike Molloy, assistant editor features. Molloy won it hands down in what became known as the battle of the parrot suit. Cudlipp liked parrots and their assorted relatives and had once given Marje Proops a mynah bird as a present. He heard nothing for months so he decided to ask her what had happened to it.

'Had to go, dear, I'm afraid. Quite unsuitable.'

'Why?' asked Cudlipp. 'Wouldn't it talk?'

'Oh yes,' replied Marje. 'That was the trouble. I think it must have belonged to a cab driver, Hugh dear. Because every time Proopsie [her husband] and I had guests round it used to keep on repeating the one line: "How much to the fuckin' airport then?"'

Hence the parrot suit, and the sketch which was intended to be a conversation with the parrot about Cudlipp. Taylor was the parrot dressed up in the finest yellow and green plumage. The trouble was nobody could hear a word he said, just the occasional strangled squeak coming from his beak. The sketch was a disaster. Taylor got the bird and the blame and Molloy the editorship.

Fallout from the farewell continued for many weeks, with accusation and counter-accusation about who hit who and who insulted who. A search party was sent out for one casualty, Teddy Prendergast, no relation to Peter, late man on the Manchester liaison desk and a notorious tippler, who had last been seen heading in the general direction of several Greenwich pubs. He had not made the dinner or been seen since. He eventually returned five days later saying he had had the most wonderful time, didn't realise how many excellent pubs there were in Greenwich, how did the dinner go and was he there?

Cudlipp may well have been past his sell-by date but at least he gave the *Mirror* credibility. On his departure we had only those with whom he had surrounded himself. Tony Miles succeeded Lee Howard in 1971 and he quickly became known as the editor whose indecision is final. He was unhappily married, and embarked on an affair with his secretary, which he might have kept under wraps except that he decided to take a day off and go to Wimbledon. Annie, the secretary, decided she would take the day off, too, while Tony's wife decided she would watch Wimbledon on TV. And what she saw didn't please her, but was the subject of much merriment in the office. There were Tony and Annie sitting together on the centre court in wonderful seats, right under the score board, so they appeared as regular as clockwork every three games.

Tony was a good journalist but a poor editor, torn between following the *Mirror*'s Cudlipp tradition and fighting the *Sun* which was beginning to make considerable inroads into the *Mirror*, not least because of the introduction of Page Three, the brainchild of the editor Larry Lamb, later Sir Larry. It was a time when the *Mirror* needed to be brave, brash and positive. Instead, he remained indecisive, often not knowing from one day to the next whether we were or were not going to run topless glamour pictures.

It wasn't just an inadequate editorial reaction helping the *Sun*, the *Mirror* was always the first to be hit when it came to industrial action, and it came pretty often. By the time Mike Molloy became acting editor in 1975, after Tony Miles had moved upstairs and Mike Christiansen's reign had been cut short by a heart-attack, the *Mirror* was definitely on the back foot. Molloy was to improve the paper dramatically, encouraging news investigations and living dangerously. Cudlipp had discouraged stories which might bring libel writs; he had hated giving evidence in the Liberace v Cassandra case and swore that nobody would have to go through the ordeal if he could help it. Compassionate, but it didn't make for exciting newspapers, adventurous executives or understanding lawyers.

Cudlipp had become part of the establishment he once despised, he even made King pay out £40,000 to Lord Boothby after a front page *Sunday Mirror* story linking the Conservative peer anonymously with the gangster Ronnie Kray and rent boys. Cudlipp was furious that King had taken an editorial decision to publish the report by Norman Lucas, the paper's crime man with excellent Scotland Yard contacts, while he was away on holiday and demanded the paper apologise, which it did. But the *Sunday Mirror* was right, Kray and Boothby had been involved in gay sex parties together, yet Cudlipp preferred to cave in rather than face the wrath of the fix it and fiddle it set, led by the lawyer Alan Goodman.

In spite of that, the 11 years I had reporting on the *Mirror* were action-packed, thrilling and never more fun than when travelling around the dark side of our rulers, the rich, the powerful and the famous. There were no rules around the dark side. They would have you if they could when you started to get close. But all that was to come later – for the time being, I was just happy to be a reporter on Fleet Street at last.

* * *

There is nothing like your first by-line on a national newspaper. Your name on the story, even if the subs have mucked it about and slashed it to ribbons, it's there staring out at you. You're famous, everybody in the street must be looking ... I'll just put the paper down here, open at the page ... It never quite wears off; the reporter who has given up looking for his name is the reporter who should be put out to grass. There is nothing wrong in being by-line hungry. For the next 11 years I would maintain my appetite before deciding on a change of diet. During those years I married Penny, the best thing I ever did – I was lucky to find the one person in the world who would put up with me – and had three wonderful children – Emily, Hannah and Christopher – who have also coped with a life undreamt of outside a lunatic asylum, as if it was quite normal, often to the consternation of their friends.

But all this was in the future when I started work on the dog-watch shift from 9.00pm until 4.00am, where by-lines usually came either very big or not at all. All the junior reporters got the late, late show; it wasn't a bad idea because it gave you a chance to shine with a late story, you got to know the night editor and his production team and you weren't lost in a sea of daytime reporters all looking to be sent out on the big one. There was one shift worse than the 9–4 and that was the 2.00am until 9.00am where your job was to field the early morning cranks, set up stories if they had broken overnight and prepare the newspaper digest for Hugh Cudlipp. Mercifully, you didn't get lumbered very often; the shift belonged to Bill Sellwood, an author and former reporter who had fallen foul of the taxman. Bill was so short of money that he frequently didn't have enough to get home to Seaford each morning so he tramped up to Hampstead Heath, found a bench if it wasn't raining and went to sleep. Then he tramped back again, after eating little or nothing, arriving back at the *Mirror* for a canteen packet of chips before settling down for a three-hour kip in Donald Zec's office. He always reckoned Zec's office had the best sofas, presumably well upholstered to take sensitive showbusiness bums.

There were two ways I could go when I eventually rejoined the rota staff doing days and nights. I could stay on the rota, doing all the jobs that are handed out by the news desk, and the law of averages means that you will get some good ones and a few decent foreign trips, too. Or I could follow my own nose; it didn't mean I got out of the rota, but it did mean I had the satisfaction of finding my own stuff. People like that are known as self-starters and that was my chosen path. I believed then, and I still do, that reporters are the eyes and ears of their newspaper. They are the troops who can change the world for the better by exposing degradation, corruption in high places, hypocrisy, fraud and double-dealing wherever they might find it, which is frequently in the gutter. You are unlikely to be handed a sex or financial scandal by the Archbishop of Canterbury. Too many reporters – too many editors, too, for that matter – are easily seduced by the rich man's hamper or the politician's bauble. Jeffrey Archer didn't hold his shepherd's pie and champagne lunches just for fun.

The *Mirror*'s objectivity at the end of Wilson's first six years as Prime Minister was not helped by the bulk of the journalistic hierarchy being members of the House of Lords. My natural inclination was to set my face against both respectability and a cosy inside track; that is why, much later, I turned down the chance to be both the *Mirror*'s chief political correspondent and head of the New York bureau. The first meant you had to join the lobby and accept its odd and self-serving rules; the second meant you had a great time, but it wasn't real reporting That took place at home where, if you were lucky, you could burrow right to the heart of a story and come out with something smelling rather different to roses. Yet at home the job of the general reporter was coming under threat, too; this was a time when the National Union of Journalists chapel (union branch) power was at its height. In-house agreements were negotiated with individual newspapers replacing the across-the-board deals which tended to be set at the levels of the financially weakest. As the *Mirror* was seen as the goose that laid the golden egg, the journalists managed to forge themselves a good deal, not just on pay but on a four-day week and sabbaticals as well. That meant every four years we were entitled to take a month off on full pay to broaden the mind, a heroic idea but in practice it was no more than an extra month's holiday.

I hated the four-day week; I couldn't see how reporters could work with any continuity on running stories. It was a deal made for soft, easy-going hacks who were only too happy to sit back and take the money, although there was an argument for sub-editors working a four-day week as the longer shifts meant continuity over a day's edition. Eventually I rebelled and refused to work the new rota and, as a result, actually had my stories blacked by the office NUJ, something of an embarrassment for the management as it could hardly refuse to back a reporter who wanted to do more work. I, in turn, refused to pay my union dues and this argument seemed to be heading for the cliffs when the dues were paid by the union's national representative at the *Mirror* and the copy blacking withdrawn. I carried on working a five-day week, but the damage was done. The *Mirror* got an even bigger reputation for being a feather bed, a prejudice that was to stick for years after it was no longer true.

My first success was to expose Britain's biggest private waste disposal firm which claimed to be the world's 'leading exponent of scientific waste management'. In fact, the firm was dumping indiscriminately, flouting planning laws and contaminating water supplies. The story was to lead to the tightening of dumping laws and the company itself being taken over.

Less successful were my attempts at becoming a foreign reporter. I was twice sent to Uganda, first to cover the coup by Idi Amin which toppled Milton Obote. That went off all right, but the *Mirror* rapidly lost interest when it became clear that, much to my relief, there wasn't going to be a massacre. I did manage to interview Julius Nyerere of Tanzania who startled me by going into a brilliant impersonation of Edward Heath, then the British Prime Minister. Nyerere had just returned from the Commonwealth Prime Ministers' Conference where Heath had been in full flow.

'It is about time,' said Nyerere thumping the table, but speaking with Heath's plummy voice and wide vowels, 'that the British Government started looking after the British.' Not much ideology difference there between Heath and Thatcher. And again, 'We will drop Africa and you will never find the pieces.'

Yes, well, up to a point, Prime Minister.

My second visit was a disaster, for me at any rate. Amin was kicking out the Ugandan Asians and he was in an ugly mood. He was unpredictable, but not half as unpredictable as the spooks around him, most of whom were hopped up on the local grass and extremely trigger itchy. Everything was going well, even though Amin's spies were monitoring our phonecalls by the simple but effective way of listening in at the hotel switchboard. I was covering for the *Sunday Mirror* one Saturday when the mood was tense and potentially ugly because the idea that British paratroops might be flown in to remove Amin was being floated in London. It had not gone down well in Uganda. I wrote a story for the *Sunday Mirror* and thought no more about it until very early the next morning when I received a call from the British High Commission asking what the hell the *Sunday Mirror* thought it was playing at. Right across the front page was a headline in the biggest type possible screaming 'HE'S NUTS' and a particularly loony-looking Amin staring out of the page next to the report, written from the safety of the *Sunday Mirror*'s fifth-floor office in Holborn. The paper was now in Uganda; by a quirk of flight schedules and early Sunday paper deadlines the papers arrived in Uganda at 8.00am on Sunday morning. Apparently, the High Commissioner Richard Slater had a well-placed spy in Amin's headquarters who could keep the *Sunday Mirror* away from him for a few hours, but that would be all. In the High Commissioner's view, this would be all Amin would need to either throw British journalists into the slammer or out of the country. My position was worse, he said. I should get out now while I could. The hotel spooks knew I had been writing for the *Sunday Mirror* and would not believe I had nothing to do with it. There was nothing for it but to get out and quick.

I was replaced by Don Wise, the *Mirror*'s veteran foreign man and an old Africa hand. Wise was magnificent; he looked and behaved like David Niven and was entirely fearless. He was not only contemptuous of African dictators' brutality but he had no qualms about showing it. In Biafra, that most bloodthirsty of civil wars, a particularly unpleasant officer who had ordered two French journalists to be flogged, was ranting to the assembled press corps about what they could and could not do and finally asked if there were any questions. Sensibly, everyone remained quiet until Wise untangled his legs, heaved himself up to his full 6ft 4in and said in his most exaggerated colonial accent, 'Would the colonel like a banana?' The colonel was left speechless and just walked out. Wise stories can be found anywhere in the world where there is a press club. His breed has died out now and we are the poorer for it. I will leave you with his immortal description of an animated conversation in the Vietnamese language: 'Like two ducks fucking, old boy.' Wise and the rest of the British press were duly slammed up in what Don insisted on describing in old patois to his captors as 'the King George Hoteli' but they had the last laugh, John Dowling of the *Daily Express* showed extraordinary courage by keeping his camera with him and somehow shooting the scene inside. It was great photo journalism from a very brave journalist.

My finest hour abroad came when, together with photographer Kent Gavin, I was sent to the Arctic Circle as part of a series called *The Last Frontiers*. The idea was to travel to the farthest ends of the earth to find the men – and women, too, if we were lucky – who were pushing back the final frontiers of the world, in our case the discovery of oil near the North Pole in Alaska, and write about the fists and booze lifestyle that went with it. We did discover that, but we also found out that it is possible to be in the United States and the USSR at the same time. This clearly came as a surprise to most Americans because the picture showing how it could be done sold to 400 newspapers across the States. Here is the secret if you fancy having a go – fly to Nome, high up on Alaska's west coast, then hire a plane to take you to a rocky bit of nothing called Little Diomede right in the middle of the Bering Strait. This is the last outpost of the USA, two-and-a-half miles away is Big Diomede, the last outpost of what was the Soviet empire. So if you stand in the middle of the sea exactly one-and-a-quarter miles from Little Diomede you are in the USSR and the States at the same time. How do you stand in the sea? In winter, it is frozen 6ft deep.

We flew into Little Diomede on a single engine ski-plane then hitched a snowbike ride across the frozen sea, a trip I do not recommend. The sea freezes in ripples so it is as if you are riding a bike across corrugated iron at great speed in a deep freeze. The temperature, assisted by a vicious wind, was minus 60°C, I was only wearing jeans on my bottom half and they froze like cardboard. The trip out was magnificent, flying slowly over petrified waterfalls of cloud, glaciers and polar bears. Little Diomede was not quite so idyllic. Both Diomedes, great and small, are populated by Eskimos, most of them interrelated. There is a virile smuggling trade between the two, anything American for Russian vodka and occasionally vicious, drunken fights break out. One such had just taken place and there was blood and glass staining the ice. The Americans deliberately keep no force on their island to avoid any confrontation, which is just as well as the Eskimos are quite capable of provoking one. The Russians on the other hand do keep a small garrison on Big Diomede. God knows what horrors the commanding officer had to perpetrate against the people's soviet to be posted there. They even have a small wooden watchtower perched at the highest point of this forsaken part of outer, outer Siberia. In the event of invasion, the 126 American Eskimos are advised by the State Department to contact the mainland – and co-operate with the Russians. However, it seemed the most likely cause of an unseemly diplomatic incident was the battle over booze. Eskimos are voracious but poor drinkers. The nearest they came to an international bust-up was when one inhabitant, inflamed by vodka, lurched across the ice threatening to sort out the Soviet Union. America keeps a social worker stationed on the island for just such an emergency and the drunk was gently persuaded that it would not be in the best interests of the American nation for him to take such an onerous task upon himself.

Nome is an old gold rush town, a contraction of 'No Name', the rather negative view taken of the settlement when it was first discovered. It has many bars and the oldest newspaper in Alaska owned then by Albro B Gregory, a splendid eccentric in the finest tradition of frontier newspapers. Not only was he proprietor and editor of the *Nome Nugget* but outside his office he boasted the world's most northern parking meter, only just outside the Arctic Circle, and woe betide anyone who parked in Albro's space. The *Nome Nugget* – motto 'There's no place like Nome' – proudly announced that it was published 'daily except Monday,

Wednesday, Thursday, Saturday and Sunday'. Under that was the exhortation '*Illegitimis non Carborundum*' – a fine sentiment and it would have taken some bastard to grind down Albro, who looked the spitting image of Ernest Hemingway. Nobody could accuse him of not having his finger on the local scene either, even if the news wasn't earth-shattering. A typical example: 'Roy Tobuk Sr returned from his North Slope job but was observed Monday as he prepared to leave Nome again.'

We retired to Albro's favourite watering hole, the Board of Trade bar, a long, thin establishment which smelled worse the further you delved into its depths. Albro explained that Nome's licensing laws were very strict; the bars had to close between 3.00 and 6.00am so they could be cleaned, which is why the disinfectant never got down to the far end. It was here we discovered a wailing Indian, or 'native American' as we did not have to call them then. And boy was he wailing, not just weeping, he was wailing a deep, animal wail, his long, jet-black hair falling into his beer. Apparently, he was the mayor of a group of local islands and he had come to Nome to pay their taxes. Unfortunately, he had drunk them instead and now realised he had to go back and face the music. Big Diomede may have been a better option.

Back in Anchorage we plunged into the low-life, all in the cause of *The Last Frontiers*. Twelve hours of non-stop strip clubs tends to pall a bit, particularly when presented with 'the world's ugliest stripper' at Papa Joe's, a boozing joint now hopefully lost in Anchorage's effort to clean itself up and present a squeaky clean *National Geographic* image. Papa Joe's barman demanded ten dollars from any punter who asks for Sherry to 'loosen the linen', 'just to cover the cost of the punters who leave rather than watch', he explained. Sherry did, indeed, live up to her reputation – everything came off except her thick pebble glasses.

* * *

One of the most overused aphorisms in Fleet Street is Lord Northcliffe's description of news being something that someone somewhere does not want printed. Everything else, he said, was advertising. An explosion of spin doctors, public relations consultants, media men, image massagers and a host of other mincing perfumers of the truth are employed to put the journalist off the track. Too many reporters are seduced by the easy quote from the ever accessible press office, the easy steer over a couple of drinks or the 'deep background' intended to lure them into the treacherous bogs of asserting 'facts' they have never checked. Ever more stringent deadlines and 24-hour news coverage being pumped out by radio and television has meant news has become like a Big Mac, to be consumed in ten minutes and the packaging tossed away. News has become advertising, and the PR man who can put his point across better is the winner. The general reporter is in the front line of this battle, the maverick private eye of his newspaper, the one most likely to find the story They don't want you to have. But who are They? They are the quick-fix merchants, the sound-bite kings, the sultans of spin, the nod-and-wink army who tell it like it isn't. And, as Harold Wilson said, They become dictators. It is the reporter's job to stop them, but like Customs men we only know of those we catch. Here are two.

Maxwell Confait was a transvestite, a sad twilight man whose life was always teetering on the edge of the gutter. Calling himself Michelle he traipsed round the bars of London's West End looking for homosexual pick-ups. He lived his life in one lonely room in Doggett Road, Catford, and frequently took his clients back there. It was a dangerous life and he paid the price. Confait was found dead after a fire in his room. A lamp flex wound round his neck had strangled him.

The story was depressingly familiar, or it was until the police came up with a remarkable coup – confessions to murder from two teenagers who were banged up, one at Rampton for an indefinite period and the other at Her Majesty's pleasure in a young offenders' jail. And there it might have remained until the local MP took up the boys' cause and asked me to help.

I was intrigued, because the policeman in charge was someone with whom I had crossed swords before, Chief Superintendent Alan Jones. He had led the investigation into the kidnapping of a baby in Bromley for which a woman was charged – with much ballyhoo – but later cleared. He had also been in command of the delicate investigation into the case of Harold Wilson's forged signature by a man called Ronald Milhench. Mr Jones had held a bizarre press conference at which he not only provided the answers, but put the questions as well. He had also irritated the local Staffordshire police by claiming he was looking into the circumstances surrounding the death of Milhench's wife when an inquest jury had returned a verdict of accidental death. Mr Jones then was no stranger to controversy and appeared to enjoy being in the public eye.

The confessions were certainly full. One of the boys – who, it emerged later, had a mental age of eight – said they had broken into the house after midnight 'to steal from the funny man who dressed as a woman'. A struggle developed and he strangled Confait with the lamp flex while his accomplice held his hands. They then set fire to the house. But new forensic evidence from two pathologists showed that Confait could not have died after midnight and the boys had alibis until 11.45pm. All the evidence also suggested that the flex was put round his neck by someone with whom he was friendly and co-operative. In other words, it was quite possibly a sex game that went wrong. The boys were cleared in the Appeal Court and the subsequent inquiry attacked Jones for 'unfair and oppressive' questioning. 'What he did was calculated to arouse disquiet,' said the chairman. As a result, the rules governing the questioning of suspects were changed. The boys paid with three years of their lives destroyed for a crime they did not commit. But it would have been a great deal longer if the campaign to free them had not received such national coverage. Eventually, the right man was charged, and it had been a sex game that went wrong.

The case of train driver Leslie Newson was even more disturbing. Mr Newson was a Tube train driver with London Transport, whose record over six years was exemplary; he was considered to be careful and conscientious. Then he piled a morning rush-hour train into a dead-end tunnel at Moorgate, killing 42 people and seriously injuring 72. The cause of the crash was a mystery; all the usual checks showed up nothing untoward in Mr Newson's life. Police even checked the sherry bottle at his home, and the evidence all pointed him to him being a very occasional drinker.

Then suddenly, just before the inquest, news was leaked to the London evening papers that sensational evidence was to be presented to the coroner which would solve this most baffling case. Someone was trying to set the agenda for blame. The 'solution' wasn't long in coming. Poisons expert Dr Ann Robinson told the inquest that, on examination, Mr Newson's blood showed an alcohol content equivalent to five whiskies. The milk bottle found in his cab also contained traces of alcohol. Open and shut. For whatever reason, Mr Newson had been drinking heavily and that had caused the crash. But I didn't believe it, because of what I had been told when I covered the disaster. The dead-end tunnel was the length of a cricket pitch but larger than the normal underground tunnel. This meant that when the train slammed into the dead end at 40mph, the second carriage reared up on top of the first and the rest of the train cannoned into it, crushing it further. It took rescuers four days, working in fearful heat with arc lights and cutting equipment, to reach Mr Newson's body. I watched the teams at work, standing next to the pathologist Dr Keith Simpson, whom I knew from previous encounters. He told me that discovering the cause of death would be difficult, if not impossible, because of the effect of the extreme heat on the body for so long. It wasn't the sort of information you could use at the time, but I stored it up – you never know when it might come in useful.

The alarm bells were tinkling and they rang loud and clear when Dr Robinson gave her evidence. How could she be so certain when Professor Simpson said it wasn't possible? I rang him at Guy's Hospital, told him of the evidence and reminded him of our conversation. If Dr Robinson was right, this man was going to be branded with the manslaughter of 42 people, and if she was wrong somebody had to say so, and quick. Simpson was clearly perturbed. Then came his bombshell: the most likely reason the alcohol was present in the body and in the milk was fermentation caused by the enormous heat over a sustained period of four days in a confined area. He used the example of a bottle of milk left out on the doorstep in the sun. 'It ferments and, if you tested it, the milk would show traces of alcohol.' Dr Robinson tested the driver's alcohol level against that of passengers, but Professor Simpson pointed out that they would have been subject to much less intense heat than the man in the cab slammed up against the wall. Unusually, the professor agreed to go on the record, and as a result of the *Mirror* report the inquest was forced to adjourn for a day when Mr Newson's widow challenged Dr Robinson's findings. New evidence was introduced and a second expert from Guy's Hospital said he placed no reliance on the minute traces of alcohol found in the plastic bottle containing Mr Newson's milk and that the amount of alcohol in the blood was small, no more than 15 to 20 milligrams per 100 millilitres of blood, considerably less than Dr Robinson's suggestion of five whiskies. Whoever hoped to 'solve' the cause of the crash at the inquest was frustrated and driver Newson was cleared of driving his train while over the drink-drive limit.

An official inquiry failed to resolve the cause of the crash, yet but for Simpson's intervention I have little doubt that Mr Newson would have been blamed for it, a satisfactory scapegoat for all concerned. Except, of course, his family. Of all the stories I covered for the *Mirror*, this was the one that gave me the greatest satisfaction. To me it was what reporting should be all about.

7

H.L. Mencken's description of the dog and lamppost relationship between journalist and politician wasn't his only astute observation on the aggressive nature of our trade. He also said that all successful newspapers are ceaselessly querulous and bellicose; put the two together, and it should mean a healthy relationship between press and politics. But too often the bond between them is akin to that between a dog and his basket. And the lamppost is quite capable of pissing all over the dog. With one or two honourable and well-chronicled exceptions, we do not have a political press prepared to delve deep into politicians' money or motives; neither, in spite of the partisan nature of the House of Commons, do we have a political system that is prepared to question itself. The scandals of the Nineties – cash for questions, the funding of the major parties by businessmen seeking to promulgate their own agenda, the acceptance of free holidays, the quality and behaviour of MPs – are all questions which arose in the 1970s, and the House of Commons at best ignored them and at worst suppressed any meaningful investigation into the shortcomings of its members.

Harold Wilson was not a corrupt man. He spent his holidays on the Scilly Isles – which he hated – in a very ordinary bungalow belonging to his wife. In his last, fading years, he had little money and for some of the time lived in a flat in Oxford provided for him by Robert Maxwell. Yet his last months in office were disfigured by a series of honours for businessmen who not only did not deserve them, but who were extremely questionable, and in some cases downright criminal. Lord Brayley, a second-rate businessman and financial supporter whom Wilson made Army Minister, was sent to prison for fraud. Lord Kagan, another supporter and manufacturer of that hideous Gannex mac Wilson always wore, was ennobled by him and also went to prison for fraud. Sir Eric Miller, knighted by Wilson while Chairman of Peachey Property Co, was a financial backer who paid for the drink at Wilson's Downing Street farewell, and killed himself shortly before he was due to be charged with fraud and theft from his own companies. Wilson became paranoid about the security services circulating stories against him and, while most of his fears were probably groundless, there was a grain of truth in his suspicions. The security services were out of control and run at middle-management level by right-wing fools like Peter Wright, the author of *Spycatcher*. They were all cloak and no dagger.

The reason why Wilson was surrounded by so many crooks was that they all chipped in to help in the maintenance of his private office, run by Marcia Williams, later Lady Falkender. The rivalry between Mrs Williams and the rest of Downing Street has been well chronicled, particularly by Wilson's press secretary Joe Haines, who exposed Marcia's lavender honours list, named after the colour of the notepaper on which Marcia compiled it. (Actually, the notepaper wasn't really that colour at all, Haines mixed up lavender and lilac.) Her influence was considered to be so damaging and out of control that, at one stage, a member of Wilson's entourage offered, quite seriously, to have her bumped off. The root of the problem was party financing, just as it is now. And for the same reason – ambitious businessmen who want access to power and are prepared to buy it.

While Wilson didn't have enough money to finance his office, Jeremy Thorpe played fast and loose, not only with male model Norman Scott but with cash that was sent to him by committed Liberals. On one occasion Thorpe opened a letter with money in it and handed it straight to Scott. And this is the man who would have become Home Secretary if Ted Heath had brought the Liberals in after his election débâcle of February 1974. Not that he would have been there for long; the conspiracy to murder investigation into Thorpe, leading to his eventual acquittal, started soon afterwards.

The 1970s saw an explosion of fraud squad inquiries into big names. Tiny Rowland's Lonrho – 'the unpleasant and unacceptable face of capitalism' according to Prime Minister Edward Heath – faced a police investigation not only into his activities, but into those of Lonrho directors Angus Ogilvy, Princess Alexandra's husband, and former Tory cabinet minister Lord Duncan Sandys. The investigation foundered after Rowland hired the police officer in charge as Lonrho's security chief.

Robert Maxwell, too – a man, according to the DTI inspectors, 'not, in our opinion, a person who could be relied on to exercise proper stewardship of a public company' – was the subject of a fraud squad inquiry after the report into his Pergamon empire. That investigation dragged on and on for reasons still shrouded in mystery. But one of them was that the police turned up information which did not tally with that of the inspectors, so detectives were forced to cover a great deal more ground. But that, too, eventually came to naught, much to the dismay of Scotland Yard. By the middle of the 1970s there were 462 major fraud squad inquiries in progress.

The longest-running scandal, and the one that typified the turbulence and shifting morality of the '60s and '70s, was that of Reginald Maudling's business affairs. Maudling was involved with three businessmen after the Conservatives lost office in 1964. He was chairman of a company run by an American, Jerome Hoffman, which collapsed owing millions. Hoffman went to jail. Ht headed up a company run by an architect called John Poulson who was convicted of corruption and sent to prison for seven years. At the same time, Maudling sold his house to Eric Miller's property company in a deal which was of no value to the company, but which meant the former Chancellor could have a swimming pool built free of charge. We know what happened to Miller, but nothing happened to Maudling through a mixture of cover-up, indolence and good old-fashioned lying. Britain was not yet ready to put a man who came within 17 votes of becoming leader of the Conservative Party, and therefore Prime Minister, in the dock of the criminal courts. But, as we shall see, he should have been.

The unprincipled stance of the Establishment which looked the other way was captured by a wonderful anonymous adaptation of 'Macavity' from T.S. Eliot's *Old Possum's Book of Practical Cats*:

> *Reginald is a mystery cat: he's called the Hidden Paw –*
> *For he's the arch–illusionist who can defy the Law.*
> *He's the bafflement of Scotland Yard, the Flying Squad's despair:*
> *For when they reach the scene of crime, well –*
> Reginald's not there.
> *Ah, Reginald, that Reginald! There's nobody like Reggie:*
> *He's always On The Other Hand, his bets are ever hedgy;*
> *His powers of levitation would make a fakir stare,*
> *And when you reach the scene of crime, blast!*
> Reginald's not there!
> *You may seek him on the letterheads or on a boardroom chair –*
> *I tell you once, and once again, that Reginald's not there!*
> *Now, Reginald's a portly cat, he's rather tall and stout;*
> *You would know him if you saw him, for his tongue is*
>   *hanging out.*

> *Some say that this is due to greed (or, even due to sin)*
> *But others claim it's laziness that leaves it on his chin.*
> *He sways his head from side to side, with movements like a snake,*
> *But when you think he's half-asleep, he's really half-awake.*
> *Ah, Reginald, old Reginald! There's no one quite like Reggie,*
> *A tower of equanimity, a cat that's never edgy.*
> *You may chuck him out of office, you may threaten him with clink,*
> *You may call him welsher, mountebank, or charlatan or fink,*
> *He will merely beam and chortle (or, more likely, simply stare)*
> *But when a crime's discovered,* why then Reginald's not there!

In the three decades that have elapsed since the Maudling affair, we have learnt or done little to police corruption in high places. The Harrods chairman Mohamed Al Fayed can bribe MPs and neither he nor the MPs are charged because of a 'loophole' in the law which Jack Straw, then Home Secretary, said must be closed. All this was promised back in the 1970s. At the same time as Straw was wringing his hands, the Attorney General went to the High Court in support of Al Fayed's bid to prevent an attempt by Neil Hamilton to bring a libel action against him. The Attorney General, John Morris, argued the case raised 'fundamental constitutional issues' about the sovereignty of parliament. What he meant was that the courts cannot question a decision taken by MPs. Putting aside the argument that nobody had done more to destroy the sovereignty of parliament than Al Fayed with his habit of bunging brick-sized wads of £50 notes to honourable members, Morris was doing little more than trying to suppress a genuine test of Al Fayed's credibility under stringent court procedures, something that had manifestly not happened during the Commons' own cash-for-questions inquiry. There had been no cross-examination of Al Fayed, a necessity if justice was to be done, given his record of mendacity.

This has remarkable echoes back to Maudling's last attempt to find a crock of gold by suing newspapers for libel. In the last few weeks of his life he was desperately attempting to hush up damaging evidence I had been given concerning his dealings with John Poulson which would have ruined his reputation. He, too, cited the sovereignty of parliament as a reason why that evidence could not be put in front of the High Court.

This issue wasn't tested until the Attorney went in to bat for Al Fayed, speaking grandly about parliament's sovereignty based on a freedom won by martyrs over hundreds of years. In the end the High Court didn't swallow his argument, and quite right, too, for although the freedoms may have been won by martyrs, they have been abused by a succession of knaves of whom Maudling was the most spectacular. MPs may see themselves as fearless seekers after truth and honesty, but for the most part they are humdrum nonentities, tied to party loyalties and their own ambition, and when it comes to questioning their own standards they often have little grasp of the issues they are being asked to examine. If they had been less indolent and protective of their many privileges a quarter-of-a-century ago, the scandals that so scarred the 1990s, that brought down John Major's Government and have helped to tarnish Tony Blair's, could have been avoided. Even what should be straightforward parliamentary inquiries are blighted to such an extent that the Foreign Office minister Keith Vaz can refuse to answer questions from the parliamentary standards watchdog, the ill-fated Elizabeth Filkin. She upheld a complaint against him that when in opposition he had recommended a businessman for an honour without declaring the financial links between them. Mrs Filkin said her inquiries on eight further complaints against Mr Vaz could not be completed because he wouldn't answer any more questions. She recommended the Commons Select Committee inquiring into the affair summon witnesses and evidence 'to resolve any outstanding uncertainties or fill in any remaining gaps in the evidence'. Although the committee had sweeping powers to do so, it didn't, leaving an overpowering impression of the Commons once again failing to deal with its own dirty washing. It was an inevitable legacy of the Maudling affair and the reaction of the Mother of Parliaments.

What follows is the vicious brawling that breaks out when both journalist and politician want to be the dog, and neither is prepared to be the lamppost. The stakes are sky high for both – obfuscation, official cover up and threats of jail for one; the ruin of a big reputation and his place in history for the other. The loser, always, is the political and judicial process which should follow Lord Denning's edict; that 'be you ever so high, the law is above you'. But it does not. The scandal of Reggie Maudling shows that if you are ever so high, both the law and Parliament will go to quite extraordinary lengths to protect you. To this day, Parliament fiercely protects its rights to set its own standards. Mrs Filkin's reward for investigating the standards and behaviour of MPs was that she was almost universally reviled and told that when her contract came to an end she could, if she so wished, reapply for her own job, which was then immediately downgraded. Needless to say Mrs Filkin didn't want to know. Once again parliament had triumphed over those who felt the need for transparency. In a quarter-of-a-century, the Palace of Westminster has learnt nothing from that infamous night when honourable members, many reinforced by asserting their rights in the Commons' bars, decided to let off good old Reggie. The official view of Maudling is best summed up by his friend Edward Boyle, a soft-centre old Sir Etonian Tory baronet who served as education secretary in the early sixties. He wrote the profile of him that appears in the *Dictionary of National Biography*, considered to be the last word in judgement and reliability about the lives of public men and women. In it Boyle says that Maudling's business judgement had never been good and civil servants were concerned about his tendency to be careless about protecting himself from possible criticism. He worked for Poulson for no salary but the architect had contributed generously to a trust close to Mrs Maudling's heart and his business dealings with him are dismissed as less important than those he had with Hoffman's Bermuda-based Real Estate Fund of America. During his last illness, reports Sir Edward, Maudling was unwilling to undergo treatment that might have interfered with his plans for a costly libel action and which, he firmly believed, would finally clear his own name and that of his family. But the truth is rather different, nothing like as clear cut as the *Dictionary of National Biography* and Edward Boyle would have us believe. Here, told for the first time, is that behind-the-scenes story of the libel battle that eventually never was and the pressures that can be brought to protect the reputation of the powerful, sometimes from the most surprising of sources.

* * *

Everybody loved good old Reggie. He was clever, he was Tory, but not one of those red-necked ones, enjoyed life and was easy-going. Yep, good old Reggie was fun, liked a drink and had a life outside Westminster. Reggie Maudling was deputy leader of the Conservative Party, largely because he didn't make enough effort to be leader when his chance came, so the prize passed instead to Edward Heath. But there was another side to Reggie Maudling, and it all stemmed from that fatal flaw in a Conservative high-flyer – he wasn't wealthy. He wasn't poor, but he didn't have the easy come, easy go money that makes an effortless grandee.

Maudling started out on his political odyssey just before the outbreak of the Second World War. He went to see the Conservative MP Harold

Nicolson and, typically, asked him which party he should join; hardly a conviction politician. By the end of the war, he had chosen the Conservatives, but it was to do him little immediate good. In the 1945 Labour landslide he lost what was believed to be the safe seat of Heston and Isleworth. But that loss was to be Maudling's gain, for he went to work at Tory Central Office where he came under the wing of Rab Butler who was then in charge of rebuilding the party's shattered morale. Butler moved the party's policies into a more inclusive centrist position, supporting merit against privilege. Maudling was one of a powerful trio of young meritocrats, the others being Iain Macleod and Enoch Powell. In 1946 he was adopted as prospective candidate for Barnet, and four years later he was at Westminster as the Tories fought back from the 1945 disaster, and a year after that regained what they considered their divine right to rule. Maudling's rise was rocketlike. An MP at 33, by 1952 he was part of the government as Parliamentary Under Secretary to the Conservative fuel and transport overlord, a vital job in a country still reeling from the economic devastation of the war. The appointment was seen as cutting short what could have been a lucrative career in the City, which it did. Maudling was to remain a minister until Labour once again regained office 12 years later in 1964.

Reggie Maudling loved good food and drink, particularly drink. He loved it even more if someone else was paying for it. He was clever but lazy and was known to nod off in meetings after lunch. He enjoyed the trappings of power, the offices, the chauffeur-driven cars, the civil servants; not for him the cramped and inadequate facilities of the average backbench MP. By 1962, after a succession of ever more important government posts, Reggie Maudling became Chancellor of the Exchequer. He backed Rab Butler for the leadership after Macmillan's resignation, but was quite happy to support Sir Alec Douglas Home, in contrast to Macleod and Powell, who refused to serve under Home because of what they saw as the victory of hereditary squatters' rights over merit. But by 1964, Home and the Tories were gone and Harold Wilson was Prime Minister, promising the 'white-hot heat of the technological revolution'. Maudling was now well placed to do 'something in the City' as all ex-chancellors are, especially Conservative ones, but before he could get his feet firmly under a desk in the square-mile, Home resigned and he found himself head-to-head with Ted Heath for the Tory leadership. He didn't get it because of his reputation for laziness, although Home himself backed him for the unorthodox reason that he reckoned lazy men were better in a crisis.

The difference between the two candidates was summed up by Cecil King who, some years earlier, had offered Maudling the chairmanship of Reed, then a subsidiary of the International Publishing Corporation of which King was chairman: 'Time was when Maudling had the leadership in his hand – and let it slip. This time he has another chance – mainly because Heath has enemies, though for the right reason. Heath really is a positive force – a leader – while dear Reggie, though very intelligent, does like a good lunch and parties that go on late into the night.'

Dear Reggie let it slip again; Heath beat Maudling by 150 votes to 133 with Enoch Powell third polling just 15. Maudling didn't want it enough, although he was both hurt and surprised when he was beaten and, from that moment he was semi-detached from the main stream of politics, even when he came back as Home Secretary in the Heath Government of 1970. The pervading view of him was expressed, as bluntly as you would expect, by Sir Robin Day: 'Maudling is bone lazy and quite useless after lunch,' he told King.

But he did have a name that could open doors, and Maudling had spent too long with the blue bloods of the Tory Party not to yearn for their privileges and possessions. He was comfortably off but did not have the kind of wealth that came so easily to his many friends who graced the pages of *Burke's Peerage*. What he was looking for was 'a little pot of money for my old age' and if the pot was to be not so little and he didn't have to stir himself in order to fill it, then so much the better. Therefore in 1966 his prayers seemed to be answered by a tubby, bald architect from Pontefract called John Poulson who was busy building up the largest practice in Europe. Poulson wanted him to become chairman of one of his companies, and was prepared to look after Reggie handsomely for the honour of doing so. The former Chancellor was the perfect choice: big name, big appetite for food and money and he could tread the plush carpets of power with ease. Everyone liked old Reggie; Jim Callaghan had even sounded him out as a possible Governor of the Bank of England. Reggie knew everyone, the world was his friend, just the man to bring in the big bucks from the foreign governments Poulson was eyeing up. Reggie was too indolent to ask questions and too keen on the cash to look further into the world of John Poulson. It wasn't the Maudling way – ask no questions, tell me some lies, was the preferred method.

By 1968, he was not only taking his cash from Poulson, but also from a crook called Jerome Hoffman, who set up a fraudulent offshore fund called the Real Estate Fund of America which collapsed in 1970 owing investors £4 million (£37.5 million at today's prices). Had Maudling bothered to check, he would have found that Hoffman had a history; he had run a fraudulent mortgage scam in New York. If he hadn't been so busy searching for easy money, he might have heeded his own words quoted in the *Times* in October 1967: 'True pride, which is a sense of high standards consciously accepted and rigorously maintained, is no longer a force in our national consciousness as it used to be and as it should be.'

So it should. But high-flying politicians were not the only people falling short of standards they proclaimed so heartily. Journalists, too, were remarkably incurious about Maudling's activities, even though he had returned to government as Home Secretary, the Real Estate fund had collapsed and he had been named in a law suit claiming £12 million damages brought on behalf of the fund's investors. The case was entered into by a retired teacher who, as a result of the fund's collapse, had been reduced to living in a one-room apartment on New York's West Side, and it accused Maudling and his co-directors of fraud, misrepresentation and misuse of investors' cash. Maudling professed himself to be perplexed, as he had resigned from REFA in 1969 saying he had never heard of the retired teacher and had never conducted business on behalf of the fund in the USA. 'There must clearly be some mistake,' he said in a phrase that was to echo down the decades in the pages of *Private Eye*. Maudling successfully distanced himself from the scandal by suggesting the litigation was one of those American 'sue-everybody-in-sight types' and for a while he faced few serious questions about his role. Worse, however, was to come.

He and his fellow directors failed to convince a New York court that it had no jurisdiction over him. Hoffman was sent to jail for two years for the mortgage swindle and John Poulson, with inconvenient timing, decided to bow to the inevitable and filed for his own bankruptcy. Once again the press, with the honourable exceptions of *Private Eye* and a young Bradford journalist called Ray Fitzwalter, was sleeping. Fitzwalter, who was to become one of television's finest investigative programme-makers as head of *World in Action*, had started his investigations into Poulson early in 1970, two years before the scandal finally broke in the national newspapers, exposing the relationship between Poulson and T. Dan Smith – 'Mr Newcastle' – and his business tie-up with Maudling, (the TV series *Our Friends in the North* was based on Smith).

In June 1972 Poulson's public examination in bankruptcy began in Wakefield. As a measure of journalistic interest, there was not one national newspaper in court. It wasn't until *Private Eye* ran a three-page special and the Liberal Party tabled a House of Commons motion demanding an inquiry into allegations of financial corruption in public life, that the press woke up and Maudling was forced into making his first statement on his relationship with Poulson. It was to be typical of many others – the truth up to a point – but not the whole truth and certainly not nothing but the truth. He admitted he was Chairman of the Poulson company International Technical and Constructional Services. 'The fact was public knowledge,' he said. 'What was not public knowledge was that I received no payment for my work as Chairman. Before I took on the chairmanship, Mr Poulson made a substantial covenant in favour of a charity whose aims I strongly supported. I do not understand how helping a charity and running an export business can be regarded as a matter for criticism.'

Very persuasive, very selective and very misleading. The truth is that the charity was the Adeline Genee theatre trust – a brainchild of Maudling's wife, with funding guaranteed by Maudling and a charity in name only which was in severe financial trouble – to which Poulson paid a total of £29,021. Far from receiving no payment from him, Poulson paid a further £13,500 to Maudling via a different company, making a total of more than £42,000 altogether, that's £450,000 at today's values. Maudling's pay and benefits in kind were so convoluted and clearly designed to avoid tax, that five years after the last payment he was still being formally interviewed by an Inland Revenue principal inspector of taxes. On top of that, Maudling and his son Martin were among Poulson directors who spent an extraordinary £162,000 (£1,700,000 at today's values) of the architect's money on foreign travel and entertaining. After spending it, they claimed £150,000 (£1,574,300 today) in commission from Poulson to cover it. 'It was a device suddenly invented by the directors to write off the money they had spent,' bankruptcy examiner Leslie Clark was to tell Poulson's trial. If that wasn't enough, Maudling had also received free designs for a swimming pool, games room and garage at his home, the money for which was only recovered when demands for payment were made by Poulson's trustee in bankruptcy. (The pool was actually installed free of charge by a property company, whose chairman Eric Miller, the politician-friendly business who only avoided fraud charges by committing suicide.) Maudling stated the true position in a letter to Poulson in April 1968: 'The accounts sent to me set out very clearly the total cost of the Maudling family and their interest. It certainly is colossal.' Hardly the transparency of a man rigorously maintaining his sense of high standards.

In 1972, Maudling bowed to the inevitable and resigned as Home

Secretary after the Scotland Yard Fraud Squad had been called in to investigate Hoffman and Poulson's business affairs. When Heath sent for him to make him an offer he couldn't refuse, Reggie was at a party. Hardly surprising, Reggie was always at a party. But his chauffeur to Number Ten did raise an eyebrow or two. It was none other than Eric Miller who had been at the same party, which explained how Harold Wilson knew Maudling had been sacked before anyone apart from the Prime Minister and his now former Home Secretary. In his resignation letter to Ted Heath, he repeated that he did not consider his activities to be 'a matter either for criticism or for investigation'. However, there were, he conceded, 'matters not relating to me that do require investigation and I entirely agree that this should be carried out in the normal way on behalf of the Director of Public Prosecutions'. Maudling presented himself as a model of reasonableness caught up in matters that were nothing to do with him, but nonetheless a man prepared to sacrifice himself on the altar of high principle. In fact he had to be pushed out of office, angry and unwilling. From the newspaper watchdogs who had so conspicuously failed to bark came little but sympathy. 'There can be little wrong with public life in Britain when a man of Mr Maudling's position of power resigns on a matter of honour,' said the *Daily Express*. This insufferable complacency and humbug was typical if not universal, and it played an important part in the disintegration of standards in public life that we were to see during the decade. The truth was the opposite to the *Express*'s view.

Maudling escaped exposure because he worked on two levels. He fobbed off journalists with half-truths and bland denials while keeping in constant touch with their bosses. Cecil King was not the only one to wine and dine him regularly; Derek Marks, the editor of the *Daily Express*, was a close friend, so was Larry Lamb of the *Sun*, until he discovered his true love, Mrs Thatcher. Neither was he averse to threatening legal action. On one occasion, the *Sunday Mirror* settled a complaint with a payment to charity and a crate of Dom Perignon champagne. But the good life was getting to him and his drinking had become a problem. He once shocked Marje Proops, the *Mirror*'s everlasting agony aunt, when he turned up as a judge for the newspaper's Mrs Britain competition. It required an early start at the Café Royal and, realising that 8.45am is not necessarily a politician's best time, Marje and the *Mirror*'s publicity director John Jenkinson were solicitous: 'A cup of coffee, Mr Maudling?' asked Jenkinson.

'Yes, thanks … Um, have you anything to, um, heat it up a bit?' inquired Maudling. 'A brandy would do.'

Jenkinson brought the bottle which stayed with Reggie until lunch, when it was replaced by a decent claret. By mid-afternoon, Mrs Britain hopefuls were still trooping past the judges but Reggie was out of it, flat out asleep in the corner.

During the course of the next two years a succession of Poulson associates were tried, convicted and sent to prison – George Pottinger, a senior civil servant, T Dan Smith and Poulson himself. A whole load of local councillors, including Alderman Andrew Cunningham – father of Jack, the future Labour Cabinet Minister – and minor officials, felt the full wrath of the law. Lives and reputations were left in tatters. There was plenty of talk of MPs who were on the Poulson payroll, but not one of them appeared in the dock and, by 1976 when the last of the small fry was duly weighed off, it looked as if the MPs were off the hook.

But someone had been beavering away behind the scenes and the *Observer*, not a paper that had hitherto distinguished itself in the Poulson investigation, carried a remarkably detailed account of the parliamentary activities on behalf of the jailed architect by John Cordle, Tory MP for Bournemouth East. On its front page, the paper carried a report by its political editor, Adam Raphael, revealing that three MPs had escaped prosecution because of a loophole in the law which prevents MPs being charged with corruption in connection with their parliamentary duties. Cordle was obviously one, but who were the other two? Maudling certainly was not in the frame, said the *Observer*, although it carried a large picture of him. Now the paper was in trouble here, for it had made a classic, elementary mistake by using his picture so close to the headline, undoubtedly giving the impression that Maudling was one. There was an even bigger problem. Whatever the *Observer* asserted, Maudling was one of the three. So how could the paper apparently know so much about Cordle and so little about the details of the whole affair? Answer: somebody who knew a great deal was babysitting them and feeding the paper with specific but selective information.

I had known for some months that there was considerable disquiet among the Poulson prosecutors and investigators about the role of the MPs, particularly the parts played by Cordle, Maudling and a Labour MP called Albert Roberts. I also knew they had been the subject of reports to the Director of Public Prosecutions and the leading Poulson lawyers had produced an opinion arguing they could not be prosecuted for the reasons the *Observer* articulated. But if there had not been this loophole, was a prosecution justified? The answer from deep inside the investigation came out as an unequivocal yes. So the *Mirror* used all three names and said they would have been prosecuted if the law allowed it. Cordle and

Roberts did nothing, Maudling sued and I embarked on the most legally fraught, long-running and fascinating investigation which took me through not just the corridors of power, but the drawing rooms, servants' quarters, holiday homes, bank balances and hangers-on too. The question was, did Maudling use his parliamentary position, without declaring an interest, to further the business interests of Poulson over the contract to design a hospital on the Maltese island of Gozo?

The Commons decided to put the whole Poulson and MPs affair to a select committee of the House of Commons, a device which had always served parliament well on previous occasions because these committees lacked the resources, and frequently the will, to dig as diligently as they should. It also had the advantage of allowing the Commons to decide the ground rules, and two of those were that both the inquiry and witnesses' identities would remain secret, so we would have no idea how diligent the committee was, how exhaustive the list of witnesses or how comprehensive the documents put before them. The Commons 'trials' of the MPs would go against the principles of fair and free hearings in every respect. The House was in one of its most self-righteous and priggish moods; it always is when the honour of its members is challenged. Mrs Thatcher as Tory leader summed up the mood of MPs and the self-interest of her party: 'I hope that there will never be any question of propounding gossip or scurrilous rumour, if that is what it is, or [using the committee] as a means of seeing that such gossip is published and uttered beyond the House. If one has any confidence in a select committee, surely one can trust it to publish all the evidence and to make an objective assessment.' But why should we trust the committee when we had no idea what the evidence was, who the witnesses were or what the documentation would be?

There was no chance of an objective assessment. The committee didn't let Maudling off completely, but it did the next best thing. He and Albert Roberts were lightly rapped over the knuckles with the conclusion that their conduct was 'Inconsistent with the standards which the House is entitled to expect from its members'. Cordle was made the scapegoat and accused of a contempt of the House. In the Commons full debate that followed, the scene was a disgrace. There was hardly a member who understood the issues or cared to; a substantial minority had clearly taken an early evening fall on the slopes of Glenfiddich and the Conservatives had no intention of 'convicting' Reggie under any circumstances and whatever the evidence. So it was only Cordle who got it in the neck. Yet what the committee failed to investigate, and certainly failed to reveal, is that the police investigation was only into the very narrow area of corruption. Their terms of reference precluded the Fraud Squad from inquiring into either tax offences or possible charges suggested by a Department of Trade and Industry report. If the House had known, and if the country had known, that the man who came within a whisker of becoming Britain's Prime Minister was under continuing investigation by the Inland Revenue, it would have been bad enough. But the real sensation was the findings of the Department of Trade; its list of potential charges read like a litany for a common thief. The inspector, Alan Ford, found the possible offences by Maudling to be as follows: Conspiracy (with Poulson) to obtain excess monies from Ropergate Services Ltd, a Poulson company; two offences of perjury in judicial proceedings, namely Maudling's examination at Poulson's bankruptcy hearing; contravention of Section 83 of the Larceny Act, involving omissions from the audited accounts of a Poulson company of which Maudling was chairman, contravention of Section 19 of the Theft Act, conniving, making and concurring in publishing a false and deceptive balance sheet.

All this from a man who had only recently been Britain's Chancellor of the Exchequer. Mr Ford, who began investigating the possibility of other charges against Maudling, was suddenly moved, against his will, to another job in Birmingham. It was a cynical, crude and breathtaking cover-up which was not exposed until Maudling decided to push his luck with one last attempt at a bumper pay day. The possible charges suggested by the DTI are neither gossip nor scurrilous rumour, they come from the highly confidential joint opinion of the two barristers responsible for the Poulson prosecutions, John Cobb QC and Peter Taylor, then his junior but destined to become Lord Chief Justice. Cobb and Taylor spent many pages of their opinion explaining why MPs could not be charged with corruption in connection with their parliamentary duties. When shorn of the legalese, it comes down to this: in order to be guilty of corruption, you have to be found to be acting against the interest of your principal, an employer, a ministry, a local authority or public utility, for example. But an MP acting in his parliamentary capacity, the argument goes, has no principal because it has not been established to whom he or she is responsible. It is his constituents, yes, but not entirely, because he does not have to vote the way they may want him to. Party or government, yes, but not exclusively. Country, the same problem. If he has no principal – as opposed to principles – then he cannot be charged under the Prevention of Corruption Act. Nor could he be charged under the Public Bodies Corrupt Practices Act because the House of Commons is not a public body within the meaning of the Act. So however 'reprehensible' – the word used by Cobb and Taylor – Maudling's behaviour might be, from a parliamentary viewpoint he committed no criminal offence.

The two, however, made their distaste for Maudling, Cordle and Roberts clear at the end of their 26-page opinion: 'Although we conclude that there is no evidence to support criminal proceedings in any of these cases, different considerations might well apply in relation to breaches of parliamentary privilege. It is not within our province to advise on this aspect, save to say the authorities might well regard the conduct of Mr Cordle, Mr Maudling and Mr Roberts as meriting consideration in this respect.

'As the law stands, a Member of Parliament using his position to show favour to an individual for secret reward commits no criminal offence, although if he were a civil servant or minister of the Crown, he would be guilty of corruption. This situation might well be thought to be anomalous and a fit subject for consideration by the Law Commission or by the Salmon Royal Commission.' In other words, get your act together and sort this loophole out.

All this was kept from the people of Britain, even though it goes to the heart of how we are governed. An inept system of investigation and the lack of any enthusiasm for putting its own House in order led directly to the cash-for-questions scandal that helped to finish off John Major's administration. But it was MPs' love of secrecy and their determination to protect privileges which they neither earn nor deserve, but frequently abuse, that resulted in this cynical miscarriage of justice.

Not that Maudling saw it as that. He was off the hook and determined to grab as much libel money as he could. The *Observer* shelled out, but Granada's *World in Action* – he was suing the redoubtable Ray Fitzwalter over a programme on the Gozo hospital which first exposed Maudling's involvement – and the *Mirror* decided to hang in there and fight. Maudling was convinced he was on to a winner and the little pot of gold for his old age was only just over the rainbow. My problem was that, although I knew more or less what was in it, I did not have the Cobb-Taylor report. But the attitude and behaviour of the House of Commons had so outraged those who knew the full Poulson and Maudling story, that I was seen as the last hope of bringing the murkier aspects of this scandal in the highest reaches of British politics out into the open. So far the police, the legal profession and politicians had for varying reasons failed to expose the truth. The small fry – the civil servants and the local bigwigs – were all banged up, Cordle was parliament's sacrifice but the really big fish was getting away with it scot-free, potentially laughing all the way to the bank again and this time legally tax free. The only thing left was, God forbid, the newspapers, and a tabloid at that.

The phone went in the office. 'Meet me in the Duke of Wellington, Eaton Terrace, at 1.00pm. I've something I think you want.' 1.15pm; brown envelope time ... 'Don't open it here. Drink your beer, don't even look at it, it's clean, no trace from the marks on it. There are only five copies in existence, six now.'

I knew the face of the man who was giving it to me. Well he had often been on TV. I swallowed hard. He's not around any more so nothing can hurt him, but without him and people like him, not only newspapers, but those who refuse to be ruled by secrecy, bullying and the abuse of power, would be dangerously the poorer. I had the Cobb-Taylor report, now how the hell do I manage to stay out of jail? This was dynamite and I was breaking just about every law from the Official Secrets Act to abuse of confidentiality.

In the immediate future, the report was of vital importance to our libel action. Legal opinion was pessimistic and Maudling had won a psychological battle over us by going before the High Court on a pre-trial point, representing himself and winning over Lord Denning with discomforting ease. Our counsel was Robert Alexander QC, stout defender of Jeffrey Archer in his libel action and soon to be Chairman of the NatWest Bank, but he seemed unhappy with us. We desperately needed someone who believed in our case and, frankly, there weren't too many in our camp who came into that category, never mind outside. The Indians were definitely circling and Cobb-Taylor had better be the cavalry, otherwise it was scalping time.

So we changed QC for a man mountain of a lawyer, at 38 one of the youngest silks going, a prodigious eater and drinker and funny with it. My fate, and the reputation of Reggie Maudling, was now in the hands of Alexander ('Derry') Irvine QC, a rarity among the barristers' ruling classes, a Labour supporter. Even rarer, his pupil at the time was to make him Lord Chancellor when eventually Tony Blair graduated from making tea in The Temple to 10 Downing Street. Irvine was on my side; he did believe the report meant Maudling would have been prosecuted but for his MP status and, just as important, he put some much needed backbone into the *Mirror* hierarchy which, although sympathetic to the cause, was understandably more worried about the escalating costs. They were, admittedly, rising alarmingly. Now the problem was what to do with the report. Clearly, we had to disclose it to Maudling, but this would certainly create one hell of a row, and quite possibly lead to me being prosecuted under the Official Secrets Act. The court would undoubtedly demand to know my source; it had to be someone big to have access to such an explosive document. I wouldn't tell them ... that would be contempt and then ... slammer time.

The row wasn't long in coming. Alarmed by his own steeply rising costs and in an effort to settle the case, he had already started writing directly to both Hugh Cudlipp, now long retired, and Ellis Birk, senior partner at the *Mirror*'s solicitors Nicholson, Graham and Jones, who had both settled cases with Maudling before. This, however, was not a champagne job. Maudling insisted on substantial damages (he suggested £30,000 – more than £100,000 today) and said that he had been advised 'they could be astronomic' because of the gravity of the libel and his position in public life. Cudlipp was friendly but non-committal, pointing out that he was no longer involved with the *Mirror*, although in private he tried to persuade Tony Miles, then editorial director of the *Mirror*, to settle the action.

Eight months later, in October 1978, and more than a year after the publication of the select committee's report, Maudling, as a process of discovery gone through in every libel action, eventually received our copy of the Cobb-Taylor opinion, and was appalled by its contents. 'This is the first time I have seen it, which seems a little strange,' he wrote to Ellis Birk, 'as I am extensively referred to in it. My understanding was that it was a confidential document.'

Unlike Derry Irvine, he did not see anything in it which would have justified his prosecution for corruption, but he was clearly put out because it was 'compiled without reference to me by them or anyone else'. Why he feels a legal opinion on his possible criminal activities should be either seen or referred to him was not explained.

Pointedly he made no reference to the possible charges suggested by the DTI. Six weeks later, in a desperate attempt to keep the Cobb-Taylor report from the public domain, he came up with what he thought would be the killer blow. In another letter to Ellis Birk, he took issue with the solicitor's claim that its meaning would be a matter for the jury. 'With respect it will not,' he wrote. 'In so far as it refers to proceedings in parliament ... this is a matter for parliament and parliament alone. It cannot be considered by the courts ... If, therefore, the *Daily Mirror* think they can rely for their defence on disputing the findings of the select committee, they are deluding themselves. The courts are never prepared to permit a clash of this kind between their jurisdiction and the proper and complete and exclusive jurisdiction of parliament over what takes place in the course of parliamentary proceedings.'

In other words, parliament can cherry pick what it chooses to release and what it does not. A police investigation can be so structured that potential criminal acts are not inquired into, even though a government department has evidence of possible offences. Parliament can so limit a select committee that it has to operate under the narrowest terms of reference, interview witnesses in secret, and the public can not only be prevented from hearing that evidence, but even be banned from knowing who is giving it. We can be prevented from knowing what evidence has and has not been considered, even to the extent of suppressing the knowledge of potential criminal offences that may have been committed by a man who came near to being leader of his country. Prime Minister Jim Callaghan justified the secrecy by remarking that 'a lie can be half-way round the world before the truth has got its boots on'. This turned out to be remarkably correct, but in quite the opposite way to which he intended. In terms of a proper and thorough inquiry, the select committee didn't even get out of bed, and the House of Commons as a whole never woke up.

In the last days of December 1978, Maudling was clearly rattled, drinking more than ever and looking distinctly ill. Whatever his public stance he knew that, if published, the contents of Cobb-Taylor would destroy him and he was reverting to straightforward threats. In his last meeting with Ellis Birk, he said that the *Mirror*'s possession of the opinion was a gross breach of parliamentary privilege, and that unless the case was settled he would report it to the Commons Privileges Committee. He said that, as the markings on the Attorney General's copy and ours were identical, the document must have been leaked by a member of the Committee of Privileges. This would mean I would have to appear in front of the Privileges Committee, which would, of course, ask me where I got the Cobb-Taylor opinion. I would refuse ... and it is slammer time again. No wonder Maudling told Birk he might rather enjoy the battle. 'I have plenty of time,' he said.

But he hadn't. His drinking had caught up with him and there it ended; the revelations of the Cobb-Taylor opinion were the last straw for an ailing man. Within two months, Maudling was admitted to the Royal Free Hospital in Hampstead. The good life got him in the end, his liver shot through by all the free booze. He died on St Valentine's Day 1979, not quite good old Reggie but his reputation not as ruined as it should have been, thanks to a House of Commons which failed in its duty thoroughly to investigate its own. Nothing was done about the loophole in the law, if indeed there ever really was one.

John Cobb died of cancer shortly after completing the Poulson investigation. His view that MPs could not be prosecuted for corruption in connection with their parliamentary duties has never been challenged by the full rigour of legal argument, but that is largely because nobody imagined the loophole existed until he said it did. The police investigators were strongly of the opinion that Cordle, Maudling and Roberts should have been prosecuted and they remained unconvinced by Cobb's 'loophole'.

When he was dying, Cobb was visited in hospital by Detective Chief Superintendent Ken Etheridge, the policeman who was in operational command of the Poulson inquiry. The two men had grown to like and respect each other over the three-year investigation. Cobb turned to Etheridge and said, 'You never agreed with me about Maudling, did you? You think he should have been charged.'

'Yes, he should,' was the reply.

Cobb thought for a moment, smiled and said, 'You know, Mr Etheridge, we could not possibly have the Home Secretary of this country standing in the dock of the Old Bailey. We would have had to have had a 100 per cent copper-bottomed case for that.'

The usual yardstick is a better than 50–50 chance. Fortuitous, that loophole.

The future Lord Chancellor, Derry Irvine, all set to make his name in what would have been a famous libel battle, had to wait a little longer for his name to go up in lights. But that's politics. As he closed the file he said with a shrug and a hint of a smile, 'Poor old Reggie, but how typical of him to die at the Royal Free.'

* * *

It's the shiver of excitement at the back of the neck that tells you a little glinting nugget of gold has dropped into your pan. The reporter's strike. Many head up the inky Klondyke, but not too many are lucky enough to hit gold. The hair bristled then when the old black magic struck in the summer of 1974.

I was sitting opposite this cuddly, giggling fellow, whom I had gone to see at his office at the top end of Shaftesbury Avenue in the hope that he might tell me a thing or two about spies. Cuddles was Leo Cooper, the publisher husband of Jilly, and he most certainly could tell me about spies.

He was in the middle of negotiating a seriously secret deal with a former Czech spy called Josef Frolik who had absconded to the West, and did he have a tale to tell. He had already been responsible for the prosecution of an old Co-operative Labour MP called Will Owen who had got off at the Old Bailey. But Josef had a lot more to tell and Owen, he reckoned, wasn't the most important MP who had been telling the Czechs things he shouldn't. There was another, younger one, a minister who had been at the Ministry of Aviation and was one of Labour's bright young hopes. Leo would not tell me who it was, but it didn't take long to work out that he was referring to John Stonehouse, one of Harold Wilson's junior ministers, who had risen through the ranks of the Co-op movement to Postmaster General. Wilson's well-developed antennae for trouble had quivered and found him untrustworthy, so when he returned as Prime Minister to Downing Street unexpectedly in 1974, there was no place for Stonehouse who, when in opposition, had decided to try his luck in business and started to dabble in secondary banking, a dangerous pastime for experts, never mind politicians with big ambitions but shallow pockets.

Frolik was a Czech agent, a major in his country's intelligence service and at the heart of it for 17 years. Like many spies, East and West, he was an inveterate gossip and, after his defection in 1969, it was the job of MI6 to sort out the hard evidence of treachery from the gossip of countless boozy diplomatic parties. It wasn't easy, and the men from MI6 were not exactly a team of James Bonds. Frolik was debriefed in the Wiltshire hills, next to the White Horse, and the names he came out with were jotted down on the backs of cigarette packets as the spooks lounged on the green slopes in the sunshine. They must have smoked a good few packets, because the personalities Frolik named were a *Who's Who* of the British political, trade union and journalistic establishment. John Stonehouse was, reckoned Frolik, his international passport to freedom. Stonehouse, he said, had given the Czechs vital information about aeronautical technology, something guaranteed to drive the Americans mad. But had he, or was Frolik bullshitting?

It was certainly true that Stonehouse had been to Czechoslovakia as a minister and signed a technological agreement there. He had also been approached, and lunched with, a Captain Robert Husak in London. Husak was an intelligence agent and inveterate womaniser; perhaps he recognised a kindred soul. There is no doubt that Husak claimed Stonehouse as a spy contact, but then was it the kind of contact journalists claim on their expenses, where the usefulness is somewhat exaggerated to justify a hefty lunch, or was there something more sinister? It was MI6's job to find out, and with that organisation's usual masterful uselessness, their results were suitably ambiguous.

John Stonehouse chose 21 November 1974 to take his phantom swim from the beach of the Fountainbleu Hotel, Miami, leaving his clothes and a mystery behind. From his point of view he could not have chosen a better day. In Britain, it was the night of the Birmingham bombing by the IRA in which 17 people were slaughtered. The drowning of a British MP didn't rate much more than three paragraphs in the papers the next morning, but it hit me like a jug full of cold sea water. Stonehouse wasn't dead, I was sure of it. I knew from the enquiries I had already made that his business life wasn't all he cracked it up to be. He talked big, but dealt small. I also knew he was probably having an affair and was seriously untrustworthy. But the real tingle came from the place he had gone missing – Miami. It is only 90 miles from Cuba and Cuba is Communist and … it was enough to start a full-scale investigation.

The first thing we did was to get our ace New York sleuth Gordon Gregor to retrace Stonehouse's steps. It was obvious immediately that unless he was less than 3ft tall he could not have drowned off the hotel beach, it was too shallow for too far.

That was all we needed to set up a story about his mystery disappearance. The chances were that if we were right and that he had been driven out either by business troubles or spying, our story would lead somebody to hang out some interesting washing. And so it proved, as creditors and business associates started doing the dirty on him. Insurance companies weighed in with judicious leaks about six short-term life policies he had taken out with his wife, Barbara, as the beneficiary. His secretary, Sheila Buckley, came into the frame as the other woman. Meanwhile, Harold Wilson was becoming angrier and angrier with what he saw as the ritual dismembering of one of his MPs. Wilson saw conspiracies in shadows and, when we eventually published Frolik's claims he decided to act, and lambasted the *Mirror* and me in the House of Commons, even though privately he had deep misgivings about Stonehouse. It was disconcertingly easy for the Prime Minister to be led by the nose by a security service that was both lax and jealous in the protection of its own little patch. It would not be the last time that inefficiency and incompetence would be masked by the spurious claims of secrecy and a need-to-know policy that did not stretch to Britain's Prime Minister. Wilson had been told by his security chiefs that, contrary to the *Mirror* assertion, Stonehouse had not been considered a security risk and that he was not a spy contact for the Czechs. This was underlined by the Cabinet Secretary Sir John Hunt, who told him Stonehouse had been investigated but was in the clear. Fair enough, Wilson had to take what his cabinet secretary and the spooks told him. But his civil service team went further, using private briefings to float some red herrings of their own about the motivation behind the 'vendetta' against Stonehouse. This one, to the *Mirror*'s political editor Terence Lancaster, was typical, as Lancaster reported in a confidential memo to the editor: 'I have just been phoned by a high government official who advised me that any further story about John Stonehouse and espionage should be checked out very carefully. He said there were inaccuracies – unspecified – in today's lead story, and that it had been decided not to deny the story only because of the Government's special relationship with the *Mirror* ... Stonehouse was regarded as absolutely clean.'

Maybe, but it didn't take long for Wilson to bin the special relationship. The next day, he was in the Commons, stoking up the anger of Labour MPs and telling us, with a well-rehearsed chorus of 'scurrilous' from his own backbenchers, to stop hounding the MP's family with 'far-fetched questions' about this poor man's death.

But nothing at that moment was as far-fetched as the truth. Stonehouse, posing under his new identity of Joseph Arthur Markham, stolen from a dead constituent, was under constant observation by the Australian police, who had been alerted to his strange behaviour by a Melbourne bank clerk. He had helped him bank cash, but in his lunch break had seen the same man going into another bank and, he discovered, using a different identity. The Melbourne fraud squad kept watch and saw this mystery man was picking up letters from the main post office. The police steamed them open and found they were addressed to 'Dear Dums'. They were from Sheila Buckley and in code. Far from asking far-fetched questions, the coded letters were frantic. 'Front page in the local circular thing, every day line head,' as she described the *Mirror* series of revelations; we had been getting too close for comfort. She struggled to explain the Frolik claims: 'There's a defect [defector] in that material I had. George [Stonehouse] has joined the co-operative India association [CIA] ... Because of this S [Sheila] is a marked specimen ... Do you know that George was named by those other people I mentioned [CIA and Frolik] 5/6 years ago and that's why the family [government] dropped him?'

Wilson would have been mortified if he had known that within hours of his briefing against the *Mirror*, coded news of his support was winging its way to Stonehouse: 'Have just heard from Uncle Harry [Wilson] – marvellous news – he's standing by George completely – a true friend and has damned ragsville [Mirror]. Says to leave the family and staff alone [Mrs Stonehouse and Sheila] – cheers from his family [Labour MPs] – and I'm in tears of relief on that aspect. I would never have believed he would have stood by us on that aspect.'

No wonder DS John Coffy of Melbourne's fraud squad couldn't make head nor tail of the code. He tried buying the *Times* as he had seen Stonehouse reading it, but he got no clue there. Then he went to the reading room at the High Commission and read the Mirror. 'As soon as I saw that,' he was to say later 'I thought, Christ this is it. Bloody hell, we've got ourselves an ex–Pom minister.'

It would have been wonderful to be able to add to Wilson's woes by revealing the reality inside M's eyrie, which was nothing like the show of confidence presented to the Prime Minister. In spite of his strong words about the spy affair, Wilson could not know that MI6 was quaking in its collective Trumper's suedes. It had already been heavily rubbished by the CIA for its cavalier handling of Frolik, and even as the Prime Minister stood up to speak in the Commons, agents were in delicate negotiations with their opposite numbers in Washington to reinterview the defector – now living secretly in the USA – about the missing MP, which they did twice in the next six months. Wilson, who had claimed there wasn't a scintilla of evidence to back up Frolik's claims, was further embarrassed when Stonehouse himself later revealed in his autobiography that he had had a second unscheduled meeting with spymaster Husak, whom he had found waiting for him in his Prague hotel room at 1.00am, when he returned during a ministerial visit to the city. This could have been turned into a major diplomatic incident at the time if Stonehouse had reported it, but he did not. More important, he didn't tell his security service interrogators about it either. When I asked him why not, he had a surprising answer. 'Ministers are very busy men. Small things like that you just don't bother with.' You do if you've just been branded a spy by a defector, unless, of course, you have something to hide. Stonehouse was the first of 400 names Frolik revealed when he escaped from Czechoslovakia, so he clearly felt he had got the big one. He was accurate enough about Will Owen for him to be charged on eight counts under the Official Secrets Act, even if he did get off. Owen, however, admitted he had passed information to Husak for cash.

MI6 did its usual trick of telling the Prime Minister not only what suited the security services but, by happy coincidence, what he wanted to hear. Six weeks later, after Stonehouse had been found in Australia and following the two further interrogations of Frolik, Cabinet Secretary Hunt, who had assured the Prime Minister that Stonehouse was in the clear, admitted to both Wilson and press secretary Joe Haines that Stonehouse was indeed considered a security risk and that the *Mirror* story was correct. Frolik remained contemptuous and bitter about MI6. 'They did a lousy job. If I had done a job like that, I would have been fired,' he told me.

This scandal was an early example – but by no means the last – of how the security services treat their political masters with contempt. Nothing has changed and the Stonehouse affair showed how little governments learn from unexpected and bizarre events such as this. To this day, MI6, now housed in its opulent and unnecessarily large headquarters on the south bank of the Thames, plays fast and loose with the truth. It appears to be just as incompetent and just as unaccountable. The débâcle over those two misfits David Shayler and Richard Tomlinson shows it still favours hiring unstable characters as it did with Peter Wright. When that cream-and-green confection was built at Vauxhall the cost rocketed from £252 million to £547 million, but nobody told the Prime Minister, pleading national security as justification. What on earth goes on in there is anybody's guess; no doubt they are still looking in the files for the cigarette packets of Josef Frolik's evidence.

Eventually I met Frolik in Atlanta, and the arrangements were as shadowy as you would expect them to be. I had to go to the Hyatt Hotel and wait to be contacted. I was eventually given the name of a woman, Mrs Olga Malina, who would arrive at my room. She did, except that she was fat, bald and a bloke. It was Frolik himself, his female alias fixed up by the CIA, although he looked more like Roy Kinnear than Mata Hari. In two days of interviews, all the names tumbled out, the cream of the trades unions, left-wing journalists (including one of my distinguished *Mirror* colleagues) and three Labour MPs, but he hadn't one bit of hard evidence against any of them so we could publish nothing except the most general claims. Part of my deal in getting the interview was that I would make my tapes available to Leo Cooper. Somehow, a copy found its way to Chapman Pincher and then to the Tory MP Stephen Hastings who planned to name and shame Frolik's 'contacts' under privilege in the House of Commons. In those more gentlemanly days there was some honour between front benches, and the Shadow Attorney General, Michael Havers, was appalled by this abuse of privilege. He went to see the Mirror Group Chairman Edward Pickering to ask him about the tapes and what was their strength. I was called up and told him there was no evidence to back any of Frolik's allegations. That should have been down to MI6, but their spooks had cocked it up. It didn't, however, stop Hastings, but the sheer number of names was mind-boggling. No doubt, somewhere along the line there was something in what Frolik claimed and probably someone who should have known better did reveal a little too much over a bottle of vodka, but if the Czech spooks were as inefficient and as daft as ours, then British secrets were every bit as safe in Prague as they were in London.

Was Stonehouse a spy? It is impossible to tell because of the inept initial investigation by MI6, but it is quite clear that Husak knew him well and considered him interesting enough to wait in his hotel room at 1.00am without expecting to cause a diplomatic incident. In this he was right, it is clear it didn't bother Stonehouse, not sufficiently for him to complain anyway. As Minister of Aviation he could have had information, or at least gossip, that the Czechs would have lapped up. There is a thin dividing line between passing information that could be regarded as spying and passing information that isn't, as Will Owen found out. We will never know if Stonehouse was a spy, because of the initial bungling by MI6 and its later prevarication, but if he did not flirt with a bit of tasty but dangerous gossip it was to be the only aspect of his life in which he maintained some sort of grip on reality.

As for poor old Harold Wilson, his hatred of the security services turned into something close to paranoia. He once thought he had discovered a listening device behind a portrait at Number Ten, but on investigation it was found to be nothing more sinister than a temperature control. Wilson, however, was not above a bit of skulduggery himself. When Idi Amin was massacring his own people in Uganda at the rate of several thousand a week, he proposed we should kill him, something that filled the Foreign Office with horror. 'We never do that, Prime Minister,' he was told, and the idea was firmly vetoed.

Stonehouse and his crimes are now little more than a footnote to the political life of the 1970s. He showed how difficult it is to get rid of an MP – he didn't resign as member for Walsall North until after his conviction – and how easy it is to obtain a passport in the name of somebody else as long as they are dead. But he also showed how vulnerable governments are when faced with events that are in danger of running out of control. Above all, he exposed the all too easy ability of MPs to lie and cheat in a way that has since become a minor art form. Stonehouse claimed he had a breakdown; that is why he stole the identities of two of his dead constituents. It had nothing to do with removing what cash remained in his company bank accounts, leaving behind a trail of debts, his wife and children, and taking off for a new life down under with his mistress. Straightforward crookery was rationalised by Stonehouse like this: 'Although I did not fully recognise it at the time, I was operating on three levels. One, the imaged man: cool, calm and apparently in command of all his senses carrying on the life normally expected of him. Two, the original man, who carried all the heavy layers of the imaged man as a burden and despised this role, suffering deep torment as the desperation of his position became more evident. Three, the Phoenix man: a make-believe person who was uncluttered with problems and tensions and, through natural relaxation, gave comfort to the other two. The first two men had to die for the strain of living for them was too great. I wanted them to want to die. I wanted them to die. I wanted to die. There was no other way.' Unless, of course, you faked it and the Phoenix Man takes all the cash, the girl and a new identity leaving the original man with the debts.

Believe it or not, there were a few MPs who swallowed this guff and even after he was dragged back to Britain, following long-drawn-out, expensive extradition proceedings, Stonehouse refused to resign as an MP and the voters of Walsall North were effectively disenfranchised until his conviction and sentence to seven years in jail. The sentence was tough and in prison Stonehouse received no favours. He did most of his time in a closed prison, even after a series of heart-attacks. The establishment may be slow to throw you out, but when it does, expect no mercy. John Stonehouse received none, he left prison broken in health; he married and had a child by Sheila Buckley who remained devoted to him, and disappeared into obscurity. He died forgotten and unforgiven, living back in Southampton where he lived as a boy, in 1988.

The Stonehouse affair was the first of a series of scandals in public life that rocked the 1970s and laid the foundations for a cynicism and debilitating contempt that remains a blight on Britain to this day. It started in the United States with President Nixon and Watergate, but here there was a steady drip of corruption, crime in high places, financial skulduggery and sexual scandal. And whenever financial skulduggery and sex come together, you will not find Ernie Marples far away.

* * *

Ernie Marples was Harold Macmillan's spiv, his sergeant major. If Harold wanted to build council houses at the rate of 300,000 a year, then Ernie was your man. No probs squire, I know where to get the bricks. A motorway, Prime Minister? Certainly, I've got this very nice M1 going for a song built by Marples Ridgeway, a few cracks in it but we can soon smooth all that out. Top shelf, guv. Honest.

Ernie Marples prided himself as an entrepreneur, a guy who got things done, and it is true he did a remarkable job building council homes for Macmillan when he was Minister of Housing. He was the son of a labourer and the grandson of the head gardener at Chatsworth. He was largely self-educated and, after a spell as a bookie's clerk, started his own engineering company before joining up. Macmillan adored him, telling his biographer Alistair Horne, 'He was a sergeant major, never got a commission, came back, started up Marples Ridgeway. Up to a point, he was a genius. He had no vision – unlike all those people who talk – but he brought in American principles of business and construction, he introduced the first solar house,'

'In fact, Marples made me PM, I was never heard of before Housing.'

At Transport, Marples not only started building the motorways but tackled the tricky problem of restricting motorists in cities, introducing the first yellow lines. He got the traffic moving, but at the expense of incurring the hatred of drivers – 'Marples Must Go' became a countrywide slogan and for more than 30 years its fading fury could still be seen on one of the bridges over the M1.

By the mid-'70s, Marples' political career was in decline. He did not get on with Ted Heath, even though, or perhaps because, their backgrounds were so similar. Both were self-made men in a Tory Party still dominated by Eton and the big country estates. He decided to cut his losses and went to the Lords as Baron Marples of Wallasey.

Politics wasn't the only area where he decided to cut and run. For years, he had been fighting a running battle with the Inland Revenue over tax and money being fed through to his company in Liechtenstein. He owned property in Putney and Kensington, all of it was in bad repair and needed extensive refurbishment which Marples was reluctant to undertake. As a result, the properties were close to being slums. Lifts were dangerous, the properties – a block of flats and several houses – had developed serious structural faults because of neglect, and tenants constantly complained of rising damp, leaking roofs, broken windows, an unreliable hot water supply and dangerous electrics. The houses particularly, in Courtfield Gardens, Kensington, were a warren of seedy, cramped bedsits that put Marples perilously close to the slum landlord bracket, uncomfortably close if Christine Keeler is to be believed. She claims Marples used to tip off Peter Rachman about properties in West London that were coming up for sale.

By the early '70s, the vultures were circling as he tried to fight off a revaluation of his assets which would undoubtedly cost him dear, and he was prepared to enlist the help of anyone of influence. One such he assumed to be Councillor Sir Malby Crofton, Tory leader of Kensington and Chelsea Council to whom he wrote complaining about the valuation in the days when local authorities still had some clout. 'I am afraid you have addressed it to the wrong person,' began Sir Malby quietly enough. 'Perhaps your long and distinguished career in government has not extended to local government. I would have thought that you would have known that the person responsible for your assessment is not myself but the District Valuer, who is an independent officer answerable to the Treasury.' Sir Malby was warming to his theme. 'After 10 years without a revaluation, during which inflation has been rampant at a rate never before known in this country, it is hardly surprising that there are considerable anomalies between different properties. Whether your property represents such an anomaly is not for me to say. It is for you to argue the matter out with the District Valuer, against whose assessment you can appeal.' Then came the kick where it hurts: 'In conclusion, I can only say that I am absolutely astonished that someone of your experience of public life should not know these facts, though unfortunately my astonishment about the ignorance of ministers, both past and present, is rapidly lessening as I find out what sort of men they really are. I do not think they would last for five minutes in my office and I fear the standard gets lower and lower. There are honourable exceptions and, I must say, I always thought you were one.' Marples could take that as a 'no' then.

The battle with the taxman wasn't going much better. The Inland Revenue, given the tight exchange control regulations governing the flow of cash out of Britain, was taking a dim view of Marples' ducking and diving, his failure to explain his secretive Liechtenstein company and the little matter of his château in the heart of the Beaujolais wine-growing area. This from his lawyers is a master of evasion: 'The château at Fleurie is not owned by Mr Marples personally but is owned by Ernest Marples et Cie, which is a French private company. Mr Marples owns none of the shares in this company and neither is he a director, although the company recognises that Mr Marples has the final decision in regard to its activities. The shares in Ernest Marples et Cie are owned by a Liechtenstein partnership. It was unfortunate that Mr Marples should have made the impression at the meeting with the representatives from the Surtax Office that the château was owned by him personally.' Unfortunate indeed, for it made the taxman even more determined to get him.

So Marples decided he had to go and hatched a plot to remove £2 million from Britain through his Liechtenstein company, Vin International (VI). The idea was to sell the Putney flats to VI for £500,000, do them up and sell them on for £2.5 million. Capital Gains Tax would have been paid on the first deal but not the second, which meant that all the profits could be spirited way to Liechtenstein. This eventually fell through because the advent of a Labour Government in 1974 meant that the banks – and Marples – were worried stiff about new landlord and tenant legislation. So there was nothing for it but to cut and run, which Marples did just before the end of the tax year in 1975. He left by the night ferry with his belongings crammed into tea chests, leaving the floors of his home in Belgravia's Eccleston Street littered with discarded clothes and possessions.

Newspaper investigations are usually started by straws in the wind, in spite of the fondness of politicians, pop stars and footballers preference to believe they have been targeted. With Marples there were three straws. His decision to leave Britain – it was going to the dogs, he said. That usually means the complainer has been told to stump up some money to the taxman or allied trades; then there were threats by tenants to sue him over dilapidations; and the decision by his former right-hand man to sue for unfair dismissal.

As soon as I started looking into his affairs, I discovered that he was also about to be sued for £134,000 by a city trust company. Bingo! In such an atmosphere, it didn't take long to build up a dossier of his activities and, by the end of June, I was ready to confront the man himself, which I did together with a photographer who was to act both as snapper and witness. Marples held court at his château in Fleurie, a benign host showing off his excellent wine which he kept in the largest barrel I have ever seen. It covered one substantial wall and had a small tap at the bottom. This could be a rocky evening.

From the start I refused all drink, and every time Marples poured me one I passed it on to photographer Albert Foster, a splendid old pro with pop eyes, a Flying Officer Kyte moustache and a vocabulary to match. 'Hello, old sport,' was his invariable greeting.

As document after document was produced, Marples poured more and more wine, all of which was pushed over to Albert who, as he had little to do, drank for two. So did Marples. At first he denied everything, but when he realised what back-up we had, he turned belligerent. It was everybody's fault but his. He claimed he had been asked to pay nearly 30 years' overdue tax in connection with his Eccleston Street house and he had a thumping Capital Gains Tax bill on the Kensington properties. 'The Revenue said I owed them all this money. The man was a socialist I could tell. The claim was preposterous and utterly unfair. In the end there was nothing I could do, so I said, "Fuck 'em, if that's their attitude, I'm off."'

He had no time for his long-suffering tenants either. The tenants' association chairman at the Putney flats was 'a layabout … ask him when he last did a day's work,' and the local Labour MP Hugh Jenkins who had backed them, was dismissed with 'Hugh Jenkins, who is he? What has he ever done? The more votes he can get out of it the better.' Forever the realist. His view of his tenants was robust. 'They can always go elsewhere, they will shit in a place if it is not their own.' His views of me were equally candid. 'You are the worst journalist I have ever met. The most aggressive man I have ever met in my life.' But still the wine flowed with Albert by now on the ropes. 'You can come back tomorrow,' said Marples pointing a wavering finger at poor Albert who was making unsuccessful attempts to get up.

'I'll have to, old sport,' he said. 'I can't do a bloody thing now.'

The next day, we both returned and Marples was all charm. He drove us up to his vineyard where he posed for pictures. 'I thought you were banned from driving,' I said, He had been banned for driving over the limit in England.

'In England, but not here, I've got a Monaco licence,' he replied and quickly flashed me an official-looking document which turned out to be a resident's permit. Wonderful, the former Minister of Transport was driving whilst disqualified and he couldn't give a monkey's. This man was impossible to dislike. As a parting shot I asked him something that had been bugging me for years. Was he the man in the mask in the famous nude picture taken at a top people's party and revealed during the Profumo scandal, and was he ever called before the Denning tribunal because of his business dealings with ladies of the night? The answer to the first question was 'no'.

This was his story of the second – fact or fantasy, I have no idea, but as a memorial to a great rogue it deserves to be true. 'I did appear before Denning. I was in my office when I received a call saying he wanted to see me. Now Denning had absolute power, so there was no way I could get out of it. I had a pretty shrewd idea what it was going to be about. I had a long-standing relationship with a prostitute – I'll call her Maisie – and I reckoned she had been leaned on to give evidence.

'But Denning had a time limit on his investigations. He wouldn't go back beyond a certain number of years. I went to see him and there was Maisie. So I said as loudly as I could, "Well, Maisie, fancy seeing you here. How wonderful, it must be nearly ten years since we last met." I never heard another word.'

However, I did. When we published under the headline 'WHY MARPLES HAD TO GO', Marples complained to the editor that I was drunk when questioning him, but when that cut no ice, he sued for libel but never bothered to follow it through. It would have been hopeless anyway, because the Treasury, true to its unerring ability to shut the stable door after the horse had bolted, decided to throw caution to the wind and froze his assets in Britain for the next ten years. By then most of them were safely in Monaco, Liechtenstein and the beautiful hillside vineyards of Fleurie. And, quite shamefully, I was rather glad.

8

There was a stunned silence at the end of the transatlantic line. I could hear the deep breathing of a goalkeeper I had watched many times at the Manor Ground, home of my team Oxford United. Jim Barron was the kind of footballer who makes it all work. Week in, week out, he was on the team sheet for first division clubs, never making international squads but playing his heart out for the boss who paid the wages, and now he was facing the question he knew would come one day.

'I have been waiting six years for this phonecall,' he said finally, his voice shaking. 'I have been dreading it. I have gone through it over and over again and I still don't know what to do.'

The question was, did he remember the game between Nottingham Forest and Leeds United on Saturday, 1 May, the last day of the 1970–71 league season? Leeds were top of the old first division, one point clear of Arsenal and were expected to win the match without too much difficulty, but Arsenal had a game in hand and the big worry in the mind of Leeds manager Don Revie was that the title could come down to goal average as it was in those days, the difference when you divided goals against into goals scored. Revie arrived at his own solution – he would try and fix the game. This wasn't anything new to him, he had done it before and he was to do it again.

The Leeds team run by Revie was a close-knit unit, us against the world. It was unloved outside the city, garnering a reputation for gamesmanship and dirty play, thoroughly professional to the tassels on their socks and led by the toughest gamesman of them all, the red-headed Scot Billy Bremner. Bremner was the manager's man and it was to him that Revie turned. Gary Sprake, the Leeds Welsh international goalkeeper, remembered 'The Boss' telling him and others that day that Billy would go into the opposition dressing room 'to try and get the right result'. Sprake saw Bremner leave the Leeds dressing room and 'about five minutes later he came back, and although I cannot remember the exact words he used, it was clear to me that he had been in the Forest dressing room and that he had seen a few of the lads'.

Leeds were looking for a victory by at least four goals, but in the end won only 2–0. This was largely due to the goalkeeping of Jim Barron. 'But for Barron, it could be five or six,' remarked Yorkshire TV commentator Keith Macklin during his report on the game.

For obvious reasons, Jim Barron's memory is vivid about the moment he was 'tapped'. 'I was annoyed then and it annoys me now to think that people try to get games fixed. This is the only time it happened to me. What frightens me is that if I had had a bad game, then I would have been implicated. That's what has worried me,' he explained.

At first, Barron, like so many footballers, was fearful of talking about Revie's corruption. He was working in the United States during the summer with the Connecticut Bicentennials and had just landed a job back in England at Peterborough. Barron wasn't one of the game's big earners and he needed the work, so he insisted on us clearing the interview with his new manager, John Barnwell. My heart sank. I had been investigating Revie for the best part of three months and had met a wall of silence, hostility and downright lies. John Jackson, the *Mirror*'s sports news reporter and an old friend, went down to see Barnwell, and came back with unexpected results. Like most people in the game he had heard rumours of what we were trying to do, he had spoken to Barron and was waiting for our visit. When Jackson asked him to free up his new assistant, Barnwell, sitting behind his office desk at Peterborough's ground, quietly rolled up his trouser leg exposing a vivid and lengthy scar. 'Billy Bremner did that to me,' he said. 'You ask Jim Barron anything you want.' It was a decisive break.

The saga started, as so many do, on an aeroplane. I was flying to Alaska with the *Mirror*'s chief photographer Kent Gavin, to do the series on the tough guys building the oil pipeline from Prudhoe Bay, well inside the Arctic Circle, right down to Anchorage. Gavers knew and loved footballers, and he suggested a series based on the untold secrets of soccer. Among his great mates were Bobby Moore and Alan Ball, both of whom were frequently short of money. The trouble with '*Secrets Of ...*' stories is that they rarely are, and footballers, understandably, will try and prise the maximum amount of cash out of you for the minimum amount of information. They are instinctively loyal to each other, and tend to close ranks when threatened, so the chances of them coming across with anything sensational are small and, in the case of Bobby Moore, I knew it was hopeless. Alan Ball, however, was somewhat different. He had been sacked as England captain by Don Revie and was known to be hurt. He might just have something interesting to say, and after several bottles of Chianti in a Southampton Italian restaurant, he dropped the nugget which was to lead to the biggest scandal in football since three Sheffield Wednesday players were jailed for bribery.

In 1966, Alan Ball was a rising star, a huge talent which was confirmed in his triumphant appearance that July as the youngest player in England's victorious World Cup-winning team. Ball was playing for Blackpool, but it was clear a move to a big first division team wouldn't be long in coming. Don Revie was determined it should be Leeds, although Everton was also very interested. Revie made secret under-the-counter payments to Ball while he was still playing for Blackpool on the understanding that he would sign for Leeds. At the time Ball was in dispute with his club over his contract and Revie told him to keep it going. 'The best way for him to get me, he told me,' said Ball, 'was for me to continue my dispute with Blackpool for so long that, in the end, they would be glad to sell me. Then he would move in. Make yourself a real rebel, he said.'

That is about as clear a case of attempted corruption as you are likely to see, and even though Ball refused to play it Revie's way, he did take his cash. He pointed out that the longer he refused to sign a new contract, the more money he would lose. Don't worry about that, Revie explained, he would be paid for as long as it took Leeds to get him. 'And that's what happened. I used to drive on to the moors on the other side of Manchester, and Revie drove from Leeds to meet me. He paid £100 in cash on each occasion,' said Ball. But, 16 days after winning his World Cup medal, he signed for Everton because Leeds refused to increase their offer. All this eventually appeared in Ball's autobiography, but at the time he had told very few people about the deal, probably because he was none too proud of his own rather shabby behaviour.

So I started my investigation into Revie; but how to get someone – anyone – to spill the beans. By 1977 the legendary Leeds team of the early 1970s had broken up, but they were still united in their loyalty to each other and especially to the Boss who was now manager of England. There was no point in going to anyone who was still in the game or hoping for a job in management or coaching. What we needed was someone who had fallen on hard times, was short of money and felt keenly that he had been forgotten. There was one obvious candidate – goalkeeper Gary Sprake. He agreed to see me at his home in Solihull and, astonishingly, readily admitted there had been plans to fix matches, the most notorious of which was one at the end of the 1971–72 league season between Leeds and

Wolves. A win or a draw would have meant the league and FA Cup double for Leeds and the pinnacle of Revie's success as a club manager. The game was immediately the subject of allegations and rumours and, not long after, the *People* revealed that there had been an attempt to fix it. An official inquiry into the game petered out because nobody would name the middleman who had been briefed to set up a deal between the Wolves players and an unnamed fixer – who was, in fact, Don Revie. Sprake also remembered attempted fixes on fixtures against Newcastle United and Nottingham Forest; the trouble was he couldn't remember when they were, so the next task was to trail through the games season by season.

But if I thought my luck was in with Sprake, it didn't hold. Nobody else would cough and soon my questions were the talk of football and football writers, who reacted with undisguised hostility. Soccer writers, like City reporters and political journalists, see their jobs as depending on good relations with those they write about, and hate any intrusion on to their patch. Don Revie was not short of informants, and it didn't take long for Sprake to receive a phonecall from Billy Bremner offering him a testimonial at Elland Road, something Sprake had asked for before but failed to get. Now, surprise, surprise, it was all on. Not only that, said Billy, the boss wants you to go and spend the weekend with him, odd since Sprake had hardly spoken to Revie since his move from Leeds to Birmingham City four years earlier. Why should a busy England manager want to see his former goalkeeper, never mind spend the weekend with him? But Sprake was flattered and keen to do it, which would certainly have meant the end of his talking to us, as Revie knew all too well.

In the event, the weekend meeting was postponed, but Revie asked to meet Sprake at the Post House Hotel in Leicester, so we had to get him under contract, which eventually we did. Instead of meeting Sprake for lunch, Revie received a phonecall at the Post House from the goalkeeper's solicitor who gave him the unwelcome news that he had signed with the *Daily Mirror*.

Two weeks later Revie fled the country, resigned the England managership and took up a £340,000 job as soccer chief of the United Arab Emirates. He left Britain disguised in Arab dress, claiming he went in such a bizarre manner because, having failed to qualify for the 1978 World Cup, he knew he was going to be sacked and he ran before he was pushed. This was nonsense. Revie wasn't known as Don Readies for nothing and any termination of his contract would have meant a good many of those. Then he could still have gone to the Arabs. No, Revie went because he was terrified of what Sprake was going to reveal. Luckily he didn't know the truth, that we were having terrible trouble identifying the games and that nobody else would talk to us. They were simply too terrified of the England manager's power. Even Alan Ball had decided to go silent after asking Jack Charlton for advice, though Jack had no knowledge of or any part in the allegation. In fact, I was making so little progress that the night before Revie fled with only the *Daily Mail* for company, I had resolved to explain to the editor that although I was convinced the story was there, I could not get it, the wall of silence had held. All Revie had to do was to hang on for a couple more days and he would have known that he had beaten us. Sprake's evidence wasn't sufficient and we had little else on the record. But he bottled it, and once he did he was finished.

If he thought his defection would ensure self-preservation, the opposite happened. Football was outraged, and doors that had been firmly shut on us began to creak open. The ace in the hole was Bob Stokoe, universally respected and admired for his honesty both as a player and manager, and vanquisher of Revie's mighty Leeds team in the 1973 Cup Final when manager of Sunderland. As he led his team out on to the Wembley turf, Stokoe's mind went back 11 years to Gigg Lane, the rather more humble home of Bury FC. Revie, then the rookie manager of Leeds who were struggling at the bottom of the second division and in danger of relegation, offered Stokoe, then Bury's player manager, £500 to 'take it easy'. Stokoe's description of what happened is a remarkable insight into what went on behind the scenes at football grounds when managers were terrified for their jobs, and the different ways they set about coping with the pressure.

'I got out of the car and was heading for the home dressing room. We have a wicket gate at Bury which you have to step through unless the main gates are open. I had just done this when I saw Don Revie on the other side.

'"Can I have a word with you?" he said.

'I said "Yes" and he said, "I've got £500 in my pocket for you if you take it easy today."

'He was a very worried man at the time. I was staggered, amazed. I told him, '"Not bloody likely."' I was just starting a career and if something like this happens, I'm a dead man.'

'But Revie wasn't finished. He had the audacity then to say, "Well, can I have a word with some of your players?" which again made me extremely angry and more and more determined that I must tell my directors that this particular thing had taken place. For me to be asked to go out and not try is waving a red rag to a bull. This was against all the things I felt I stood for – the honesty, the fairness and the competitiveness which I have always loved. I just want to win and here was a fellow wanting to destroy something that hadn't really got off the ground yet, and I was extremely upset about that. I could have taken that money, I could have said, "Thank you very much, Don," and said nothing about it and gone and strolled around. I think I would have jumped off the Tyne Bridge if I had done something like that. I can never forgive him for it, never.'

Bob Stokoe was not to have the name-in-lights career in management that was Revie's destiny. But that day at Wembley in 1973 made up for all that. 'I felt if I could pull this one off this would be more than I could hope for to kill that particular occasion well and truly dead from the point of view of revenge.'

Revenge was sweet. Second division Sunderland beat Leeds 1–0 in one of the greatest upsets in FA Cup Final history. Even after 13 years, Bob Stokoe found talking about the attempt to bribe him a difficult, emotional experience. As he eventually told me the details in a hotel room at Newcastle's Royal Station hotel, tears rolled down his face.

After that, the *Mirror*'s investigation went from strength to strength. In all, we exposed five games Revie had tried to fix, as well as the bribes paid to Alan Ball. We presented the FA with a 315-page dossier of statements, names, dates and witnesses, an overwhelming catalogue of bribery and double-dealing that went to the heart of the game in England. Yet the FA sat on its hands. Revie sued for libel, but it was intended to be nothing more than a gagging writ. The FA set up what looked like a high-powered committee to investigate the *Mirror*'s exposure, but in truth it never did anything, claiming that the inquiry would only happen after the libel action was heard, a case they knew would never come to court. The FA used that old phoney standby of the legal action making the affair *sub judice* – something any cub reporter knows is not true until the case enters the court lists. It's chairman, none other than Sir Harold Thompson – who had lived in the St John's College don's house at the end of Museum Road when I was a boy – was convinced of Revie's guilt. But officials were fearful of what a wide-ranging inquiry would dig up, suspecting that he was by no means the only manager prepared to ask the opposition to 'take it easy', he was part of a new breed who became managers after playing in the shadow of the maximum wage, when footballers were paid a pittance for entertaining 50,000 crowds every weekend.

When Revie became a manager, he was determined to leave nothing to chance, on or off the field. He summed it up like this: 'I am a methodical man and I hate disorder. Football is more than a sport today, it is an industry, an empire of entertainment with great rewards for the successful clubs. If you want to be an important part of it, you have to plan. The slapdash approach is fatal.' So Don Revie planned and schemed and offered bribes, leaving as little as possible to chance. He relied on the loyalty of those he took into his confidence not to talk, and it nearly worked. He always believed that the *Mirror* investigation was launched in order to get him out of the England manager's job. It wasn't. Like so many things in newspapers, it started out as something else entirely and took on a life of its own because Alan Ball was sacked as England captain without even a thank you or a signed letter from Revie. The Boss had forgotten the first rule of a criminal conspiracy: know those to look after, and look after those who know.

Eventually, Revie was banned from English football for ten years, but only for breaching his contract with the FA. At the same time Alan Ball was fined £3,000 for taking illegal payments from him, although unaccountably the FA never heard the case against Revie himself. This was made even more strange by a pledge from the FA's Secretary Ted Croker that the *Mirror*'s dossier would be put to England's former manager when he returned to the country. The truth was the old men of Lancaster Gate didn't have the courage to clean up the game, so they just turned their backs and hoped it would go away. It was a humiliation for them, but nothing more than many of our informants had prophesied.

Nonetheless, control was beginning to slip from their arthritic fingers. The real power was moving to the managers, the players and their agents, while club chairmen fought between themselves to control the FA. They exerted the power of hire and fire over their playing and coaching staffs, but they could only do that at the price of a king's ransom. As with the House of Commons, their failure was to return to haunt them when once again the spectre of match-fixing overshadowed football with the disgrace of Liverpool goalkeeper Bruce Grobelaar. By then, money and its manipulation had taken over the game completely, with the FA little more than bemused onlookers. The Revie scandal was the last time the Association had any chance to stamp its authority on the game it was meant to police and lead. But the old men didn't want to go down that road, they were too fearful about what lay buried in their own backyards; better to do nothing and hang on to the vestiges of what tattered pride remained. It wasn't much, but as most of them were well over 70, they didn't need much. The legacy they left was one of deceit, rampant corruption, the stench of ancient privilege rising from the self-preservation they had practised for decades. It was a malaise that was to spread to the pitch as the England team tumbled from best in the world to also-rans. When the time came to sack Sir Alf Ramsey, they couldn't even do it face to face. The pride of the man who brought them the World Cup was so shattered that, he told me several years later, he seriously considered committing suicide.

The antiques of the FA had placed themselves and the players they were meant to protect in a Catch–22 situation. They refused to do anything because of what they might turn up. The players were frightened to talk because they feared nothing would be done about the scandal if they did. Their dilemma was summed up by Stan Anderson, then manager of Doncaster Rovers and desperate to work his way up the managerial ladder. He was 'tapped' by Revie on the phone when captain of Newcastle United. Revie's Leeds were top of the second division and had two games with Newcastle over Easter 1964. He asked Anderson to offer his players £10 each to throw the game (£120 at today's rates) – Anderson furiously refused. Like so many who had been tapped by Revie, the nightmare was revived when we approached him to confirm what happened. Anderson didn't want to know, and his explanation was, I suspect, as true a gauge of players' emotions, loyalties and cynicism about the game's administrators today as it was then. 'I want nothing to do with it ... I will deny it in court.' When Frank Palmer, the *Mirror*'s fine East Midlands reporter, pointed out that he would be denying something he knew to be true, Anderson said, 'I am still in the game. Why are you doing it? Why just go for Revie, the game is full of cheats. He was just more successful at it, that's all. I don't want to be branded as a snitch who cannot be trusted. People are panicking. We will all be involved whether we like it or not. I have already had mates from '64 on the phone panicking because they are still in the game. I am an honest man. You are asking me to get involved in something that is going to have big repercussions.' But there was another reason why he was fearful of speaking out. 'Nothing ever comes of it. It is just passed from committee to committee and nothing ever happens,' he said. On that point, at least, he was right.

Altogether, the Revie investigation lasted four months and took me across Britain many times, as well as to Europe and the United States. By the end, there were five of us working on it because we needed that many to get through the number of witnesses who had come forward. The only person in the football hierarchy who was prepared to say what he felt was our old friend Sir Harold who delighted in Revie's discomfort; the two had always hated each other. 'I know he's a crook,' he said. 'But I just want him out, all your stuff is rocking the boat.' Alas Sir Harold's boat was rocking pretty heftily, too, with persistent allegations of pinching air hostesses bums, he wasn't much help. The only good thing to come out of it was that life with the Arabs for Revie was, by all accounts, pretty dreadful. It started OK, as he was entertained lavishly – until he signed terms. Then he was just another employee with the kind of respect that goes with it. For a man who put great store by being treated properly – that's why he didn't like Sir Harold, who treated him in a very donnish way calling him Revie – it was a total humiliation, a judgement of the gods. At Leeds, the board stuck their heads in the sand and pretended nothing had happened. Now the memorial to the club's moral bankruptcy is there for all to see. The corrupt, disgraced Revie and his messenger boy Bremner are commemorated with a stand named after the former and a statue erected to the latter. The heroes now are Lee Bowyer and Jonathan Woodgate.

* * *

Other investigations followed, into pop-chart rigging and phoney wines, but it was time to move on. Running complex and long-term newspaper investigations is a solitary business, frustrating and time-consuming. I wanted to get back into the mainstream, but not any longer as a reporter. After 16 years I wanted to try my hand at something different. My mind was finally made up when I saw the cellar manager of a wine firm I had exposed in the dock as a result of our investigation. He was an elderly man, he wasn't bad, just misguidedly doing what he was told. Now he was broken and I had broken him. I didn't like it. I was getting soft, time for change. After so long on the road I made the one jump journalists rarely make, I moved from news to features, thanks to the faith of the *Mirror* editor Mike Molloy. I was about to try my hand on TV with *World in Action* when he offered me features editor of the *Mirror*. I joined the enemy twice over as far as reporters were concerned. I had not only become an executive, but I had gone to features. In the words of Ron Ricketts, the reporters' famous resident kettle drum, I was now both a weasel and a wanker.

9

Features are wankers because they wouldn't recognise a news story if it got off a bar stool and cracked them over the head with a pint glass. They are wankers because they never freeze their rocks off doorstepping for hours on end. They are wankers because whatever crap they write, it goes in the paper and more often than not it goes in unsubbed. This is the robust newsroom view, reporters will never admit it, but they are jealous of features for all of the above, and for one of their own to cross the floor was tantamount to treason. Features is also the department where editors tend to come from, or it was at the *Mirror*. Hugh Cudlipp had risen through features, so had Tony Miles and the *Mirror*'s editor at this time, Mike Molloy. Molloy had inherited the paper at a difficult time, after Mike Christiansen, son of the great *Express* editor Arthur, was forced to retire following a heart-attack. Molloy was only 34, and he set about trying to bridge the chasm between those twin citadels, news and features. He had some big successes, and my Marples and Revie investigations were cited as examples of how news and features could work together and overcome their traditional rivalries and suspicions.

The main friction is caused by a newspaper's structure which gives features control of 'the Dummy'. This is a skeleton plan for the paper, empty of everything except the adverts, and prepared two days in advance by the advertising department. It is the features editor's job to portion out the space between news, features and sport and present it to the editor for his approval. Control of the dummy means control of what gets big projection on the spreads. These are invariably done overnight, because of time limitations, and inevitably that is down to features as the news of the day hasn't yet happened. Features and sport – the latter known with varying degrees of enthusiasm as the toy department – are the only two areas which have the power and satisfaction of thinking up the ideas, allocating the writer, editing the material and projecting it into the paper. But whereas sport is limited in both space and on-the-night commitments, features can range over any subject and continent in the world, subject only to the editor not throwing a wobbly. No wonder Mike Molloy told me that whatever future job I held, features would always be the most enjoyable. With the job came The Writers, who worked – well, inhabited – a room not dissimilar to the set of one of those American comedies set in the scriptwriting offices of a big-time TV show. A dart board, secret bottle store and tattered dictionaries vying for space with frayed balloons coming from dog-eared photographs containing some long-forgotten joke about one of the faded grandees who should be occupying a desk but wasn't in today. Or yesterday, and probably not tomorrow either. This crumpled, mostly highly-talented, self-regarding, jealousy-riven crew ranged from megastar John Pilger through to the appallingly behaved but sweet-writing Paul Callan, from the famous, friendly but dangerous-when-crossed Marje Proops to the straightforwardly loony Bill Marshall who, on his day, could write so brilliantly that after one of his interviews the darts player Jocky Wilson refused to come out of his dressing room when he heard someone from the *Daily Mirror* was around.

Between them Marshall and Callan were capable of creating more mayhem than the rest of the staff put together, as they were both enthusiastic drinkers, and even though they had suffered many points defeats and knockouts from the fists of Bacchus, they constantly staggered from the canvas for more. Marshall tended to get married when drunk, so he had made several attempts at matrimony, the most famous of which he apparently spent entirely under the snooker table of the Liverpool Press Club, only coming out for a divorce. His other great love was cars, which was a pity because he was a useless and terrifying driver. He had one he was mightily proud of, a great big American job, which was unfortunately clipped by a truck. The damage wasn't bad, but Marshall saw it as a fatal flaw in his virgin bride. With tears in his eyes he pushed the otherwise pristine car into the Mersey.

His other weakness was showbusiness and, once, an impresario was foolish enough to offer him a part as a cowpoke extra in *The Greatest Little Whorehouse in Texas* at Drury Lane, the idea being that he would write about the experience. However, Marshall's overacting so unsettled the cast, not to mention the audience, that the whole show was thrown out of balance during his brief but memorable appearance. If he had actually been required to speak, it is doubtful whether the show would have survived. He had a great love, for Elaine Paige who at this time was staring in *Cats* where she sang the hit song 'Memory', composed for her by Andrew Lloyd Webber. Marshall loved this song and would, to the distress of everybody else, sing it loud and long after an equally loud and long lunch. So his interview with Ms Paige at Langan's was always going to be a bit of a tester. All was going well until, towards the end, Marshall, tongue loosened by several bottles of red wine, could contain his secret no longer. 'Elaine,' he said, 'Will you do something for me?'

Elaine was not unnaturally guarded: 'What?'

'Sing "Memory" for me.'

Which is what she did, right there in Langan's. Marshall was so moved that at the end of the lunch he bashed on to several other places, singing 'Memory' with the introduction, 'She sang it for me ... for me.' He wasn't seen in the office for several days afterwards.

That didn't matter much in features. A legend called Eric Wainwright was at the end of his career when I arrived. For a brief period he had been a household name, writing a regular feature called *Try Anything Once, Wainwright*, in which he would do anything from entering a lion's den to parachuting. The one thing Wainwright hadn't tried once in recent years was going into work, never mind actually writing anything. Occasionally, there was a panic and the cry went up, 'Anyone heard from Wainwright?' but someone usually had, from a pub in Soho where he now held court. This time, however, it was different. Nobody had heard from him in weeks, and he was in none of his regular haunts. This was serious. The editor was told, and he called in Tony Miles, the editorial director. As befits the editor of editors, he knew exactly what to do. Check with the cashiers, see if he has collected his expenses, ordered Miles. Relief! He had, bang on the button, Thursday morning, regular as clockwork. Now Eric was retiring and, as befitted a man of such long service, he was given a full features lunch. I had been on the paper for 12 years but, at the beginning of his farewell speech, Wainwright introduced himself to me and 'anyone else who may have no idea who I am'.

Paul Callan was different. There were many occasions, particularly after lunch, when you wished he would not come into the office. It was then that Callan's deep insecurity tended to manifest itself, usually in the form of complaints that others were getting the jobs he should be doing. On his day he was superb, a fine writer with an elegant touch, witty, sharp and a pleasure. At other times, when he had been worshipping at the wine shrine El Vino, the best thing to do was to scarper. He once overturned my desk when I expressed some doubt about his Eton schooling, insisting that he had, in fact, been a pupil in form 4B at West Norwood County Secondary School with PJ Wilson who had heroically kept quite about Callan's guilty secret. But Paul had so perfected his Eton persona that even those who had actually been there swore he was their contemporary. This may, of course, say rather more about the addled brains of Old Etonians than the inventive one of Callan. He took a lot of public stick over his Old Etonian inventions and it hurt him deeply; there wasn't much harm in a little manicuring of the truth, but journalists, particularly the gossip columnists – or diary editors as they like to be called nowadays – love the scent of blood and Callan's was rich feeding.

One of his many saving graces was that Callan could laugh at himself. Months later, when he was returning to London from the North by train with reporter John Penrose, later to become famous as Mr Anne Robinson, they stopped at Rugby. 'Rugby, Rugby? Wasn't I at school here?' asked Callan of a mystified first-class carriage. He also played a vital but unsung role in a superb picture by the *Mirror*'s brilliant animal photographer Arthur Sidey of the Guinness toucan in full flight. Arthur had waited for hours in the vain hope that the toucan – which had just been pensioned off by Guinness – would fly. But it would not, until Callan crept up behind it and jammed his pen firmly into the bird's bum. The result was the natural world at its regal best.

In any sane business Callan's antics would have merited instant dismissal, but the *Mirror* was tolerant of such madness on the grounds that life was richer for him being there. He surpassed himself one day when he got into a 'Don't call me a prick, you prick,' argument in the features pub, the universally famous Stab in the Back, with his arch *Mirror* rival John Edwards. Edwards, who was both a committed Welshman and drinker, gave back as much as he took, as Callan accused him of making up stories. They both decided this deserved the judgement of Tony Miles who was now not only editorial director but Chairman of the Mirror Group. Sadly, this time his soothing magic failed to work. Visitors to the ninth floor were somewhat surprised to see two middle-aged men rolling around the floor trying to punch each other's lights out.

The next day, my phone at home went early with the usual Callan overture when he was really in trouble. 'Callan here, old boy, I think I could be in the soup.' He was yellow-carded, but that was all.

John Pilger was altogether more difficult. He had made his name, justly so, for his searing reports from Vietnam during the war there. He was one of the first to question the American involvement and, as the years and the slaughter dragged on, his reports became more and more graphic and angry. He led public opinion, he didn't follow it, and without question his dispatches were among the finest to come out of that grisly war, not least because for so long he was a lone voice of dissent against the USA and its armed forces' frequently less-than-heroic actions. It was campaigning journalism at its very best, and Pilger well deserved all the accolades that came his way.

He had arrived at the *Mirror* as an itinerant Australian journalist and was plucked from the subs bench by Hugh Cudlipp in true Fleet Street tradition, but by the end of the Vietnam War in 1975 Cudlipp had gone and the *Mirror* was facing ever-greater pressure from the *Sun*. When Saigon fell to the North Vietnamese and the Viet Cong, there was a last minute panic to clamber aboard the last of the massive Jolly Green Giant helicopters as they left the American Embassy compound for warships stationed in the safety of the South China Sea. This should have been Pilger's supreme moment of triumph – alone among the British journalists, he had reported favourably on the army now about to sweep into the city, victors over the greatest war machine in the world. But, inexplicably, he was on one of the last helicopters out, instead of staying in Saigon where, clearly, the eye witness report of the arrival of the victorious Army was the story. For Pilger, the result was catastrophic. Not only were eyebrows raised that he had made his escape aboard a helicopter of the Army he had so despised, but, that he had left the story an open goal for John Edwards, then of the *Daily Mail*, who stayed in the city and filed top-class, dramatic and fascinating reports. It was a great disappointment for Pilger's war reporting fans that they were deprived of his dispatches at the moment of Ho Chi Minh's victory.

Although Pilger went on to do other stories, I felt he never really overcame either the highs or the lows of his Vietnam coverage.

In 1982 his credibility and confidence took a further knock when he wrote, as part of an expose of child labour in Thailand, a heartrending story in the *Mirror* about 'buying' a five-year old girl called Sunee and telling the story of how he returned her to her mother. In fact he was hoaxed, Sunee was a Bangkok schoolgirl and had been living with her mother there. The story led to a protracted libel action by Pilger, backed by the *Mirror*, against Auberon Waugh who, Pilger claimed, had suggested in a *Spectator* article that he was a party to the hoax. Eventually the action was dropped with both sides paying their own costs, but there is no doubt that both for Pilger and the *Mirror* it had been an embarrassing period. His muscular prose brought complaints at home too, where, on occasions, the subjects of his reportage did not altogether agree with his interpretation of the facts. He particularly infuriated a mining community, when he reported a miner's funeral much as if it came straight from a D.H. Lawrence novel.

Shortly after I became features editor he was briefly to star once again with his *Death of a Nation* shock issue on the massacres of Pol Pot in Cambodia, but by this time it was clear that he did not take direction, but neither, as Mike Molloy explained to me, was he a highly energetic self-starter. The upshot was that he did less and less and what he did usually came down to the same thing – it was either the fault of the Americans or Coca Cola. Solutions that may on occasion have had some justification, but with Pilger's reports it became a somewhat monotonous explanation that was easy to caricature and increasingly difficult to take seriously. This was later refined into his Hidden Agenda theory, thus when he appeared in the *Mirror* again for the first time in 15 years to pronounce Tony Blair's War on Terrorism a fraud, the effect was spoilt by his claim that the driving force of the United States was its quest for oil. George W. Bush's concealed agenda was to exploit the oil and gas reserves of the Caspian Sea and pump it through Afghanistan, he insisted. The agenda remains concealed to this day.

Gradually, Pilger fell out of love with the *Mirror* and the *Mirror* fell out of love with him. There were claims he was sacked or 'purged' by Maxwell, a handy tale, but not so. There was no hidden agenda; he was sacked by me after I became editor in 1985, because all areas of the company were facing job cuts and the journalists were no exception. Pilger had done little of note for months, apart from appearing on Maxwell's Meet the People train, and once again went off to Australia. It is convenient to say he was fired because Maxwell hated him and his views, but it is not the case. When Maxwell arrived at the Mirror, he called up both Paul Foot and Pilger for a glass of champagne, and told them he wanted them to stay. Foot pointed out that he was happy to continue his column as long as Maxwell didn't interfere. While I was editor he didn't, and Foot produced one of the finest campaigning columns in tabloid journalism for another nine years. Pilger hung on for another 18 months and contributed very little of real worth; that is why he went.

After he left, he telephoned Mike Molloy – reverse charges, to his home, from Australia – to ask for his help in getting extra cash from the *Mirror* as he was not a member of the pension scheme. I went with Molloy to Maxwell to put Pilger's case.

Maxwell: 'But he's only going to piss all over us, why should we give him any extra?'

Us: 'Because, Bob, in the past he was a terrific asset to the paper and we should recognise that.'

Maxwell: 'All right, but he will still piss all over us.'

In the end, Pilger got £63,000, considerably more than he was entitled to under the redundancy agreements that had been negotiated. And Maxwell was right, he did piss all over us and has continued to do so on and off until Piers Morgan reintroduced him to that paper.

When I gave up investigations and went to features, Mike Molloy suggested we hire Paul Foot as my replacement. I was iffy, not because I didn't reckon Paul, I did, but because his experience had been on *Private Eye* and the *Socialist Worker*, publications with a quite different agenda and readership to the *Mirror*. I needn't have worried. Mike's decision was an inspired one, and Paul's column over the next decade was a greater contribution to the art of pejorative investigative journalism than mine ever was. The trick was finding the right format for the column, a mixture of investigation, campaigning and good old-fashioned rant. It was terrific, and much of this was due not just to the sheer hard work, professionalism and passionate conviction of Paul, but of the legal manager, old Harrovian Hugh Corrie, who always referred to Foot as 'your leftie friend'. Foot and Corrie had much in common – good public school education, a love of cricket and a natural patrician background. Their politics, however, couldn't have been further apart, unless you take the view that the political spectrum is not made up of two wings but a circle with the far left and the far right joining up. In that case, Foot and Corrie were rather close.

One afternoon, Corrie decided to take Foot to the Oval to watch a test match against the West Indies. Corrie, naturally, had good seats, and was surrounded by braying city and legal folk taking a day 'orf'. After an hour or so, Foot could stand it no longer and decided to head for the West Indian section of the crowd over the other side, in what is known as the Ganja Stand because of the exotic smoke rising from it. As Foot made himself comfortable in these more desirable surroundings, the man next to him, no doubt suffering from hallucinations caused by the smoke billowing round him, failed to see the light of Foot's Liberal conscience and was unimpressed by his all-embracing Trotskyist zeal. After studying him for a moment, he delivered his verdict: 'Hey, honky, why don't you fuck off back where you came from?'

Over the 13 years, his column ran in the *Mirror*, Foot won numerous campaigns and awards. He was more than just a columnist, he was the uncomfortable conscience who would not go away, something every newspaper needs. Too often, in the rough and tumble of producing a newspaper every day, we lose sight of injustices, ignore lies and turn a blind eye to brutish behaviour which tramples those who have no voice.

Foot was that voice, eloquent, insistent and persuasive. He wrote many wonderful columns; together – him investigating and writing it and me projecting it – we even managed a first when we accused an unconvicted man of murder. When Tony Miles saw it he nearly choked to death on his glass of chilled Chablis. But Foot was spot on, and several years later the man he exposed was jailed – for murder.

At the end of 1986, he announced he was sending 13 Christmas cards that year, all to men and women he believed to be in jail serving life sentences for murders they did not commit. Nobody cared about them, except their families and him. It took time, but every single one of them was eventually cleared and freed. That is great journalism. He won countless awards and for me, both in features and later as editor, he was the paper's pride and joy. Only the *Mirror* would dare run Foot; only the *Mirror* would care enough. At the *Sun*, Kelvin MacKenzie couldn't see why we bothered. Of course he couldn't, that was one of the reasons why the *Mirror* was never the *Sun*, not until David Montgomery arrived, anyway.

Foot's column eventually came to an end when he wrote a savage page condemning the sackings and blood-letting at the *Mirror* under Montgomery's régime, and put it forward for publication. It was a magnificent way to go out, made even better by the editor, David Banks, a Montgomery admirer, claiming Foot was loony and needed 'professional help'. By that stage, Banks and Montgomery had so emasculated the *Mirror* that it was the paper itself that desperately needed professional help.

Newspaper lore reckons that if you have a good, vibrant features team you are likely to have a good paper. It is the only department that has to rely entirely on its own wits to produce material, and for that you need a constant stream of new talent. I was lucky; one way or another I found it in spades and, curiously, all of it was female. When the Mirror Group's old-fashioned weekly *Reveille* closed, it was everyone into the lifeboats. *Reveille* journalists were not noted for their national newspaper potential, and a communal groan went round heads of department when they were told they were required to haul in survivors. Nowadays, they would be given a few months' redundancy and told to get lost. In features, I was lumbered with what looked like a frail 24-year-old schoolgirl whose previous features experience had, for some reason now totally forgotten, been posing as a traffic warden in a Ho Chi Minh mask. But this girl had enormous talent, even though it took a few weeks to convince her. Christena Appleyard was a superlative writer with an extraordinary ability to get even the most difficult and taciturn of people to talk. For her we introduced a series called *Women Talking* in which she would interview apparently ordinary women who just talked about their lives. It was riveting and became the template for countless imitations in women's magazines. No other newspaper would have had the originality or the talent to come up with either the idea or the writer, it was the uniqueness of the *Mirror* that did it. Christena went on to win the British Press Awards Feature Writer of the Year – as Bill Marshall did before her – later becoming deputy editor of the London *Evening Standard* and then the *Daily Mail* before being made editor of the *Mail on Sunday*'s *Night and Day* magazine.

Christena was followed on to the staff by Noreen Taylor and Mary Riddell, both top-flight writers with razor-sharp observation and that elusive ability to coax rather more from their subjects than they might in retrospect consider wise. Mary, who came to us via editing the fish prices on the *Aberdeen Press and Journal*, is now the most accomplished interviewer in Fleet Street and her decision to give up her career as a newspaper executive when *Today* closed – she was deputy editor – is journalism's loss. Is it just coincidence that these three young women should shine through, while new young male talent was nowhere to be seen? I don't think so. At the beginning of the 1980s, the *Mirror* started pioneering interviews which gave readers the feel that they were actually in the room with their subjects, whether they be film stars or prostitutes. Up until that time, interviews had been conducted largely on the lines of 'Isn't it fabulous to be in this palatial suite with Liz Taylor and Richard Burton telling us all about being rich and how much they are in lurve with each other?' True, there were a few, like Donald Zec, who could make it readable, but they were still pedestal people, not flesh and blood. Wall-to-wall television had changed all that; we needed the smell of our celebrities, we wanted them to laugh and cry. We wanted them angry, or drunk, vulnerable or behaving like tosspots. These girls could get under their skin, behind the image and to some pretty raw truth. It was great stuff and, most satisfying of all, their success drove Callan mad.

In spite of the influx of female talent, we did not have a women's editor. There was a reason for that and it can be summed up in two words – Marje Proops. Marje had been queen of the agony aunts for 30 years. She was probably the most famous name in journalism, although she didn't actually start writing her *Mirror* column until the 1960s, when all the sexual, moral and family values of the past were challenged, and largely discarded, in an explosion of youth culture which brought in its wake huge riches, power and a freedom unknown to previous generations. Most newspapers were scandalised, run as they were by middle-aged men used to telling people how to behave, even if they couldn't take their own advice. Marje Proops and Felicity Green were the exceptions, writing graphically about the Pill, pre-marital sex and, God forbid, pubic hair.

But by 1980, these standards were not only accepted, but old hat, and Marje, although she never revealed her age, was by then an old-aged-pensioner. However her plans didn't include retirement, nor did they embrace a successor or even a deputy. Hence no women's editor. It also explained why we didn't have a female columnist of any quality or profile; Marje was going to have no sapling growing under her branches. We did try with Bel Mooney, but she didn't translate into a tabloid columnist – too rambling – and Marje was not displeased when she was eventually given the heave-ho. 'Never right, dear, I thought, although I would never have said so.' Of course not, Marje, never.

It was at this stage that Anne Robinson re-entered my life. I had known Annie for ten years as the occasional stormy partner of my great friend John Penrose, *Mirror* reporter, interior designer, boozer, lover of good restaurants, anything Italian and running up American Express bills he couldn't possibly pay. My first memory of Annie isn't actually of her but her sporty car, a present from her mother, an older version of her daughter, a woman, so the story goes, with such a well-developed sense of social snobbery that when feeling ill in Knightsbridge one day she crossed the road in order to faint in Harrods.

Annie was the first of my friends to acquire a personalised number plate – AR 21, to mark her twenty-first birthday. She made the mistake of lending it to Penrose – everybody calls him Penrose – to go to a party in Oxford to which I had invited him. Naturally, he had too much to drink and, unwisely, set off for home with his equally drink-ravaged friend for company when he considered himself to be sober enough, although others might have thought he still had some hours to go. He managed to smash the exhaust when he took a shortcut over a roundabout instead of using the more orthodox route, thus necessitating a drastic reduction of speed for the rest of the journey to London. He was just navigating his way over the Hammersmith flyover when he was stopped by the police and breath-tested. Penrose protested on the grounds that the only reason he was stopped was because of his slow speed caused by the car injury. The police, equally strenuously, insisted this was not so. 'Why have you stopped me then?' challenged Penrose.

'Because, sir,' explained the world-weary cop with a sigh, 'Your passenger is wearing a lampshade on his head.'

For much of the 70s Annie was drunk, the result of her marriage to Charlie Wilson, then the northern editor of the *Daily Mail*, falling to pieces and breaking up in the most acrimonious of circumstances. As she revealed in her own searing and painfully honest book, Annie had taken to the bottle in a big way, was rarely sober and had reached rock bottom. She was close to death. It was a pitiful sight to see her unable to stand, being helped to taxis where the drivers took one look and refused to take her. Her marriage was disastrous because Charlie wanted a traditional wife and Annie wanted to be a traditional journalist. She would rather be covering the war in Vietnam than doing the hoovering, she famously told the judge at the bitterly-contested custody battle with Charlie over their daughter, a battle she lost.

Her attitude to Charlie, a bruising Scots skinhead but first-rate journalist, was summed up by her story of the time they went to the races and came across Arthur Brittenden, then editor of the *Daily Mail* and Charlie's boss. 'Charlie was wearing a flat cap and he doffed it to him. It was then I realised I had married a jockey,' she said.

Her book reveals the extent of her obsession with Charlie Wilson and the injustice she felt about losing custody of their daughter Emma. But anyone who knew her at the time would not have questioned the judge's decision. Not only was Annie incapable of looking after Emma, but Charlie, in spite of his own enormous ambition, was a caring and coping father who was under enormous pressure. The custody battle was long and bitter and showed Fleet Street up in its worst light, even though the proceedings were in private. It was an open secret that Charlie had among his witnesses people who worked for him and were therefore not entirely neutral. Even Penrose gave evidence for him – something he reproached himself about for years – after finding Annie smooching with her solicitor. In spite of her terrible drink problem – or perhaps because of it – she loved sex, and on one more than one occasion finished up in strange beds; sometimes she didn't even know the city, never mind the man on the other pillow. But she remained a terrific reporter, first for the *Daily Mail* and then Harold Evans's *Sunday Times*. She was not cut out to be the little wife at home entertaining northern reporters of the *Mail*.

For much of that decade, I sat next to Penrose in the reporters' room and often took her long, rambling drunken calls. I have no doubt that Penrose, with both patience and great love, played a large part in saving her from the gutter and an ignominious early death. The other person who deserves great credit is Annie herself. With an enormous effort of will she returned home to Liverpool from London, where she had been slowly killing herself, acquiring such a reputation that nobody would employ her, and set about sorting herself out, privately, quietly, no doubt with great pain, self-doubt and certainly great will-power.

The result was that, by 1979, she had a column on the *Liverpool Echo* and a good one it was, too. Penrose brought her cuttings in to show me. I wanted her on the *Mirror*, Marje didn't, and she had plenty of supporters who outranked me. 'Still drinking is she?' was the inevitable first question. 'They never get over it you know, she'll start again as soon as she's in the right environment,' was the next line. And the *Mirror* was certainly the right environment. 'Let her work from home, dear, not in the office. Don't want her to make a fool of you, do you, dear?' Thanks, Marje.

But Annie was simply too good to ignore. Gradually, she began to spend more and more time in the office. A staff job as women's editor followed, the first time Marje had been overruled. Their relationship was one of armed combat ever after. Eventually, when I went to head up news, Annie became assistant editor in charge of features but I don't think it was really her. The writers were wary of her, partially because she was such a good one herself, but also because there was a sizeable chunk of her that wanted to be the star, and you can't do that if you are in charge of writers. Your success is making them stars. I think the same problem would have prevented her from being a great editor, although there is no doubt that she had the technical equipment for the job. I suspect Annie recognised this, too; her battle against the booze had left her with enormous self-knowledge, but also a tendency to dismiss quickly those with whom she became impatient. She was not always right and it tended to leave her department demoralised. Staff began to become wary of the Robinson Clump, as it was known, the sound of Annie's purposeful walk down the newsroom in search of some poor writer to scourge. What, however, was blindingly obvious to me was that she had all the makings of a great female columnist. She could write well, held forthright opinions and was not afraid to put them. I suggested to Mike and Tony Miles that she was the answer to a problem that nobody had solved. The reason was obvious when Tony came up with the first question: 'What will Marje say?'

This time, however, Marje bowed to the inevitable. It was obvious Annie had enormous potential and, however jealous she was of her own patch, Marje was a consummate journalist and office politician. She agreed, though it didn't stop her sniping from the sidelines occasionally, particularly when in one column Annie had what Marje considered to be a dig at her when she referred dismissively to people with cats who live in Putney, where Marje lived. Annie was shocked and surprised, or at least she said she was. Her *Mirror* column started what was to be a meteoric name-in-lights career, and a thoroughly deserved one, too. Nobody can know what devils she had to defeat in the lonely hours of the night to come back from the dead, but that she did is beyond question. Her columns, for the *Mirror*, *Today*, the *Sun*, *Express* and the *Times*, have always expressed that witty, spikey, infuriating mixture of harridan and unsure girl, hard career woman and soft mother earth that make up Annie Robinson.

Her battle against drink left scars. Her obsession with success, fame and money became more pronounced, too many people knew too much about her past for her to care what they thought, and this manifested itself in a presentation to the world of a woman who knew what she wanted and didn't care much how she achieved it. In the clubby atmosphere of the *Mirror*, the Robinson touch was like a big sheet of heavy-duty sandpaper, but nevertheless she brought a valuable new dimension to the paper, a female punch that the ageing Marje was now unable to deliver.

Annie's is a remarkable story and you would have to be cold-hearted indeed to begrudge the beautiful Cotswold farmhouse and London townhouse that have come from her success on *Watchdog* – which she based on the *Daily Mirror* consumer investigations by Jan Walsh – and the extraordinary world fame *The Weakest Link* brought her. It is curious to watch her on that; it is as if she is playing a caricature of herself, an exaggerated version of the real Annie, or at least one side of her. Fame has softened her, but she still feels the need for reassurance, which is why she constantly talks about the amount of money she makes. It is a reminder to Charlie Wilson that she was right all those years ago to take the Vietnam option and forsake the dusting.

Their daughter Emma, as fiery as either of them, has survived remarkably well, considering the damage that such a bitter divorce and custody battle could have inflicted. It could also have soured Emma's relations with her mother. That they haven't is a tribute to the resilience of a feisty young woman and the searing honesty of her mother about dark days she would prefer to forget, but is brave and honest enough not to.

For Annie and Penrose, life together wasn't to be all sweetness and light. When Annie decided to pursue fame, Penrose found it wasn't to his taste and the pair split up, but neither was happy. It was Annie who eventually cracked. Weeping over her typewriter one night she decided she didn't want to be alone any more and called Penrose. She told me they had decided to get back together. Why, I asked. 'Because I love him,' she said. It was a simple statement of fact from a scarred and difficult woman who, as she said it, looked once again like a girl of 18. Penrose has been described, unkindly, as the perfect Mrs Robinson, but he was a great deal more than that. He bandaged her insecurities, massaged a deceptively fragile ego, and provided the artistic side to the formidable Robinson front, which hid a softer and sometimes confused woman with a fierce pride and will to win. Most important, he knew the dark side better than anyone else. And he had been in love with her since the first moment they met in the tatty North London offices of John Rogers' news agency. It was the nearest to a love story our craggy old trade could manage.

Threading his way through this carnival of jugglers, contortionists, fire-eaters, high-wire acrobats, two-headed women and drunks, was Keith Waterhouse, whose genius managed to combine the lot. His *Mirror* column was the finest example of sustained writing in Fleet Street over two decades and even now in the *Mail* it is something others aspire to and rarely attain. Mercifully Waterhouse wasn't on the staff, so he only came in to deliver his column for the following day on Sunday and Wednesday. It was impeccably typed and grammatically unchallengeable, and woe betide the sub-editor who did. Waterhouse always wrote his own headlines, and once a casual sub altered it on the stone without anyone knowing. The explosion from underneath the Waterhouse thatch was a joy to behold, particularly because he gave the distinct impression that his TV creation Worzel Gummidge had come to life in the newsroom and that the features department had become traditional Aunt Sallies, rather than the object of Worzel's infatuation. There was nothing you could do but sit back and admire the invective.

Much of Waterhouse's play *Jeffrey Bernard is Unwell* was based on the *Mirror*; the egg trick executed so expertly by Peter O'Toole loomed large in Waterhouse mythology and was always on display at Labour Party conferences where Waterhouse held court at Yates' Wine Lodge in Blackpool. This was tempered by tram trips to the Fleetwood kipper shop which was not only the end of the line, but within whiffing distance of the Fisherman's Friend factory, where he would inhale enough of 'Oop North' to refresh his column for another year. On returning unsteadily to his room at the Imperial, Waterhouse would invariably ask for an early morning call in order to compose that day's column. 'Ring me at seven,' he would command in that clipped Leeds accent. 'But Mr Waterhouse …' came the reply from the front desk.

'Seven please.' The tone brooked no argument, as the great man sashayed towards the lift. 'But...', 'Seven, on the dot,' as he fumbled with the lift button.'
'Mr Waterhouse, I can't ...'
'Yes, you can,' as he lurched into the lift.
'No I can't.'
'Why not?' ... Lift door closing.
'Because it is twenty past seven.'
Doors slam shut.

Running news was not half as much fun as running features, because, for the most part, news runs itself and it is only possible to have a marginal influence on it. Nonetheless, one appointment was to make a lasting impact, if not on journalism, then certainly on the politics of the late twentieth century. Every year the *Mirror* used to interview trainees from our graduate scheme in Plymouth, the Plymouth Brethren as they were known. This was an excellent idea, encouraging bright young men and women into a journalism career – not half as popular, in those days, as the ubiquitous media studies courses have made today's profession – but the difficulty was placing them at the end of the course. The Mirror Group could only take a few and these places were much prized. The successful candidates were chosen by executives of the three newspapers – *Daily* and *Sunday Mirror* and the *People* – from a short-listed group of the brightest and the best who travelled up to London for inspection. Most *Daily Mirror* executives tried to dodge this examination, mainly because they hated interviewing potential staff for jobs, and partially because they did not believe the Plymouth Brethren should be allowed to go straight on to the national papers. I had managed to avoid being on the interview panel but in the evening I found myself in the Stab in the Back having a drink with John Penrose. A tall young man was standing on his own with a pint of lager. Was he one of the Brethren? I asked Penrose. He didn't know but said he would find out, which he did. The name rang a bell. Isn't he the one who hit Bob Edwards? Bob Edwards was the editor of the *Sunday Mirror* at the time, and any member of the Brethren who had the balls to bop an editor couldn't be all bad. It also explained why he hadn't made the candidates' shortlist, even though after a short conversation with him it was obvious that he was possessed of a quick intellect, easy charm and a mind of his own. He was in the Stab because his girlfriend was on the shortlist and he was waiting for her. This was my first meeting with Alastair Campbell.

He intrigued me. It was wrong to keep him off the shortlist purely because he had hit Bob Edwards. Understandable, but wrong. If we used that as a yardstick, some of Fleet Street's finest would be on the dole or in the slammer. But he was forthright, underawed by the fact that he was talking to the *Mirror*'s head of news and deputy news editor, and he was young and bright. The newsroom was getting old and we needed fresh talent, so I told him to come in for a shift.

'I can't, I haven't been selected,' he said.

'Yes you have, just now. Come in, tomorrow'.

But he didn't, so Penrose tracked him down and asked him why.

'I thought you were joking,' he said.

'Well, come in now.'

So he did. A quarter-of-a-mile away in the Temple, Tony Blair didn't know it, but his right arm had just been born.

Campbell's first stay with the *Mirror* was cut short by the lunacy of Maxwell's first year. He and his great friend John Merritt hated the way in which the *Mirror* was being traduced, and hated even more the derision with which it was being treated by its rivals. Both decided to leave; Merritt for the *Observer* and Campbell for *Today*. When I rejoined the *Mirror* (after a spell editing the People, see next chapter) I tried to persuade them life would get better, but neither was prepared to wait and see; I could hardly blame them. For Campbell, it was to prove a searing experience, as his drinking tottered out of control, leading to a drunken lost weekend and a nervous breakdown. Why should a man with such a reputation for control have left the rails in such spectacular fashion? Campbell needed figureheads, and at *Today* he didn't have one. At the *Mirror* he had been treated very much as a favoured son after I left to go to the *People*, and I think it was a potentially fatal mistake. He believed top jobs were there for the taking, and so they were, but not the way he was going about it. Hard graft was the way to do it and Alastair thought he could stroll through the opposition. He couldn't. At 29, he lacked the breadth of experience needed to succeed in the job he had taken on. He was overpromoted, out of his depth, confused, unhappy and terrified that he had not only made a mistake but that there was no way out of it.

When he finished up a physical and mental wreck in hospital, suffering from depression and too much booze, it was John Merritt who went to see him and gave him half-a-dozen marbles. 'Here you are, don't lose them again,' he said. It was a seminal moment in Campbell's life, and with the help of Merritt – who was to die a brave and premature death from leukaemia, depriving Fleet Street of a potentially great reporter – and his partner Fiona Millar, he gradually came back to the land of the living. He came to see me and asked for his old job back, admitting he had made a terrible mistake, that he had given up booze and realised he had all but ruined his life. He returned to the fold, teetotal and desperate to make amends, but wary of how he would be received by his former colleagues. He need not have worried. Alastair went from strength to strength, through the *Mirror*'s political department under the guidance of Joe Haines, to the *Sunday Mirror* as political editor and then back to the daily in the same position. He never lost those marbles Merritt gave him.

Campbell had much in common with Annie Robinson, and turned to the same solution when his ambition was thwarted. He saw his progression as breaking through a series of glass ceilings and he tried to smash his way through newspaper executive structure. But top-class newspaper executives have to be able to motivate staff, and both Alastair and Annie were both too personally ambitious to do that. They wanted to be stars, whereas the best of newspaper editors star through their staff. Alastair, I think, realised this when he left the *Mirror* for *Today* in the mid-80s where he was to become the night news editor, a position he neither liked nor excelled in. It was his equivalent of doing the hoovering and not covering the Vietnam war, and it was this that drove him to drink in excess and finally to the lost week which led him to give up drink and return to the *Mirror*. Like Annie, the quest for power was closely allied to panic. Alastair, too, needed mentors and attached himself to them, starting with the *Mirror*'s West Country reporter Syd Young, through me and on to Neil Kinnock and his family and then Peter Mandelson and Tony Blair.

Both Alastair and Annie had a barely suppressed rage about them, both were impatient of lesser talents and could be abrasive when expressing that impatience. But sometimes that rage could be turned against themselves, and it led them both to uncontrolled drinking, and the spectre of their careers disappearing when they had barely started. Although ambition may have driven them to the brink of destruction, it also brought them back. Both had the discipline, the focus and the honesty to realise that if they were to be as powerful and successful as they believed was their destiny, the booze would have to go. So it did.

By 1983, I was assistant editor in charge of both news and features, and the paper rollocked on with journalists having a high old time and the printers earning whatever they asked. The management was powerless to either curb excess expenses from editorial or excess pay demands from the print trade unions. There were 13 different unions in Holborn Circus, and the board was powerless to control any of them, which resulted in a shoulder-shrugging attitude to our industrial problems, a balance sheet that was a disgrace to any company – less than £1 million profit on £200 million turnover – and an exasperated main board at Reed International.

We were not unique; the rest of Fleet Street was in a similar position, but the *Mirror* with its *laissez faire* approach and its history of being the golden goose was the problem writ large. It was the last days of the old empire, with everybody grabbing as much as they could. Sub-editors in features, for example, worked a four-day week but the same hours as they did when working five days. They put in expenses although they never went out on jobs – all agreed by a management too chicken to say no.

Mike Molloy had become steadily more disillusioned. A journalists' strike in 1977 after the *Mirror* produced three blockbuster series – Joe Haines on the Wilson years and the lavender honours list; Chris Hutchins on the truth of Tom Jones' and Engelbert's sexual excesses; and the Revie match-fixing scandal – had sent the circulation crashing after the three series had seen it soar. The *Sun* passed us and we were never to regain our lead. Behind the parties and the laughter, which were becoming steadily more manic, was a stolid hopelessness that nothing could be done.

My gloom was deepened by Tony Miles offering me the deputy editorship of the *People* under Nick Lloyd. It would have been a disaster; Nick and I saw eye to eye on nothing, including each other. Not only that, deputy editor of the *People* was no better than what I was doing at the *Mirror*, so I turned it down. 'You only do that once,' said Tony. 'You won't get an editorship y'know, cock.'

One Thursday evening our diary editor Peter Tory came into the pub and said, 'This is crazy. I'm a bit short this weekend, so I've taken out a chit for £100 and the cashiers have paid it without a murmur.' Good old cashiers, we all lived on tick there. It couldn't last and deep down we knew it. That's why the parties got longer and the hangovers bigger. We were still capable of producing some great papers, and often did. But the business was going down, weighted by overstaffing, overpayment and trades unions demands that became ever more absurd; the more outlandish, the more the management caved in. Sabotage of the printing presses was a regular event, the papers rarely came out on time and when they did it was a collectors' item if the editions went to the right places. You lose readers quicker by putting a Liverpool football match report into Manchester and vice versa, and we did it all the time. At Reed, Chief Executive Les Carpenter was running out of patience and wanted shot of this troublesome parent which caused so much angst for so little reward. Reed had only once interfered with editorial matters, when the *Mirror* was asked as early as 1983, to rein back on it's coverage of Charles and Diana's marriage. Sod's law operated immediately. The next day Kent Gavin produced a haunting picture of the pair that said more than words ever could. The *Mirror* didn't use it, but Reed's intervention became known. They never said another word. The Reed board was fearful of selling the group on to someone unsuitable and incurring the wrath of the Labour Party. Yet the *Mirror* had to go, so they came up with the idea of floating it away; all they needed was a chairman with enough clout in the City to carry it off. The warning signs should have been plain enough when they couldn't find one, so they asked Tony Miles and Douglas Long, the *Mirror* Chief Executive, to come up with an idea. This was lunacy as neither of them had any City weight or knowledge, so they turned to Robert Head, the paper's respected City editor to find one instead. Madness piled on madness, the party was nearly over.

10

Nobody bothered to ask me whether I was interested in editing the *People*. It was the relative nobody talked about at the *Mirror*, they were ashamed of it, rather like an old aunt who is locked away 'for her own good'. The paper was banished to Orbit House on the other side of Fetter Lane, and to reach it you had to cross the Bridge of Sighs. *People* people were considered odd, not one of us, a feeling strengthened by the long-term stewardship of Geoff Pinnington who had changed an investigative newspaper with a fine record into a 'Spot the face of Christ in George's cabbage patch' type paper, folksy and irrelevant. It had been allowed to go soft because nobody knew what to do about it. It was an embarrassment, and always had been, because it was given houseroom reluctantly by Cecil King's International Publishing Corporation when he took over Odhams, which he did in 1961 for its stable of magazines. With them came the *People*, the *Daily Herald* and *Sporting Life*.

The Odhams takeover was not sufficiently thought through. Both newspapers and magazines were at the top end of their popularity and they came with enormous overheads, not least on the printing side, and their acquisition was to make an already difficult situation worse. The main problem for the *People* was that it was a direct competitor of IPC's *Sunday Pictorial*, later the *Sunday Mirror*. Inevitably, Hugh Cudlipp preferred the *Pic*, the only Mirror Group paper he ever edited, so the *People* was left to its own devices with Cudlipp dismissing it derisively as the *Pee-ople*. It became a dumping ground for clapped-out *Mirror* executives and a testing ground for new ones. This meant that no young *People* blood was coming through, and by the time Pinnington retired it showed all too clearly.

But it had not always been like that, even under IPC stewardship. Cudlipp appointed Bob Edwards as editor when the legendary and long-serving Sam Campbell died. Edwards proved to be a superb editor, producing exposées in its finest tradition, from the massacre of 25 Malayan villagers by British troops to the widespread corruption at the top of Scotland Yard. It was the stuff the *People* did best, and the kind of thing I wanted to revive. The trouble was, it didn't look as if I was going to get the chance when Nick Lloyd decided to up sticks from the Mirror Group and take on the job of turning the *News of the World* into a tabloid. I assumed the curse of Tony Miles was still on me, until I had an idle conversation with Mike Molloy who told me that Miles was about to ask Lloyd Turner, currently editing the *Daily Star* and doing a good job there, if he wanted it. I said nothing.

'You don't want it do you?' he asked. 'You don't want to go to the *People*, surely?'

I pointed out that it was an editorship, they didn't come up very often, and there was no chance of going any further where I was. I also liked what I felt the *People* should be and could be again. Mike clearly thought I was mad, but was generous enough to recommend me to Tony. Within 24 hours the job was mine; it was the most crucial move of my journalistic life and one that was going to shape the rest of it. I was appointed on Friday, 14 January 1984, 21 years to the day since I first walked in through the battered blue front door of the *Bucks Herald* to start what had turned into a big, bruising, glorious switchback of a ride which seemed destined to go faster and faster.

With Nick Lloyd gone, the staff was led by his deputy Ernie Burrington, an accomplished newspaperman but one all but destroyed by drink. The real power was Lloyd's protégé David Montgomery, who ran everything. Montgomery was a slick operator but was loathed by the staff, which had become rather cosy and complacent after years of Pinnington. There were exceptions – Laurie Manifold, who had exposed the Yard corruption – was still as creative as ever, even if his material was falling on stony ground, and John Smith, a first-rate journalist who had been consigned in the Pinnington years to constantly touring the world. Montgomery was a production man with an eye for a headline which often, sadly, was not matched by the story underneath. There were many complaints of copy being changed to fit a preconceived idea and front-page stories being stolen from opposition papers rather than backing your own bet. There is nothing new about that, and nothing wrong either if the story is big enough, but it was happening to such an extent that morale had dropped dangerously low with many staff feeling the stories being replaced were often better than those being nicked. However, it wasn't a problem for long. Monty was always going to join Lloyd, which he did within a few weeks.

Ernie hadn't been too bad but he was still boozing, and I was due to go to the *People*'s Christmas party in Manchester which, for some perverse reason, was held in the new year. Penny and I went up there to meet the troops, little knowing that Ernie was starring in an assault course of his own back in London. The *People* was a mass of warren-like offices, built up over the years by executives defending their own little patches. Ernie had got well oiled at lunchtime and had decided that it was time for a cosy chat with Christena Appleyard who had come with me from the *Mirror* as women's editor. She didn't see it that way and locked herself into her office and, at the moment I checked in to see if everything was all right, Burrington was trying to scale the wall and drop in over the partition. He only stopped when she shouted out that the editor was on the phone.

The next day I read him the riot act, saying he reminded me uncomfortably of my father, a good operator when sober but a total waste of space when drunk. If he was going to carry on like that – and he had been doing it for years – then he could go somewhere else and do it. Ernie was one of those drunks who knew no fear when pissed and retained no memory of it when sober, an alarming Jekyll and Hyde. To his great credit, I never saw him drunk again.

My editorship of the *People*, or *Sunday People* as it was then – the name is always being changed, a measure of its instability – coincided with the arrival of a new chairman. Reed's had bitten the bullet and decided to get rid of us, but Alex Jarratt, the same chairman who had been so roundly booed at Cudlipp's farewell, wanted to wash his hands of the Mirror Group. The profits were abysmal – still less than £1 million on a turnover of £250 million – the union problems insurmountable, at least by the present management, and tabloid papers were not his cup of tea anyway. But Jarratt didn't want to upset the Labour Party – in 1983 he must have been about the only person in the country who didn't – and therefore pledged he would not sell it to an individual. That meant only one person: Maxwell. The Mirror board was asked to come up with a name who would have enough clout in the City to make a flotation credible, a difficult trick given the state of anarchy that existed downstairs. The Mirror board was no more than a branch management office in terms of City players and hadn't got a clue who to approach. All Chief Executive Douglas Long wanted was to hire a chairman who would sort out the float and then take a back seat, allowing him to run the Mirror Group in much the same way as before. Unrealistic, but nobody said we were living in the real world.

The solution of Long and Miles, the Group's current chairman, was to ask Robert Head, the *Mirror*'s long-serving and highly-respected City editor, to come up with a list of names. In among the great and the good was one, Clive Thornton, general manager of the Abbey National Building Society, a current darling of the square mile. Thornton, a small man with a big ego and a limp caused by the amputation of a foot when a child, arrived at the *Mirror* at the beginning of 1984 in what was to be a tumultuous year. But, for the moment, it was hail to the new chief, or in the words of Paddy O'Gara, the *Mirror*'s art director, 'In the land of the legless, the one-legged man is king.' He was to turn out more like Cecil King, vainglorious and ignominiously sacked, but that was still six months down the line.

Thornton faced an awesome task. The industrial problems were terrible. Staff overmanning was bad enough, not just in the print areas but throughout the company, including editorial. Management was appallingly weak, in spite of tough words; strikes and stoppages were invariably settled rather than allowing lost production, which meant revenue gone for ever. But the surrender method of dealing with disputes was as bad, the company simply being screwed for more next time. On the Sunday papers, the situation was anarchic as a result of both union malpractice and management incompetence. At the end of the '70s, the *Mirror* had attempted to modernise the antiquated hot-metal system of producing newspapers by introducing full-page composition bought from an American company. It was a disaster on every front. The technology was intended for straight up and down column layouts used by American papers, not the tightly subbed and intricate layouts of British tabloids. The printers couldn't – or wouldn't – take to the skills required and, anyway, the computers were constantly on the blink. In the face of the unions' inevitable opposition, management immediately gave in over job losses but hammered out a productivity deal, an agreement that the printers produced more for the same money. That never materialised but then neither did the new technology. The *Sporting Life* was chosen as the guinea pig, a disastrous decision, as the technology suffered a comprehensive nervous breakdown when confronted with column after column of figures. For some reason nobody ever figured out, all the computer would set was John Wayne's obituary, which it did time and time again. The *Sporting Life* didn't appear for several days until full-page composition was finally abandoned and the papers reverted to 'cut and paste' where the computer produced the type and it was cut out and pasted on to the page by a compositor. This gave us the worst of all possible worlds.

The *People* expected to be at the wrong end of all this and was. We were a hybrid, half 'new technology' and half hot metal. This meant that on Saturday we got the dregs of the National Graphical Association's membership which was every bit as bad as you would expect it to be. It could often take six hours to make up the front page and then it was full of misprints, transposed lines and ill-fitting headlines. On more than one occasion the 'comp' in charge could not even speak English, never mind read it. If you complained, it was seen as victimisation and the paper was stopped for a mandatory chapel meeting. It was a nightmare of horrifying proportions from which one never woke. It is no wonder journalists became increasingly cynical and prepared to rip off the management themselves with inflated expenses and long lunches spent entertaining each other.

So Thornton had a problem. He had to clean all this up if he was going to have a hope of producing anything like an attractive prospectus for flotation. He tried being nice, he tried being tough and even nasty with the printers. No dice. At the same time, he was alienating both senior management and the journalists. Thornton had come from the important but unglamorous job of running the Abbey National, where the most exciting thing was answering thousands of letters received at the Baker Street office about Sherlock Holmes whose mythical home was where the building society headquarters stood. Holmes would have recognised instantly that Thornton suffered from an overdose of what James Whitaker describes as 'red carpet fever', a sweat of importance manifested by proximity to royalty, in Thornton's case the oxygen of publicity caused by being catapulted into such a high-profile job. While often justifiably attacking journalistic and managerial vanity about unnecessary expense, he would be quick to point out that he himself was humble enough to use his own ancient Jaguar. But he insisted that his driver wore a proper chauffeur's uniform and cap, the two suits he required cost £250 each and they were never worn. This was a needless expenditure, particularly from a man who was preaching good housekeeping.

But his greatest problem was that he was the wrong man for the job. He preached sobriety, reason, prudence and caution in an industry which had grown successful and powerful enough to threaten governments on drink, excess, daring, wild genius and low cunning. You can't be a ringmaster if you don't want acrobats, clowns, high-wire acts and dangerous animals in the show.

Nonetheless, much of what Thornton was saying was right, even if it was getting up everybody's nose. After less than four months in the job, he was caught between a rock and a hard place; he was respected neither by unions nor managers while both felt their Old Spanish Customs threatened. A strictly private and confidential note to the board summed up his dilemma:

> I have asked Lawrie Guest (finance director) to provide me with details of the expenses incurred up to the end of the fiscal year and I am appalled to find that the amount is £5 million. It is even more disappointing to learn that £1.348 million is attributable to business entertaining. On further checking this, I have been provided with a list of those people whose expenses currently exceed £8,000 and it is staggering to find that many who have recently had a review of salary which did not take into account the expenses factor are claiming what must be regarded as a considerable additional sum.
>
> I cannot continue to present a bleak picture to trade unions and ask for restraint against this background. I think we must, as a matter of extreme urgency, turn our minds to bringing about a substantial reduction in this item. My feeling is that in the current financial year this figure should be halved and I would like your advice as to how this is to be achieved.

Thornton went on to say that he was quite prepared to discuss the £8,000-plus cases at a board meeting but it 'seems this would be a source of embarrassment'. In other words, some board members were as guilty as anyone and I'm sure that didn't exclude editors. The problem was that expenses were built into the system by managements which had traditionally underpaid journalists while bundling out the cash to printers. The printers claimed they should have the cash because they didn't have the journalists' lavish expenses. It was a Fleet Street wide abuse, but the only paper aiming for flotation and, therefore, City scrutiny, was the *Mirror*. The City may have applauded his motives, but it wanted action, and the more Thornton talked of worker participation, share ownership, the new presses the papers desperately needed – particularly in Manchester where pictures looked as if they had been printed on blotting paper – plus a golden share to prevent any one owner taking over, the more it didn't like what it heard. All this made an already problematic flotation more difficult, and Reed, which had been looking for £90 million, had lowered its expectation to less than £50 million.

There was an even bigger poison pill. Our Manchester plant, antiquated and falling to pieces, was owned by Thomson's who decided to close it down. But because of an extraordinary agreement, all the redundancy payments would fall on the Mirror Group, so once again Thornton would be faced with the worst of all possible worlds.

Meanwhile, Jarratt and Reed Chief Executive Les Carpenter were becoming increasingly restless. It was clear Thornton's love of publicity and his failure to keep his mouth shut meant that the valuation of the float to Reed had nosedived. The atmosphere at Holborn Circus grew first of all sour and then outright rebellious as Doug Long became openly contemptuous of Thornton. Thornton, in turn, distrusted both him and Tony Miles, and believed his plans for the flotation were being leaked, quite possibly to Maxwell. I was the junior member of the board, a new editor and totally consumed by my job of running the *People*. I was also physically removed from the action by the Bridge of Sighs and was kept unaware, deliberately or not I do not know, of what was going on behind Thornton's back.

Anyway, whatever plots were being hatched I didn't want to be a part of them; I was having a fantastic time finding out what it was like to be an editor. My one contact with business reality, apart from boring and time-consuming Mirror Group board meetings, was the once-a-month lunch with Les Carpenter at Brown's Hotel off Piccadilly with the editors and Tony Miles. Carpenter always insisted he would never sell to Maxwell, he didn't trust him and, anyway, he was a '£50 million man', nothing like the £90 million Reed was looking to make from the float. But the decision wasn't Carpenter's or Jarratt's to make. By deciding on a flotation, the Reed pair had effectively put the *Mirror* into play whether they liked it or not, and their promises not to sell to one man weren't worth the paper they weren't written on. Maxwell may have been a £50 million man but he was one who did his homework. He knew that the Holborn building alone was worth £90 million, and in the end he paid only £113 million for the whole group, and that included the extremely profitable *Daily Record* and *Sunday Mail* in Scotland.

The last Mirror board meeting resembled the final knockings of Kerensky's provisional government before the Bolsheviks swept him away. The order Thornton so prized vanished, as futile attempts were made to concentrate minds on a flotation that was looking increasingly like a mirage. Maxwell's tanks – or at least his accountants – were camped out in the Ritz Hotel opposite Reed's headquarters, the Holborn building was a buzz of intrigue, rumour and treachery, but over the bridge I remained strangely detached. I was never taken into the confidence of Miles or Molloy, or of Bob Edwards of the *Sunday Mirror*, an old friend of Maxwell who would have no problem with him taking over.

A week before Maxwell finally bought the papers, Miles and Molloy went to see Neil Kinnock, a vain attempt to enlist the Labour leader's support in a last-ditch 'stop Maxwell' assault. It was a meeting, amazingly, suggested by Carpenter, who wanted a statement from the Labour leader opposing Maxwell's bid. But politicians are notoriously wary about that sort of thing; they know which side their bread is buttered, and the Labour leader wanted unstinting support if Maxwell did take over. He was sympathetic, but non-committal.

In spite of his trip to see Kinnock, Molloy was ambivalent about a proprietor. In a *Guardian* article, he pointed out that the *Mirror* had 'lacked the kind of autocratic player who can take his seat in the Fleet Street poker game'. This Maxwell saw as a green light from the Mirror Group's chief editor.

I decided to pin my colours to the mast.

In the six months I had been editing the *People*, we had published some good investigations, one of them was into the employment of Mark Thatcher who, according to Cementation, the company that employed him, had been vital in helping to build a new £300 million university in Oman. This deal had led to a row in the House of Commons over a select committee's refusal to investigate MPs' doubts about the relationship between the Prime Minister, her son and Cementation. We had been virulent in our attack on the Commons – shades of Reggie Maudling again here – and had demanded a proper inquiry. The *Observer* had been covering similar ground and when Maxwell was considering buying that paper, three months before he eventually bought the *Mirror*, he said he would have 'stamped on' the investigation. If Maxwell was to own us then he might as well know where I stood. So in the last paper printed before he bought the group I wrote a leader under the headline: WHOSE FREEDOM MR MAXWELL?

> When Robert Maxwell, the multi-millionaire publisher, was trying to buy the *Observer* in April, he made one complaint about the newspaper's editor. He objected to his coverage of Mark Thatcher's business dealings in Oman and said, I would have stamped on him for that. The *Observer* was not the only newspaper involved in that investigation. The *Sunday People* revealed several aspects of it, including the amount paid to the Prime Minister's son.
>
> Now Mr Maxwell is trying to buy the Mirror Group which includes the *Sunday People*.
>
> New stamping grounds perhaps?

On 11 July, two days before Maxwell bought us, Clive Thornton sent me this note: 'I thought your editorial on Sunday took the kind of courage that seems to be markedly lacking these days and I am grateful and applaud you for it.

'I am sure you know that if we do not succeed you might be joining me in the dole queue.'

It was a gracious note from a man who must by then have known his fate. But it did not take courage to write that leader, it is what editors must do if they believe in the staff who have the courage and ability to go out and dig out stories like that. Newspapers and their editors are nothing if they cannot stand up for what is right when it matters personally to them. You cannot ask others to stand up and be counted, whether they be Prime Ministers or England football managers, if you are not prepared to do the same.

As for the dole queue, I was about to find out.

11

Alex Jarratt couldn't bring himself to meet Maxwell to conclude the deal he promised would never happen. He presided over the Reed board meeting which bowed to the inevitable when it became clear Maxwell's offer was £40 million more than the Group would have made from a flotation, but he left it to Les Carpenter to hammer out the details of the deal with Maxwell over the road at the Ritz. Jarratt was too fastidious and refined for the rough, nasty world of newspapers and, even right at the end, Pilate-like, he washed his hands of the problem. The boos of 1973 at Cudlipp's farewell must have echoed in his ears, the audience may have been drunk, but its long-term vision was unimpaired. Cudlipp had turned to Reed to prevent a takeover of IPC and, in the end, he precipitated it because of Reed's failure to take on the trades unions. They weren't the only ones of course, Thomson did the same, presenting Rupert Murdoch with the *Times* and *Sunday Times*.

Carpenter completed the deal just before midnight on 12 July 1984, and shook hands with a man he didn't trust an inch. Maxwell proposed to pay for the Mirror Group with a banker's draft from the NatWest, but Carpenter refused to accept it, fearful that Maxwell would go straight to the Mirror, provoke a strike, and the deal would unravel. It was settled by Hill Samuel, Maxwell's merchant bankers, passing over a cheque to Reed's on the personal OK of Sir Robert Clark, Hill Samuel chairman. The deed was done, Reed had sold the Mirror Group to a man it did not like or trust, and a man with whom the company's two top executives had always sworn they would not do business. It was about as big a betrayal as it was possible to perpetrate and the reputations of neither Jarratt nor Carpenter ever fully recovered.

Maxwell's first act as the new owner of the Mirror Group was to break his word. He had promised Carpenter he would not go down to the Holborn Circus headquarters, but he did, arriving not long after midnight and heading straight for the ninth floor executive offices where Long, Miles and Molloy were waiting for him. Bob Edwards had been phoned personally by Maxwell and told to go to his headquarters in Worship Street, a drab part of the City nestling next to the East End and Liverpool Street station. Edwards did as he was bid and was picked up and taken to the Mirror by Maxwell's Rolls-Royce. He had already telephoned the company secretary and, on Maxwell's instructions, organised a board meeting for 1.30am, thus cutting out both Long and Miles. 'By 2.15am all but one of the directors had arrived from their beds and probably the only board meeting of Mirror Group Newspapers to be held at that hour began,' wrote Edwards in his autobiography.

The one missing director, and no doubt conspicuously so, was me. Nobody had phoned. Tony Miles was to claim later that he had tried but my phone was off the hook. It wasn't. His secondary explanation is probably more truthful; he thought that I might resign on the spot after that week's *People* leader and he didn't want me to over-react. I wouldn't have done, but the thought was nice.

I didn't meet Maxwell until lunch the next day when he took the editors and Miles to lunch at Claridge's. It was a lucky break because it gave me time to plan my strategy for the *People*. I had no doubt he would try and interfere, and I had even less doubt that he did not have an aptitude or feel for the editorial side of the business. By lunchtime I had decided what to do, and over an enormously inflated cheese souflée, in cruel contrast to the deflation felt round the table, I kept silent as Molloy and Edwards told Maxwell about the horrors of the print unions and the ineffective management of Reed and Thornton, who had already gone – petulantly and publicly tearing up a copy of the *Mirror* as he left. It was a fitting epitaph.

Eventually, Maxwell came round to me. He had been well briefed about the *People*'s recent run of successful stories – presumably by Derek Jameson, who was his public relations man at the time – and started, in what I was to discover was his usual way. 'Why so silent, mister? What have you to say?'

So I started distancing myself from the two Mirror titles. The *People* was an investigative newspaper, that is why I was so disturbed by his comments about the *Observer*. We must be allowed to get on with our own stories and, as long as they were fair and accurate, we should not be inhibited by worrying about internal pressures.

Maxwell's reply was immediate. 'Your case is completely different to the *Observer*'s. I have no problems with your enquiries into Mark Thatcher, they were very good. You must continue to do what you think fit, you have my absolute backing.'

You couldn't ask fairer than that, even if it was obvious that he had no idea what our investigations into Mark Thatcher had been and that they were not in any way different in approach to that of the *Observer*. I pressed home the point that the *People* was not only different to the two *Mirrors*, but should be seen to be. This, I hoped, would mean that he would deal with us at arm's length, which is more or less what happened.

At Claridge's, however, Maxwell's reputation had preceeded him. As we headed for the cars at the end of his champagne welcome, the hotel manager scuttled after us. 'Mr Maxwell, Mr Maxwell come back, you haven't paid,' he cried. Maxwell waved him away telling him to send the bill to the office. 'You always say that and you never pay, you must pay now,' insisted the manager wringing his hands. Eventually Maxwell coughed up. It was a valuable lesson in how to deal with him in the future.

The first test of my alienation strategy came immediately, with Maxwell's statement of intent published all over the *Mirror*'s front page the next day under the headline Forward with Britain. Mike Molloy had suggested to Maxwell that the *Mirror* should reintroduce its famous slogan 'Forward with the People', but Maxwell had changed it to 'Forward with Britain', as bland an aspiration as the original, but lacking the Socialist conviction. Maxwell wanted his piece, written by the soon-to-be ousted political editor Terence Lancaster, to be all over the front pages of both Sundays, too. He had quickly got a taste for the grandiose pose and front-page picture, but I played my semi-detached card and convinced him it should go on page two. The price I paid was a secondary piece exhorting *People* readers to tell us of good works 'in this smashing country of ours', stories of ingenuity and selflessness that new newspaper bosses always like, but more cynical hands always dread. You get a few genuine cases to start with but they rapidly tale off into a dribble of bores, nutcases and self-publicists. Nonetheless, it was a small price to pay for a significant victory.

Maxwell had arrived at the Mirror with little good will inside but a great deal outside. From the heart of the military establishment came this salute from Major General Trythall, managing director of Brassey's, the defence publishers: 'Your success in the battles to obtain a major national newspaper appear to owe at least something to the application by you to the principles of war – particularly mobility, concentration of force, offensive action and maintenance of the objective.' From a pillar of City respectability, Aubrey Jones, a former chairman of the Prices and Incomes Board, came a letter expressing his delight and congratulations and his pleasure 'that you outwitted the shuffling Jarratt'. And the budding pornographer Richard Desmond's admiration went beyond the pull of gravity. He wrote a fulsome letter congratulating Maxwell on his achievement for which he said he had 'the greatest admiration'. He felt sure that the Mirror was the perfect forum for him to further his success 'You must indeed be very proud and elated by this major coup and I am sure the synergy that your new company will have to offer will reap even greater rewards in due course. Who is going to be the first communications company on the moon?' he wondered ...

A more down-to-earth view, and one many shared, was expressed by the Prime Minister, 'A dose of Maxwell will do you good,' Mrs Thatcher told the *Mirror*'s Julia Langdon.

There was no doubt that the trades union anarchy needed to be sorted out. No less than 13 unions and 52 FoCs squabbled with management and among themselves. We had double the employees we needed, casual staffing and payment was out of control – managers had no idea who was employed on Saturday shifts and frequently 'workers' would clock on in the name of Mickey Mouse and go and work somewhere else, or even do a shift as a cab driver. For us on the *People*, it was a scenario from hell, made worse by the Father of the Chapel being a regular employee on the *Sun*, who worked on the *People* for no more than two days a week. This time was spent almost exclusively on union business which meant much of his resources were spent on reducing hours, increasing pay or bringing in more people than we had already. If he couldn't get that, he organised a strike. For this, we paid him £400 a week.

When Maxwell arrived, the unions were presented with a stark choice – either to engineer a dispute and face him out with a long strike or sit back and see what happened. They opted for the latter, and throughout 1984 the papers enjoyed a comparatively industrial action-free period. There was some fly posting in the lifts warning us about Maxwell being after our pensions, but few took much notice.

The phoney peace with the print unions was a mixed blessing, as Maxwell turned his interest on the content of the papers which, unfortunately, included large chunks of self-publicity. It started with the launch of a new game – Bingo by any other name – called Who Dares Wins. Maxwell had called in the group's two advertising agencies, Young and Rubicam, and Grey, for a presentation on potential games at Headington Hill Hall, his Oxford home and headquarters of Pergamon Press. Whatever spiel they came up with we knew it was going to be a version of Bingo, so it was interesting to see what glitter and gloss they could put on it. The contest was won hands down by Y and R's boss

John Banks, who produced a masterstroke of vanity stoking in a private aside to Maxwell which I earwigged. 'There is only one thing people think about when you say Mirror Group now, Bob,' began Banks in an urgent whisper. 'It's you. I know this might sound ridiculous, but you are the biggest celebrity around, you should be fronting this game. That is why we are calling it Who Dares Wins. You have dared and you have won. It is the personal guarantee of the Publisher and his personal imprint which will sell this big time. I urge you to do it Bob, you are the man to lead this campaign. Quite honestly nobody else can do it, you are the unique selling point here.'

Banks was the first, but certainly not the last, to discover the joys available from the cunning use of constructive brown nosing, an art form that was to be taken to new heights by a succession of senior managers and trade union leaders during Maxwell's ownership of the papers, usually when it involved some form of pay or promotional prospects. It goes something like this: 'Now, I'm telling you this straight, Bob, and anyone will tell you I'm a straight-up guy who doesn't take shit from any bugger and that includes you, but I'm telling you to your face because that is the way I deal ... you're a bastard, Bob, but you are a fair bastard, who is the best thing that has happened to this business in a long time. Right, I've said it, do what you like, fire me if you want, but I've got it off my chest and I don't care who knows it.'

Banks's proposals were met with nods and then a beaming smile from Maxwell. 'I have come to the conclusion you are right,' he said, announcing to the assembled meeting that 'Mr Banks has come up with a winning suggestion'. Indeed, nobody could match it and poor Grey, which had, in fact, come up with the better mechanic for the game, lost out completely – Who Dares Wins, the Win a Million game, as it was slugged – was put all over the papers. None of us could avoid the front-page treatment and for a week it sold a massive amount of extra copies, feeding Maxwell's vanity and sense of unconquerable public popularity. The first sign of this was when he had the print run of the Who Dares Wins cards stopped because, he said, they were folded the wrong way; his picture was on the inside and he wanted it on the front. The extra cost was fearful. Banks's brainchild did well for Y and R, but had dealt a blow to the Mirror Group of hideous proportions. Maxwell was off on his ego trip, helped by the good wishes of many who might have been expected to know better, including Hugh Cudlipp, who wrote to him saying that until he took over, reading the *Mirror* was 'like shaking hands with an empty glove'. Maxwell loved that, and

Cudlipp's blessing gave him the licence he was looking for to interfere in the editorial content of the paper. Maxwell really believed he was blessed with journalistic flair.

For Mike Molloy, Cudlipp's ill-considered letter turned a difficult situation into an impossible one. Each editor had his own way of dealing with Maxwell. Mike took the view that, as owner, Bob had a right to do whatever he wished, he could advise but, in the end, he either had to put up, shut up or get out. He was also more sanguine than I was about having a proprietor appearing so often in the paper. He thought it a good thing that the *Mirror* was being talked about and being noticed with an owner who was prepared to pump so much cash into it. Mike had been editing for almost a decade by this time and he was hardly in his first flush of enthusiasm, there had been too many false dawns for that, and like so many he had been worn down by the omnipotence of the trades unions. He did little to oppose Maxwell's meddling, instead he took refuge in writing crime novels, shutting himself away in his office often for hours on end. Tony Miles went soon after Maxwell arrived; there was no point in him being there, caught without power between Maxwell's non-stop involvement with the *Mirror* and Bob Edwards fast consolidating his role as editorial adviser, a position that was formalised with Edwards being made 'Senior Group Editor', an odd title for an odd job.

Edwards was an accomplished, intelligent and humane editor who had a fatal flaw – he loved powerful proprietors and was in awe of them. His first love was Beaverbrook and he saw much of the Old Man in Maxwell, a view those of us who never knew Beaverbrook found hard to justify. At the start Edwards genuinely believed Maxwell could be a force for good at the *Mirror*, a view no doubt encouraged by the fact that he himself would certainly take Tony Miles's job. Over the next two years, he was to be reduced almost to incoherence, often changing his views in mid-sentence if, as he frequently did, Maxwell interrupted him to put a counter point. He ran Edwards ragged and it was embarrassing to see a man in late middle-age with a distinguished record behind him being treated in this way.

One Friday evening there was a crisis in the *Daily Mirror* because for some reason now lost in the mists of time, Maxwell had decided he didn't like crime 'backgrounders' – big crime projections run at the end of particularly notorious trials – and Molloy had pulled several pages inevitably causing immense production difficulties. We also had planned a big background for Sunday, so I decided to have the row with Maxwell sooner rather than later. I found him drinking champagne and eating dinner with

Molloy and Edwards, which annoyed me, so I waded straight in, refusing to eat and drink with them. I told him that I intended running all our stuff, that it was right for us, but Maxwell insisted he was right and I was wrong.

'Nobody wants that kind of stuff any more,' he said.

'If I knew exactly what people wanted I would be the biggest genius newspapers ever knew Bob,' I replied. 'But this is good stuff and I'm going to run it.'

Maxwell looked thunderous, but the tension was broken by a phonecall. While he took it, Bob Edwards turned to me and muttered, 'A bit of advice ... you have done well, but now let him have his way. It's the best thing, believe me.'

But I wasn't in a mood for compromise and refused to back down. For a moment, Maxwell stared hard at me and then said, 'You are the editor, have it your way, but I'm right.'

He wasn't, and everyone round the table must have known it, but not only had Mike and Bob Edwards gone along with it, in my view they had become active participants by sitting down and drinking champagne at his table while the paper was being torn to pieces six floors below. This was consolidated by their support for Maxwell's ill-conceived High Court action for contempt of court against Kelvin MacKenzie over a bought-in book by Peter Bogdanovich about the death of a *Playboy* bunny which the *Sun* decided to rip off in time-honoured Fleet Street tradition. But Maxwell and the *Mirror*'s unctuous, self-righteous tone grated on everyone – including the judge who decided there hadn't been any contempt. The *Mirror*'s humiliation was compounded by Maxwell, Edwards and Molloy being pictured leaving the court after their defeat in a white convertible Bentley, not the best image for the paper that champions the working man. It was a low-point in the paper's fortunes. Maxwell had owned the *Mirror* for just ten months and it was now a laughing stock. Three years earlier it had been voted Newspaper of the Year.

Everything was going wrong. Circulation plunged as he appeared more and more in the paper. His mission to save Ethiopia from famine – we all got lumbered with that on the front page; my alienation strategy didn't work – was a toe-curling embarrassment. But, mercifully, I avoided the triumphant picture of his arrival which showed quite clearly that he had pissed down his trousers. He also led an abortive mission to end the miners' strike. There were endless pictures of him doing something or other irrelevant, and frequent reports of meetings with world leaders were destroying the paper. Even worse was his decision to take a train around the country to find out what people thought, accompanied by all the ballyhoo the *Mirror* could muster and a trail of shamefaced writers who showed all too clearly they would prefer to be somewhere else. What he did discover was that not many people cared, and huge halls rarely catered for more than 20 people. All this was made infinitely worse by an extraordinary new design that was introduced into the *Mirror* which dictated that no headline should be wider than three columns, the antithesis of what mass, brash tabloids should be about. This was accompanied by local pages not just for regions, but for cities, which somehow had to be filled, usually with the most excruciating garbage. No part of the paper was sacrosanct on this, not even the pop column then run by John Blake. He was so short of stuff that on one memorable occasion he was reduced to reporting that a nightclub in Bristol had changed its sofas.

Molloy retreated more and more into his office to write his books. Following his empty glove letter, Cudlipp had been brought back on board. When the editors were asked their views, Miles, Molloy and Edwards all agreed that he should be asked to return as a consultant. I voted against on the grounds that he was too old and, anyway, he had abandoned the Labour Party for the SDP.

I said earlier that I was lucky to be over the bridge and largely out of mind. The policy of divorcing myself from the two *Mirrors* was working reasonably well, although I had failed to prevent the page-one nonsense of Who Dares Wins, which, although Bingo in a different guise, was not seen as such by the readers, particularly when nobody appeared to win the £1 million. After an initial huge jump in sales, public interest had rapidly declined, not least because the *Sun* had quickly matched the £1 million in prize money but had also paid out. Maxwell had handled everything himself and it had all turned to dust. He announced the £1 million prize at a press conference in the fond but ludicrous belief that rival newspapers would not take the piss or use it to launch their counter bid. The *Sun* did both.

In his book on Maxwell, Joe Haines remembers a conversation he had with Bob Edwards when he suggested that the press conference was a disastrous decision. 'Really?' replied Edwards, 'Bob Maxwell and I and Bob Head took it.'

'It was a dreadful mistake,' said Joe.

'What do you think I should do about it?' said Edwards.

'You should tell him you made a mistake.'

'Oh I can't do that,' replied Bob, clearly fearful of the reaction. 'I know, I'll tell him that you think he has made a mistake.'

Maxwell had to agree to a £1 million winner or face humiliating ridicule. You can produce a winner easily by triggering key numbers and this the *Mirror* did shortly before the Labour party conference in Blackpool. The lucky winner was an elderly widow called Maudie Barrett who, apart from having an enormous family, also had a dog called Thumper. Thumper accompanied Maudie everywhere, including Blackpool, whence he travelled courtesy of Kent Gavin's brand-new Jaguar with beautiful leather seats. Gavin was not best pleased, particularly as Maudie developed car sickness and he was forced to stop and get her out, prompting an agonising phonecall to his partner Gloria with the immortal words, 'Ere Glor, what the 'ell do I do? She's abaht to Ralph on me doeskin.'

Thumper had an even more torrid time. Paul Callan trod on his paw at the Imperial Hotel. Thumper was not the first to be sent off limping after a party conference encounter with Callan. To make matters worse, at the cheque presentation in Blackpool's town hall, Marje sat down not knowing that Thumper's rear end was already occupying part of the seat. As she did so, she pinioned him, but as neither could move, the squeals of Thumper and the protestations of Marje held up the ceremony for several minutes. His fate was no more ignominious than ours, forced to travel in an open-topped bus along the Prom with the jeers and catcalls of Fleet Street colleagues whistling in our ears. At least Thumper got his revenge on Marje. As she tried to negotiate the swing doors at the Imperial, Denis Healey came through them at pace from the opposite direction, catapulting Marje out on to the pavement.

Although I had taken a few knocks with my policy of keeping the *People* and myself out of the way as much as possible, it hadn't worked too badly. We had avoided the worst excesses and humiliations. The circulation gap between the *People* and the *Sunday Mirror* had reduced considerably and we were generally considered to be pretty good. The staff certainly produced some great stories, two of which were to have lasting effect and were tributes to the finest traditions of tabloid Sunday paper reporting. The first was a system of illegal cash payments made to Lester Piggott. The exposure of these payments was the first crack in the Piggott financial scandal which was eventually to lead him to jail for failure to disclose secret cash deals to the taxman. This report was run in the face of enormous opposition from the racing establishment because it was, as one racehorse owner said, 'the tip of the iceberg'.

The second was an even more remarkable piece of painstaking journalism by the *People*'s chief reporter Fred Harrison. Over a period of eight months, Fred had been making visits to moors murderer Ian Brady in the isolation block at Gartree Prison. Over packets of Gauloises cigarettes, Brady told Harrison about his life in jail, his feelings – or lack of them – for Myra Hindley and eventually what Fred had come for and what nobody else had been able to get out of him, his admission to the murders of Pauline Reade and Keith Bennett. This led to Brady being taken back to the moors and the eventual discovery of Pauline Reade's body. Brady claimed to Harrison he had done other murders – 'of course, there were many more deaths,' he said. This was tabloid journalism at its best, skilled, patient and sensational.

So was our investigation into the legacy of the Christmas Island nuclear tests in the 1950s. The *People*'s Alan Rimmer produced a catalogue of cases where not only had the national servicemen who witnessed the tests contracted cancers and leukaemia, but more than 100 of their children had been born deformed or were suffering from debilitating disease. The Government refused to admit any responsibility for this and still does, in spite of overwhelming evidence to the contrary. More than 15 years after we first revealed this scandal, and half-a-century after the tests, it remains unfinished business. The Labour Party, which in opposition promised a full-scale inquiry into the after-effects of the explosions, turned its back on the scandal and the suffering as soon as it came to power. Britain is now the only country which took part in the tests to have done nothing about their veterans and it remains a vivid stain on the record of successive administrations.

No editor could ask for more challenging and vital exclusives from his staff, but we remained undercapitalised, with no colour magazine and damaged by a newly-invigorated tabloid *News of the World*. We were consistently undervalued as a newspaper, yet we were doing a lot better than most pundits expected and we were, by general acclaim, the paper other news editors picked up first on Saturday nights, the ultimate accolade.

By mid-1985, the uneasy industrial peace was beginning to collapse; so was the circulation of the *Daily Mirror*. When Maxwell arrived in July the previous year, circulation stood at 3,547,247, but this had been artificially inflated to encourage the flotation. Who Dares Wins had swollen it to 3,683,746 by the end of October, but the increase fell away quickly and by the time the *Mirror* was into its witches brew of too much Maxwell, too little news, daft layouts and regional pages to make a local freesheet blush, the figures were plunging. So was morale, as the *Mirror* became the whipping boy of Fleet Street.

By July '85, one year after Maxwell took over, the circulation was down to 3,102,427, a loss of almost 450,000 copies a day. Maxwell's bankers were getting restless: What was he going to do about the unions and overmanning? He had failed with his editorial initiatives, when was he going to start making the hard yards and take on the unions? It was a good question and one he couldn't put off much longer, but neither could he do it while his flagship remained in the mess he had largely created.

On the evening of Cup Final day in May 1985, I was in the office waiting for the paper to come up. It was a week after the Bradford football ground fire in which 52 people died. Maxwell and I had a minor bust-up that night, because he wanted to put Oxford United's promotion to the first division – he owned the club – on page one. The *People* sponsored Oxford and it was a great achievement, but there was no possible way that story could be anywhere near the front with such a disaster dominating the news. It would have to take its chances, I told him.

He rang off in a huff, but nothing mega, and at the regular Tuesday lunch with the editors I escaped unscathed. Even Maxwell had recognised the enormity of the tragedy and anyway, he was now busy getting himself into the *Daily Mirror* by organising medical aid. On the Saturday he went to the Cup Final, and when he returned to the office he asked me to go and see him. This was unusual so I packed my usual grumpy bits – it was always worthwhile having something to complain about if the conversation took a turn for the worse – and headed for the ninth floor and a large Scotch. After a while, Maxwell asked me out of the blue what I thought about the *Daily Mirror* and, more specifically about Mike's editorship. I told him I did not like the new layouts and that I wasn't going to talk about fellow editors on the group. I wouldn't like them talking about me behind my back and I wasn't going to talk behind theirs. Maxwell said he wasn't happy with the *Mirror* and mentioned a few pieces, the majority of which I knew he had inspired. He had obviously been talking to someone who did know about newspapers, and who had read his fortune without fear or favour. Good for him – or her – whoever they were.

The next week, I went to see Mike in his office, something I rarely did now because the *Mirror* had become embarrassingly bad. He must have been going through agonies, caught at the centre of a web of old men, Edwards, Cudlipp and Maxwell. He was in the middle of writing one of his books. I was blunt. 'The knives are out for you, Mike,' I said. 'This isn't gossip, I know it. I am sure Maxwell is thinking of getting you out, you must do something about it.'

Mike seemed unperturbed. He was OK, he said. Maxwell was happy with the way things were going. He was getting what he wanted, he thought the paper was doing well.

But what about you ... are you happy with it?' I asked.

Mike wouldn't be drawn; everything was OK and so was he. I think he had so far withdrawn that he wasn't even admitting the truth to himself. He had been editing now for ten years and that is really enough for anyone. It was the cruellest of fates to be lumbered with Maxwell at the end of what had for some years been a fine editorship. He had relied on Maxwell being an ogre, but a talented and reasoned ogre, and it had not turned out that way. Everything Mike had stood for had been ground into the dirt and much of it he had accepted with hardly a whimper. It was a tragedy of Greek proportions that was threatening to engulf the *Mirror* itself. Lloyd Turner's *Star* was making inroads into both circulation and staff, while over the other side of Fleet Street MacKenzie's raucous cackle of delight could be heard in every wine vault and printing hall by those with stomach enough to listen. The *Mirror* staff was openly contemptuous of their paper which Maxwell had reduced to rubble.

Towards the end of July, I was attending a farewell party for a reporter who was going to the United States, when the phone rang in the pub. It was Maxwell. Could I 'pop up' and see him?

He was in magisterial mood. 'I have decided it is time for a change of editorship at the *Daily Mirror*, and I am minded to put you on the shortlist. What do you think?'

I didn't think. 'I have no intention of going on any shortlist, Bob. Everyone round here, including you, knows what I've done, what kind of paper I run and what I did before during my time at the *Mirror*. You can make your mind up from that. If you are offering me the editorship of the *Mirror*, that is a different matter, as long as I do edit it.'

Maxwell went quiet, then said, 'Right, I am offering you the editorship of the *Mirror*, do you accept?'

'Yes,' I replied, then added, 'But I want to put down on paper what my thoughts and feelings are. If you agree with them, fine; if you don't, then you will have to find someone else.'

He nodded and that was it, I went back to the party.

During the next month, I thought long and hard about the *Mirror*; not just how I would change it but how it would change me. I was under no illusions about Maxwell, I did not think I could change him and I knew he would probe for my weak spots and exploit them mercilessly for his own ends if he found them. I knew, too, that the pressure, much of it unpleasant, would be turned not only on me but on Penny and the children.

The task was daunting: a newspaper with a smashed morale, plunging circulation and reputation all but destroyed by a proprietor who had become a figure of fun for those lucky enough not to work for him, and a tyrant for those who did. I was well aware of all this and I was aware, too, of how I had managed to avoid much of it by being on the far side of the bridge. On the other hand, the *Mirror* was my paper as much as his, I had put 17 years of my life into it and I believed in all the best things it stood for. I was proud of both the *Mirror* and what it had allowed me to do and I hated the way it had been traduced. If I walked away, I would be walking away from the challenge of both bringing the paper I loved back into the real world again and facing up to Maxwell. I wasn't sure I was up to either, but I knew that I would regret it for the rest of my life if I turned my back.

I took the family down to Plymouth to stay with old friends, Dick and Penny Page. Dick runs a general practice at Yealmpton close to the beautiful River Yealm and the old smugglers' cove of Newton Ferrers. It was a suitably conspiratorial place to work on new dummies for the paper. Dick and Penny were the only people apart from my Penny who knew what was happening. Dick's a good GP; he can keep a secret.

Much has been written about what I did or did not say to Maxwell about keeping him out of the paper. According to Bob Edwards, I said that page two was his but the rest of the paper was a no-go area. Maybe I did, but I wasn't even prepared to surrender page two; it would have been the thin edge of the wedge. What I did was to compose a memo which was typed in the patchy secrecy of my office at the *People* by Gill Hemburrow, the secretary who was to stay with me throughout my *Mirror* executive career and the sort of person I could – and often did – trust with my professional life. Gill managed to keep it secret in spite of scores of trained eyes trying to find out what she was doing. The trickiest part was addressing the problem of Maxwell's involvement in the *Mirror* but it had to be done, so, after itemising the details of changes I would bring in, I went on:

> Those were the particulars. But they will mean nothing unless they can be forged together to produce a pugnacious, highly charged tabloid that pumps iron on every page. That is my job and no one else's. I stand or fall by my ability not only to create the paper, but

also the atmosphere whereby it is not just possible, but second nature. To do that, I have to have the confidence of the staff and they have to know that the editor has the complete confidence of the publisher.

I said to you when we discussed my appointment last month that full control was essential and that the job could not be done without it. It is very important for you to realise that this is not because of some pompous journalistic article of faith, but because a newspaper cannot work in any other way. Only one person can be in charge of the paper's editorial content, either publisher or editor, but not both. One of the main reasons for the attack on the Mirror's *credibility and morale over the past few months has been the alarm created by what many people inside and outside Fleet Street interpret as confusion over the two roles.*

Finally, I outlined my view of what the fundamentals of the *Mirror* are:

Caring, championing the weak, passionate, fearless exposure of injustice and over-privilege, uncompromisingly left of centre. We must inject fun, cheek and the irreverence of youth. In short, we should be glad to be alive.

We care for everyone and are frightened of nobody, we are prepared to laugh at everything and anything, to weep and not be afraid to show it, to shout with glee and not care who hears it. We should court the sensational revelation and never apologise for it.

Maxwell accepted all this without demur; I heard nothing from him for a week, and edited what turned out to be my last edition of the *People* from Manchester, because industrial strife had once again broken out in London. Manchester followed suit so we had no paper. It was a sad anti-climactic end to a wonderful 18 months, where a staff dismissed on the *Mirror* side of the bridge as being loony, sozzled, second-rate and out-of-date had produced a newspaper of high quality week after week. They had taught me a great deal more than I had taught them.

At the beginning of the TUC Annual Conference in Blackpool, Maxwell decided to announce the change of editorship, making Mike editor-in-chief and Bob Edwards deputy chairman. Naturally, he didn't tell me of his plans until I received a panic phonecall asking where I was. Eventually I made it and Maxwell took me into his bathroom to tell me he had spoken to Mike, and what I should do now is sack all the executives.

'I don't think so, Bob,' I said.

'They must all resign, so you can appoint whom you like,' he said, sitting down heavily on the lavatory.

'No, Bob, it would be a disaster and send quite the wrong message. It's my throne and you're sitting on it already, even in here,' I insisted, pointing at him perched on the lav. He laughed, got up and clapped me hard on the back.

I had just signed up for the biggest Big Dipper ride of them all, and it wasn't going to be on the Golden Mile.

12

The first thing you noticed about Robert Maxwell was the smell. It came from his hair, not the jet-black dye but the bay rum he used to oil it. Then there was the sheer size of him – enormous body, of course, but a huge head too, with small, even teeth. Small, almost dainty feet and green-brown eyes, fierce and primeval. When angry, they would narrow with threatened violence. His voice was deep, and could move from persuasion to threat in less than a sentence, usually accompanied by a chopping motion of his arm being brought down hard on the desk. It was the emperor's sign that discussion was at an end. But it was the raw power he exerted, the ability to kill and the knowledge that he would use it without thinking twice, just as he had done during the war, that made him disturbing. His language was coarse and littered with swear words and, when in full fury, he didn't care who took the blast. The only way to deal with him was with absolute candour, look him unblinking in the eye – he would always try and stare you out – and not be scared. Such honesty, you knew, he would repay with obsessive secrecy, lies, and if necessary, the firing squad. It wasn't easy to psych yourself up to it every single time but you had to, he could smell a rabbit instinctively and took full advantage of it. The world is now littered with those who claim to have stood up to Maxwell but, in my experience, those who did, either in the boardroom or on the editorial floor, can be numbered on the fingers of one hand and few of them survived.

All those who fought him did it in their own way; mine was to dance round the ring attempting to wrong-foot him, either with jokes, keeping my distance from him where possible, or occasionally flat refusals to do what he wanted, and always telling him the truth, whether he liked it or not. He would lumber round the ring after me and frequently land some heavy punches. But the distant memory of the remnants of Gordon Hazell's old boxing ring technique came in useful: never get caught on the ropes; if you do, turn your opponent by catching him off balance. If you take a big punch go down, clear your head and come back punching – he won't expect that – always look him in the eyes and always do the unexpected. I may have gone down, but I did not go out. He was not, as some fondly supposed, the kind of man who appreciated people standing up to him. He didn't like it at all, but he was prepared to accept that my loyalties were entirely to the *Daily Mirror* and everything I did was intended to make it better, more successful and, once again, make it win the respect of its rivals.

Maxwell's personality was a mass of constantly opposing forces, tangled from his birth in Solotvino at the centre of the bitterly poor area of Ruthenia, which has variously been in Hungary, Czechoslovakia, Poland, Romania and the Soviet Union. He was born into a large, superstitious Jewish family when the town was in Czechoslovakia and was forced to write right-handed with his natural left tied behind his back. Being left-handed was believed to be a sign that you belonged to the devil. His writing was illegible and he remained deeply ashamed of it until his dying day. The majority of his family were murdered in Hitler's concentration camps and, depending on which story you believe, he somehow made his way to France where he joined the Czech forces fighting there. He was eventually evacuated on a British destroyer and landed in Liverpool in July 1940 with, he insisted, a rifle in his hand. 'I was not a refugee.' Whatever happened to Maxwell in the first 17 years of his life – and much of that is still shrouded in mystery – only half of it needs to be true for it to have been deeply traumatising for a boy cast out into a world at war with no family or friends. It must have coloured the rest of his life and inevitably led to a philosophy where looking after his own interests against all-comers and all pressures was his only and all-consuming concern. Everything else had its place, including family, but he remained obsessed by self. He was generous but never kind; far-sighted but, on occasions, blind stupid, cunningly subtle yet numbingly unpleasant. Unhappy, lonely, terrified of boredom, constantly wining and dining the great and the good of the world but never truly liking or trusting anyone. Nervous, uncertain and insecure, which he dealt with by being decisive to the extent of lunatic folly, secure in the belief of his own infallibility even when presented with incontrovertible evidence to the contrary, and charging through people and events like a demented rhino. He could have had all the money he ever wanted, but he threw it away, quite literally, sometimes on the gambling tables. He had a deep-seated fear of being left alone with nothing but himself for company, and he would go to the ends of the earth, usually by telephone but later by helicopter and yacht, to avoid it. He surrounded himself with the trappings of the multi-millionaire but he wiped his bottom on bathroom towels and dropped them on the floor for his staff to pick up. He pretended to watch his diet, but his ballooning weight belied it. Often in the night he would raid the enormous kitchen he had in his penthouse flat next door to the *Mirror* and in the morning the kitchen staff would open the door to a mass of empty packets and tins and food littered all over the floor.

His manners and habits had not come far from the poverty of the village he was brought up in, yet he powdered his face, used mascara on his eyebrows and dyed his hair. He claimed to be humble, but he was vain and remained convinced of his attraction to women as if he still possessed the filmstar looks of his wartime years. He was contemptuous of the City financial establishments yet relied on them to an unhealthy and eventually fatal degree. He was, in every meaning of the word, a monster, untameable, dangerous, unpredictable, with power over all he surveyed, and he revelled in it. Most of those who had their heads snapped off were those who went too close in the belief that they had a 'special relationship' with him, something he encouraged the unwary to believe. The opposing forces deep within tore him apart and his instinctive reaction was to tear apart everything around him. His effect on the Mirror Group, so long feather-bedded in every department, was devastating.

Why, then, work for him at all? The answer was, I considered myself to be working for the *Mirror*, not for Maxwell. I believed in what the *Mirror* stood for – social justice, decent and honest standards in public life and the rights for people with small voices to be heard loud and clear. The *Mirror* believed in, and campaigned for, better schools and hospitals, and remained steadfast to the Labour Party when all about it were deserting. We did that because we believed our principles were our currency as a newspaper, and the readers appreciated us for it. In the years that followed, it was to be the rock on which the *Mirror*'s foundations remained intact, in spite of the horrors waiting in the wings. This strength had been built by two generations of journalists and I was proud to be a torchbearer of the third. Maxwell had not built its greatness, its circulation or its success. Nor was he a natural newspaperman, although he did possess the journalist's sense of mischief and piracy, which other newcomers like Lords Stevens and Hollick did not. I really did think it was more my paper than his, that I had put more into it than him and I knew more than he ever could about how to rescue it from the editorial mayhem he had created in such a short time. This may have been arrogant or naïve, but without a fierce self-belief there was no chance of success.

The first thing I did was to tell all the executives that if Maxwell came on to them then they should tell me immediately. If anybody had to face him up then it would be me. He had the habit of phoning anyone on the paper, a practice known as 'being Captained', that destabilised departments and reduced the authority of the editor. No doubt that was one of the reasons he did it.

For the first few weeks all went well, even though he had insisted on being in on negotiations with Sara Keays over the serialisation of her book detailing the affair with Cecil Parkinson, the birth of their daughter, Cecil's promise of marriage, subsequent jilting and his return to the bosom of his first family. It was great stuff and just the thing to start off a new editorship, particularly as it would be published during the Tory Party Conference, so I wasn't complaining. Anyway, Sara Keays wasn't easy and liked the idea of dealing with Maxwell.

She had a reputation for being difficult; not surprising considering the traumas she had been through and, in spite of Maxwell's claims that he had sorted her out, the deal was still far from clinched when I went down to her home near Bath, together with the *Mirror* lawyer Hugh Corrie and Joe Haines. She was wary of journalists waving big cheques, but I had what I reckoned was a hidden weapon – the Old School Tie. Sara Keays had been at Clifton High School just up the road from Clifton College and would have been there at the same time as me, although somewhat younger. That meant she would have been there with the wonderful Caroline. I asked her if she remembered her. 'Oh yes,' she said. 'Wasn't she involved with someone from the school ... a bit of a scandal I think?' She was indeed, I nodded. You're looking at him. From then on, there was no turning back.

The first test of my concordat with Maxwell was bound to come – I had not carried out one of the reforms I had promised. He said: 'Don't piss me about, mister. I've let you get on with the job and you must do it.'

He was right, I hadn't; it was to do with the relocation of the leader column and I had changed my mind, which is what I told him. No changes of mind, he said. Oh yes, if the ideas are better, I replied, by this time in his office with a layout pad, pencil and Stanley knife which, inadvertently, I was waving in his face.

'Put that down or you will slash me,' he said. 'You are mad, go away before you do me damage.'

A hasty retreat; round one to the Stanley knife.

For the next six months, Maxwell was taken up with the *Mirror* 'Survival Plan' – big redundancies in every department. Nobody could justly complain they were unfair; we were overstaffed and overunionised. Mrs T was right there, a dose of Maxwell would do us good. We desperately needed new presses and Maxwell was determined to bring in colour, but the cost would be in excess of £300 million. To finance that, we had to show we were capable of putting our own house in order and this, unlike editorial interference, was something he knew about.

In a statement about the *Mirror*'s future – issued at the same time as I was made editor – his words were prophetic: 'Fleet Street is facing a revolution in work. Not some time in the distant future but within the next 18 months to two years at the most. Those who understand that are those who will prosper. Those who turn their face away will lose.'

The task was enormous. There were 52 chapels in the *Mirror* and job losses were to be across the board, 1,600 in all from a staff of 6,000.

Rupert Murdoch is today credited with leading the Fleet Street revolution. But it was Maxwell who set it in train. He was using all the weight afforded him by the courts, new trade union legislation and the fact that he had bought the group cheap which made his claim – that he could shut the papers and still make a whopping profit – credible. By the end of the year he had achieved a notable first: printing and getting out 28,000 copies of the *Mirror* during an official strike. Not much, but a foothold on the slippery mountain of industrial anarchy that loomed over Fleet Street. As a new editor I was only vaguely aware of what he was trying to do. I was more concerned about the lack of papers, for every day we could not print we lost more readers, and that was something we could not afford.

Mirror morale, particularly among executives, was on the floor. Most of them had been hounded by Maxwell who kept them constantly in fear of their mortgage. There was no confidence among the senior staff, who had started to try and second-guess what he would want, a disastrous course. Worse, they felt defeated and demeaned and saw no way of curbing his influence in the newspaper. There was no self-respect or respect for the paper they were creating.

My return to the newsroom after 18 months was like entering a journalistic Belsen, with staff cowering in their own little corners and one department literally cutting itself off from the rest of the paper. Maxwell's preoccupation with the *Mirror*'s industrial relations meant he had less time for grandstanding in the paper, although we did have to swallow chunks of anti-union propaganda which must have bemused the vast majority of our readers. But at least it was genuinely important, an improvement on the nonsense the paper had to endure in his first year.

Murdoch's move to Wapping wrong-footed him; it was always to rankle that Murdoch walked off with the glittering prize, so there were many attacks based on how 'un-British' News International's tactics were. They were tactics Maxwell would have revelled in, and that made him even more bitter and frustrated.

It was at this time I found out who had recommended me as editor of the *Mirror* – it was Bruce Matthews, the managing director of News International. Bruce was the architect of NI's flight to Wapping and a great newspaper manager. When I eventually broached the subject of why he had suggested me for the *Mirror* editorship, he said a strong *Mirror* was in the interests of the *Sun* and he felt Fleet Street would become dangerously destabilised if the Mirror Group was to collapse under the weight of its mismanagement and overstaffing. He also felt that Maxwell making trouble with the unions would be more significant if his paper was not held in such contempt.

By the end of 1986, we had begun to pull back from the brink. Maxwell's dealings with the paper, apart from a few lapses, were confined to either me or Joe Haines. Joe has taken a lot of stick over his biography of Maxwell and clearly wishes he hadn't done it, but as a leader writer, political columnist and lightning conductor with Maxwell he was invaluable. Maxwell always talked by diktat – 'instruct', 'authorise', 'insist' and 'require' were his favourite words. So if we disagreed about a leader, there was nothing for it but confrontation. With Joe there the cogs were oiled and he invariably managed to smooth over the differences. It also meant I was freed up to deal with the rest of the paper.

We returned to more traditional news values, stopped the non-stop Maxwell campaigns which bored the readers into cancelling the paper and introduced new sections and strong promotions. We were the first daily paper to introduce extra-value weekend sections and, by the end of the year we had been voted Newspaper of the Year by Radio One and Capital Radio – important for us as it was essential to capture a new, young audience. The next big improvement was to be the introduction of colour presses to replace the clapped out black-and-white elephants which gave us reproduction that looked as if all our pictures were taken in a very deep coalhole. Colour was to be Maxwell's single greatest achievement at the *Mirror* but, characteristically, when presented with an open goal, he took his eye off the ball and missed it completely.

His decision to buy new presses from Germany was seen as foolish and unnecessary by Murdoch. 'It will make the paper look like a comic and lose them 100,000 in circulation,' he told Kelvin MacKenzie. Murdoch was not alone in this view. No newspaper of a similar size to the *Mirror* had re-equipped in colour successfully. Only one national in Britain had attempted it at all – *Today* – its founder Eddie Shah tried to do it on the cheap with terrible juddering results known universally as 'Shahvision'. The established wisdom was that colour would be good for sport, fashion, royalty – particularly Diana – glamorous showbusiness events and advertising, but precious little else. It should be avoided for hard news stories, especially disasters. All this was drummed into me by a series of 'colour consultants' brought in by advertising agencies and a twittering raft of marketing men with glossy and expensive research. They were usually American-based and had no conception of British newspapers. In the end I stopped going to the meetings after I told one overpaid consultant that all we needed was 'bloody good pictures' and they would leap off the newsstands like a Jack-in-the-Box. He looked at me sadly, shook his head and said that I would 'never understand the psychology of colour'.

Maxwell was at his best over the introduction of the colour presses. The technical guys were understandably nervous and when the techies get nervous it means they will start overcompensating by bringing forward deadlines. Their first attempt was to suggest the front page should be ready for printing by 2.00pm. I pointed out that we might as well pack up and go home now if that was to be the way of the wind. I told Maxwell that colour would be a good servant but a bad master; there was no point in saying how clever we were if all we were going to show was a dateless picture of a clown throwing coloured balls up in the air while at the same time we failed to get football match reports to Manchester and Liverpool. Everyone expected us to fail with colour, I said, and we would if we went down that route. To his credit, Maxwell agreed and the technical departments were told they must have realistic deadlines and the flexibility to change editions, even if it meant postponing the colour launch. He was right; colour launched gradually, region by region, without a hitch and the circulation began to grow, supported by the only themed television advert I have ever known to work, created by Dave Trott of Gold Greenlees Trott. The theme music was the 1974 hit 'You Ain't Seen Nothing Yet' by Bachman-Turner Overdrive, backed by cheeky, iconoclastic graphics designed to attract a young audience that had grown up with colour. Even Maxwell could find nothing wrong with it. By this time the three newsrooms had been rebuilt to cater for direct input by journalists, although we were still some way from the total removal of compositors. Maxwell was immensely proud of the vast, computerised newsroom and was only too happy to show visitors around it, sometimes with unforeseen results. One day, Charles Lyte, the education, religious and gardening correspondent – there is a common thread somewhere – decided to give an exhibition of the Egg Trick, the one immortalised by Peter O'Toole in Keith Waterhouse's *Jeffrey Bernard is Unwell*. Lyte is the only equal to Waterhouse and O'Toole as an exponent of this immensely complex trick, which requires a raw egg to drop into a glass of water after several convoluted preliminaries. The downside is that if the trick fails, nowhere within ten yards is an egg free zone. Lyte was very good at it, but there was a drawback – he could only do it when enlivened by drink. One afternoon, he did it to christen the new *Mirror* newsroom. A suitably impressed crowd was gathered around him when right at the other end, I saw Maxwell heave into view, followed by a gaggle of what on closer inspection turned out to be Japanese bankers. The trick was too far advanced to halt, so I went up to Maxwell and said in an urgent whisper, 'You have arrived, Bob, at one of the most famous ceremonies in journalism. It is known as the Egg Trick and is performed only on the introduction of a new newsroom. We have to have absolute silence; it is very much a sacred ritual for us.' I think I must have been carried away by the sight of the Japanese.

Maxwell looked at me as if I had gone mad, but eventually turned to the Japanese and said, 'Gentlemen, you are privileged to be watching one of the most sacred rituals in British journalism, it is known as the Leg Trick. I must insist on absolute silence.'

Lyte, no doubt unnerved by Maxwell's presence, or maybe the fact that he was sober, failed miserably and egg was splattered all over the newsroom floor. Maxwell looked at me curiously and swept out with, 'You better get that cleaned up. By the way, where did the leg come into it?' There is no record of what the Japanese businessmen thought.

Colour was to be proved the best newspaper printing innovation since the rotary press, not because of all the window dressing advocated by the 'experts' but by the cutting edge of hard news. There were four dreadful disasters in quick succession – Lockerbie, Hillsborough, the Clapham train and Kegworth air crashes. Each was graphically illustrated by colour, giving a new urgency and shock element to the papers on the counter. On each occasion, the *Mirror* far outstripped its rivals in quality of coverage and sales. Hillsborough proved to be both controversial and heart-searching, as well as opening up a debate on the ethics of using disturbing pictures given a new impact and shocking intensity by top-quality colour printing.

Hillsborough was not the first disaster to be covered in colour, 1988 had seen both the Clapham rail and the Kegworth air crashes. But it was the most horrible because the suffering of so many people was viewed close-up by photographers on the other side of the iron cages penning in the hapless fans. The colour pictures were deeply disturbing and the question was whether they should be used at all. The Saturday television cameras had panned away from the trapped fans and had fallen back on the use of general shots only. But this missed the terrible point and scandal of the tragedy. There was no escape for the supporters because there were few emergency exits on to the pitch, and those there were remained closed until it was too late. The only way out was to break down the railings, which was eventually what happened. Our pictures showed this in a brutal and uncompromising way. During the course of Sunday, the full extent of the disaster became clear as the death toll mounted, but nobody expressed the sense of outrage the pictures deserved. Railings erected to prevent hooligans invading the pitch had sentenced people to die like trapped animals; little thought had been given by the English football authorities to crowd safety and the pictures showed the horrible legacy of that.

I felt we had to use them, and to use them big, which is what we did. The idea was to shock the country into a proper debate about the deadly nature of soccer grounds. In that, we were successful; the pictures so shocked everyone that our headline Never Again became the rallying cry for the forces of reform. But in Liverpool especially, they caused deep anger and resentment. Many felt the pictures were intrusive and deeply offensive to those who had lost relatives in the disaster. Liverpool went on the offensive and copies of the *Mirror* were burnt in the street. Other papers had used similar pictures but none had the intensity of the Mirror's colour. It was now possible to see the expressions on faces 15 rows back in the crowd and the effect was devastating.

I went on the local radio to defend my decision to publish – it was the least I could do – but, apparently, I was the only editor to agree to stand up and be counted. I explained that the only way we could force the authorities to confront the appalling neglect and cavalier attitude to safety by the English football clubs was to confront the issue head on and show people what the end result of such failure was. That was the only way to stop it happening again; if we had turned our backs we would have been as guilty as the men we were indicting. Liverpool is an emotional and tribal city and it gave me a fair hearing in spite of the baying for *Mirror* blood. Many still did not agree with my decision but they were generous enough to give me credit for being prepared to stand up in front of them and say why I did it. The mood began to change, but it was the *Sun* that swung the city behind us.

On the Tuesday evening after the disaster a piece of agency copy dropped, claiming that police in Sheffield were blaming drunken yobs for the disaster and that they had even robbed the dead. The copy came in at a notoriously dangerous moment, shortly after the evening conference and just in time to whet the appetite of the night editor whose mind is turning to the front page. News editors, too, looking for something fresh with which to entice the editor, are always attracted by new stories, too late for the evening papers and the notoriously slow TV news bulletins. Our news editor Tom Hendry was no exception as he hurried in with the report. But to me it stank of a rearguard action by policemen determined to get out from under, not the top men but others who had seen the way the wind was blowing and didn't like what they smelled. Instead of running the story straight, I asked for it to be put back to Liverpool and see what the reaction was. It was one of predictable outrage and that was what we ran. The *Sun*, which had already floated the idea that the fans were to blame, ran the allegations under the headline THE TRUTH.

In terms of lasting effect, it was probably the biggest single editorial misjudgement in newspapers for years, and the *Sun* has still not recovered from it. Up until that time its sale in Liverpool had been strong, but overnight circulation crumbled, never fully to return. By Thursday, the pitch at Anfield was covered in flowers, even copies of pictures from the *Mirror*. The same editions which, at the beginning of the week, had been burnt in the street, were now laid out in tribute on the turf. It was a stunning and moving sight and we took a spectacular panoramic shot of the scene by using a photographer hovering in a helicopter at the other end of the ground to give the picture elevation and width. We ran the photograph across 13 columns, taking up the whole of the front and back pages under the headline 'YOBS? THAT'S NOT WHAT THE FLOWERS SAY'. The picture was so big we could not fax it to Manchester, we had to fly it up and process it there.

Even so, by the end of the week most commentators were praising the *Sun* and pouring scorn on us. In the *Daily Telegraph* Frank Johnson said it showed how the *Sun* was in touch with its readers while we were not. It was a good example of why editors should never listen to pundits who pretend to have their finger on the pulse, especially if it is a *Telegraph* writer claiming to understand the Liverpool working classes. What is nearer to The Truth is that MacKenzie psyched himself into his mistake because the *Mirror* was setting the agenda by its uncompromising use of colour, and as a result was consistently outselling the *Sun* on big news issues. He could only fight back with words; pictures were a dead duck until he got colour. He over-reacted and paid a penalty which is still being exacted today.

His second disaster came with his rent boy allegations against Elton John. Maxwell demanded that we lift the story when it arrived in the *Sun* first edition, but it was obvious from a quick reading that it was seriously short on facts. One fact stood out, however – a date when Elton was said to have met the rent boy. Our own pop columnist John Blake set to work to discover what the singer was doing on that day – only to find quickly that he was in New York and there was a picture in the newspapers there to prove it. It was pay up time for Kelvin. Such experiences should have made Maxwell wary about making snap judgements on stories, but they never did. He always felt he had to make a decision and as far as editorial was concerned, it was invariably the wrong one. When the *News of the World* revealed that Jeffrey Archer had used a middle-man to hand over £2,000 in cash to a prostitute – actually it was probably considerably more, nobody had time to count it – he ordered the *Sunday Mirror* and *People* not to use it, and then phoned Archer to tell him what he had done, adding that no Mirror newspaper would report the story. We did, but not until Monday.

Everything he decided had to be absolute, ridiculous in a grey world where we dealt in all shades of human activity and the one constant was the ability of human nature to surprise, thrill and shock. Our world was one of uncertainty, sensation and revelation, Beaverbrook's clattering train, careering off in directions often undreamed of at the start of the day. Maxwell attempted to control it by edict – I say it is so, therefore it is so. A classic example of this was when he rode to the rescue of the Commonwealth Games in Edinburgh, which was all but on the rocks. The British Establishment, too, showed its ambivalent and hypocritical attitude to him. Everyone involved from the Queen and Thatcher to the British athletic world were lavish in their praise for him stepping in and preventing what would have been a major embarrassment. Nobody else was daft enough to do it, but Maxwell revelled in being centre stage in such a theatre. He had a special blazer made, but his party was slightly spoiled by some nations boycotting the games, not an unknown phenomenon. One such was India, and the news came through as Maxwell was making a speech. At the end of it he was asked about the boycott. He was incensed, he said India would never be mentioned in the

Mirror again. When I suggested to him that this would be a little difficult when it came to Test matches – England versus an un-named country doesn't have much of a ring to it – famine, flood, assassination and the myriad other reasons we might wish to mention India in the paper, he said he had added an important rider to his instruction: 'Except when the editor orders it!' He hadn't, of course, he just thought if he banned India from the *Mirror* the sub-continent would disappear from the face of the earth. At least it was a touching belief in the power of the press.

In spite of the occasional Maxwell foray, the new colour *Mirror* was working well; readers were being attracted to it on the newsstands and, undeniably, the sensational element of so many major disasters meant many more people were sampling us and, judging by the steadily increasing circulation, liking what they saw. But Maxwell was always hovering, and calamity was never far away.

One such was the serialisation of the Joe Haines biography. This book on Maxwell has been much denigrated but it tells an interesting story, and Haines's attempts to describe Maxwell's complex and ultimately unfathomable personality are pretty good. But in the end he was beaten by Maxwell's deceit, secrecy and treachery. He, too, made the mistake of getting too close. Joe always loved power; it was an aphrodisiac and the powerful men who exercised it fascinated and mesmerised him. Inevitably, when the candle guttered, Joe was burnt.

Not so Tom Bower whose book *Maxwell: The Outsider* he tried to suppress by hefty legal action. He claimed he did it because the book contained many inaccuracies, and maybe it did. But before Bower extensively rewrote it after Maxwells's death, it struck me as being not all unsympathetic. Charles Wintour, a former editor of the *Evening Standard*, felt the same way. In his book *The Rise and Fall of Fleet Street*, he writes that in some ways 'Maxwell emerges as a more sympathetic, vulnerable and human figure than in the Haines biography'.

By the end of 1986, Maxwell's appearances in the paper had been considerably reduced although not eradicated – I never achieved that. I continued to insist that all attempts to get himself into the paper were referred to me, so there was no chance of him ordering the backbench to put something in without me knowing about it. It didn't stop him trying, but it did mean he had to face the hassle of an argument and often he decided it wasn't worth it. One area where I did back off slightly was sport, where I had some pretty hefty defeats, usually something to do with Manchester United – which he tried to buy – or pieces praising his friends and launching vendettas against his enemies. He only withdrew when he did manage to put in a piece which I had previously warned him was libellous. Sure enough we had to pay out.

The Haines Maxwell biography, however, was in a different league. The first I knew of Maxwell's determination to serialise it in the *Mirror* – he had tried at first to sell it to the *Sunday Telegraph* for £250,000, an offer wisely refused – was when he suggested I 'pop up' to see him and there he was with Joe and Mike Molloy, the editor in chief. He had clearly been discussing the plan to put it in the *Mirror* and I was aghast. I told him the *Telegraph* was a much better bet – Joe Haines agreed with that – and that publication in the *Mirror* was neither the right place, even if he wasn't the owner – nor would it be looked on favourably by the readers.

Maxwell was very sensitive in this area. Invariably, when he met readers on the rare occasions he actually went out, they liked seeing him, asked him for fiver and generally took the mild piss. He loved that and thought it showed him to be a man of the people. The readers didn't mind him being the paper's owner – most saw him as a bit of a card – but what they didn't like was him appearing in it. He could never understand this distinction and therefore ignored it. I was clearly going to get no support from either Molloy or Haines for my argument that we should not run the book. Both remained ominously silent as I put what I saw was an increasingly hopeless case. It wasn't right for the *Mirror*, it would create a backlash and damage our credibility, something we had been painstakingly rebuilding for more than two years. The circulation decline had stopped and we are actually increasing – timidly, true – but at least it was going in the right direction. The book would stop all that, I said. Maxwell looked more pained than angry. He really believed, or at least he said he did, that the book would put on circulation.

'It won't, Bob. It will kill it stone dead,' I was growing sullen.

'Trust me, Richard, it will put on 30,000.'

No point in looking round the table for support; Joe wanted his book in the paper and Mike was with Maxwell. I told him it wasn't true and that we were throwing away the chance of building up our readership. But Maxwell insisted his book would sell the paper. It was Who Dares Wins all over again and, apart from jacking in the job, there was nothing I could do. I had been stitched up.

Worse was to come when, with Who Dares Wins no doubt in his mind, his faithful Young and Rubicam lieutenant John Banks was drafted in to do the television advert, which only added to the gloom. It was full of phoney mock heroics about this dynamic leader of men, etc. Maxwell loved it and, so fortified, bet me a crate of champagne the circulation would show a sharp increase. He spent £250,000 of our promotional budget on the advert; no wonder old Banksie loved going over the top with him.

Maxwell was still unhappy, though. He had been unable to convince me that I had a fantastic property on my hands and started ringing me, still more in sorrow than in anger. At least I managed to convince him we should do the book as a pull-out rather than taking up half the paper; that would mean readers could throw it away if they so wished. It was at this time Maxwell decided to announce he would not be leaving his children any money, much to their consternation. That, at any rate, turned out to be true, along with my circulation prophecy. In spite of the huge TV spend, we dropped more than 40,000 copies in a week and it took us six valuable months to win back the readers. I was mortified and for the first time considered resigning. It was my first major defeat. He had clearly interfered with the paper and damaged my credibility. But what would be the point in quitting? He would just get someone who would do everything he told him to and the paper would be up the creek again. Lose a battle and win the war – or at least try to. And to add insult to injury, you've guessed it, I never got the champagne.

Staff confidence and pride was beginning to return, although Maxwell was quite capable of making destructive interfering forays into the paper's operation. He rarely did it during the day, preferring to attack my deputy Phil Walker or one of the assistant editors standing in on a Sunday or late at night when he thought he had a better chance. When Christina Onassis died the unlucky victims were John Penrose, now assistant editor in charge of features, and associate news editor Phil Mellor. Mellor's memo of what happened perfectly encapsulates the frozen terror atmosphere Maxwell could engender:

> *After morning conference on Sunday 20 November 1988, the hotline from the Publisher rang and Mr Maxwell asked me what I was doing on the Onassis story. I told him we had staff in London, Peter Stephens in Paris* [Stephens was a veteran Mirror bureau chief with superb contacts in Paris where he had been stationed for four decades], *Stuart Dickson in New York, other stringers and, of course, the agencies working on the story. I also said we were focusing on Athina, the surviving Onassis child, and how much she was worth.*
>
> *To this I was told 'I was fucking useless ... where is the editor?' I told him you had rung and we had discussed the story. He then*

asked who was the duty editor. When I answered John Penrose, he said we should come up and see him. John was talking to Peter Jay [Maxwell's chief of staff] *and then to you. I then got another call from Maxwell saying, 'If you want to continue working for me, come up here quick.'*

In his office, we were asked to sit and he asked me to tell him when I had first heard of the Onassis death. I told him at 10.30pm approx on Saturday night, I had seen the news flashed on Ceefax. He said she died on Friday. I interrupted and said it was Saturday night, which seemed to displease him. We discussed who was covering the story and then both John and I were roundly abused. We were called 'schmok' and other unsavoury insults. He then said we had done nothing on this story, why hadn't he been phoned? Did we not know he had an agency and TV station in France? We, of course, answered yes. He then berated me for using Peter Stephens. 'Who the fuck is he?' said the Publisher. The fact that Peter Stephens had worked in Paris for 35 years and had covered many Onassis stories seemed of no help. He then asked about pictures and was told we had good colour pictures taken recently of Christina and her daughter. He said that if they were from Gamma we should get a special deal as Maxwell Communications owned it. I was then grilled on who the godparents and the trustees of Onassis were. I said we were still working on that. Why hadn't I rung him? Did I not think he could help? John said that we didn't ring him on every story. I suggested that he might care to help me now with any names, but he said he would give details to the Express *in the morning ...'*

This last sentence shows up another side of Maxwell, his petulance. There was never any likelihood of him having any useful names or information, it was just that it was a Sunday, he was bored, the story involved a rich, powerful person and he wanted to be involved and be seen to be involved. His practical usefulness was zilch, but his ability to instil fear and loathing was enormous.

The next day, I went to see him and told him how badly he had behaved. 'These people have mortgages, Bob ... you are terrifying them by behaving like that. You must not speak to employees in such a way, it destroys everything we are trying to do with the paper'.

I was steamed up because of the rubbishing two senior men had taken on my behalf. Phil Mellor was tough, but John Penrose was vulnerable and Maxwell knew it and he knew why. Within two days, John decided he had had enough and left the paper, heading for a highly successful career looking after the business interests of his wife Annie Robinson. Annie, with characteristic balls, went and demanded a pay rise from Maxwell to compensate her for losing Penrose's salary. She got it, too.

A year earlier, Maxwell had sued *Private Eye* over a piece of gossip suggesting that he had acted as paymaster for Neil Kinnock in return for a peerage, an unlikely tale, although there was one part of the story which was true. Maxwell had employed Nick Grant, Labour's previous director of publicity, at Pergamon Press to take him off the Labour leader's hands. Kinnock always distrusted Maxwell, while Glenys actively hated and was repulsed by him. At the annual *Mirror* lunch for the leader of the Labour Party during the conference season, she always used to change the seating plan, or get me to do it for her if he was watching, so she didn't have to sit next to him. She once lumbered a female Norwegian politician into poll position instead, a lady nobody – including, I suspect, Maxwell – knew. These lunches were a nightmare because Maxwell was at his most pompous. 'We are honoured by your presence with us here today, Neil. You are dining with the élite of the élite. What can we at the *Mirror* do for you and this great movement of ours?'

Kinnock, like Wilson before him, was obsessed with newspapers, which is hardly surprising given the coverage in the Murdoch papers that swung between the unfair and distorted to the downright lie. So he asked for a series of campaigns on anything from education and health – we did those anyway – to the more esoteric reform of the Labour Party and constituency planning. Important for him, but hardly likely to rivet *Mirror* bums to seats. Maxwell loved it, and agreed we would do everything he asked. Luckily, we adopted a rearguard action of masterful inaction and soon the commitments were forgotten in the rough and tumble of a new parliamentary session.

There was much interest when the case against *Private Eye* came to court, and on the first day, when Maxwell's QC opened the case, it received a lot of coverage. The next day it was *Private Eye*'s turn and this, too, was reported but not as extensively.

That evening, Maxwell rang to see 'what's cooking', his usual greeting, and I told him that we were continuing to report the *Private Eye* case. He was furious. 'Get it out. It's all fucking rubbish. I don't want that in the paper.' It had to go in, I pointed out. If it didn't, *Private Eye* would almost certainly point out the omission the next day in court.

'You get it fucking out, mister. You do what I tell you.'

I saw red. I pointed out to him that he should listen for a change, that I was not taking it out and that, worse, if the judge knew what he was ordering now, he would take a pretty dim view and his case would be down the tubes. He was quite wrong to do what he was doing, and very, very stupid.

This seemed to shut him up, and then, petulantly and with only a hint of menace, he added, 'Nobody else will use it, you see. You will be alone.'

'On the contrary, everyone will use it,' I said. At this moment, the *Times* first edition dropped and I started scrabbling through it to find the report, praying it had been used. Mercifully, it had. 'Right, Bob, I'll bet you a fiver that another paper will use it,' I said.

'Done,' he replied. 'You can pay me tomorrow.' Click.

The next day was the weekly editors' lunch. Five newspapers had used the report in the end and, without saying anything, he handed me £5.

'No, no Bob,' I said, 'Fiver a paper. That's £25.'

Worth it from his point of view. If I had grassed him up to the judge, it might have cost a damn sight more.

Maxwell eventually won the case and was awarded more than £50,000 damages. To celebrate, he decided to produce a newsprint spoof of *Private Eye* called *Not Private Eye*, which, predictably, turned out to be embarrassing and rather leaden. Peter Cook, *Private Eye*'s largely absentee, hands-off owner, was at his best in times of financial crisis and decided to hit the *Mirror* where it was most vulnerable. He invited John Penrose, who with Mike Molloy had put *Not Private Eye* together, out for a few drinks. Both Cook and Penrose got plastered and Penrose, unwisely, decided to take Cook back to the *Mirror* for a couple more. Cook couldn't believe his luck when he found himself in Molloy's empty editor's office at the *Sunday Mirror* where he had become acting editor. It was late on Monday night so there was nobody about in the newsroom. Penrose and Cook raided Molloy's bar and set about demolishing it. Eventually, Penrose did what Penrose always did when he had drunk more than enough, he fell into a deep, untroubled sleep, curled up on a sofa looking like a peaceful dormouse. Cook was made of sterner stuff. Just as pissed, he started spraying graffiti on Molloy's windows and walls. Then, after a couple more large ones, he grabbed Molloy's phone and placed a call via the switchboard to Maxwell in New York, giving him the none-too-welcome news that he was getting back his £50,000 by drinking his way through Maxwell's booze. He told him where he was and exactly what he was doing as he sprayed yet another 'Maxwell is a Wanker' message across the editor's window. Maxwell phoned his Girl Friday Jean

Baddeley to find out what the hell was happening and she phoned the *Daily Mirror* newsdesk two floors below the action. Alastair McQueen, the night news editor, went upstairs to look. The scene of mayhem was appalling. Empty bottles everywhere, a smashed phone, the graffiti, overturned glasses, floods of drink on the floor, but no Peter Cook. He had staggered off into the night. There was, however, a John Penrose, flat out, gently snoring with a cherubic smile on his face. McQueen rang me direct from Molloy's hotline. Alastair is very close to the SAS and had yomped across the Falklands with the Paras, and this was definitely a case for Who Dares Wins. Baddeley, in the absence of a return call from McQueen, was on the warpath and had phoned security at the *Mirror*'s front door. But the guy there, too, was compromised because he had let Peter Cook in. He telephoned the newsdesk and we told him we would sort it out.

Together, McQueen and I cleared up Molloy's office as much as we could, but it still left a lot to be desired. Baddeley, however, was tenacious; she had brought in the *Mirror*'s security chief and his men were on their way up in the lift. There was nothing for it, we had to cut and run with Penrose carried, still comatose, between us, his glasses hanging off one ear. We puffed our way to the far end of the *Sunday Mirror* newsroom as the lift doors opened at the other end and the office spooks crashed in. We heaved our way down two flights of the back stairs and dumped Penrose under a pile of coats in the photographers' room.

I fled back to my office gasping for breath just as the spooks arrived at the newsdesk to be confronted by an irate McQueen who had somehow conjured up an urgent story which required his undivided attention. The security men came to see me, with the pompous PC Plod approach they adopt while pursuing their enquiries, to ask what I knew about the atrocities being committed against the Publisher's person in Mike Molloy's office. The Publisher required an immediate answer. With the self-importance editors adopt when out of breath and guilty as hell of protecting a massively drunk colleague who is without doubt severely in the brown stuff, I replied that I ran the *Daily Mirror*, I was not responsible for the *Sunday* and it was their job to make sure no undesirables got into the building, not mine. Now would they kindly sod off and leave me to run a great national newspaper.

It worked, they knew Penrose was somewhere around but they couldn't find him, although by now his snores had reached heroic proportions and in the photographers' room the coats were rumbling like the beginning of an earthquake. Maxwell had lost his man, although he still asked me to sack him. 'On whose evidence?' I asked.

'Yours,' should have been the answer. But from then on, John was marked; it was only a matter of time.

It was John and Phil Walker who were lumbered with what became known as the Great Burma Shock Issue affair. I was about to go on my summer holiday so I went to see Bob with a special plea – please don't sack my deputy when I'm away.

'Why would I do that?' he protested.

'Because you always do, Bob.'

'Do I?' He seemed put out.

'Yes, you do, and it is very dispiriting for everyone, particularly him.'

'Right, I promise, no sackings,' he said, and I set off for our family flat down in the South of France.

The phone was ringing when I opened the door. It was Phil.

'I've been fired,' he said.

As soon as I had left, Maxwell had decided he wanted to do a shock issue on Burma. Shock issues are, or were, one day's paper devoted almost entirely to a single subject. I had already done three – on crime, education and the health service. They can be extremely powerful weapons if you have strong pictures and poignant words, but the subject must be sustainable. They were one of Cudlipp's finest innovations and set the *Mirror* apart from other newspapers as well as confirming our own agenda. On every count Burma did not fit the bill, it was about the looniest idea Maxwell had managed yet. But what on earth was I to do about this? A shock issue was grotesque, and Phil had more or less told him so. That's why he had been fired.

I told him to get back to Maxwell and show him that he was taking action on his suggestion. Send McQueen to the Burmese border – he wouldn't get in – and say you are waiting for his report back from the front line. Maxwell, who still maintained a sentimental attachment to the military, would like that and it would give us a couple of days to fight him off. Maxwell had a bee in his bonnet about Burma because he believed, mistakenly, that it was about to open up and he wanted to take advantage of it. So the shock issue would, in reality, be a paean of praise to Burma's unsavoury military régime. The situation was going from bad to worse; once again he was threatening to destroy our credibility for the foreseeable future. Our best hope was that he would be sidetracked into something else, but even that faint hope was dashed over the weekend, when he decided to redouble his interest and sack Penrose as well.

I phoned Maxwell and pointed out that he had reneged on his promise already. 'Really, what is that?'

'You've sacked my deputy, Bob. Not only that, you've sacked the number three and threatened to fire the entire newsdesk.'

'It is only because they have failed to act on my instructions to complete this very exciting prospect of a shock issue on Burma.'

I took a deep breath and cast off. 'It's a crap idea, Bob. Firstly, it is August and you don't do shock issues in August. Secondly, shock issues are formed round photographs and the only pictures worth publishing out of Burma are ones showing Japanese prisoners of war, those who worked on the Burma railway and a general file under the heading Abuse of Human Rights. Thirdly, most of our readers who know anything about the country hate it because of the way they were treated during the war. Fourthly, my father had been on the Burma railway and it was an insult to his memory [As you know, he hadn't at all, but I was desperate and I hoped the real Burma veterans would forgive the lie in pursuit of the greater objective]. The idea in short would kill the paper stone dead.'

There was silence at the other end, then a sigh. 'If you really think so ... you are the editor. But we must have a leader praising Burma's march towards freedom.'

Done! But what *Mirror* readers thought the next day when, for no obvious reason, we ran a leader on Burma, God only knows, particularly when we carried the line 'Burma, a country we have ignored for far too long ...'

Meanwhile, in the drama of the liquidation of the paper's senior staff, everyone had forgotten about McQueen who, by virtue of his SAS techniques, had actually managed to make it into Burma, a remarkable achievement. But I wasn't going to tempt providence and use his report. We had escaped by the skin of our teeth and inventing my father's war record, I had no intention of revisiting the charms of Rangoon.

Maxwell had a highly-developed respect for the military, probably because his MC was the first recognition the British gave him and, he believed, the only time he was ever appreciated for being himself, which was probably true. When my father-in-law died someone showed Maxwell his obituary in the *Daily Telegraph*. Late in the war Penny's father was shot down in a Lancaster raid over Brunswick and had been in Stalag Luft III. For six months his family did not know whether he was alive or dead, although the rest of the crew in the plane had been killed. Lancasters were so uncomfortable that the fliers used to sit on their parachutes instead of wearing them, in spite of repeated warnings that it was potentially lethal to do so. Sir Colin was the only one to be wearing his and managed to escape as the Lancaster twisted with engines ablaze towards the ground. He was deposited at the camp only ten days before the Great Escape, but was not allowed to take part in it because he arrived only shortly before the breakout and all newcomers were regarded with suspicion. Instead, he was ordered to give a lecture on the stage while tunnelling took place underneath it.

The film was a source of great family merriment, for Penny's dad is presented as being a boring old buffer giving a lecture on birds; in fact, it was on aircraft design, and Sir Colin was anything but boring. As the end of the war approached, he and the other inmates were force-marched across the country, away from the advancing Russians towards the British and American forces coming from the west. Many died on the way and stragglers were shot. When an increasingly bedraggled and starving group eventually ran into a British tank column, the first words of the NCO in charge to the prisoners of war was to ask which of the guards were 'the bastards'. One in particular was singled out. He was shot on the spot.

After the war, he flew around the world in a light aircraft deliberately seeking out bad weather in order to test out radar reliability, his constant companions being balls of St Elmo's Fire which danced around the cockpit during particularly vicious storms.

In a letter of sympathy, Maxwell wrote to Penny, the only letter we ever received from him. He spoke of the 'gallant war record [which] tells us all what he did for his country'. I am sure the war was the only time in his life when Maxwell was truly happy and comfortable with his adopted life.

Maxwell decided to rekindle his love affair with the army by having a replica made of his wartime captain's uniform, for a visit to Poland to celebrate the fiftieth anniversary of the outbreak of the Second World War. One morning I was asked to 'pop up' to his headquarters in the building next door to the Mirror. 'What do you think?' he boomed, rising from his desk at the other end of his Mussolini-sized office. He was a mountain of khaki, captain's pips, medal ribbons and Sam Browne belt with which he had a problem. He was so big he was having trouble getting it across his shoulder and round his back, and the exertions were swinging both the belt and his body round in circles. I started to snigger and helped him thread the Sam Browne which, like the rest of the uniform, had been specially made. 'Pretty good, eh?' he wheezed from the exertion of fixing the Sam Browne.

'You need some brown brogues, Bob,' I said, catching sight of his black slip-ons under the desk.

'Get me some brogues,' he thundered to his secretary. He looked like a massive Captain Mainwaring. Then a thought struck him. 'Is this Sam Browne on the right way?' I had no idea and, without thinking, suggested he ask Sergeant Haines. Finger on the buzzer again; Joe answered. 'Sergeant Haines, would you pop up?'

'I'm not your Sergeant, Bob,' came the testy and entirely predictable reply.

By this time, the Captain's travelling companion for the Polish trip had arrived, and Field Marshal Lord Bramall, KG, GCB, OBE, MC, former chief of the defence staff, was not amused. 'He can't wear that,' he said. 'He was only a captain, he can't wear a uniform. Not only that, his Sam Browne's the wrong way round. Someone will have to tell him.' He looked at me.

'You're the Field Marshal. Order him to take it off,' I said.

Bramall retired in good order to plan his campaign. Whatever the Field Marshal did, Maxwell wore his uniform in Poland, a visit that gave rise to the legend of the anniversary ceremony there. The story goes that Maxwell realised during the service that he had forgotten his wreath as a tribute to the dead, so he commandeered the one of the man standing next to him, who just happened to be the American Ambassador. The US Ambassador realised his had gone missing and nicked that of the man next to him. And so on down the line until the last representative of a presumably small, impoverished nation could do nothing but bow in front of the memorial to Poland's war dead but offer nothing in the way of a wreath. Whatever the truth of it, Field Marshal Bramall did not volunteer for any more forays into foreign territory with his fellow MC.

An extension of Maxwell's love of military lore was Peter Jay's title – Chief of Staff. It was the former British Ambassador's job to make some sense of his Captain's chaotic affairs, a task more Herculean than running our embassy in Washington. Jay's suits were always rather shabby and Maxwell was none too happy with the evidence of several Jay lunches on the lapels, so legend has it he gave him £500 to buy a couple more. No point in being a chief of staff unless your kit sparkled, although evidence of Garrick Club lunches remained on Peter's frontage. One of his many jobs was to sort out the *Mirror* car park, almost as thankless an operation as running Maxwell's business affairs, and even worse if your own car has been vandalised.

At one of the editors' lunches where the subject of the car park came up yet again, Peter complained bitterly that the hubcaps of his car had been stolen. Dreadful, appalling, we tutted, and none more so than me who was responsible for the theft. One of the many perks of being an editor is that you have a car and driver, which is just as well because, left to our own devices, we would undoubtedly be a traffic hazard. Drivers in newspaper offices are not be trifled with because they always know what is going on; it is a strange fact of life that people in the backs of cars seem to forget drivers have ears and, as a result, they are extremely well informed.

There are many stories of Maxwell and drivers. He had, on a number of occasions, become impatient with his chauffeur taking the orthodox route across London and decided to drive himself. This involved going down a number of one-way streets in the wrong direction; one driver refused to get in the car with him again. On another trip he decided he would stop for fish and chips which he devoured at shark-like speed, throwing the wrapping out of the window. Much to the merriment of his driver, the car was going so fast the tattered vinegar and fat-stained paper flew right back into Maxwell's face. One poor man was so terrified at having to stand in for his regular driver that he sat quaking in the Vanway – the internal drive at the *Mirror* where the vans line up to be loaded with newly-printed papers – waiting for Maxwell to arrive. He had been told he was on his way down and that when he was about to get into the car he would hear his cough, the door would open and close and once he did that, you were on your way. No messing. Simple. It all went to plan – the cough, door open, door close, and the driver sped off … only to hear a thunderous 'Oi!' from the Vanway. Maxwell had decided to have a pee against the Rolls-Royce's rear wheel and had been left in glorious isolation and full cascade.

My driver was a legend of the garage, utterly fearless, utterly loyal and, like many of the best chauffeurs, on occasion barking mad. John Brockington was a fanatical jogger, always in training for the London Marathon, and one day he decided to run the 14 miles to our home to pick up Penny for an evening function, having left the car there earlier in the day and travelled back by train. When he arrived, he was knackered and had to be revived by the children, but he still wasn't up to driving the car back to London. So Penny drove, with Johnnie Brock propped up on pillows in the back.

On one occasion when he was actually driving, we were sitting in a traffic jam as a motorcyclist started making frantic signals to him outside the window. Johnnie was oblivious to this, intent instead on listening to Jazz FM. I, as usual, had my head deep in a newspaper. The signals turned to rapping on the window, but still no response from the driver who was being transported by a particularly fine lyrical passage of Gerry Mulligan. Eventually, I tapped him on the shoulder and he reluctantly opened the window to face a screaming helmet. We had been parked, Johnnie, me and a Daimler, on the motorcyclist's toe.

Peter Jay and I had the same kind of car and one morning Johnnie Brock was fuming. Two of our hubcaps had been stolen.

'That's no problem,' I said.

'Nick Peter Jay's.'

Johnnie was swift and covert. They had gone before Peter left for home and hence the roar of outrage. Maxwell naturally blamed Jay for the lack of security in the garage. We never gave them back, but were more than helpful in giving Peter the name of a supplier.

Peter had a genuine respect for Maxwell, strengthened by his hatred of Rupert Murdoch. Maxwell treated him like a skivvy, but Peter did an impossible job with as good a grace as he could muster. He was short of money from the débâcle over TV-AM and Maxwell was a much-needed lifeline, as he was for Derek Jameson after he lost his libel action against the BBC that left him all but bankrupt. Peter is undoubtedly clever, immensely so, but I wonder about his common sense. When he first arrived he tended to be dictatorial, or try to be, provoking me to put a question that had always puzzled me: 'How is it, Peter,' I asked, 'If you are one of the cleverest 100 people in the world, why didn't you wear a condom when getting your leg over the nanny?'

He thought for a second and then replied, 'Do you know, Stotty, I have often wondered that myself.' A friendship was cemented.

Maxwell always claimed that he wasn't interested in material goods, but he was being persuaded. Gradually the yacht, the helicopter and the plane appeared. Grand parties were held at Headington Hill Hall with its spectacular view over my home city to celebrate his wedding anniversary, Pergamon's fortieth birthday and his sixty-fifth. Brother John used to do the catering for Maxwell back in the 1970s and the Pressed Steel or Morris Motors brass band used to provide the music. Brass bands need a lot of refreshment, or these did anyway, and John was always good at providing it, beer for the band was always packed on the truck. The problem was that although Headington Hill Hall is a fine-looking house, there is only one downstairs lavatory. And when 40 members of a brass band want to release three pints of best Morells at the same time it causes a bit of a queue. So John told them to nip off into the rose garden, under cover of darkness, and use that. Unfortunately, they were spotted with their cornets out and John was fired on the spot.

I was reminded of this when queuing for the lav at one of Maxwell's parties and decided it was time to restore the family honour. I went off to the rose garden and completed the job the brass band couldn't, only on my return to the marquee to encounter Maxwell. 'Hope you haven't been pissing in my garden,' he said with a snort of laughter.

He was becoming more grandiose and ever more frenetic in his bid to catch up Rupert Murdoch in the mogul stakes. It was a hopeless quest; he had started much later and did not have the broad base on which to launch himself into the United States. Neither did he listen to the best advice – he was convinced of his own infallibility and he trusted nobody. The *Mirror* was going well, but not as well as it should, for he had failed to press home the early advantage going into colour had given us. For the first time for many years, we had the *Sun* on the back foot; Thatcherism, in spite of her decisive victory in 1987, was beginning to pall; our opposition was looking tired and, by early summer of 1989, we had reduced the gap between the *Sun* and the *Mirror* by more than 350,000 copies a day.

Towards the end of 1988, I suggested to Maxwell that I would like to buy the *People* from the Mirror Group if he would sell it; the *Mirror* job would not last for ever. It wasn't as far-fetched an idea as it sounded; he had already sold the British Printing Corporation to its employees and the *People* continued to sit uncomfortably with the Mirror Group. Maxwell had not sorted out the problem of having two competing Sunday newspapers any more than previous managements had.

I went to see him one evening and he was already in his shortie dressing gown but without his pyjamas, a difficult job to stay covered when you are his size. I tried to keep my mind – and eyes – on the subject, but it became increasingly difficult as Maxwell, standing in his study, put his foot up on his chair, revealing equipment which would not have disgraced a Smithfield champion. He liked the idea of the buyout and said we should talk further and suggesting, rather quickly I thought, that David Montgomery might be a good editor for the *Mirror*. Too right-wing, I said, but happy he was not against the buyout idea. A few days later – at John Penrose's farewell party – he rang me to confirm his interest. 'I like this idea ... only I could do it, you know.' Then I heard nothing more of it.

Our relationship was becoming increasingly fraught, boiling over into an outright row about the delivery of his first edition papers. He had blown up yet again at the newsdesk because, he claimed, his newspapers had not been delivered on time. Yes they had, said the night newsdesk, they had been sent up to his flat. With a flurry of the usual language he rang off saying that everyone was fired.

When I got home at around 11.00pm, the phone was ringing and Maxwell was in full flow. 'What sort of bloody circus do you run, mister? I don't interfere with you and you treat me like shit. Well, fuck you, I'll get an editor who can get me papers on time. Don't you fucking defend those cunts on the newsdesk, they are worse than fucking useless and I've fired them. Sort it out.'

There is a difference between being roundly abused in the office – par for the course – and being screamed at while at home. It makes you feel soiled, furious and demeaned, as if the attack had been made on your family. I checked to see what had happened and, as usual, the papers had been left outside his door because he wouldn't answer; nobody could get in because he didn't trust anyone with a key. I phoned him back and let him have it non-stop in much the same language he had used, ending with, 'You make this job a misery, Bob ... you can stick it. You don't deserve the loyalty of the staff you have,' and I slammed the phone down before he could – his favourite trick.

The next morning, he was on the phone. 'We have something to talk about. I always accept resignations.'

'Good,' I said and slammed the phone down again. I went to see him at around 11.00am and he seemed genuinely nervous. 'How are we going to resolve this?' he said. He was strangely timid and quiet.

Oh, sod it, I thought. 'You are going to apologise for behaving so badly, I'm going to accept it and we are going to have a glass of champagne,' I said. 'The alternative is that you sack the editor of the *Daily Mirror* for the messengers failing to deliver papers to you which were there all the time but you couldn't be bothered to pick up. It won't look very good, Bob,' I said, and waited.

He cleared his throat, coughed, then went to the fridge and opened a bottle of Krug. 'I'm sorry,' he said. 'I was wrong.'

Bloody hell, it was the first time with him that anything had gone as the script intended. But from now on it was only going to be a matter of time. In the darkness of the night and the turmoil of his mind, he would come back to that conversation and begin to feel as I had done, demeaned and humiliated. Was he not the Publisher. Had he not, single-handed, saved the paper, killed the power of the trades unions, brought in colour printing against all the best advice, including Murdoch's, turned an overmanned loss-making mammoth into an efficient, big bucks company? Yes, he had done most of that, but when it came to running a newspaper he had a tin ear, and he hated it. He loved the buccaneering nature of journalism; he loved the mischief-making and the camaraderie, the intrigue, the excitement and the living dangerously. It's just that he was no good at it, and that was the unkindest cut of all. He had control and success in every area of the *Mirror* except the one he craved. He would have it back, it was time to seize the initiative again. It was only a matter of time. But we weren't finished yet. There was still the mystery of the great Berlin Wall graffiti.

Charles Griffin was the *Mirror* cartoonist, a brilliant caricaturist, and like so many of his breed, eccentric. He had been known to put Maxwell in crowd scenes and, on one occasion, he was doing something obscene – even for Maxwell. But when the Berlin wall came down, a sharp-eyed reader had noticed that among the forest of graffiti in Griffin's cartoon version was the legend 'Fuck Maxwell'. Sod's law dictated that the reader wrote to Maxwell rather than me and he, not surprisingly, ordered an inquiry. This didn't worry me unduly as I was convinced Charles didn't do it. The retouchers who prepare the cartoon for publication in the paper had all been issued with notices that week – their jobs made redundant by new technology – and I assumed one of them had done it as a parting gesture. But I had not counted on the forensic skill of John Pole, Maxwell's chief spook. He had the cartoon X-rayed and claimed it showed the writing was on the rough drawing underneath the completed ink version, pointing the finger at Griffin as the culprit. Pole, in true Chief Superintendent fashion, demanded Griffin help him with his inquiries but, in the ensuing interview Griffin refused to move from his desk. A nonplussed Pole was forced to conduct a non-interrogation with a man who refused either to stop drawing or take off his earphones on which he always used to listen to his beloved operas. Maxwell pulled back from the brink; he didn't sack him in spite of merciless coverage in rival newspapers and, in fairness to him, Charles has always maintained he didn't do it.

The second time Maxwell acted with great caution, wisdom even, was when he was facing industrial action from the National Union of Journalists at Pergamon and pickets were manning the barricades. This was too much to resist for Paul Foot who, even before right-wing columnists without an ounce of his integrity or courage, started sniping at him about showing solidarity, had decided to join his brothers and sisters. He was pictured outside the gates of Headington Hill Hall. I was once again asked to 'pop up'.

'Your mate is taking the piss out of me,' he said before I was even through the door.

'What's that, Bob?' I affected not to know what he was talking about.

'Foot. Foot and mouth, that's what I am talking about. He's picketing my offices and he bloody works for me.'

'Well, up to a point, Bob, up to a point.'

'He should be fired,' he said, but without the cure-all conviction the words usually carried, and definitely, I noticed, no chop of the arm.

'Oh no, I don't think so, you see they would love that, wouldn't they, Bob? Fire him and you confirm all their prejudices; ignore it and it will eventually go away.'

It was one of those rare moments when Maxwell saw the sense of what someone else was saying. 'Tell your mate,' – a good sign this; 'Listen, mister' would have been bad news – 'He's bloody lucky he's got a merciful and compassionate publisher.' I was out of the door before he could change his mind.

With the circulation stabilised, Maxwell was becoming increasingly determined to run the paper and cut back on editorial spending to finance his growing American interests. He believed the hard work had been done, but the hard work is never done when you are up against as unremitting a foe as the *Sun*. With his usual lack of editorial touch, he started to save money at the very time he should have been pressing home his advantage. In August I decided to take the family to the United States; it was a grand tour of California and Arizona as it was the last year we would all be together before elder daughter Emily launched herself into an unsuspecting world. As soon as I was on the runway at Heathrow, Maxwell launched himself into what was billed as 'Play It Again' Bingo, a cheapo production where readers were told to use their old Bingo cards instead of being issued with new ones. It was an absurd idea made even worse by the presentation in the paper, which the hapless Phil Walker was powerless to prevent. The readers were furious, seeing it for what it was, a cheap con to circumvent an expensive Bingo relaunch the next month.

Maxwell was also taking away in-paper supplements we had been gradually building up over the previous three years and which had definitely been a circulation booster. It is a remorseless fact of newspapers that while add-ons may not increase your circulation, if you remove them it will certainly be reduced. Maxwell was also desperately keen to run an investigation we had launched into claims of misuse of the miners' strike funds by Arthur Scargill. Two close associates of Scargill were spilling the beans, but I was still unhappy with what we had unearthed, although I was keen to publish if we could stand everything up. Maxwell wanted to go with it now, but I was resisting that; we had not copper-bottomed it

Top: With Czech spy Josef Frolik at our secret meeting in Atlanta, Georgia. It was so cloak and dagger the CIA gave him a woman's alias. His trousers are almost as bad as my suit. I bought it in Melbourne when chasing John Stonehouse. It's seersucker. They certainly did ...

Bottom: Don Revie and Bob Stokoe lead out Leeds and Sunderland for the 1973 Cup Final – rather different to their last confrontation at Bury when Revie tried to bribe him to lose a match.

Top: Chilling out 20 degrees below zero in a 60mph wind for a picture that went round the world. Kent Gavin, the great *Mirror* photographer (*far left*) and me (*far right*) with Eskimo guardsmen. Gavin is in the Soviet Union, I'm in the United States and we are both standing in the middle of the Bering Sea. It can be done – honest!

Bottom: Reporter of the Year 1977 for the exposé of former Leeds manager Don Revie for corruption. (*Picture by Doreen Spooner*)

Less happy times for Charles. This is the 1983 Kent Gavin picture the *Mirror* wouldn't use. It proves two things: Charles and Diana's problems started early on in their marriage; and the old cliché is true – a great picture is worth a thousand words.

Top: Editor of the *People*, 1984, and watch-your-back time. (*Left to right*) Ernie Burrington, my deputy who went on to become chairman; Bill Hagerty, later Editor of the *People*; me; and David Montgomery, who believed he should have been Editor and later fired me when he became Chief Executive. Love that body language.

Bottom: Editor of the *Daily Mirror*. Jobs don't come any better than that ...

Top: ... he wouldn't agree, of course – With Kelvin MacKenzie, Editor of the *Sun* in typically boisterous mood.

Bottom: It had been a tough day ... Maxwell had taken to wearing bow ties because he reckoned it looked more publisher-like.

Top left: Man of the People, John Smith – columnist, foreign correspondent and ex-variety artist – in full Maxwell mode at a *Mirror* Christmas party. In the background John Jenkinson, publicity director (*left*) and former *Mirror* Editor Mike Molloy (*right*).

Top right: At Headington Hill Hall for Maxwell's 65th birthday party with (*left to right*) John Penrose, Annie Robinson, and Penny. I later exacted revenge on his rose beds for the sacking of my brother as his caterer.

Bottom: Diana asks me how we are managing after the Maxwell scandal broke. 'Are you going to bail us out?' I asked. (*Picture by Kent Gavin*)

Top: Alastair Campbell on his beloved bagpipes in our kitchen before he started calling the tune in Downing Street.

Bottom: Always used to tapdancing, Peter Mandelson (*left*) lets rip at our 25th wedding anniversary party with Fiona Millar, Alastair's partner. On the right is Nichola McAuliffe, the brilliant actress wife of *Mirror* reporter Don Mackay.

Top: Interviewing Tony Blair in 2002 aboard his RAF jet for the *Sunday Mirror*.

Bottom: They get it from their mother ... Three wonderful children, (*left to right*) Emily, Christopher and Hannah.

and I had asked for a string of further enquiries to be put in train. He thought this unnecessary and was growing dangerously impatient. All the warning signs were there, that once again he was convinced he knew how to run the editorial side of a newspaper.

The crunch came, as oddly it so often does in newspapers, over Christmas. Romania was in open rebellion against its dictator Nicolae Ceausescu, one of the numerous Eastern European leaders with whom Maxwell had conducted a series of embarrassingly sycophantic and interminable interviews for a grandly-named series of publications called *Leaders of the World*. After a show trial, Ceausescu and his wife Elena were taken out and shot and by Boxing Day pictures of their bloodied bodies, Ceausescu wearing a red tie, were sent across the world. It was a sensational news picture, as well as one that symbolised the violent death of the old Communist order, an order the Maxwell series had done much to perpetuate by giving their leaders a spurious respectability.

Christena Appleyard, by now a *Mirror* assistant editor, was in charge that day and we had already discussed the projection of the picture when she phoned to say that she was being 'Captained', the shorthand for interference from Cap'n Bob. He wanted to put an appeal for cash for the Romanian people all over the front page, a disastrous idea from every point of view. Maxwell always wanted to make an appeal for cash on any major story where it might be remotely apposite, but it is a tool to be used sparingly and certainly not immediately after Christmas on behalf of a country whose people would not naturally come at the top of the *Mirror* readers' list for support from their own hard-earned cash. Especially when the main reason for helping them was that they had just executed their leader in the most savage of circumstances. It would be made even worse by the inevitable reaction, that it was the same Maxwell launching the appeal who only a few years earlier had been grovelling before the hated Ceausescu.

Maxwell decided to call a 'summit meeting' of all editors, executives and so on, a sure sign that he was bored and we were in for a rocky ride. As it was Boxing Day, very few were contactable but I went in to make sure we weren't made to look ridiculous the next day. We had a house full of relatives due and it was the only time Penny showed any impatience with my life. She actually kicked the furniture; I had never seen anyone do that before and was rather impressed.

I was in no mood to compromise, so I told him that Ceausescu was the page-one picture splash and his appeal would have to go inside. He said I was wrong, the picture was 'a load of shit'; I told him that was nonsense.

This was history.

'You'll be sorry you did that,' he said.

I said I wouldn't, then the phone rang. It was Roy Greenslade. I knew he had been offered the editorship of the *People* and had turned it down. I also knew he fancied the editorship of the *Mirror*; he had suggested himself for it when he turned down the *People*.

'What do you think he wants?' Maxwell asked, looking rather guilty, although it was pretty obvious he must have instigated the phonecall. Roy wouldn't be phoning Maxwell on Boxing Day otherwise.

'He probably wants to edit the *Mirror*, Bob,' I said. Maxwell put the phone down promising to phone him back. Later that day, he offered Greenslade the editorship of the *Mirror* which Roy accepted. But he had already made his first mistake. He thought Maxwell was tameable and that he was the man to do it. Maxwell thought he had hired a tame editor.

The next morning, shortly before 7.00am, he phoned me to tell me he had decided to activate the *People* buyout immediately. 'Great news, Bob,' I said, determined he wouldn't have the gratification of registering my shock. In truth, I hadn't thought about the buyout for months and the *People* had been going through some hefty trauma of its own under Wendy Henry, fired by Murdoch for turning the *News of the World* into a paper he loathed, and fired eventually by Maxwell for running a picture of Prince William having a pee, although I don't think he saw anything wrong in it until Joe Haines complained that it was disgraceful.

So that was it. I was now a putative newspaper owner, although I was well aware that Maxwell's promise and his performance were two entirely different things. He was having an 'everything must go' clearout. Peter Jay went as chief of staff and former Beecham's executive Patrick Morissey, his ineffectual Mirror Group managing director – he was a football referee and expected journalists to accept his decisions without question; instead, they behaved like several teams of Paul Gascoigne and Vinny Jones rolled into one – was also given the red card.

Whatever the battles he fights, however brave, cowardly, good or bad to his staff, however truthful or duplicitous, weak or strong an editor may be, there is only one way, justly or unjustly, his tenure in office is finally judged – sales. I inherited a paper in Roy Greenslade's words 'in freefall' at the beginning of September 1985, when the latest Audit Bureau of Circulation figures for August were 3,064,667. By August 1989, they were 3,137,778. By contrast, the *Sun*'s for the corresponding time were 4,165,933 and 4,073,102. During that time we had succeeded editorially in spite of Maxwell and, as a business, because of him. We had sharpened the news coverage, the features staff contained the best writers in Fleet Street, Joe Haines was a political commentator of the highest order, sport had improved under the noisy but talented Keith Fisher and the paper was clearly identified as an iconoclastic, ballsy campaigner of the left. The colour presses were the best in Fleet Street and business practices, staffing and profits had all been improved immeasurably. In five years, the Mirror Group had been transformed from a dinosaur gradually being killed by the weight of its own history and success into a highly profitable modern newspaper group with state-of-the-art technology, a modern newsroom and a circulation going the right way. Much of the credit for that belongs to Maxwell. But much, too, belongs with the *Mirror* staff, which put up with the monstrous behaviour of a man who was out of control yet produced a paper to be proud of in the teeth of a publisher the like of whom nobody had remotely experienced before.

I left the train set in a damn sight better condition than I found it and Maxwell was about to kick it over again. Meanwhile, by giving the green light to the *People* buyout, he had given me the chance to show that the lunatics really could run the asylum. Hadn't he?

13

At my first press conference as a potential newspaper publisher I was described by the *Daily Telegraph* as a pugnacious little man who seemed uncertain about the details of his deal. Uncertain? I hadn't a clue. The truth was that I had been bounced out of the editorship of the *Daily Mirror* with the promise of the buyout. Once Maxwell realised the publicity potential of this, he warmed to his theme. 'I am giving him the chance to be his own publisher,' he boomed to the assembled hacks. And in an echo of the last time we had spoken about the possibilities, when he rang during John Penrose's farewell, he added, 'I do not think any publisher has given any journalist that chance before in the United Kingdom.' True, but would he do it? Both staff and the City were sceptical. Yet I was snowed under from merchant banks and venture capitalists offering their services, the most serious of which was Michael Stoddart, chairman of Electra, the venture capitalists who had masterminded the buyout of BPCC from Maxwell by John Holloran.

Maxwell reckoned the buyout would take two years if 'market conditions were right' so he gave himself plenty of leeway. He was also planning to float the Mirror Group, too, and the first question the City wanted answered was which would come first. He never gave a satisfactory answer.

The interest in the buyout was surprising but gratifying. Since I left the *People* almost five years earlier, circulation had continued to decline, it was now 2.64 million and still diving, half-a-million fewer than when I had been there in 1984. The paper had also gone through an unsettling number of editors, always a sign of distress and of a management unsure what the answer to the problem was. At least the buyout idea had never been tried before.

Ernie Burrington had followed me, and John Blake followed Ernie. Blake, a former pop page editor, had turned out to be a better editor of the paper than many thought he would be, but that wasn't enough for Maxwell. When Wendy Henry was fired from the *News of the World* by

Murdoch, Maxwell was determined to employ her for the worst possible reason – he thought it would make Murdoch furious. Why he should think that when he had fired her nobody could quite fathom, but she was not an ideal choice for the *People*. She had talent but was from the Look At This Baby With Two Heads school of voyeur journalism. It did not work on the disapproving, predominantly northern readership of the *People*. She eventually lost her job after the Prince William having a pee picture. She blamed me for moaning to Maxwell, but it had nothing to do with me. It was, as he has frequently pointed out, Joe Haines who said it was a gross invasion of privacy. Up until that moment, Maxwell had thought nothing of it.

There was little anyone could do about the continuing slide of the *People*, in spite of its impressive past. It should never have been brought into the Mirror stable. It was unloved by the vast majority of senior *Mirror* men; I was an exception. Over the years, the staff had grown older and wearier as they adapted to one editor after another and coped with relaunch after relaunch, none of them done with either enough promotion or conviction. The Sunday market was shrinking as the nature of Sunday changed. Huge circulations had been built on a Sunday afternoon spent reading a pile of papers with nothing to look forward to until Harry Secombe launched into *Songs of Praise*. No soccer on the TV then, no shops open and the pubs restricted to two hours at lunchtime. The large circulation Sundays made a fortune, led by the *News of the World* which topped 8 million at its zenith, a temple of titillation full of scout masters, errant teachers, Soho pimps and tarts and naughty housewives. The *People* was not expected to follow suit; it was intended to be a counterpoint to the *News of the Screws*, two notches more serious but still expected to reveal its fair share of sex scandals. As Sunday opened up, the popular newspapers stayed more or less the same until the broadsheet *News of the World* launched its colour magazine in order to stop it falling behind the more up-to-date tabloid *Sunday Mirror*.

My idea for the *People* was to turn it into the mass-market equivalent of the *Sunday Times* and the *Mail on Sunday*, a comprehensive package newspaper, colour magazine and several newsprint supplements, the complete popular Sunday with everything from travel to personal finance, from regional sport to the biggest names in the top leagues, consumer investigations, property guides and a new advertising venture based on an exchange market, a kind of bartering car boot sale. I believed it was the only way the paper could make itself felt in a market where, apart from the *Observer* in those days, it was the only newspaper without a daily stablemate. Maxwell was enthusiastic, but his mind was back on the *Daily Mirror* where, once again, he had decided to come out to play, which he did with a vengeance when the paper finally ran its investigation into Scargill. The consequences of his interference were depressingly inevitable; the investigation finished up confused and unsatisfactory, even though it was clear Scargill had a lot to answer for. Maxwell's involvement blurred the issue, as did a *Sun* spoiler run shortly before the *Mirror*'s report was published.

During my years away at the *Mirror*, it had become increasingly difficult to improve sales, even with a traditionally spicy Sunday paper story. One such was the attempt to blackmail the Chairman of Manchester United, Martin Edwards, a persistent and enthusiastic womaniser who lived dangerously enough to keep extremely compromising sex pictures of one of his married conquests in his office safe. Nor was he above getting his leg over on expenses. Before one game at Chelsea he entertained one of his mistresses at Langan's restaurant before taking her off for a little extra training at the Royal Lancaster Hotel. Manchester United picked up the bill for both the away games that day – the team's overnight stay and Edwards's £200 for a night in his own special theatre of dreams. The blackmailer, another mistress, demanded £100,000 – only a week or so's wages for David Beckham – from Edwards within seven days 'as a reward for not speaking to the press about his affair'. The dirty pictures, one of which President Clinton would not have considered inappropriate, were further evidence of Edwards's remarkably successful record playing away from home. All this is perfect mass tabloid Sunday fare, but the increase in circulation was modest rather than sensational. When Edwards attempted unsuccessfully to sell United to Sky, he had the brass neck to suggest that the club would be run 'in the same way as it has been for the past 18 years by me'.

Once again the *People* and its staff were showing they could break stories, and big ones. And, once again, Maxwell was showing his ability to prevaricate. We eventually relaunched the *People* in September 1990 but, sadly, we went off half-cock. He would not advance the funds for more than half of our ideas, so we finished up with an in-paper supplement of only marginal extra value and a magazine revamped by Frankie McGowan who had joined the buyout team from her job as the successful launch editor of *New Woman*. Frankie's magazine was a class act, but it was too thin to make a real difference. It suffered from the problems of all Sunday newspaper magazines – it lost a fortune. That launch issue of the paper carried the story that would eventually lead to the downfall of David Mellor. This was not the revelation about his affair with an actress but the exposure of his freebie holiday with Mona Bauwens, the daughter of the treasurer of the Palestine Liberation Organisation just before the Gulf War. The PLO supported Saddam Hussein. The immediate effect of the relaunch was to give us a big lift in sales, which we maintained for three or four weeks before it started dropping off again. We simply had not made the package big enough to be noticed, although the reaction to what we had done was largely favourable. Once again, the *People* was suffering from being Tail-End Charlie.

We still ruffled feathers, though. During the Conservative Party Conference in Bournemouth, our political editor Nigel Nelson happened to find himself at a table next to Cecil Parkinson who was dining with two political journalists. It was a convivial do and Cecil began to relax, waxing eloquent about the current Cabinet under Margaret Thatcher, whom he adored. He was dominating the room in a way I had seen him do before when sounding off about Sara Keays. Once, when he was in charge of Trade and Industry, we had gone out to lunch at Beoty's in St Martin's Lane – a favourite haunt – and at 5.00pm he was still going strong, an uncomfortable contrast to the silence he enforced on Ms Keays and their daughter. So compelling was his conversation that virtually nobody had left; the free entertainment was well worth the extra charge for the brandies. This time, Cecil's view on the Cabinet was equally stringent. 'If the Cabinet was a racehorse, I wouldn't put a bet on it,' he said. This was accompanied by some thumbnail sketches of a number of Cabinet members, none of them complimentary, particularly his view of the then Agriculture Secretary John Gummer. We decided to splash the story but not before we told Cecil, who naturally denied saying any such thing. 'What I said was, "If the Cabinet was a racehorse I would put a bet on it,", he said.

No you didn't, Cecil, I objected. In the end, we came to a deal; I left out one of his more astringent observations and he swallowed the story. I always had a soft spot for Cecil even though he was Thatcherite through and through. He was gossipy and funny and made me uneasily guilty of enjoying his indiscreet company in spite of his Dickensian treatment of Ms Keays and their troubled daughter Flora, whom he treated as a non-person himself and, through the disgraceful use and connivance of the law, managed to force the world to treat her as such, too. Cecil remained immensely attractive to women, but he was essentially a weak man dominated by three tough cookies in his life. Mrs Thatcher, his wife Anne and Sara Keays. Mrs T was always a sucker for the filmstar looks – Cecil has the Redford look about him – and I always thought she was a little bit in love with him. He told me once that he was sent on a mission by her private office to explain that the Churchillian V sign was presented with the palm of the hand outwards, not inwards as she was in the habit of doing, a message to the country many felt she was delivering all too successfully. Now Mrs T was naïve in the jargon of sex – 'Every Prime Minister needs a Willy', being her most famous remark. Less famous is her sitting on a gun in the Falklands during her lap of honour there and, when it fired, exclaiming, 'It really jerks you off, doesn't it?'

So Cecil's mission was tricky, but it was rendered impossible when he entered her office to find her reading *Private Eye*, a magazine which has a coded language all of its own. One of these phrases is 'discussing Uganda', code for having sex. As soon as Cecil entered, the Prime Minister was in her pulpit. 'I have said for years, Cecil, that girls in the House of Commons are worth more than just working as secretaries. Look at this, here is one – and she named the secretary to a well-known MP – who has stayed up late in order to discuss Uganda with him. That is the kind of girl we want in the party, an interest in foreign affairs.'

Cecil, of course, was the last person to contradict her. When asked by an eager front office if he had managed to broach the touchy subject of the V sign, he had to admit that the time had not been opportune.

A close examination of Cher is not something one would normally expect to encounter in the day-to-day running of a newspaper but Mary Riddell, who had come over to the *People* with me as an assistant editor, managed to land an interview with this magnificently preserved specimen. It was her preservation that was worrying her and, in order to counter constant speculation about how much of her remained real, Cher went for a full examination to a Harley Street plastic surgeon, for a thorough MOT prior to the interview. This was his report and the state of Cher's body; at least it was on the 19 October 1990:

> This patient has consulted me because the media are repeatedly mis-reporting information regarding any surgery which she may have had done to her body and, in order to clarify this indisputably, she has undergone examination from a consultant plastic surgeon, myself. I can confirm and certify that she has never had any surgery to her upper and lower eyelids, nor has she ever had any surgery to her cheekbones, such as the insertion of implants; nor has she had any similar surgery to her chin such as implants or other re-

contouring of the bone. All these areas represent her natural, well-developed good looks and have never been touched by surgery.

Further examination shows that, contrary to certain reports, she has never had any surgery to her ribcage in order to enhance her figure, nor are there any operative scars whatsoever on her abdomen or ribcage. Examination of her buttocks, thighs and lower legs show no evidence whatsoever of any surgery. She has no operative scars of any kind in these areas which confirm that she has never had any surgery to remove any skin or fat with the object of improving the shape of these areas. She does, however, have slim legs of athletic appearance and she can confirm that she has maintained her excellent figure through regular exercise and discipline with her diet.

So there you are, everything she had was absolutely real.

This obsession with plastic surgery can lead to some strange places, not least Michael Jackson's nose. A year or so later, the *Mirror*'s great photographer Ken Lennox took an amazing picture of Michael Jackson in concert. It was a shattering image, so extraordinary that Jackson first of all said it had been doctored – it hadn't – and then sued for libel. The Jackson entourage was so upset that on a subsequent visit to London one burly bodyguard encouraged fans to tip horse manure all over Lennox, an eloquent tribute to the power of the news picture. The case dragged on for years until a judge decided that he would halt proceedings until Jackson agreed to be examined by the *Mirror* team. Much to our surprise he agreed and plastic surgeon Christopher Ward and *Mirror* lawyer Charles Collier-Wright flew to Los Angeles in great secrecy to have a look at the world's most fascinating face. This they did in a suite of rooms on the eleventh floor of a hotel just outside Universal studios.

The first thing Charles noticed was that Jackson spoke in a perfectly normal voice, not the simpering whine he produced for his public utterances. Unfortunately, the strange vagaries of our legal system prevent me from telling you any more about the visit or the trip around Jackson's face; both are covered by a confidentiality agreement. I can't tell you what the examination revealed, but I can say that, as a result of it, Britain was prevented from witnessing one of the finest libel spectacles for many a year, much to the annoyance of George Carman, who we had hired to represent the *Mirror* and was working himself up for a thriller of a cross-examination.

By the end of the year, the vibes for the buyout were not good. Maxwell was evasive and, by now, heavily into his plans to float the

Mirror Group, giving characteristically different signs to the *Observer* and the *Sunday Times* about whether the *People* would be allowed to go its own way. At Electra, Michael Stoddart was getting restless and put a sale price of £15 million on the paper; Maxwell rejected it out of hand. Unknown to me, he had already valued us at £50 million in a document he produced for the banks in October. It was a ludicrous overpricing. At the same time, it was becoming clear he was tiring of Roy Greenslade at the *Mirror*. He had wanted to fire him as early as July after only five months in the job, but had been persuaded from doing so on the obvious grounds that five months in charge is far too short a time for an editor to be judged. Maxwell had always had a soft spot for Roy's wife, the highly talented feature writer Noreen Taylor, and was constantly suggesting she should interview his acquaintances. He was trying to set up an interview for her with Raisa Gorbachev and one morning phoned to give her a progress report. Noreen told him that she was off to Sotheby's to view some paintings and he asked her if she intended to buy. It was too much for Maxwell the tycoon. He told her to buy some and, with his wholehearted agreement, she spent £80,000. He then asked her to hang them in his flat, which she did. The problem here is that Maxwell starts to believe he owns you and, however innocent the intentions, you go down a notch in his estimation. He believed that money seduced everything, and with seduction, came disdain. Roy, however inadvertently, had allowed himself to become too close. It was a small point but one that weighed heavy with Maxwell.

When he first decided to sack Roy, prodded by a frank appraisal of her editor by Anne Robinson, he thought up the idea of a *'troika'* running the *Mirror*. Joe Haines as executive editor, in much the same way as an American editor; Mike Molloy, the former editor in charge during the day, and Bill Hagerty, Greenslade's deputy, drawing the short straw as editor at night. It was a useless idea but it would have had the advantage of Maxwell being able to divide and rule himself – 24 hours a day. Nothing came of it, which was just as well, but his relationship with the *Mirror* editor was down the tubes; it was only going to be a matter of time. Roy had not learnt the best way to handle Maxwell – how could he? – and assumed that the *Mirror* was run in much the same way as Murdoch ran the *Sun* where he had been a MacKenzie lieutenant for some years. He had not encouraged Joe Haines as an ally, and therefore either had to take on Maxwell himself on every occasion, give in to him or allow his executives to deal with him, especially at night, thus encouraging him to come back for more.

The final straw from Maxwell's point of view was an interview Roy gave to the trade paper, *UK Press Gazette*, which Roy saw as a 'hard, rational look at the tabloid marketplace' and Maxwell saw as him 'expressing a large amount of pessimism about tabloid newspapers'. It may well have been a rational look at the marketplace, but it was strong enough stuff for Jean Morgan, *Press Gazette*'s chief reporter, to ring Roy back and ask him if he wanted to withdraw any of it. Certainly, it was not the kind of interview a newspaper proprietor would encourage his editor to give on the eve of launching a flotation of the business. It was, I suspect, the interview of an editor who knew his time was up and wanted to get his retaliation in first.

Roy had never come to terms with the worst facet of editing a Maxwell paper; Maxwell came with the territory. You had to deal with it the best way you could, and that meant taking a load of flak from other newspaper editors who were lucky enough never to be brought face to face with their own courage, or walking away from the job. Roy did not lack courage, but he did not possess the mad loyalty to the *Mirror* which was necessary if you were to face down Maxwell. Nor was he a natural tabloid editor, a view held by many on the staff of the paper. When he arrived he adopted the *Sunday Times* policy of 'line' management, which led to vital columnists like Paul Foot feeling they did not have direct access to the editor, essential, in my view, for a column like his to work. He had to feel the editor was four square with his campaigns, cheering him on enthusiastically from the sidelines. Line management may work in a juggernaut Sunday paper, but not a tightly edited and packaged daily tabloid. Running a paper like the *Mirror* requires a tightrope walk every day; you have to balance the serious side with gossip, fashion, royal stories, good sport and a fair smattering of soap opera-led TV. It isn't easy and we all overbalanced, but the *Mirror* under Roy was in danger of becoming worthily dull, a paper which pleased his friends on the heavies, but was not altogether acceptable to the readers. This can be dismissed as the sour grapes of a former editor – it is an occupational hazard of all editors to be rubbished by the one before – but it was a general view of many *Mirror* executives and staff at the time. What is certainly true, and probably inevitable, was that Maxwell had bullied his way back into the paper, largely because Roy had decided against using the black arts of Joe Haines as a weapon to keep Maxwell at bay. In November, Maxwell tried and failed to hire David Montgomery as editor, a daft idea as they don't come much more right-wing than Montgomery.

By this time, the grey men in grey suits from the City were swarming all over the place compiling their long form report, the state of the company to be presented in the flotation document. Staffing, costs, overheads, lavatory rolls and the amount of bacon sandwiches sold in the canteen, were all checked. When they came to see me, I pointed out that the *People* was being bought out from the Mirror Group, therefore would take no part in their inquiries. If The *People* was to be part of the float, it would be so without me. I had edited it before and I had edited the *Daily Mirror*, I had no intention of staying on purely as an editor. This caused consternation in the ranks of the suits and a report was fired off to Maxwell asking him to 'bring me into line'. But he did nothing, and neither did I. Maxwell now had a serious problem with the flotation and, as we were to find out less than a year later, he was in desperate need of money. He was on the verge of firing his flagship editor, sales in the latter part of the year had slipped behind those of the previous one, and in December – a notoriously bad month at the best of times – the figure had dropped below three million. In February and March it was to drop below again, never to return above the magic three. On top of that, he had an editor at the *People* refusing to co-operate with his flotation because he had been promised a buyout which Maxwell clearly wanted to renege on. The impasse was broken by Michael Stoddart who went to see Maxwell in New York where he had launched himself into negotiations to buy the *New York Daily News*, crippled by a strike which showed no signs of ending. It was clear the gap between Stoddart and Maxwell's ideas of a fair price was unbridgeable and Michael rang me to tell me so. The idea of the lunatics being in charge of the asylum and the slaves shedding their chains was over before it started. Did he ever intend to allow the buyout or was it just a convenient way of getting me out of the *Mirror* without sacking me? The answer to both questions is probably 'yes'. Like so many things with Maxwell, he intended to carry them through right up until the moment he didn't. He was bucked by the idea of being the first proprietor to give the slaves their freedom, but he wouldn't give me a price. He did to the banks, valuing the *People* at £50 million as an asset for disposal to me between October 1991 and June 1992. Although this was circulated widely to the financial institutions, he never once indicated to me either the price or the timescale. It wasn't until cornered by Michael Stoddart that he came across with it.

So that should have been that. But, of course, it wasn't. Once again he asked me to 'pop up', but this time I had to point out that he was in New York – he had forgotten – so I would have to 'pop over'. I went with the group's technical and printing director Ian McDonald, whom he wanted to examine the print set-up of the *Daily News*. It was to be a memorable trip.

I knew by this time that Maxwell was not only going to can the buyout, but wanted me to return to the *Daily Mirror*. Charlie Wilson, who Maxwell had brought from News International after he was sacked as *Times* editor by Murdoch, was put in temporary charge. Maxwell even flirted with asking him to edit it permanently, a crazy idea from every conceivable point of view. Wilson was an accomplished journalist, but he had never edited a mass circulation popular paper and he was an out-and-out Thatcherite with no sympathy for either the Labour Party or the *Mirror* cause. With an election on the horizon, his appointment would have been a disaster and, if Maxwell didn't know it, Wilson certainly did.

McDonald and I flew out to see Maxwell in New York where he had hitched his wagon – his yacht the *Lady Ghislaine* – to the East Side Pier near 32nd Street and the Manhattan heliport. As we arrived, he was showing a group of schoolchildren around the boat. When he saw us I spotted something I had noticed once or twice before – a sense of relief and almost pleasure came across his face for an instant, then the mask was back. I do not think it was because he was delighted to see us especially, it was because we were faces he knew, and for a moment the loneliness of a man, who delighted in meeting everybody and knowing no one, showed through. It was the uncertainty and deep insecurity of the true outsider, a man who feels he has been precluded from the world of others and has therefore determined to build his own, with his own rules for his own game. Fanciful nonsense possibly, but I had seen that look on his face before and it seemed to me to be a key to the bubbling mess inside.

So it was on to the boat. Be careful to take your shoes off before you sink into the ankle-deep pile. The *Lady Ghislaine* once belonged to Adnan Khashoggi and was furnished in what I can only describe as 1970s Playboy Baroque, all leather and tubular steel, deep fluffy white carpets and enormous bed, but strangely cramped for such a large yacht. We were then whisked to the famous old *Daily News* building on 42nd Street, model for Superman's *Daily Planet*. Ian McDonald was asked to look at the pre-press technology, although technology was rather a grand word for equipment that must have been creaking when Superman was a baby in Smallville. The staff was in much the same boat. We found one in the camera press room flat out asleep, too drunk to wake up. This we were assured was quite usual and acceptable; we were back in the dark days of Fleet Street in the early '80s. Ian's eyes boggled as he was told of the manning levels – three times that of the modern *Mirror* – the antiquated black-and-white presses and the enormously slow state-of-the-ark composing room. The Fleet Street scenario was completed by the fact that the print unions were just finishing a long and destructive strike which the previous owners, the Chicago Tribune Group, had failed to solve. Like Reed International at the *Mirror* seven years earlier, all they wanted to do was get out, and they paid Maxwell $60 million to take it off their hands. New Yorkers swing from deep gloom to elation easily, and Maxwell was hailed as the saviour of the *Daily Noos*. A cab driver really did lean out of his seat at 2nd Avenue traffic lights and shake hands with Maxwell, 'because I wanna shake da hand of d'man who saved d'*Noos*'.

But could he? It would mean taking on the Teamsters Union among others, and New York was a blue-collar city. There were all sorts of dark stories about the *News* delivery vans being used as drug couriers by the Mafia, a wonderful distribution network if you think about it, rushing to all corners of New York City in the dead of night, totally unmolested. The Teamsters' made the National Graphical Association and SOGAT look like the Royal College of Nursing and, with its history, a negotiating ploy could well include being dumped in concrete in the East River. But none of this worried Maxwell, he was living for the moment and New York loved him. He was pictured on 42nd Street flogging the paper from a news vendor's stand wearing the obligatory baseball cap and, once the strike was over, he ceremoniously restarted the presses – two hours late because pre-press was so slow and he had increased the cover price at the last minute. Before that, he had decided to have a celebratory dinner at Fu's, one of the city's most fashionable Chinese restaurants, where he ran into New York's former mayor John Lindsay who was immediately offered a job on the *News*.

Then, together with Bob Pirie, the Rothschilds' chief in New York, it was over the river to the *News's* printing plant in Brooklyn with a cab driver who had no idea where he was going and all Pirie's impressive repertoire of swear words didn't make any difference. Eventually we found it and, while Maxwell was making his speech about bygones being bygones and working together as a team in a new age of hope for the *Daily News* etc., fights were breaking out among print workers and editorial staff, some of whom had worked through the strike. The new deal hadn't quite reached the shop floor yet.

Maxwell asked me to attend a *Daily News* editorial conference which I did with some diffidence. I knew how I would feel if some upstart from over the water, brought in by a new proprietor, suddenly muscled in on my patch. But all was smoothed over and I joined the Sunday edition team which turned out to be more like an army. The conference went on and on for well over an hour-and-a-half with a good 30 people all having their say at great and boring length. It may have been a good meeting, but there was no way it was going to make for a great and incisive newspaper. It cemented me in my view that American newspaper men and women's biggest fans are themselves, and far too often they confirm it at enormous and tedious length in their own papers.

By now, America's newest newspaper baron was where he liked being best, on the front pages. And he was to be anointed at America's grandest journalistic shindig, the Gridiron Dinner in Washington. The Gridiron Club was a venerable old Washington establishment, originally all-male until the bastion was stormed by John Knox's monstrous regiment. It didn't capitulate at the first blast but, in 1975, bowed to the inevitable and women were admitted. The dinner maintained its distinct men-only university flavour with journalists and politicians alike doing their skits and satires of each other. The guest of honour was the President of the United States; this year it was George Bush, fresh from what he thought was an election-winning campaign in the Gulf War, and virtually all his Cabinet went with him. Maxwell was squeezed in at the last moment, and so was I.

There was, however, a problem; the dinner was a seriously dressy do and men had to wear white tie and tails. Maxwell travels with an extensive wardrobe, but white tie and tails were not his natural companions. We did not know until 24 hours before the dinner that we were to go, but I managed to borrow my kit in New York from an open-all-hours hire shop. Maxwell, being no known size, couldn't, and anyway he wanted his medals. So his Man Friday, Bob Cole, was ordered to hop on the first available Concorde to Washington with Maxwell's gear. That night, I left my suit on the *Lady Ghislaine* – 'It will be safe there, Richard, much better than your hotel room; after all, I'm paying for it' – and disappeared with Ian McDonald to show him the sights of New York while Maxwell retired to the charms of his deep-pile bedroom. We finished up in the newspapermen's bar, Costello's, far too late in every sense, it was a ghost bar, a sign of Fleet Street's changing times. The old team of barmen had gone, so had the journalists, long removed from their cosy jobs in New York bureaux. Even the famous James Thurber cartoons were covered in a thick layer of dust.

The phone rang impossibly early three hours later as I emerged from a hangover and the sun dazzled over the East River.

'You've fucked it now,' boomed an all-too-familiar voice.

'Morning, Bob,' I croaked.

'Why did you allow your tail suit to be stolen?' he said.

'But it's on your boat, you said it would be safe there.'

'Fuck you, it's gone. So have my shirts.'

In spite of the throbbing head, I started to laugh.

'It's not funny. You better pop up.'

The thought of some quick-footed thief wandering around Harlem or the Bronx wearing a white tie and tails and several shirts the size of tents was funny and, I assumed, likely to attract some sort of attention. Apparently, they had been left on the deck to be packed into the helicopter the next morning and had disappeared without trace. What wasn't funny was that I had to get another one and pay the price of losing the first. Not only that, there was a run on white tie and tails because of that evening's dinner. I managed to get the last one in more or less the right size, but my plastic was now groaning with more than £1,000 worth of white tie and tails to support. When I saw Maxwell as we prepared to board the helicopter to fly to Washington, he was in testy mood. 'I've bought you two dress suits now ... I hope you realise how generous I am.'

'Er, you haven't Bob. You have cost me God knows how much because you lost the first and I've had to pay a repeat fee for hiring the second.' He ignored me and climbed aboard.

The row over the white tie and tails had obscured the fact that we had not yet discussed what I was there for – to be told officially the buyout was off, which he announced in the helicopter taking us to his new toy, the Gulfstream jet which had been on permanent standby at a private airfield just outside the city. Once in the helicopter, together with *Daily News* editor James Willse, he shouted to me that the buyout could not go ahead because of the Mirror flotation. I shouted back that I had heard as much from Michael Stoddart. As we clattered our way over Manhattan, he startled me by shouting back, 'I want you to edit the *Daily News*.' This was a bit of a stunner for two reasons – I hadn't expected it, and the present incumbent was sitting next to me, pretending not to hear. It was a crass piece of unnecessary behaviour and I rejected his offer instinctively, pleading that my son Christopher was at a crucial time in his schooling and I did not want to up sticks and move to New York. Neither did I think an Englishman would make much of an editor of what was a New York local paper. Subsequently, Martin Dunn of *Today* did go over there and do a good job, although he admitted to me it was often hard for him to find the New Yorkers' wavelength.

The Gulfstream was Maxwell's pride and joy. Uniformed stewardesses and pilot, luxurious upholstery with a front section that could be shut off from the rest of the plane, the seats turning into a huge bed for Maxwell. On take off, he sat in isolated splendour while the rest of us, secretaries, Josef his butler, James Willse and myself, were packed into the back. Once we were airborne, he asked me to 'pop up' and started to explain in more detail why he was abandoning the buyout. In the end it came down to two things: Stoddart was not offering enough money – 'he is taking the piss' – and the flotation of the group. I told him that those were his decisions to make and there was obviously nothing I could do about it, but I had no intention of staying on as editor of the *People*. I had made that clear when we agreed the buyout and I had not changed my mind. 'What are we to do then, where do we go from here?' he asked.

I knew he wanted me to go back to the *Mirror*, but I realised that his pride would not allow him to ask me. He wanted me to offer to do the job again so he could dictate the terms. 'Pay-off time I would have thought, Bob,' I said.

This was a reckless gamble on my part, because I did want to go back to the *Mirror*, it was my one true love and there was no point in denying it. I did not want to be out on the street looking for a job I knew would be second best to the one I was now in danger of losing. So I hesitated and then added, 'If you want, I will go back and edit the *Mirror*. But not in the same way as before, I want some guarantees.'

Cautiously, Maxwell agreed, but he wasn't too keen on the guarantees so he didn't press me as to what they were. This was just as well because I hadn't formulated any; it was done to stop him laying down his own conditions.

We booked into the Capital Hilton over the road from the White House and the hotel where the dinner was to be held. Maxwell immediately started on a string of meetings with everyone from presidential staff to the Prime Minister of Turkey who, for some reason, wanted to see him. It was only late in the afternoon he realised his white tie and tails had still not arrived; Concorde had been delayed. On checking my gear four floors below Maxwell's suite, I found I did not have black socks to go with my suit. All the shops were shut so I went in search of Josef, Maxwell's brilliant butler. Josef was Portuguese and was an efficient, intelligent version of Manuel from *Fawlty Towers*. He had the ability to be the perfect butler but was quite capable of taking the piss out of Maxwell even while serving him. He did not treat him altogether seriously, which was just as well considering the way Maxwell could treat his staff. 'Josef,' I said. 'I need a pair of black socks.'

'But, Mr Stott, I only have the pair I am wearing.'

'I'll swop you, I need them,' and handed over a blue pair of my own, dark enough for Maxwell not to notice. The deal was done.

An hour before the dinner was due to start, Bob Cole arrived bearing Maxwell's gear. Fifteen minutes later I went up to his suite for a drink, only to find Bob Cole in tears of frustration running down the corridor. 'He definitely told me white tie and tails,' he wailed. 'But when I get here, he shouts and screams at me saying, "You've brought the wrong fucking suit, you idiot, it's dinner jacket. Go and get me one." Where do I get a dinner jacket his size at this time of night?'

I calmed him down, he had brought the right suit, Maxwell's brain was fusing – something that was happening with increasing frequency by this time. Maxwell had, of course, sacked Cole, who had been with him for almost three decades, but by now he was used to that. It was the frustration of Maxwell insisting that he was right when he clearly was not that had got to him. Bob Cole reassured, I went into the suite to find Maxwell in the white tie and tails complete with medals and shiny shoes – but no socks.

'You look good,' he said.

'Don't look too bad yourself, Bob,' I said. 'But aren't you going to wear any socks?'

'That fucker Cole didn't bring any.'

'Oh, you'll have to wear black socks Bob, part of the uniform.'

He looked at me. 'Where did you get yours from?'

'Your butler. It was his only pair.'

Josef, who was pouring the drinks, lifted his trousers to show he was wearing my blue ones. Maxwell looked from me to him and back again. 'He's my fucking butler, I should have those socks.'

'Well I'm not taking them off, Bob, I've done a deal and Josef has got my socks.'

'That's right, Mr Maxwell, Mr Stott asked to borrow them much earlier,' insisted Josef with a shrug. We both stared at him, then Josef relented. 'I'll see what I can do, Mr Maxwell, maybe one of the hotel waiters can help.'

Maxwell gave him a $100 bill and Josef went in search of the most expensive pair of black socks in newspaper history, which he discovered in double-quick time leaving one Capital Hilton waiter very happy, even if he did have cold feet for the rest of the night.

After the Gridiron dinner, we flew back to London in the Guifstream with Maxwell tucked up securely in his bed by an air stewardess and the rest of us huddled in blankets at the back. Maxwell didn't allow cooking on the plane because of the smell, so Josef and I amused ourselves by making cocktails in the galley. It was interesting to see how Maxwell tried to sleep; you could get the occasional glimpse of him when the curtain opened. He tossed, turned, coughed, cleared his throat every five minutes and went to the lavatory on several occasions.

Back in London, he told me he was about to announce me as the editor of the *Mirror* again and assembled what members of the board he could find late on a Monday evening. I had to cut him short and remind him we had unfinished business; I was determined that I was going to get my guarantees – by now I had thought of some – however worthless they may turn out to be. We retired to his study and I told him that I was not doing the job this time with stars in my eyes, that the loss of the buyout was a great disappointment and that I wanted guarantees of spending money on foreign travel and series – Maxwell had always insisted on sanctioning both, although in practice we had found ways around that – and I must have a free rein. He agreed, he always did, and offered me £30,000 as a golden hello, which I turned down. If I had accepted, I would have been at his mercy, and however much I could have done with the cash it would never have compensated for being compromised by his wallet.

With that we agreed and shook hands, both of us wary. 'Welcome to the *Daily Mirror*,' he said.

'I've been there before, Bob,' I pointed out.

'So you have, so you have.'

I was back where I had always wanted to be.

14

When I moved my desk and chair back down the corridor to that old familiar office on the third floor overlooking Holborn Circus, flotation was seven weeks away. Two years earlier, eight months before I left, circulation was 3,242,508. A year later it was 3,143,683, and in the month I went back it was 2,935,137. We were back on the slippery slope and this time there was going to be no colour to help stop the slide.

It wasn't just us. The *Sun* had dropped from 3,953,790 to 3,688,645 in the same year. Bingo had nothing like the pull of ten years earlier and television advertising, already hideously expensive, provided little more than a very short-term sales boost. Certainly not worth the outlay of £300,000 for a heavyweight weekend exposure. The problem for the *Mirror* had always been that the *Sun* responded much better to competitions, giveaways and games. It was the paper born of the TV game show age we live in and it reaped the benefits. The *Mirror*'s strength, an instantly recognised personality, pro-Labour, working class, campaigning, was also its weakness if you turned over the coin; too political, northern, old, worthy. Colour had helped us change that perception to a degree, but Maxwell, shifting his interest to the United States once the launch was successful, failed to turn the screw on the *Sun* by deciding to cut costs at the precise moment he should have been adding investment. If he had done so, the newspaper history of the next 20 years may well have been radically different. News International was more than a year behind us on colour, and even when they got it failed to use it properly. Murdoch still remained unconvinced of its editorial advantages and his views tended to influence those of his senior executives. Whatever the cause, our greatest rival's use of editorial colour was uncharacteristically poor.

The flotation was a nightmare for the editorial production staff. Everything had to be examined and receive the good housekeeping seal of approval from both the financial advisers, Samuel Montagu, and their solicitors. In one way it was helpful; it meant Maxwell couldn't change the copy, although it didn't stop him trying. When I say 'everything' I mean everything, even the cross-heads which are used to break up the type had to be approved. 'GET SET FOR THE GREAT MIRROR SHARE OFFER' was definitely not all right. 'ALL SET FOR THE MIRROR SHARE OFFER' was. The crosshead 'WONDERFUL' caused immense trouble.

All this took up an enormous amount of time and energy with Maxwell huffing and puffing in the background demanding more space and me fighting a rearguard action, daintily treading the tightrope of not going over the top while remaining enthusiastic about the flotation, which I was. If the institutions had spent as much time making sure the prospectus was accurate as they did complaining about captions in the paper and threatening hapless journalists – I was told if sub-editors made another mistake the culprit would have to be fired – then the subsequent scandal could have been avoided. They spent hours writing memos complaining about the editorial staff, but didn't mention in the prospectus the fact that the Maxwell private companies owed £980 million to the banks at the time of flotation on top of substantial borrowings from Maxwell Communications Corporation and the pension funds. If these figures had been published, the flotation – or at least one with Maxwell retaining 51 per cent of the shares – would have been dead in the water. From our point of view a partially publicly-owned company, even if he did control that 51 per cent, was better than nothing at all. For if he was properly regulated with all the constraints brought about by public listing, he might be more manageable as far as I was concerned.

We rarely saw the flotation suits unless they were asking questions or moaning that we had cocked something up. However, one day the top guns of Samuel Montagu paid me a visit and I said, jokingly I thought, that when the Mirror went public, Bob would have to have more than one signature on the cheque and that he wouldn't be able to carry on selling things to himself. No problem with that, they said. All was taken care of, we've got his measure. The *Mirror* has been properly ring-fenced, away from the maze of Maxwell private companies. In order to ensure this, two independent, non-executive directors were to be appointed. The first was Sir Robert Clark, recently retired deputy chairman of the TSB Group and former chairman of the merchant bank Hill Samuel who had OK'd Maxwell's cheque when he bought the Mirror from Reed. The second was Alan Clements, a former finance director of ICI.

I had been given an insight into Clark's position when I happened by chance to stand near his wife during a football festival being held at Charterhouse public school in which my son and her grandson were both playing. Lady Clark has a loud and penetrating voice and she announced to the group she was with that her husband was one of the few people who could handle Maxwell. 'He will make sure Bob does as he is told, he will have no problem with him, there's no need to worry about that, no need at all, he knows how to handle him,' she said.

The flotation was managed by the skin of its teeth, much of the share issue being taken up in the United States. In Britain the City was cooler, largely because of Maxwell's 51 per cent stake. Journalists naturally want to blow the trumpet for their newspaper, and tabloid ones will want to do it in the style of the paper. The *Mirror* had always had a close relationship with its readers, fostered over the years by Marje Proops and her advice column and the Readers' Letters service which Maxwell axed. We wanted the readers to be able to buy shares, and we wanted them to make money from being part of a successful company. If the ring-fence was in place, if the auditing of the Mirror's current position by Cooper Lybrand was careful and accurate, and if the rigorous and tight control of Samuel Montagu was as diligent as it was when it came to shouting and screaming about cross-heads in the paper, then there should be no problem. But it would have been better if newspapers were prevented by law from carrying editorial on their own flotation, the information should be carried by advertisement only. That way no editorial pressure can be brought to bear; the cumbersome method of signing off editorial reports made it no better than an advert anyway.

But at least some good seemed to have been achieved; Maxwell had once again demanded staffing cuts and I was told to make them. Charlie Wilson, the newly-installed editorial director, passed on the news and left me to do the nasty bit. The journalists, however, decided on action, and I must say my sympathy was with them. There had been precious little discussion and the management seemed as ill-prepared for the fallout as I was. I told Maxwell there was no way I could get them back to work and suggested the board might like to explain its position, because I couldn't. Clearly the board couldn't, and Maxwell – who was out of the country – retreated, leaving me to issue a statement that no further action would be taken on voluntary and compulsory redundancies until 'the Publisher has had an opportunity to discuss the position further with management and the chapel'. He never did, and it was a singular victory for the NUJ chapel and a humiliation for the new board which Maxwell castigated roundly for 'not having a fallback position', even though it was his idea in the first place. He backed down because he was fearful of the public reaction to his newly floated business. But, less happily, it was also an indicator that the rest of the board had no mind of its own and that going public had not succeeded in encouraging any independence.

Maxwell was now spending much of the time in New York dealing with his rapidly expanded interests in the United States. This suited me, the calls were fewer, apart from the occasional ritual demand to cut costs. On one occasion he demanded the immediate sacking of all casuals – part-time workers who supplement staff – particularly in sport, where there was a complex system of regional editions during the football season. Part of the reason was nothing to do with the need to cut costs, it was because casuals can vote in NUJ meetings and Maxwell wanted to reduce the chapel's power, casuals do not necessarily have the same commitment to the paper as staff men. He would do this in a roundabout way, usually through the editorial manager who would fire off a memo to me. I then pointed out to the editorial director, Charlie Wilson, that if I carried out this instruction the paper would stop immediately. Wilson's reply was: 'It's his train set, matey, no point in talking to me about it, you'll have to take it up with him.' But, of course, it wasn't his train set any more – only 51 per cent of it was, but he continued in the same way as before and the board of directors made no effort to stop him. Many owed their positions to Maxwell, particularly Ernie Burrington, the managing director in London, who was about to be sacked as *People* editor in favour of John Blake when Maxwell asked myself and Joe Haines about his decision. Ernie had been badly burned in the shares department on Black Monday and we told Maxwell he would be in some difficulty if forced out. There was little prospect of him getting employment elsewhere. The next thing we knew, Maxwell had made him deputy Publisher. He had a soft spot for Ernie, who was one of the first journalists he grew to know well because he was seconded to smooth the passage of the Who Dares Wins game in Maxwell's early days.

There were two Ernie Burringtons, and it is necessary to meet them both to understand why he was never taken seriously as a senior management executive by the editorial departments, who knew both of them well. First, Ernie the extremely talented journalist who was blighted by drink. He spent much of his time drunk, whisky – or 'red eye' as he described it – was his downfall and when drunk he knew no fear. On one occasion, he had to be pulled off the desk of the *People*'s women's editor Pat Boxall by the deputy editor Alan Hobday after a red-eye session. Hobday had received an SOS message from Ms Boxall's secretary as she tried to fight off Ernie's attentions. Drink promoted the idea of a bit of slap and tickle for him, but sadly destroyed the performance.

The second Ernie was Ernest Burrington, bridge-playing friend and confidant of, amongst others, Lord Harris of Peckham, the carpet king, living on a private estate in Orpington with his charming wife Nancy.

Ernie was shrewd and clever and, if he had managed to stay off the booze would have made editor long before he did. He gave up after his first binge when I was editor of the *People* and, as far as I know, he has never touched a drop since. But he owed his position and his £170,000 a year to Maxwell – he had been given a £20,000 pay rise four months before the flotation – and however journalistically skilled he was, he was a naïf as far as high finance was concerned. All this Maxwell knew and, far from discouraging him, it probably determined his decision to make him joint managing director. Maxwell asked Vic Horwood, the chief executive of the *Daily Record* and *Sunday Mail* in Scotland and a good newspaper businessman, to suggest a managing director for the flotation. Horwood suggested Burrington because, he told Joe Haines later, 'I decided Bob wanted to be his own managing director.' From the old Mirror board, only Lawrie Guest as finance director and Horwood, joint managing director with responsibility for the Scottish titles, were financially experienced, but Guest – a mild, affable chartered accountant, at home nursing a gin and tonic in a suburban golf clubhouse – was no match for Maxwell's financial bullying. He was a former finance director of Reed and had already been terrorised by Maxwell in the years leading up to the flotation. His position was made even more precarious by the appointment to the Mirror board of 42-year-old Michael Stoney, a Maxwell man through and through, who was deputy managing director (finance) of Robert Maxwell Holdings and finance director of Pergamon.

Charlie Wilson was brought on at the handsome salary of £110,000 a year; as a former editor of the *Times* he would be appreciated in the City, and was useful to Maxwell in his dealings with the *Daily News* in New York. Wilson was a Murdoch man to his fingertips; he had originally been hired to edit the *Sporting Life* – with his racing and journalistic flair he would have been superb – but had never got round to doing it. Like so many of Murdoch's top men, he was eventually discarded and left to kick his heels in Wapping, so when the Maxwell call came it was too good to resist. But he had no feeling either for the *Mirror* or its traditions. Every other executive director was a former Mirror Group executive, except for the deputy chairman, Ian Maxwell. Ian was an easy-going, nice enough bloke, but totally under the thumb of his father. There was never any chance of him standing up to the old man.

We relied for good governance on the ring-fence which Samuel Montagu and their legal eagles were being paid a fortune to construct. After all, there was nobody who was not aware of that damning judgement by the DTI inspectors. We relied, too, on the Mirror audit by Cooper Lybrand being thorough about our relationship with the other Maxwell companies, which it was not.

Maxwell's first fast one came as soon as the flotation was over and he bowled the board all ends up. At the first board meeting, he slipped past them a resolution giving him sole signing rights for an unlimited amount at a new bank account with the NatWest. Nobody noticed the decision, buried in a sheaf of minutes of previous meetings and, in effect, the board had handed him the keys to the Mirror coffers. At the same time he separated the powers of his two financial men. Lawrie Guest, the long-serving Mirror finance director, was put in charge of accounting, the book-keeping department, while Stoney was handed the treasury, the investment arm of the Mirror, a move either the directors did not know about, or those who did failed to spot the significance. It was vital if Maxwell was to use Mirror cash to prop up his ailing empire.

It wasn't only the empire that was ailing. During the summer, there was a marked deterioration in Maxwell's physical condition. He had a constant cold and cough, his face became more florid, necessitating the use of more powder. He was also becoming more isolated. His marriage was, to all intents and purposes, finished. Betty was reduced to faxing his office complaining that she never saw and rarely spoke to him. On two or three evenings, he had talked to me about the legacy he wanted to leave; he was proud of his achievements at the Mirror and he had good cause to be, but he was now in the grip of two obsessions – his determination to out-Murdoch Murdoch and his love for a young girl. He had become infatuated with his secretary Andrea Martin, who, although she had left full-time employment, still came in on Sundays. In his isolation and increasing fantasy world, Maxwell was deeply and hopelessly in love with her. She wasn't his first obsession but she was certainly the one that became all-consuming and out of control. For all the bombast and bullying, there was a part of him that was nothing more than a lonely, sick, overweight elderly man, pining for a handsome youth that had long gone. Even his love for Andrea was unreciprocated. She was in love with the *Mirror*'s foreign editor, the twice-married Nick Davies, a frequent companion of Maxwell on his trips. It was a fraught tangle which could only lead to Maxwell's humiliation.

Maxwell's world wasn't the only one that was turning topsy-turvy. He had infiltrated Mikhail Gorbachev's inner circle by promising to back the

Gorbachev-Maxwell Institute for Environmental Research in Minneapolis, yet another idea that came to nothing. A year earlier, Maxwell had been screaming at Greenslade over Gorbachev's decision to send Soviet tanks into Lithuania with all the bloody violence that followed, something the publisher refused to accept on the bizarre grounds that Gorby would ring him first.

Come the revolution in August 1991, I was on holiday in Crete. As soon as I heard, I set off for the *Mirror* leaving Penny to struggle home as best she could with two of the children, Hannah and Christopher. Nobody ever said editors were thoughtful human beings. At Athens Airport, I telephoned the office only to find that Maxwell had banned any reporters from travelling to Moscow on the grounds that he would be the first to hear anything of interest. I went potty and asked to be put through to him. From his first words, I knew he was feeling guilty. 'How do you think I am handling this story while you are away enjoying a well-earned rest?'

'I'm on my way back, Bob, and at the moment you aren't handling it at all. We must be in Moscow, that is where the action is.'

'No, listen, I know Gorbachev.'

'You may know him, Bob, but he's in-bloody-carcerated and I bet you fifty quid to a rouble he hasn't phoned you. We've got to go, Bob, and we've got to go now. Not only that, I'm bloody melting in here, it's over a hundred degrees in this phone box and I'll die within the next minute and then you'll be sorry.'

'Oh, fuck you, do what you like,' he replied and slammed down the phone. I came out of the phone box dripping with sweat from top to toe, only to be greeted by a round of applause from a group of Greek matrons who had been listening to my shrieking.

I was wary of what would happen when I got back to the office. The prospect of Maxwell directing everything from his command centre filled me with gloom. When I arrived, it looked every bit as bad as I had feared. Maxwell had decreed that Gorbachev was the story. He certainly wasn't, because by now Yeltsin was storming the Russian parliament building in full glorious movie colour. Maxwell asked my deputy Phil Swift – he had come with me from the *People* – to 'pop up'. I went with him and he was surprised to see me back so quickly. Gorbachev was the story, he said; he was sure I would agree. I didn't.

'No, this is the story, Bob.' I showed him the pictures of the shelled building. Maxwell looked threatening and asked Phil to leave. Here we go, I thought. The Russian parliament isn't the only one that's going to get a pounding. He set off on a long ramble about knowing everyone and everything about the uprising, he had his contacts, they would give us world exclusives.

'Well, they might, Bob,' I replied. But I have to deal in what I've got and I'm telling you the biggest thing I have is this picture, it is the stuff of history.' This was becoming an uncanny rerun of the Ceausescu execution. I held his gaze, crunch time again. But he was in no mood for a fight. 'You've just got to trust me, Bob,' I said before he could; it was one of his favourite phrases.

He shrugged, 'You're the editor.' And the battle was more or less over.

Over the next two or three days I visited him frequently in his office after being asked to 'pop up' to be given new information from his contacts. But doors which used to open to him were closing. He would sit alone for hours at the round ebony conference table in the middle of his office phoning government officials in Moscow. They were never in and they never returned his calls. The information he was passing on to me was coming from CNN, I had it on in my office too. There was no fight in him, illness, a hopeless love and mounting financial pressures were taking their toll, now even his friend Gorby was deserting him.

The fall of Gorbachev was quickly followed by more bad news. *Panorama* was planning a programme on Maxwell's business affairs and he was jumpy about it. When it was broadcast, the programme contained little that was new but, apart from undermining confidence in his companies, it also revealed that a *Mirror* Spot-the-Ball contest had been fixed to avoid the payout of a £1 million jackpot. There was nothing especially new about this either; all newspaper Bingo games are fixed to the extent that in order to have a winner every week, certain 'trigger' numbers are held back to produce a regular payout. When the *Mirror* launched its Bingo game in the early 1980s in response to the phenomenal success of the *Sun*'s promotion, we launched 'honest' Bingo – in other words, we played the game as it would be in the halls, calling the balls by lucky dip rather than by computer. The result of this was that we might go two weeks without a winner and then produce a dozen. The readers hated it; they much preferred the *Sun*'s controlled version and we were forced to follow suit. All newspaper games are a variation of this. The problem with the *Mirror*'s Spot the Ball – introduced as a spoiler to the *Sun*'s version, always a dubious investment – was that some of the wording in the paper, usually carefully worked out by the competitions department, had been rewritten, but not by Maxwell. There was also one crucial difference to the normal game – the missing ball had to be placed in the picture and, on his own admission, the *Mirror*'s editor Roy Greenslade himself placed it in the most unlikely positions. What on earth he was doing getting so involved is a mystery to me, in all my years as an editor I never became involved in such a way, particularly as he had contemplated resigning over the issue because he hated the idea of fixing the game. Yet here he was, conspiring to make the competition as difficult to win as he could. Whatever the reasons for the intimate involvement of the editor, it gave Maxwell the chance to disclaim responsibility himself.

Unfortunately, he was determined to sue *Panorama* and set up a meeting with myself, the former competitions chief John Jenkinson, Ernie Burrington and Roger Eastoe, the director in charge of advertising and marketing. Before we met with Maxwell, I told the two directors that from what I had been told by John Jenks and read for myself in the Spot the Ball editorial copy, the allegations made by *Panorama* were largely true. We should resist any attempt by him to make the paper claim it was not, although if he wished to say so himself we would report what he had to say. I asked for their support and they promised they would give it.

At the meeting with Maxwell, John Jenks told him that the *Panorama* allegations were correct and that part of the problem was the in-paper promotion material which had been rewritten. I agreed with him, then Maxwell turned to Burrington and Eastoe, who suddenly seemed to have been struck by severe speech defects. Maxwell then cleared the room leaving him and me together, where I repeated my view of what had happened and told him we should come clean as the quickest way to lance the boil. He didn't agree, but he didn't insist on a statement by the *Mirror* either, preferring to rely on his own indignation to carry the day. In the end, the Spot the Ball fury died down, I suspect because newspapers in glass houses realised they couldn't throw too many stones.

But our respite was short. Seymour Hersh, a Pulitzer Prize-winning American reporter, claimed in a new book that Maxwell and foreign editor Nick Davies were Israeli spies and that Davies had been involved in the kidnap by Mossad of Mordecai Vanunu, an Israeli scientist sent to prison for blowing the whistle on his country's secret nuclear weapons programme. As a result of this book, two MPs – Rupert Allason and George Galloway – put down motions based on it on the House of Commons order paper, thus protecting themselves from any libel action. The pro-Arab Galloway claimed Davies had been involved in substantial arms sales to Iran and other countries over a ten-year period. He was, said the MP, 'a long-standing and highly-paid Israeli intelligence asset' and that he 'betrayed the whereabouts in a hotel in London of Mordecai

Vanunu to Mossad'. Allason claimed the *Mirror* and Maxwell 'have maintained a close relationship' with Mossad.

Both Davies and Maxwell flatly denied the claims, some of which had surfaced two years earlier. I have always detested the practice of MPs using parliamentary privilege to make allegations of which they have little or no personal evidence, and we decided to go in to bat for Nick Davies. Maxwell could look after himself and anyway everybody knew he was on gossiping terms with Israeli leaders and was no doubt frequently the conduit of unofficial communication between them and other world leaders, particularly the Russians. Hardly spying, but it tended to muddy the waters of what we saw as an unfair attack on one of our own men. Anyway, Maxwell would have been a terrible agent. He was used as the go-between by the Israelis and the Russians over the agreement to allow Soviet Jews to leave the USSR and went to Russia with the outline of an agreement between the two countries ... or at least he should have done. He left that protocol behind on his bedside table and a major document in the history of the Jewish state had to be faxed to him from the *Mirror* newsroom to his Moscow hotel. Some spy.

Meanwhile, Nick Davies assured me there was no truth in the allegations, first made by a strange shadowy figure on the fringes of the Israeli espionage world called Ari Ben-Menashe. He was, depending on which point of view you took, either Israel's Oliver North who reckoned he had brokered a deal between Ronald Reagan and the Iranian government, or, in the words of Israeli government officials, 'an unreliable, exaggerating damnable translator.' Ben-Menashe was to surface again ten years later when he set up the Zimbabwe opposition leader Morgan Tsvangirai in an alleged plot to bump off Robert Mugabe. It was no surprise to many that the apparently damning tapes had been heavily doctored. That Ben-Menashe knew Nick Davies I don't doubt, but that made him neither a spy nor an arms dealer. Nonetheless I should have been more careful in my response. He said there was nothing to come out which could embarrass the *Mirror* and that Hersh had got it round his neck. So we went in with all guns blazing with a big front-page attack on the two MPs. With hindsight I recognise I went over the top, but it was me and not Maxwell, or Maxwell inspired. I had certainly made the paper a hostage to Nick Davies's fortune and we were to pay for it to the tune of £200,000 into the pocket of Allason, an inveterate litigant who made a fortune from suing newspapers until the Stott law of libel – that the true nature of someone will come out eventually – damaged him when he was branded by a judge as one of the most dishonest witnesses he had seen. That wasn't until almost a decade later.

But with my knowledge of Davies I should have known better and acted with more caution. In the next couple of days his former wife revealed she had found letters at their home suggesting he had been doing a deal over arms in Ohio. Nick responded by saying they were fakes, he was being set up and that he had never been to Ohio in his life. We had nothing to worry about, he was 100 per cent telling the truth. But he wasn't. At the time, he was in Harare covering the Commonwealth Conference and, on his return, he came to see me to thank the paper for all our support. Shortly afterwards, we heard that the *Daily Mail* had a picture of him with the arms dealer's wife in Ohio. At this, Nick appeared to think for a while, put his head in his hands and said that he may have strayed over the Pennsylvania-Ohio border. I pointed out to him that this wasn't straying over the border it was well inside. Then he admitted he may have met a dealer at Cleveland Hopkins Airport. At this point I exploded and said he must be the only foreign editor in the world who didn't know Cleveland was in Ohio.

For the next couple of days, we were covered from head to toe in several barrel-loads of old nasty as the other papers had a field day. The *Sun* carried a front-page splash branding Davies a liar and Maxwell demanded I run a leader attacking the *Sun*. I refused, because much of the *Sun* report was correct and this would just stack up more trouble for us. Maxwell then threatened to sack me. This was too bizarre so I shouted back, 'Great, you want to sack the innocent in order to protect a liar.' He banged the phone down.

Eventually he calmed down and agreed to Nick being suspended. I still didn't believe that he was an arms dealer – nobody had produced a shred of evidence to support the claims. I thought he was capable of living in a fantasy world of nods, winks and behind-the-hand muttering, but a world where nothing very much actually ever happened. He may well have had some minor dealings with Mossad – he wouldn't have been the first foreign editor to do so – but he was so conspiratorial, devious and gossipy, he couldn't have been of any great consequence. But he had lied, continued to lie and made the paper into a laughing stock and, worst crime of all, compromised our credibility.

I knew Maxwell was stalling and I knew why. He wanted to save Nick because of Andrea, the foolish and sad obsessions of an old and sick man were coming home to roost. Eventually, he agreed that Nick should put his case to myself, Joe Haines and Charlie Wilson, which he did. But he only succeeded in convincing all three of us that he was piling lie on lie and that he should be fired. Meanwhile, Maxwell had been promising

Nick that his job was safe, but he realised he couldn't win and, Andrea or no Andrea, Nick would have to go.

It was an episode from which nobody came out with much credit. I shouldn't have leapt in so early and aggressively; I knew Nick of old and I knew of his labyrinthine and conspiratorial mind. When I left the *Mirror* the previous year, I had written to all the executives thanking them for the work they had contributed to the *Mirror* during my time as editor. To Nick, with his close relationship in mind, I wrote, 'Perhaps you will permit an old colleague one word of advice. Don't sit too close to the fire. You get burnt.' I should have listened to my own advice.

However, I was still irritated by Hersh's claims, little of which had been backed by evidence. The Pulitzer Prize-winner is one of America's most famous journalists and his investigative technique is considered a model for other reporters. Hersh, like many well-known American journalists, takes himself very seriously but, in this case at least, his investigative qualities let him down badly. His technique should indeed be studied by all aspiring investigative reporters, but not for the reason Hersh would wish. As a consequence of the row over his book, he was comprehensively conned in a way that would not have happened if he had checked the facts properly.

Hersh and Matthew Evans, the chairman of his publishers Faber and Faber, thought they had hit the jackpot when they announced, in the face of increasing scepticism over Hersh's claims about Davies and Maxwell, that they had new evidence to link the two of them to the kidnap of Vanunu.

They claimed Davies, operating under a false name, met secretly in a Geneva hotel with Israeli intelligence operatives and a private detective in an attempt to arrange telephone tapping of the home and offices of a *Sunday Times* reporter working on the Vanunu revelations. To support these claims, the private detective supplied the two men with logs of Davies's phonecalls from the hotel as well as records of calls by the Israeli agents. Davies was accompanied on his trip by Frank Thorne, a *Mirror* reporter. Pretty impressive, except the whole story was a concoction from start to finish. The private detective was a well-known conman called Joe Flynn who had met the Faber chairman at Amsterdam airport. He had never met Hersh at all. But for such an experienced reporter, the alarm bells should have been ringing. Frank Thorne was contacted only hours before Evans and Hersh went public and easily proved that it could not have been him at the hotel and, crucially, Thorne's business card, produced as 'evidence' by the man claiming to be a private detective, wasn't printed until a year after the 'meeting', which meant the private detective must have been lying.

All this Hersh could have discovered very quickly, but he was so keen to prop up his story he ignored all the basic rules, something he accepted when he admitted to the *Sunday Times* he regretted not checking the facts by meeting the man who claimed to be the private detective.

So how was Mordecai Vanunu finally kidnapped by Mossad? Andrew Neil, editor of the *Sunday Times*, which ran Vanunu's story, is in no doubt. After the paper asked the Israeli embassy for an official reaction to the story, their agents began staking out Wapping, the newspaper's headquarters then under siege from sacked workers, disguised as TV crews. Eventually, Mossad managed to follow Vanunu and his minders and from then on he was toast. It had nothing to do with Nick Davies.

Anyway, the thought of Davies being an Israeli spy is inherently absurd. He was an inveterate gossip, quite unable to keep a secret and living in his own make-believe world. Mossad could either be the best, most professional espionage service in the world, or it could employ Davies as a big-time operator. It could not manage both.

But already a much bigger drama was beginning to take shape. Six floors above the *Mirror* newsroom, Burrington, Horwood and Guest had become increasingly worried about cash being moved out of the Mirror Group, ostensibly into money-making investments. In September and October, two huge chunks of company cash – £47 million and £50 million – disappeared from the Mirror.

Burrington had further reason to fret. On 24 June only weeks after the flotation, he had co-signed a Mirror bank transfer for £11,032,012 on the say-so of Kevin Maxwell, acting, he said, for his father who was out of the country. Yet Kevin was not even a director of the Mirror. He had caught the managing director at lunchtime and impressed him with the urgency of the need to get the money on to the markets straight away. Kevin had already drawn the cheque and signed it – even though he was not authorised to do so. He went to see Burrington and told him it was 'damned urgent'. He went on, 'You're not to worry, there is no problem about signing this.'

There was. As an unauthorised signatory, Kevin was the problem. Inexplicably, the NatWest bank honoured the transfer, although within six weeks they were beginning to have doubts about the honesty and integrity of both Kevin and Robert Maxwell. Burrington was now having severe second thoughts about what he had done, and Lawrie Guest's anxieties, first voiced on 29 August, increased his suspicions that all was not well. Short-term deposits of £40 million worth of Mirror cash, reported Guest, had been placed with US investment banks, but no supporting documentation had been produced. The finance director of the group did not know the interest rate, repayments date for the cash or even the currency it was in.

But in spite of this, there was vital dithering among the three directors in the know – Burrington, Horwood and Guest. The joint managing directors took the most optimistic possible view of the transaction, that it was a misunderstanding brought about by Michael Stoney's determination to assert himself in his new position and that it could all be resolved by him and Guest establishing a better working relationship. What they should have done was inform the non-executive directors about their concerns as soon as they realised money had gone walkabout and they hadn't been a given a map explaining where it had gone. They discussed resignation but did nothing when they should have called a full meeting of the board. It was only the force of Maxwell's personality and the hold he had over his directors that stayed their hands. They could hear the rumble of the approaching train, they could see its lights and hear the wail of its siren, but they remained stranded on the track, dazzled in the headlights.

By early October, Guest was so concerned he was putting everything down on paper, unaware that all his spoken thoughts were already being recorded by a secret bug installed in his office. He was not only at loggerheads with Stoney, the Maxwell private side-business money man brought on to the board by the chairman, but in effect, Guest's power over the Mirror coffers, unbeknown to the majority of the board, had been removed and handed to him. He didn't like what he suspected was happening. Guest fired off a private and confidential memo: 'As you know, I have been increasingly concerned with regard to the lack of information on the short-term deposits made to American banks ... it is essential that you keep me fully briefed on the money transfers ... without this information we cannot write up the books properly ... we do not even know interest rates applicable to the transactions ... I hope I have kept you abreast of financial matters, but I don't think you have done the same ... I must insist that further treasury transactions are accompanied by a note telling us the type of transaction, interest rates and other relevant information required to keep a proper financial record ... please give me your written agreement to the contents of this memo before the weekend.'

This note was also sent to Maxwell, Burrington and Horwood. Stoney fired back: 'I regret you chose to ignore my request not to circulate inaccurate information to colleagues before showing me a draft of what you intended to say in order that any misunderstandings or errors could be avoided.' He denied the thrust of Guest's argument and demanded a meeting 'to correct some of the unfortunate impressions given by your memorandum and to do this in a way that restores harmonious relations all round'.

But Lawrie Guest had been silent for too long and in the middle of October – 11 days after the memo spat – he had a face-to-face with Maxwell in the presence of Burrington and Horwood. He was asked to state his problems. Guest took a deep breath and waded in. Promised repayment had not been made, shareholders cash was being used speculatively and he questioned the use of pension money and the investment return it appeared to be yielding. 'After discussion and my stating that I was totally dissatisfied with the information flow, and the number of transactions going through MGN's accounts, I cited a £20m transfer to Robert Maxwell Group, *Daily News* $2m taken out of *Racing Times* account, the chairman stated there should be no problems and that I should obtain all information from Michael Stoney and I would have a separate discussion with him. My removal would be a disaster to the group and not in the interest of anybody,' wrote Guest in his notes of the meeting. 'The chairman, after expanding how brilliant a corporate finance man Michael Stoney was, said that the next board meeting would appoint him deputy managing director (finance).'

In the subsequent meeting 'Stoney was very flushed,' reflected Guest. 'I am now convinced that MGN resources have been used to support other parts of the group, but I have no proof,' he wrote. 'I think I have frightened the chairman but my main concern must be to get the money back. I think I am in a situation that nothing more will flow out although I don't have the mechanism to stop it. At a subsequent meeting with Vic Horwood and Ernie Burrington, it was agreed that I should try and nail Stoney firmly in writing. However, this will not achieve the objective of getting the money back.' Guest was also becoming worried about the activities of Bishopsgate Investment Management, a private company which was running the massive *Mirror* pension fund.

So the suspicions were well and truly there. Maxwell was getting nervous and Stoney's role was under the microscope. But the lid remained on the scandal. Meanwhile Maxwell had attended the Labour Party Conference in Brighton. He looked worse, had difficulty in breathing and constantly returned to his latest theme, how he was going to make everybody millionaires through the Mirror flotation. Penny, whom he called Duchess but is in fact a practice nurse at a GP's surgery, saw him for the last time and reckoned he looked a prime candidate for a heart-attack or stroke. Ernie Burrington was threatening resignation and wanted to go as soon as his pension rights had been agreed. He came down to the Metropole to sort out the last rites with Maxwell but confided his fears of what was going on in the company to nobody, even though Joe Haines, a non-executive director, had a room close by. Haines and Burrington had fallen out over a six-year back tax demand on the editorial drivers which Maxwell had originally agreed to pay and then reneged on. Haines had called Burrington 'a spineless bastard' for what he saw as his complicity.

At his last lunch for the Labour leader on the Metropole's top floor, Maxwell took a desperate gamble. He led Alastair Campbell, by now the *Mirror*'s political editor and a close friend of Neil Kinnock, out on to a small balcony perched high at the top of the hotel overlooking the sea. Maxwell talked quickly and urgently telling the bemused Campbell that enemies were out to get him, and if they were out to get him then they were out to get the Labour Party as well, so Neil Kinnock must be warned. He talked of BOSS agents and Mossad and enemies in the City, all were out to get him and he was insistent – Warn Kinnock. Campbell passed on Maxwell's ramblings to the Labour leader who was as confused as his messenger. Campbell was convinced that Maxwell was going mad; nonetheless, it is an extraordinary coincidence that, less than three weeks later, he was to be accused of being a Mossad agent and, in little over a month, was dead. The most likely scenario, however, remains that he knew he was facing imminent exposure and wanted to get in some groundwork with the Labour leader.

Less than a week later Maxwell was visited by Ian McIntosh and Andrew Galloway, the two Samuel Montagu men who had masterminded the float of the Mirror Group and who had said so loudly and so often that it would be ring-fenced from Maxwell's other businesses and fondly believed it was. Just before the start of the Labour conference, Burrington and Guest had shared their concerns with Samuel Montagu about the money flowing out of Mirror Group, for which they still had not been provided with supporting documentation. But although the merchant bankers did talk to Maxwell, the Mirror men never heard back from them. Hardly surprising, as Maxwell did a snow job on McIntosh and Galloway, pointing out, presumably with a straight face, that money could hardly go walkabout because the *Mirror* was ring-fenced. He promised to get back to them after 'investigating' what had happened, but did nothing of the sort. Five days later, he said some of the money had been repaid and airily dismissed their concerns about the rest.

At the same time, Guest decided to bring in the two non-executive directors – Alan Clements and Sir Robert Clark – both of whom had extensive financial knowledge and experience. But he couldn't locate them. In spite of his run-in with Stoney, Mirror money continued to flow from the company coffers. Less than a week after Maxwell's rooftop talk with Campbell, a further £36.5 million was moved to a Maxwell company, ostensibly to buy gilt-edged securities. The next day, a further £2.3 million went the same way.

By now, Galloway, too, was worried that Mirror money was going to support private Maxwell companies and he relayed his worries to Clements. Clements claims he talked to Guest, but neither Guest nor Galloway can recall it – and although Clements was suffering from a bad back at this time his lack of action hardly indicated a sense of urgency. Sir Robert was also involved and the two men resolved to tackle Maxwell after the board meeting the following week. Meanwhile, Maxwell himself had moved once again to placate a by now extremely concerned Guest. He told Maxwell he could not sleep because of the huge sums being moved out of the group. 'Don't worry,' soothed Maxwell. 'You are losing sleep and that's not right. You will receive everything. Don't worry.' But Maxwell wanted Guest neutralised and carried out his plan to promote Stoney to deputy managing director (finance), thus, in effect, putting him in charge of all financial matters, whereas before the treasury and accounting functions were split equally, with Stoney in charge of the treasury and Guest running accounting.

Guest would have lost even more sleep if he had known what Maxwell was to do next. Three days after their conversation, he called a hurried lunchtime board meeting to renew the lease of the *Mirror*'s Holborn headquarters. The plan had been to move the offices of the three newspapers to Great Dover Street in a rundown area of South London close to the Elephant and Castle. Editorial departments were opposing the idea – not least because it had the highest rate of muggings in London – so Joe Haines in particular was pleased when he heard the *Mirror* was to stay in its old headquarters at a reduced rent. He and the other board members present – they didn't include either Guest, who was abroad, or Burrington, who had gone to lunch and said he wasn't coming back – passed the resolution without a murmur. Burrington's absence was most unfortunate because he strongly opposed the plan, but his view that lunch was more important than the meeting reinforced the view that it was routine. Maxwell himself attended by telephone and the meeting was chaired by Stoney. Because of the short notice and odd timing, neither Clements nor Clark were there, so there was nobody with sufficient knowledge of this complex leasing agreement or its financial implications present, apart from Stoney. The upshot of this new lease was that the building's owner, Robert Maxwell Estates, was able to winkle out an £80 million loan from its bankers.

So by the time of Maxwell's last board meeting on 29 October, five executive directors of the board – Maxwell, Burrington, Horwood, Guest and Stoney – knew at the very least that all was not well. So did two of the four non-executive directors – Clements and Clark. So did the two top men of the company's merchants bankers, McIntosh and Galloway. Therefore, half of the 14 board members who assembled in the ninth floor boardroom of Maxwell House were aware that something was seriously wrong. They also either knew, or strongly suspected, that the company was in breach of its flotation pledge over dealings with the Maxwell private companies. Yet at this board meeting, not one word was mentioned about the seriousness of what was happening to the Mirror Group. Instead, Ernie Burrington contented himself by talking of profits being up £3.5 million on the previous year. Vic Horwood was happy to report Scottish profits were £2.8 ahead of the business plan. Lawrie Guest said the September profits were £5 million below plan. He talked of associated Canadian companies, but not a mention of why he was losing so much sleep. Maxwell talked of the sacking of Nick Davies and how it had become inevitable. Ernie Burrington, a great friend of Davies, said it was generally agreed that he had damaged the reputation of the *Mirror*, but not a peep about the much more terrible damage Burrington had suspected for more than two months. From Clements and Clark, the shareholders' watchdog, not one single growl.

In less than six months £98 million had disappeared from the Mirror Group and half of the men sitting round Maxwell's table that autumn afternoon knew all was not as it should be. The only sign of anything remotely untoward was Clements and Clark's private meeting with Maxwell once the official board business was over. They told him there had to be an audit committee established to examine financial controls within the group. Clements said he would draft the terms of reference and Maxwell brought the conversation to a close, pleading he was late for a meeting.

But still Maxwell wasn't finished. Later that day, he telephoned Clements to tell him that Stoney would be drafting the terms of reference.

Now there's a surprise. But why did the two financial watchdogs refuse to come out of their kennel and tell the other two non-executives, Haines and Lord Williams of Elvel? Clark's reason, given to the DTI, is breathtaking. They were uncertain of their independence; in other words, they would fink to Maxwell. But why not bring the cash loans up at the board meeting? Again, Clark blamed others: 'Maxwell would either go into a tirade or turn to his cronies and say, "This is all right, isn't it?" They would have all said "yes", and nothing would have happened. So we said we would see him on our own afterwards, which we did.'

Again, this does not bear examination. From evidence given by Clements to the DTI, Lawrie Guest was by this time in an appalling state. His hands were shaking and he was chain-smoking. If all four of the non-executives had brought the matter up, Guest would have been only too relieved to tell what he knew. Clements met him for lunch shortly before the board meeting and could, and should, have told him the missing money was going to be brought up at that afternoon's meeting. Burrington by now was sufficiently frightened to have handed in his resignation and Horwood was well aware of the suspicions. It is highly unlikely – dilatory though they were in the earlier stages of the developing scandal – that they would have sat on their hands and said nothing.

The DTI inspectors rejected Clark's reservations about Haines and Williams, so that meant seven of the 14 board members would be more than likely not to support Maxwell. It would not have been beyond the realms of persuasion for Burrington, Horwood and Guest to convert Roger Eastoe, Charlie Wilson and Endell Laird, representing the Scottish editors, to the cause. As it was, Clements and Clark saw Maxwell separately and, on both occasions, he was 'totally charming', explaining that the money paid out from the company to 'purchase gilts' was a one-off transaction which would be repaid shortly. Clark reported Maxwell as saying: 'Oh, I have got an answer to all these questions, it's being rectified. I will see you next Tuesday, if that's all right ... I'm going off in half an hour.' In other words he fobbed off a former director of the Bank of England and a director of several blue-chip companies with the same bland assurances he had given Guest only a few days earlier.

However Clark tries to dress it up with the benefit of the hindsight he professes to deplore, he and Clements allowed Maxwell to escape without answering to his board of directors. He had agreed only to an audit committee report which at least had bought him a little more time, as opposed to an immediate boardroom challenge which would not. If he had been confronted and defeated in his own boardroom, it is likely the crisis would have been precipitated there and then and he would have been unable to fly off to the *Lady Ghislaine*.

In fact, he showed no sign of the full extent of the disaster about to befall him, his family, his businesses, pensioners and staff as he prepared to fly out in the Gulfstream to the yacht berthed at Tenerife. He had been doing this more often in recent weeks as his health was visibly declining. This time he didn't even take Josef with him, he went alone.

The last time I spoke to him was on the evening of 4 November when I told him the gap between the *Sun* circulation and that of the combined *Mirror* and *Daily Record* in Scotland was once again too close to call. He chortled and betrayed no sign of distress or preoccupation. He had been less trouble since I returned to the *Mirror* and he had even more or less behaved himself over the Nick Davies affair, although I still thought he might try and reinstate him to please Andrea. On the other hand, if he did that he would have had serious problems not only with me, but with Joe Haines and Charlie Wilson.

I was mulling over this scenario the next day at around 2.00pm when the phone went. It was Ernie Burrington. Could I go up immediately to the chairman's office. Bloody Davies, I thought, he's swung Maxwell round. I'm going to fight this all the way to the dole queue if necessary, I thought to myself, as I made my way through the *Mirror* building, through the pass door into Maxwell House next door and up in the lift to Maxwell's palatial office. I saw Ernie and, from the look on his face, I could tell it had nothing to do with Nick Davies. I thought he must have either resigned or been removed, but it was neither. With his habitual manner of coming at you sideways and speaking out of the corner of his mouth, he said, 'Bob's gone missing. He's gone over the side of the boat.'

My reaction was immediate. 'Thrown himself, or did somebody push him?' I asked.

But Ernie didn't have any answers. Would I keep it quiet until the Stock Exchange had been informed? An announcement would be made within the hour.

I was rather shocked by my own reaction. I felt no regret; indeed, my first reaction was an overwhelming sense of relief. I had beaten him, I had outlasted him at the *Mirror*, I had been here when he arrived and I was here when he went. I never expected that. He might have handed me a few drubbings, and I had certainly lost a few rounds, but at the final bell I was standing and he wasn't. Totally selfish, but it wasn't until he was gone that I realised how much he had dominated my life for more than seven years. Running a newspaper is a tough enough job on its own, but running it while trying to keep him at bay was well nigh impossible. Yet he had saved the *Mirror*, whatever the knockers and piss-takers said. Those of us who lived the *Mirror* every minute of the year, knew he had. He was appalling but he had turned a puny profit into big bucks, he had revolutionised the workplace and smashed the print unions, most of it in the wake of Murdoch's Wapping, but he had played a considerable part and, above all, he had introduced colour, encouraging people once again to take a look in the *Mirror*. On that Guy Fawkes day, if you judged a newspaper proprietor by whether he leaves the paper in a better state than he found it, then Maxwell, for all his many faults, had been a successful owner.

Now it was back to the office and the next day's paper. I told John Jackson he was going to be babysitting Betty who was already preparing to fly out to Tenerife. They left in the helicopter from the roof. By now, the news was spreading like wildfire. Most of the staff looked shocked, but a few could hardly disguise their glee. The columnists queued up to pay their glowing tributes, many of them so fulsome in their praise no doubt because of an overwhelming sense of relief that he was gone. There was a curious cocktail of emotions, and we were tempted to see only the good bits.

In spite of the terror, the *Mirror* had come through largely intact; things could only get better, couldn't they? I wrote the front page headline – THE MAN WHO SAVED THE MIRROR – setting the tone of much that was to appear inside. Every other newspaper – with the notable exception of the *Independent on Sunday* – was generous in its praise of this most extraordinary man. By the evening, both Ian and Kevin Maxwell were in my office waiting for news from the search teams off Tenerife. There was something odd about them, but I couldn't quite put my finger on it. I didn't have time to dwell on what it was, but they were odd. Definitely.

When they left, I suddenly realised what it was. Ian was sad, naturally, but he was already relishing his new job as publisher. He was decisive in his reactions to requests for information. Kevin, on the other hand, was quiet, withdrawn, preoccupied, unsure of himself, indecisive. He was clinging on to the hope that his father was still alive, whereas Ian had accepted the reality, and although there was as yet no body there was no realistic chance of their father being found around. They were reacting in precisely the opposite way to what I would have predicted and the way they had behaved when the old man was alive. Just before he left for the night, Kevin asked me to let him know if his father was found.

The rescue helicopter found his body when Kevin was driving home,

I phoned him and told him the bad news. There was a long silence on the other end of the phone. Then, a very small voice just said, 'Thanks, thanks a lot.' Kevin Maxwell was on his own now, and only he knew just how alone.

That night, I appeared on the ITN News and, when asked how Maxwell sounded the last time I spoke to him, came out with the unintentional, immortal line: 'He was in very buoyant mood.' But already the questions were being asked about the viability of the Maxwell Communications Corporation of which I knew nothing. I only knew that the *Mirror* was in great shape, making a great deal more money than it had for decades and had a circulation figure that was once again narrowing the gap with the *Sun*.

I was surprised that with such a success story to tell, there were no Mirror Group directors on hand to address the media throng. Where on earth were they? Vic Horwood had phoned from Gatwick Airport on his way with his wife to the Caribbean on a prize she had won in a *Mail on Sunday* competition. Should he come back, he had asked Ernie. No, no need, Vic. Enjoy your holiday, have a great time. There's nothing you can do here.

That evening my secretary Gill tried to get hold of Ernie Burrington in his office. We were told he had gone home to play bridge.

15

The days following Maxwell's death were eerily calm. Ian settled into his new job as publisher easily. The first decision he took was to ban the dirty phonecall adverts we had continued to take under his father and something nobody, apart from the advertising department, wanted in the paper. The ads, which looked like refugees from a London public phone box, brought in a considerable revenue, but it was a bit like pimping. Ian won a few editorial hearts with that. But reports that all was not well within the Maxwell Communications Corporation started as soon as Maxwell was reported missing. With the publication of a *Financial Times* investigation, it was clear the corporation was heavily debt-laden and Kevin as the new boss there was coming under great pressure from his creditors to explain all. Nobody thought these problems applied to Mirror Group because of the ring-fence; if we thought of it at all, it was in terms of the Maxwells possibly having to sell off their 51 per cent in order to bale out MCC. This was clearly in the mind of Lord Hollick, too, for the man who was to buy the *Express* had already approached Joe Haines at the Labour Party Conference before Maxwell died about the possibility of buying the *Mirror*. Hollick had close links with the merchant bank Hambro and was beginning to catch stray straws in the wind.

The main question intriguing everyone was, and still is, how did Maxwell die? There were four possibilities. He was pushed overboard, and therefore murdered. He fell during an early morning walk and toppled over, an accident. He suffered a heart-attack and fell in, natural causes. Or he came to the conclusion that the game was up and decided to end it all, suicide. All four theories have their supporters and all four can be backed by circumstantial evidence.

Murder – there were countless potential candidates with a motive to see him gone, from creditors to Mossad, from the racketeers on the fringes of the *New York Daily News* to the personal enemies he had made over the years, and the criminal gangs beginning to flourish in Moscow. Maxwell had been the go-between in the secret negotiations over the freeing up of Soviet Jews to emigrate to Israel. But none of the candidates look as if they had an overwhelming motive, although it does seem certain from the forensic evidence that at one stage he did try and hold on to the safety rail of the *Lady Ghislaine*. The muscles at the back of his shoulder were torn and bleeding, as if he had been attempting to pull himself back on to the boat but couldn't do so because of his great weight. It could have been the result of a last struggle with his killer. The crew were all closely questioned and given a clean bill of health and none of them saw any stranger come aboard. However, there was the strange coincidence of the rooftop conversation with Alastair Campbell at the Labour Party Conference which certainly indicated that Maxwell wanted it to be known by Neil Kinnock that he thought somebody was out to do him harm.

Accident – Maxwell was in the habit of wandering about during the night in the nude. He could have stumbled and pitched over the side, managing to hold on to the rail at the last moment. One crew member reported he had nearly done the same thing at the spot where Maxwell is believed to have gone overboard. The *Lady Ghislaine* had a shallow draught and could pitch, although there was nothing untoward about the sea that night.

Natural causes – his health had been deteriorating rapidly for some months and it would have surprised nobody if he had succumbed to a heart-attack or stroke. From his inability to sleep – he had suffered from insomnia for years – and his request to the crew to turn the air-conditioning up and down, he was obviously restless, which, given the state of his businesses, was hardly surprising. It is possible that he went outside naked to what Betty Maxwell described as his 'quiet place' on the boat. We know from the post mortem by Dr Iain West of Guy's Hospital that Maxwell had 'undoubtedly' suffered from a degree of heart damage but that 'there is no evidence to indicate that this is more than a potential cause of death'. However, we also know that he frequently used to pee over the side of the boat and the desire to urinate often preceeds a heart-attack. It is possible he pitched over the side during an attack and desperately tried to hang on. The crew ensconced on the bridge were highly unlikely to hear any cry for help.

Suicide – the most obvious choice unless you knew him. There was certainly plenty of motive to end it all. The bankers, notably the Swiss Bank Corporation, had started calling in his loans and were threatening to go public. He faced an audit committee at the Mirror which would certainly tighten up financial controls and would, almost as certainly, unearth his unauthorised borrowings and fraud within the group. If the whole pack of cards came down, Scotland Yard would not be far behind and Wormwood Scrubs would be beckoning a crooked finger. Maxwell's contempt for the British financial establishment had meant that, unlike Murdoch, he did not go to the banks to reschedule his debt-laden empire. He tried to do it by money market gambles and shifting cash and commitment around the labyrinth of Maxwell companies. But he had always done that, bluffing his way to a position where he was monarch of all he surveyed with a multi-million pound yacht and private aircraft. He had faced financial disaster many times and had always managed to escape.

But on the day before he died Maxwell was hit by four hammer blows. Eugene Fife of Goldman Sachs, which for far too long had been propping Maxwell up, telephoned Eddie George, then deputy governor of the Bank of England, to tell him that the next day the company was to announce it was selling off its MCC shares held as security for loans to Maxwell companies, an unmistakable sign that all was far from well. Citibank told Kevin that it, too, would be starting to call in its security and the money brokers Lehmans served recall notices on the Maxwells, which, in effect, meant they had to repay some $80 million within 24 hours. On top of that the *Financial Times* was planning an exposée of the debt burden of Maxwell companies and investigators from the paper were due to see Kevin about it the next morning. More than enough there to push him over the edge. Yet if it was suicide, why did he decide to hang on to the side of the boat, why not just jump?

Dr West has an answer to this. 'One sees this pattern of injury on occasions in individuals who kill themselves as a result of falling from high buildings. Whilst some jump or let themselves topple over a balcony or out of a window, others will actually ease themselves over the edge and hold on for a time with one or both hands before letting go.' This could be explained by Maxwell changing his mind at the last minute and trying to clamber back on to the boat. He frequently reversed decisions as soon as he had made them and, on occasions, was seriously indecisive. He was, as I observed earlier, quite capable of intending to follow a course of action right up until the moment he didn't.

What militates against suicide is his character and his belief that he could win through. But time had now run out and there was no prospect of the cavalry riding to his rescue. The MGN board had taken an extraordinarily long time to summon up the courage to question him, but the die was now cast. The bolt holes were closing fast, and the United

States was about the only place left where he might obtain further cash. He may have calculated that his death would wipe the slate clean as far as his sons, particularly Kevin, were concerned, yet he left no note exonerating him. If he thought his death without any further explanation or *mea culpa* last words would be enough to prevent the scandal, it was a remarkably optimistic view.

The search for the truth of how he died was confused by the Spanish post mortem which did not over-impress the insurance team when it came to examine the corpse. By the time our Dr West came to the body – sent to examine it only hours before the funeral as the family stood to gain £20 million if he died either by accident or foul play – much of the potential evidence had been destroyed or damaged and West's eyes were constantly watering because of the embalming fluid. The heart was in a particularly bad state, having been cut up by the Spanish pathologists.

Unlike the Spanish authorities, Dr West took the view that Maxwell probably drowned and that suicide was the most likely explanation. The one thing that remains constant is the probability that he did cling on to the side of the *Lady Ghislaine* until his weight forced him to let go. Dr West thought a heart-attack unlikely as the cause of death because he would have fallen down and not rolled into the sea. However, he did not know of Maxwell's habit of peeing over the side. That would be consistent with a heart-attack and pitching forwards off the boat. Surely, though, if he had finally made up his mind to die, he would have jumped. This was a man who had won the MC for leading a fearless attack on Germans he cleared out of occupied buildings 'showing no regard for his own safety'. He was not lacking in physical courage. He was also an inveterate gambler, both on the tables and in his business affairs, and gamblers always believe something will turn up. In the absence of any evidence of murder and the unlikelihood of his death being a pure accident, the choice is between suicide and natural causes. It is a close-run thing, but the arguments for suicide are powerful, although the evidence of his torn muscles and ligaments suggest he clung on, and clinging on signifies a will to live. This is backed up by the fact that when found, his hands were tightly clenched, as if he had been hanging on to something. Dr West concluded that 'he had probably climbed over the boat rail, gone to jump, changed his mind and tried to cling on, then, when his muscle tore, he fell into the sea. It made murder a very unlikely proposition and suicide likely'.

As in so much of his life, Maxwell decided on suicide right up until the point of no return, and then changed his mind. This time he left it too late and was unable to hoist himself back on to the boat. But that's not suicide, it has to be an open verdict.

A good outside bet is the alternative scenario. The existence of a heart problem and his obviously deteriorating health during his last year, plus the strain of imminent exposure and his restlessness through the night, were causing great agitation. He clearly felt uncomfortable – hence the requests about the air conditioning – and, feeling unwell, went out on deck to his favourite spot and decided to pee over the side, suffered a heart-attack at that moment, keeled over but managed to hold on to the ship's guard rail before either having a further attack and falling or being forced to let go by the weight of his own body. Although there were criticisms of the Spanish post mortem, the pathologists were unequivocal in their findings. Two days after Maxwell was winched from the sea by helicopter, the investigating judge, Luis Gutierrez, said, 'Mr Maxwell was dead when he fell into the sea. He did not die by drowning, nor were there any signs of violence.' He could, he said, 'find no complications whatsoever'. It was only after the scandal began to unravel that the Las Palmas authorities started to have second thoughts. As with so many things surrounding Maxwell, we will never know the truth for sure and he died, as he had lived, like Churchill's description of Russia, a riddle wrapped in a mystery inside an enigma. One thing, however, I am certain about. I am delighted we were not faced with the problem of him being around when the scandal broke; the prospect of editing the *Mirror* with that lot engulfing us and him trying to manipulate the news would have been impossible.

As it was, the tributes poured in from all over the world. Gorbachev was 'deeply grieved' and Israel's Prime Minister Yitzhak Shamir spoke of his great sorrow, adding 'God bless his memory'. The Hungarian President Arpad Goncz said he was a born politician who had played an important part mediating behind the scenes in the emergence of Eastern Europe from Communist domination; no mention there of how much he had done previously to prop up that dominance. In New York, Mayor David Dinkins said Maxwell 'had done a lot for our city'. Within a week, he was buried on the Mount of Olives, but not before several last-minute dramas. His zinc-lined coffin was too big and heavy to get on to the Gulfstream – altogether it weighed 32 stones – so another aircraft had to be hired to take him to Jerusalem. Then the underwriters of his £20 million life insurance insisted on another post mortem, the one carried out by Dr West. Eventually, the funeral was held, but he was almost too big for the grave. By tradition, he was buried naked and without a coffin, returning to the earth as we all arrive, with nothing. But his enormous size, made even more bulky by the two post mortems which had displaced most of his organs, meant he entered the grave in a sitting position and a grave digger, out of sight of the family, was actually in the pit heaving and pulling to straighten him out. It was a suitably bizarre end to a bizarre week and a bizarre life.

Israeli President Chaim Herzog spoke the epitaph as the sun set over the Mount of Olives. 'He scaled the heights,' he said. 'Kings and barons besieged his doorstep. Many admired him, many disliked him. But nobody remained indifferent to him.'

His doorstep was about to be besieged again. Back in London, accountants discovered that Mirror pension fund money had gone missing and share certificates could not be found.

About ten days before the storm actually broke, some board directors were made aware of the problems within the Mirror pension fund, but decided not to inform the Stock Exchange or ask for a suspension of share dealing. They didn't even think it necessary to inform other directors. This decision is made even more puzzling because the pensions shortfall was not an isolated event – as we know, Burrington, Horwood, Guest and Stoney were aware of the problems within the company accounts. It should have set alarm bells ringing loud and clear that money had disappeared wholesale from both the *Mirror* and its pension fund. Surely at that stage the Stock Exchange should have been informed and the shares in MGN suspended. Directors' silence would be extremely difficult to justify to investors who bought shares in the last ten days before the dam burst.

In the event, when it became apparent how much was missing – on the weekend of 30 November and 1 December – the board was in barely concealed panic. I was aware that there were a series of emergency meetings going on in Maxwell's headquarters next door but, like everyone else, I assumed this was to do with the Maxwell Corporation. I had been in the office that Sunday and late at night, back at home, I received a furtive phonecall. 'The four horsemen are in the Vanway,' I was told, before the phone went dead. The Vanway was that area where Maxwell had been left in full stream by his nervous driver; it was the heart of the *Mirror* and the agents of destruction, war, pestilence and famine were upon us.

The next morning, there was no official word from the board of directors, but eventually I was seen by Burrington, Wilson and Haines that afternoon and asked to reassure the staff that the pension fund had not collapsed. I asked for details, but few were forthcoming, although Joe Haines was unofficially feeding me what details he could. I also asked if money was missing from the company. Again, I was told nothing. I said I wanted the two Sunday paper editors present – they have Monday off – and I also wanted the newspaper's lawyer to be there and I asked to see Ian Maxwell; after all, he was the chairman. At that the meeting was abandoned; I gave no assurances to the staff because I had been given none. The three were so vague – they had been given board approval only to tell me in 'broad terms' what the situation was – I feared the worst, the four horsemen were indeed in the building.

That evening, Ian Maxwell came to see me in my office and I asked him to assure me that no money was missing from the company and that the pension fund was intact. He could do neither, but continued to repeat the mantra that the paper must continue and that I must reassure the staff that all would be well. The situation was unclear, he said, but the staff would be all right. I told him that nothing he had said reassured me and therefore I would not reassure the staff. He had done nothing but waffle and talk in the vaguest of terms.

The next morning the pension story broke in the *Guardian* and predictably caused consternation throughout the building. By now the board was in almost constant session as the full extent of the horror began to unfold. Ernie Burrington feared a stoppage of the paper unless a statement was put out to 'tranquillise the fears' of Mirror staff, an unfortunate phrase. But there was precious little tranquilliser available. By now, the board was aware that at least £50 million had gone missing from the *Mirror* and that £426 million was missing from the joint Maxwell and Mirror pension funds, of which £350 million belonged to the *Mirror*. But, as yet, the news had not broken publicly of the cash missing from the company nor the extent of the catastrophic rape of the pension funds.

In spite of all this, when the three wise men came to see me again that afternoon, they asked me once more to reassure the staff. Again, without assurances from them I refused to do it, pointing out that they were asking the same of me as they had done the previous day and the position had materially altered for the worse.

By now I had my own deep throats operating on the ninth floor – home of the board – and information was beginning to stream into my office. I was told of money missing from the *Mirror* itself and that the pension fund was in serious trouble. I began to prepare a story for the paper and, when it was ready, I read it to Charlie Wilson who didn't want me to run it. 'Christ, you can't publish that,' he said. Neither would he confirm the amount missing – I had been told more than £20 million at that time – but I told him I was going ahead anyway unless he specifically denied it, which he didn't.

That evening, Ian Maxwell and Michael Stoney resigned and Andrew Galloway, the man who was so proud of his ring-fence, had to tell the board that another £50 million of Mirror money had tunnelled its way out.

In late October, a £50 million loan from Bankers Trust to MGN had been transferred into an account at New York's Chase Manhattan Bank in favour of the Robert Maxwell Group, but in a statement that evening, the board only admitted to money missing from the pension fund. It was becoming clear to me from my ninth floor moles that there had been colossal movements of money out of the Mirror itself, and that it had been going on for some time. It was also becoming evident that what was happening was not a total surprise to all members of the board. I had no idea where these revelations were going to take us, but I resolved that wherever they went, we would be leading the pack, not skulking at the back.

There were several reasons for this: it was natural for a newspaper to want to break news; it was right that in order to maintain our own self-respect we made the running wherever we could, that to hang back might imply we identified with the board of directors which we most certainly did not. It was no less than the readers, shareholders and pensioners deserved, particularly as all three groups had invested in the flotation which we had promoted, and without an aggressive stance of our own, the board would attempt to gag us.

So as well as running the MILLIONS MISSING FROM THE MIRROR story, I wrote a leader to go with it, pledging our commitment to the truth of this affair: 'At the moment nobody, not the board, not the bankers, not the staff, can tell where this will take the *Daily Mirror*. However, we promise you that we will bring you the truth on this matter – as on all matters – as and when we know it, warts and all if necessary.' It did not go down well on the ninth floor or with the directors' advisers. That day, I met with the staff to tell them the truth as I saw it, and by now it was becoming pretty clear. I told them we had been mugged but we would recover, and the response was magnificent. Far from confirming the board's worst fears that they would stop work, they went back to their desks with a will; once again it was us against the world and this time we were fighting for our livelihood.

The next day, we carried further revelations about the full extent of money missing from Maxwell companies – remarkably accurate at £526 million – and the method by which he did it, 'late-night meetings succeeded in moving many millions – and involved very few authorising signatures. Few knew what was going on,' the *Mirror* reported. We told, too, of the £100 million we now knew was missing from the Mirror itself, most of it removed in September and October. Other newspapers scrambled to catch up; that at least was gratifying. More was to follow, and with it came the most serious confrontation yet, a clash between the board's advisers and the right of the rest of the world to know what was happening.

I interviewed Lawrie Guest who was clearly shell-shocked. I had known him for a long time, he was a decent man and he knew he was in the firing line. I had obtained the documents showing his row with Stoney and the damning notes of his meeting with Maxwell – 'I am now convinced that MGN resources have been used to support other parts of the group' – and asked him about them. He told me of his meeting with Maxwell and how he had been told he would get everything back. I think it was a relief for Lawrie to get it all off his chest.

I had told both Charlie Wilson and Ernie Burrington, now the new chairman, that I would check stories with them for accuracy only, not for vetting. This time the advisers went bananas, claiming the story would significantly damage the group. 'I hate to be the nigger in the woodpile, but you can't possibly run this,' I was told in a meeting I was called to attend by the board and its advisers. I pointed out that the company was already significantly damaged and that was largely due to the ineffectiveness of the ring-fence placed there by the same advisers who were among those now telling me not to run the story. The room was full and Ernie was asked for his view. At that day's board meeting, Andrew Galloway of Samuel Montagu had told the meeting that if the group made any hard fact statement as to its liabilities, then its shares would be relisted. Any announcement should be a 'collective initiative' culminating in a circular to shareholders, he said. Ernie Burrington agreed that any announcement would only be made in consultation with Galloway. But he had to tell the Montagu man the hard facts of newspaper life, pointing out that the business should be run vigorously with the *Mirror* keeping ahead of the field with this story. Ernie was torn between his advisers and this position, which he had adopted at the last board meeting. He agreed the paper should have the right to publish, but asked me to consider whether I thought it in the interest of the *Mirror* to do so. Although it may not have been in the interests of the directors, I had no doubt it was in the

Mirror's interest, even though it certainly drove a coach and horses through Galloway's 'collective initiative'. Ernie suggested we leave the decision to Lawrie Guest, who decided he did want to talk. We ran the story all over the front page, and once again at least had the satisfaction of watching the rest of Fleet Street trying to catch up. By now, other papers were trying to stop us cleaning up on the story and pointed out, quite reasonably, the contrast between our headline the day after Maxwell died THE MAN WHO SAVED THE MIRROR and MILLIONS MISSING FROM THE MIRROR. Even though both statements were correct, the critics were quite right, there had been a king-size U-turn, but we knew a hell of a lot more now. Neither were we the only ones; every other newspaper had done the same thing, as one correspondent to *The Times* pointed out. He asked how the paper managed to reconcile its view that there should be little sympathy with the banks' loss because they 'ought to have known what kind of man they were dealing with' when shortly after his death Maxwell had been 'the type of immigrant buccaneer of whom British industry seems in chronic need'. There is nothing newspapers like better than a big dollop of *schadenfreude* and some commentators were so prissy about the *Mirror* that they managed to push themselves into taking up the most ridiculous of positions. 'There is something deeply vulgar about how this rudderless newspaper now deals with its own, as well as its ex-owner's shame,' wrote the *Guardian*'s Ian Aitken from the lofty position of never having had to fight his owners and stick his job on the line. There is something deeply absurd in a journalist suggesting others in his profession should shut up about a scandal on their own doorstep while comfortable columnists, who have never looked over the crumbling edge of catastrophe, pontificate about their shortcomings.

By Saturday, we had exposed the most eccentric story of all. Maxwell was found to have bugged not only his own offices but those of Burrington and Guest, too. To do this, he used John Pole, the same Pole who had run the abortive investigation into Charles Griffin the cartoonist.

It was at this time that I decided to attempt a buyout of the *Mirror*, a quixotic gesture to many, but it was aimed at providing some sort of protection for the staff and the future of the paper, both of which had been continually denigrated and ill-served by successive appalling managements. I could not see a way the current board would survive; after all, the bottom line was that within six months of flotation, £100 million had been removed from under their noses and, at the same time, £350 million had disappeared from the employees' pension fund. Hardly a great stewardship. The danger was that another Maxwell would leap in with an offer which the fleeced banks would be only too happy to accept.

The banks, in turn, appointed an administrator, a keen Morris dancer called John Talbot, whose job was to get their money back. The Mirror board, discredited at least in the eyes of their staff, was virtually powerless. It was a recipe for anarchy and only the staff stood between the *Mirror* and meltdown. It was a remarkable tribute to everyone – middle management, journalists, clerical staff, printing, advertising and circulation departments – who refused to be phased by either the incompetence of their board or the sniping of the opposition. They all deserved better than yet another dictator.

I was joined in the buyout team by Ian McDonald, who had done such a marvellous job overseeing the introduction of colour; circulation director Ian Herbertson, who had made sense of the blackest newspaper art of all, managing the seemingly impossible by sending the right editions to the right areas, a must if you are to have any chance of building a loyal sports readership; and ad director Mark Pritchett. We were also backed by many of the staff, but we ran into problems when the *Record* and *Sunday Mail* in Scotland decided to follow suit and attempt to go their own way; understandable, but a downer for us. Of the board, Charlie Wilson said he was 'in with both feet, matey', Joe Haines supported us and Roger Eastoe was ambivalent. Bill Hagerty, editor of the *People*, was with us, too, and so, we thought, was Bridget Rowe of the *Sunday Mirror*. She, like Wilson, backed both horses, board and buyout. Once again, the buyout was being managed by Michael Stoddart's Electra, and former British Rail chief Sir Peter Parker was brought in to lead it. But the Mirror board would not help us, and the banks were working to their own agenda. They wanted a share price of 170p for their 54 per cent holding before they sold out, although they did not tell us that. Just as well, as we couldn't offer anything like that price, but we could offer a properly run company, vibrant and cash-generating enough to meet its liabilities both to its creditors and pensioners.

There was, however, a further complication. The leading bank with the biggest exposure to Maxwell was the NatWest, the same bank which had honoured a transfer of £11 million signed by Kevin Maxwell, who was not a director of the company. The bank was also refusing to hand back pension fund shares pledged to it illegally by Maxwell. The NatWest was, in effect, in possession of stolen property, an odd position for a bank chaired by Lord Alexander of Weedon, a former chairman of the Bar Council.

Meanwhile, armies of advisers, investigators, lawyers, accountants, actuaries and policemen were crawling all over the Mirror and what remained of the Maxwell private companies. The first complaint of the Fraud Squad was that an enormous amount of shredding had taken place around MCC's offices, so much so that, at one stage, the fuses blew.

For the first six months after Maxwell's fall circulation of the *Daily Mirror* held up well, a great deal better than that of the *Sun*, although both were on a falling market. The six-month figure for the first half of the year showed the gap between the two papers as the lowest since the *Sun* launched Bingo ten years earlier. The relationship between the board and those who actually ran the papers from day to day was virtually non-existent; we rarely saw any of the executive directors, which suited the editorial floor fine. Then came an explosion. Chairman Ernie Burrington announced a 3 per cent pay rise across the company. 'It is the absolute limit we can afford in this exceptionally troubled year,' he wrote. This would be paid 'to all members of staff, irrespective of their position within the company'. What he did not reveal was, only two weeks earlier, the board's remuneration committee had increased his salary from £170,000 to £200,000 in recognition of his new job. Vic Horwood's money had been raised from £80,000 to £125,000. The committee recommended the salaries be backdated to the beginning of the year. Both Burrington and Horwood had failed to stop money haemorrhaging from the group before Maxwell died, and Burrington still had the little matter of the £11 million cheque he co-signed with the unauthorised Kevin Maxwell on his conscience.

Two months after this big rise, Burrington resigned as chairman, and his pension was fixed to his final salary. The timing may have been coincidental, but a couple of weeks before he stepped down, chartered accountants Ernst and Young produced their draft report on a review into possible prospectus claims and criticisms. The report makes it clear that Burrington, Horwood and Guest had been aware of unsupported transactions using Mirror money. In this report, Ernst and Young said, 'We were struck during our interviews of directors and staff by the enormous dominance of the personality of Robert Maxwell. The fear of being sacked and possibly sued undoubtedly affected, to a varying extent, the way in which directors and staff conducted their duties. The same fear may have affected the advisers, though we have not spoken with them.'

If they had, they would have found Galloway claiming that Samuel Montagu was blameless – a view decidedly not shared by the Department of Trade inquiry – because Maxwell had to break the law to breach the ring-fence he had put in place. But the ring-fence itself was fatally flawed. Not only were there more than enough Maxwell private company men in vital positions, but the company secretary, too, was a Maxwell man of many years standing. Alan Stephens had been with Maxwell for nearly 30 years. After Maxwell's death, it became clear that a £50 million loan facility from Bankers Trust of America to MGN had been obtained by Maxwell and Stoney by the simple expedient of passing a committee of the board off as a full board meeting and by claiming they were directors of subsidiary companies, which they were not. The loan actually went to a Maxwell private company. The minutes of these meetings were all signed off by Stephens who protested his innocence of any conscious wrongdoing. Stephens was required to resign because the board had lost confidence in him, not least because he transferred to the Mirror pension scheme on the day Maxwell died, from the much more unstable Maxwell works scheme.

It was clear that flotation had not changed Maxwell's *modus operandi*, he still treated shareholders' money as his own and totally ignored the arm's-length pledge. To do this, he first obtained board permission, less than a month after the flotation, for two directors — one himself — to act as a committee of the board. Along with the single signature resolution he had smuggled passed directors, this gave him further room to manoeuvre and manipulate by using Stoney and Stephens and effectively by-passing the directors. It was a fatal decision and one which surely should have been rejected by the two financial non-executive directors Clements and Clark. Samuel Montagu had indeed erected its ring-fence, but it was designed to keep out the enemy. What McIntosh and Galloway failed to realise was that the enemy was already inside and eyeing up the treasure. Far from clambering over the fence and into the citadel, all he had to do was tunnel out with the loot, which he did all too easily.

The Ernst and Young report is damning of the failure of MGN directors to live up to their flotation pledge to keep Maxwell's private companies at arm's length, a great deal more damning than the eventual finding of the DTI. Stoney, of course, was a Maxwell private company man and put in charge of treasury – investment – functions at the Mirror. Neither Burrington nor Horwood challenged this, preferring, at least in the beginning, to believe there was a personality clash between Guest and Stoney.

Ernst and Young identified six areas in which MGN directors were open to criticism: failure to introduce a system whereby these transactions were brought to the attention of independent directors, as promised at flotation; allowing funds to be moved from the Mirror on the authority only of directors who were representatives of Maxwell companies; the length of time it took to identify these transactions; failure to keep proper account books; the announcement of interim results which may have been materially incorrect; and the fact that, on at least two occasions, bank instructions relating to unsupported transactions were actually authorised by current MGN directors – Burrington and Guest. Lawrie Guest protested about the draft report, pointing out that no independent Mirror director could be sacked by Maxwell under the company Articles of Association. 'I felt resignation would only make the position worse and Ernest Burrington and I had several discussions on the subject of resignation,' he wrote. If that was the case and the two men felt suspicious enough to contemplate quitting, then why on earth did they not approach the non-executive directors Clements and Clark earlier? That was precisely why they were there. Anyway, the fact they could not be sacked strengthened their hands – certainly it was a luxury not afforded to others who had to steel themselves to stand up to him – and a threat of resignation would have scared Maxwell and possibly prevented money flowing from the company. But neither man did anything. However much Lawrie Guest might complain, the Ernst and Young report was damning stuff, the two directors resigned at the next board meeting, Burrington with a pension option of either £120,000 a year or £80,000 with a £250,000 lump sum.

The Burrington and Horwood pay rises were the nearest the journalists came to outright revolt following Maxwell's death. There is no doubt they were doing bigger jobs and Horwood was underpaid, but it was crass and insensitive to either offer or accept such enormous rises when the roles of both men were central to the operation of MGN when the cash was walking out of the door. Charlie Wilson – the man who was in the buyout with both feet – told a worried board that 'a number of people on the editorial floor were associated with the management buyout and wished a destabilisation of the present board of directors believing that to be in their favour'. This was nonsense. The staff needed no bidding from the buyout team to vent their fury and, in the eyes of the journalists, it would be impossible to discredit the board any more than it already had been.

The directors' tenuous hold on newspaper reality was underlined by their next act – increasing the price of the *Mirror* by 2p. All price increases bring circulation declines, that is why newspaper groups had a secret – and illegal – pact to put up prices at more or less the same time. For the *Mirror*, the timing could not have been more disastrous. Circulation was holding up well in a declining market, the readers were showing great sympathy to the paper and were immensely supportive of our pledge to report the scandal 'warts and all' and, as a result, the *Sun*'s sniping was having no effect. Seven months after he died, the joint *Mirror* and *Daily Record* circulation was 88,000 in front of the *Sun*, market share was increasing and, in some areas of England, sales were running neck and neck. The *Sunday Mirror*, too, had increased its market share, and Bill Hagerty's *People* had stabilised its sale, a remarkable achievement for a paper with so many problems.

But the price increase was to change all that. It came immediately after the row over the pay rises for Burrington and Horwood and the revelation of punitive interest rates being paid to the banks for loans, the same banks that had lent money to Maxwell so recklessly. I was appalled by the boneheaded stupidity of raising the price at such a time, particularly as it wasn't just to generate more cashflow but to help re-equip the *Daily Record* plant in Scotland, an absurd priority given the beleaguered state of the company. I wrote a memo to Sir Robert Clark, the new chairman following Burrington's resignation, pointing out my concern:

> *I believe it could seriously damage the* Daily Mirror, *perhaps for years. For the past six months, we have fought back against the* Sun *to a current position where the six-month difference between the two sets of circulations is the smallest for more than ten years. This position cannot possibly be maintained if the* Sun *does not follow us and increase price. All previous history has shown that when the* Sun's *circulation is under threat – as it is now – Murdoch protects it to the exclusion of any other consideration. Therefore, to assume he will increase his price is a very large gamble ...*
>
> *There is also the question of staff morale, extremely brittle throughout the company, as I'm sure you are aware. The price rise will be seen as an attempt to pay for the refinancing of the company by the banks at interest rates that have already raised many eyebrows in the press. It will also be seen as using the* Daily Mirror *to finance the re-equiping of the* Daily Record *at a time when the* Mirror *needs all its resources to protect itself.*
>
> *Finally, the timing could hardly be worse. We are entering a traditional time of intense* Sun *promotion when they would naturally expect to regain market leadership (over the joint* Mirror *and* Record *figure) they will not, in my judgement, risk a price rise during that period, but will heavily attack the* Mirror *for costing more and probably throw in a few grenades about the legacy of*

> Maxwell etc. It seems to me that we are dangerously exposing the future wellbeing of the Daily Mirror *with no adequate safeguard to buttress the inevitable downturn in circulation. It is a policy that led to the eventual discrediting of Reed International as* Mirror *owners and was largely responsible for the continual downward spiral of* Mirror *fortunes throughout the Seventies and early Eighties.*

But the directors would have none of it. 'The interests of the company would be better served by making this modest increase,' explained Sir Robert. This showed his ignorance of newspapers in general and *Mirror* readers in particular. Two pence may be a modest increase for a millionaire merchant banker, but it is a lot for a family struggling to make ends meet when the paper bill has to be paid at the end of the month. It also maintained the fiction that the directors were in charge of Mirror financial policy, when, in fact, they were now the puppets of the banks. Clark may have had no knowledge of newspaper mechanics, but there were plenty on the board who did and must have known what was likely to happen.

The *Sun*'s reaction was swift, launching a poster campaign suggesting readers were now being asked to pay for Maxwell's fraud, a charge made even more effective because it was largely true. But it seemed to take the directors by surprise. At the next board meeting, Sir Robert talked of the *Sun*'s vitriolic attack and Roger Eastoe, who had been a keen advocate of the price rise, talked defensively of the retail trade being 'incensed' by the *Sun* campaign and that 'generally' it was behind the *Mirror*. This was hogwash, the trade took its sales wherever it could and would agree with any rep's suggestion from whatever source. However, there was no disguising the truth. The circulation had been hit hard and the *Sun* was regaining momentum. Newspaper readers were being reminded once more of the *Mirror* legacy of Maxwell and that they were being asked to pay the debts; old wounds were reopened. It was a lethal combination and the directors were blind to it. They had failed to spot the millions flowing out of the company when Maxwell was alive, now they failed to spot the disastrous consequence of their 'modest' increase.

The *Mirror* was never again to be as close as it was at that time to the *Sun* circulation; from that moment on the gap widened and, although there were to be other reasons for the *Mirror*'s decline, it was this price rise at such a crucial time that allowed the rot to set in. The board had managed to supplement its record of watching the company brought to its knees, by setting in train the process by which the same thing would happen to the paper.

By the end of the year, the gap between the *Sun* and the *Daily Mirror* had stretched to more than one million copies a day, an increase of more than 300,000 in six months, and that in spite of the famous Fergie and Johnnie Bryan holiday pictures which sold an extra 1,500,000 copies of the paper in just three days.

Meanwhile, the battle to save the Mirror pension fund was on. At the time of the flotation, the pension fund surplus was £149 million, and that without Maxwell paying a penny in contributions since he bought the company in 1984. It was a good scheme but, gradually, pensioners, under the redoubtable leadership of former Mirror director Tony Boram, had become dissatisfied with the annual increases being paid out. Tony was assiduous in lobbying the *Mirror* and had written to me about it, a letter I passed on to Ernie Burrington. I had even broached the subject with Maxwell who told me the rises were in hand. Sadly and wrongly, like most people on the staff, I took little interest in pensions, assuming that Maxwell couldn't get his hands on them even though there had been plenty of fly posting around the *Mirror* building warning that he could. Pension finances were so obscure and remote and the problems of dealing with Maxwell so all-consuming that the last thing most senior editorial staff worried about was their pension. On the rare occasions we did see Trevor Cook, the pleasant, unassuming pension fund manager, he never gave any cause for concern and, on Tony Boram's complaint, assured me and others it was being addressed, although Maxwell was proving difficult.

Maxwell spirited £450 million of pension fund cash away from the Mirror and Maxwell pension schemes in much the same way as he removed funds from the company. He set up a private company, Bishopsgate Investment Management, to oversee pension fund investments, but once in BIM's clutches they were moved to the private side and either sold or pledged as securities for loans. One such was £25 million worth of Teva Pharmaceutical shares, the ones pledged to the NatWest Bank, which was Maxwell's principal debtor. The NatWest refused for six months to give the shares back, even though by then the bankers were well aware they were stolen from the Mirror pension fund. Neither did the bank adequately explain, when it must have realised Maxwell was in financial difficulties, how he suddenly became the proud owner of such blue-chip shares that were now pledged as collateral.

The shares were only returned after a big public campaign when the

Mirror came close to suggesting readers might like to move their accounts elsewhere, something that did not endear me either to the bank or the board.

The pension fund stock lending began as early as 1985 and, according to Trevor Cook, there appeared to be no problem at that time. But as Maxwell's cash position worsened, he began to scoop deep into the fund. At the same time as Burrington and Guest were being told of misunderstandings over company money that had gone walkabout, Cook was being given the same treatment over pension cash. Maxwell assured him all was well. When the full extent of the losses were revealed, the *Mirror* staff acted with remarkable calm. Once again industrial action was considered and rejected on the reasonable grounds that stopping the paper would only make the situation worse. In fact, much of the pension fund money was recovered and today, with the assistance of a big contribution from the company, it is able comfortably to meet its pension commitments. Maxwell pensioners, many of whom had been paying into their own works schemes that had been taken over by Maxwell, didn't fare as well and endured years of uncertainty before receiving pensions inferior to those they had every right to expect. They are still suffering today.

By now, it was clear the banks wanted a big price for the *Mirror*, the best asset in the crumbled Maxwell empire. But shares were still languishing at half of the 125p flotation price. What they wanted was a campaign of massive cost-cutting across the company and editorial casuals were targeted. The editorial strength was much the same as that of the *Sun*, but we had more casuals because we produced more supplements and more editions, particularly in sport which was proving to be a big success with readers. Not only were we getting the right editions to the right areas courtesy of Herbertson's improved department and McDonald's streamlined press room, but sports editor Keith Fisher had perfected a way of managing to do them in colour, something the *Sun* could not match. We were winning that battle, especially in the football-crazy north, but it was labour intensive and therefore expensive.

The board wanted to chop the casuals, I resisted on the grounds that we were already suffering from the price rise, and a reduction in the quality of our sports coverage would be disastrous. At the same time it became increasingly obvious to me that our buy-out would never be able to fund the share price the banks wanted before getting out, at three times the price at which it was currently stuck. The only way to achieve that would be huge cuts in staff which had already been so badly traduced by the company and I wasn't prepared to do that. In effect, we were dead in the water.

But there were two people lurking in the shadows. Lord Hollick put his close relations with Hambro's Bank, where he was a non-executive director, to work. As we know, Hollick fancied buying the *Mirror* before Maxwell died, hence the approach to Joe Haines. Now he had his chance, but he needed someone at the sharp end. David Montgomery had always wanted to be his own proprietor and had persuaded Murdoch to allow him to be both managing director and editor of *Today*, which Murdoch had bought from under Maxwell's nose. But Montgomery, after some initial success, had damaged *Today* with an off-the-wall relaunch which was an editorial and technical fiasco. He had been sacked from both his jobs and was looking for another chance to prove Murdoch wrong. In this, he had an identical ambition to Charlie Wilson, who had also been sacked by Murdoch from the chair at the *Times*. Sir Robert Clark, at the age of 68, had been hoping for a few non-taxing, non-executive City sinecures, but found himself fighting to save his reputation in the autumn of his years. This could only be achieved by getting the banks out from under, so the staff were to pay the price for saving his reputation.

In the end, he was roundly criticised by the Department of Trade inquiry for failing in his duty. He and co-non-executive director Alan Clements should have 'found out much more about MGN before the flotation and asked what had been done to pass control to the board'. It is typical of Clark's unfortunate view of his responsibilities that he refused to accept the DTI's condemnation of his lack of action. The report, he said, 'doesn't take any account of the situation as it was in 1990. They talk about corporate governance, which is a word that wasn't used in 1990, it wasn't invented then.' But this is unrealistic; the whole point of Clark and Clements being on the board was to control Maxwell, and if Clark didn't know that, then his wife clearly did from her boasting on the side of the Charterhouse football pitch. And what was the ring-fence for if it wasn't to stop Maxwell doing exactly what he did?

The Maxwell era came to an end, seven years and four months after he first barrelled into the Holborn building and almost two decades since he was branded a man unfit to exercise stewardship over a publicly quoted company. That should have been enough for him to be disqualified as a company director, but he wasn't. Far from it. Prime ministers, presidents and Cabinet ministers all came to eat at his table. The American evangelist Jesse Jackson came and, desiring to be fed with a few crumbs which fell from the rich man's table (Luke, Chapter 16,

Verse 21), didn't dissuade his son from pocketing Maxwell's Cuban cigars from the humidor while he was out of the room. Edward Heath was Prime Minister when the first DTI report was published – he came for lunch. The President of the Board of Trade at the time of the inquiry was Peter Walker; he became a non-executive director of MCC, Maxwell's publicly quoted company, and was about to become chairman when he took an extremely handsome pay-off of £100,000 and a £30,000 Mercedes after only four months in the job. Mrs Thatcher came to lunch, as did former Trade and Industry Secretaries Norman Tebbit and Lord Young. Very little was heard from the semi-house trained polecat until he savaged Paul Foot for working for Maxwell's *Mirror*, no mention, though, of his own dining at the captain's table. Jimmy Carter came to lunch and Maxwell was received at the White House by US Presidents Bush and Reagan. From the world of the law, Attorney Generals Silkin, Elwyn Jones and Havers all worked for him, the latter two were both Lord Chancellor as well, the highest legal post in the land. Sir Peter Archer, the solicitor general who oversaw the troubled 1970s Scotland Yard fraud squad investigation into Maxwell, was appointed Mirror Ombudsman. Every Labour Party leader back to Harold Wilson accepted invitations to dine and listened intently to his views. High finance paid court, too; Norman Lamont was a frequent visitor and entertained Maxwell at Number 11 when Chancellor of the Exchequer. It was as if the DTI report of the early '70s never was.

Alex Jarratt and Les Carpenter put Reed's shareholders before the employees of the *Mirror*, knowing full well Maxwell's dubious reputation. The excesses of Fleet Street hastened his arrival; we had created an uncontrollable monster of our own and it required a bigger and more brutal monster to bring it down, a beast that turned out to be even more destructive and uncontrollable. The board of directors Maxwell appointed to his publicly quoted Mirror were at critical times little more than puppets, and the auditors called in to examine the books clearly inadequate. The City men, so proud of their ring-fence, had produced paper bars to cage a tiger. All of them – directors, auditors and bankers – had done too little too late, condemning shareholders and staff alike to lost savings and lost jobs while banking huge salaries and fees themselves. Those who had lent money so recklessly demanded repayment by the loss of jobs of the innocent their greed had put at risk. And, in the end, the only ones to suffer were those who had to be sacrificed so the banks could have their money back. There were no criminal convictions and no fines; the only ones to pay the price were to be *Mirror* staff and casuals out on the street looking for jobs, as well-heeled money men and Mirror directors looked anxiously for somebody else to blame, while engineering huge fees and massive pensions.

The scene was set for one of the worst bloodbaths in Fleet Street history. David Montgomery was slouching towards Holborn Circus to be reborn.

16

Clive Hollick thought it was a winning formula when he teamed up with David Montgomery to take over the running of the *Mirror* although there was little evidence to support his belief. Montgomery was a journalist who had failed in his first managerial enterprise, as editor and managing director of *Today*, the job given to him by Rupert Murdoch after Montgomery had persuaded him to buy it. Murdoch liked the idea because it was a poke in the eye for Maxwell, who had telephoned him to tell him he had got it, but he also had vague thoughts of establishing a mid-market newspaper, the one area where he was not represented in Britain.

Montgomery is a right-wing Ulsterman, a journalist who learnt his trade on the *Mirror* training scheme in Plymouth and joined the *Daily Mirror* as a news sub, first in Manchester and then in London. He quickly acquired the reputation of being a newspaper obsessive, badgering Derek Jameson, the northern editor, and, on one memorable night, changing the splash without telling anyone. On another occasion he had to be rescued by northern news editor Leo White from the clutches of an irate Alastair McQueen, another Protestant Ulsterman, who took grave exception to his copy being rewritten in a way he felt had not only been inferior but inaccurate.

In London he was seen as a loner, constantly hanging around the edge of a group in the pub nursing a half-pint of beer. He married a girl he met on the training scheme but the marriage was soon in trouble.

When I was features editor he did an exchange visit from news only to be sent off with a flea in his ear after he decided to have a go at redesigning Marje's page by producing a layout dominated by a massive graphic of a telephone. This had the interesting effect of reducing Marje's letters and replies to a quarter of the usual content and his attempt to persuade her of the excellence of his idea lasted less than a minute. 'Not right for us at all, dear. Not right at all.'

However, he was right for Nick Lloyd who took him to the *People* when he succeeded Geoff Pinnington as editor. Monty went ostensibly as number four but in reality was deputy to Lloyd and his wife Eve Pollard, as well as babysitter for their young son. Ernie Burrington was actually number two but the Lloyd triumvirate ignored him. At the *People*, Monty was cordially disliked and distrusted and, on more than one occasion, was the subject of complaints that he was writing the headline and projecting a page before he had properly read the story. It was something I experienced during my few weeks with him on the paper before he left to join up with Lloyd again on the relaunch of the tabloid *News of the World*. He then passed out of our lives before re-emerging as editor of the *News of the World*, where old hands reckon he was one of the best of the many editors to take the chair before making their excuses and leaving.

But editing was not what he wanted to do. He wanted to run a paper, to own it if he could, and that is how he came to *Today*, the Eddie Shah colour newspaper that had already been through a fraught and unsuccessful youth with terrible colour problems and uninspiring editorial. Monty thought he could create a 'yuppie' newspaper to reflect the growing number of young City whizz-kids being created by deregulation and the Thatcherite get-rich-quick, fill-your-boots' philosophy of the 1980s. For a time it worked, and the circulation was pushed up to a peak of more than 600,000 with the serialisation of Michael Jackson's autobiography for which he paid £275,000.

Murdoch became increasingly worried about Monty's massive spending commitments, so he decided *Today* should be moved into Wapping from its offices in Vauxhall Bridge Road. After the Michael Jackson peak, the paper began to decline; there wasn't a yuppie market and certainly not for a paper which kept on about them. The whole point of yuppies was that they were dedicated to being upwardly mobile and therefore would hardly read a newspaper which branded them as such. The mood, too, was beginning to shift from pure Thatcherism to a rather more inclusive approach, so Monty changed *Today's* stance. Indeed, he changed it often, quite frequently twice a week in an effort to catch the wind of change. All he caught was a circulation cold as *Today* plunged to a three-year low of below 500,000. In Wapping, Monty's relaunch – both technical, with new equipment, and editorial, now based loosely on *Hello!* magazine – was disastrous. The first month's circulation was lower than the pre-launch figure and Montgomery was fired.

Suffering the fate of all Murdoch's rejects, he was put in charge of future projects – in other words, nothing. He eventually took the money and ran and tried unsuccessfully to launch a local radio station. It was during this operation that he impressed a firm of stockbrokers which, in turn, recommended him to Lord Hollick and Anthony Beevor, executive director of corporate finance at Hambro's, who were putting together a consortium to buy the *Mirror*. Insufficient checks were made with News International about Montgomery's fitness to run a big business. If they had been, Hollick and Beevor would have found that there were considerable reservations about his business ability which is why *Today* was brought into Wapping and he was stripped of his financial controls. Murdoch's view was that the experiment had not been a success.

As soon as it became clear Monty was being touted as the *Mirror*'s new chief executive, the editorial floor erupted in anger. There were a number of refugees from his régime at *Today* who were under no illusion about what he would do. Joe Haines resigned as a non-executive director; he had written a vitriolic leader about Montgomery when *Today* tried to promote a boycott of the *Mirror* for advocating that troops should be withdrawn from Northern Ireland. The board was split on whether to approve Montgomery's appointment and, if Haines had stayed, he might have been prevented him from getting the job, although it would have then been put to an extraordinary meeting of the shareholders who would, no doubt, have welcomed him with open arms as the majority shareholding was held by the concert party of debtor banks. Montgomery had convinced them he could cut costs and up the share price, and as long as they got their money back and a bit on top, they weren't too fussy how he did it. Neither was he.

For the first time since Maxwell's death, the editorial floor rebelled, holding a series of meetings demanding, first of all, Montgomery's removal, and then assurances about jobs and union recognition. On two occasions I persuaded the staff to go back to work against their better judgement; on the second, they only did so after Montgomery had signed the following pledge:

'During the course of today, the following issues have been raised and I wish to take this opportunity to give certain assurances for which you have asked and which I have no difficulty or reservation in giving you.

'The editorial independence of our newspapers will be preserved and vested in the editors, with continuing support for the left of centre and tradition (sic) of all titles. I have definitely got no plans for job cuts in editorial departments, nor has the board considered any.

'We will create the conditions in which the journalism will flourish and increase the value for money quality of all titles.

'Union recognition will continue.

'The editors of all titles remain in their positions. Our aim is to build a strong independent company.'

Few trusted Montgomery's commitment. Indeed, when I brought down his guarantees I told them I felt uncomfortably like Neville Chamberlain returning from Germany with his little piece of paper, and many wanted to organise a sit-in at the *Mirror* that first weekend of his rule. But the situation was hopeless – he was already negotiating with the Sunday papers, in effect splitting the NUJ. In the end, the staff could do little but hope the new chief executive would keep his word, although those who knew him were deeply sceptical. Nonetheless, what he did showed a breathtaking disregard for keeping his word and a merciless savagery unheard of even by Fleet Street's bloodsoaked and hypocritical standards. Within weeks, every one of his assurances had been torn up. Two editors gone, staff both regular and casual summarily sacked, union officials victimised and forced out and the papers in chaos with circulations plunging.

Bill Hagerty at the *People* was the first to go, followed a few days later by me. For three weeks, there had been a phoney peace between me and Montgomery. He had praised the paper but I was wary of him. It was obvious he had been brought in to get the banks their money back and he had the full support of the rump of Maxwell's discredited board. Wilson, the man who backed the buyout, Roger Eastoe and Robert Clark were now 100 per cent Montgomery men. Clark stayed on as chairman, useful to Montgomery because he was a lame duck figurehead, as anxious as the banks that they should get out with money in their pockets, in order to save what remained of his own reputation; if it meant the price was the jobs of scores of staff then, well, that was the way of the world. I was not surprised by my removal, whatever other motive Montgomery might have had leading the buyout was justification enough for a new chief executive to be wary of his senior editor. I probably knew too much about him, anyway, for him to be entirely comfortable with me at the helm of the *Mirror*.

He walked like a crab, almost sideways, often with his hands clasped in front of him and when he spoke he turned his face so he spoke to you sideways in his broad, clipped Ulster accent. He was a small, rather fussy man, dominated by a large pair of spectacles. He took care of his appearance and was always expensively dressed. His spiritual home was with the Red Hand of Ulster, hard-line Protestant, a natural descendant of Carson. He had a burning ambition to succeed and prove to Rupert

Murdoch that he had been wrong to sack him. His most successful time as an editor had been at the *News of the World* and, initially, at *Today*, but he lost his way. His problem as an editor was that he had no core beliefs beyond the Ulster protestant right; he would chase his tail, constantly hoping that if he aimed at enough targets, he would eventually hit a bull's eye. He was a talented newspaper man but not a natural editor; he was too keen on the quick fix, the catchpenny headline and the cynical, artificial, 24-hour campaigns which came from a lack of belief in anything and an underlying contempt for the rest of us who practised his chosen profession.

Two days before I was fired, I heard rumours that David Banks was saying in Australia that he had been asked to edit the *Mirror*. I went to see Montgomery and confronted him. No, David Banks was coming to edit the *People* he said. 'The *Mirror* is going well ... it is the one paper we don't have any problems with. You are the editor and you are doing a good job. I like the paper.'

'So I have your assurance,' – that word again – 'that Banks is not coming to edit the *Mirror*?'

'Certainly you do.' Another breathtaking untruth, as less than 48 hours later he called me to a meeting at Claridge's to discuss a 'matter of national importance'. By the time I met him, I knew that casual staff were being locked out of the building. I had been told on the phone on my way to the West End, so it was clear what my meeting was to be about. When he arrived, he asked me to have breakfast – I refused and told him to get on with it.

'I feel it is time for a new broom at the Mirror,' he began.

'Really? That's not what you said on Friday,' I replied. 'You thought everything was going very well,' I pointed out.

'I was tap dancing,' he replied with a sheepish half-smile.

'But everything is going well, what is your problem?'

'You can't control those lefties in features,' was his only explanation before repeating that the paper needed a new broom.

This was rubbish. Until he arrived, not one newspaper had been lost through industrial action by journalists, in spite of being threatened with the loss of their pensions and livelihoods. On the contrary, if the journalists, printers, advertising staff, secretaries and everyone else on the payroll and not buckled down to the job of saving the *Mirror*, it would have gone out of business long before Montgomery arrived. The board of directors had no control over them; they did it to save not only themselves but the papers as well. As for the lefties, Montgomery revealed his blind prejudice. There were lefties in every department, even sport. That's what happens when you run a left-of-centre newspaper. When I pointed this out rather forcibly to him, Montgomery just shrugged and looked away.

By the time he gave his first interview a couple of days later, he had refined his line. 'There is nothing wrong with Richard,' he said. 'He is a capable and dynamic editor. He represented a culture of decline that existed before, during and after its takeover by Robert Maxwell.'

The decision to fire me, he told the *Independent,* was in order to change the culture of the newspaper so it could seize the initiative from its arch rival, the *Sun.* In other words, he was about to launch himself into a bloodletting exercise that had no parallel in Fleet Street history. His excuse, parroted by his yes-men on the board and in the editors' chairs, was that the papers were overstaffed – not true, the *Mirror*'s staff was almost identical to that of the *Sun* – and that we were overrun by casuals. This, too, was nonsense; the reason we had them was to produce the supplements and the numerous football editions now printed in colour and one of the main reasons for the *Mirror* closing the gap with the *Sun*.

Wilson emphasised the new authorised version: 'There is much more to this than the fact that Stott and Montgomery do not get on. Banks is a very worldly and experienced journalist with a great deal of talent and enthusiasm, who will adopt a more modern approach to the *Mirror*'s political coverage.'

Ah. So that meant the *Mirror*'s politics were now in the hands of two ultra-right-wing Thatcherites – Montgomery and Wilson – and my successor David Banks, a bleeding-heart liberal – his description – who hadn't lived in Britain for almost seven years and had scant knowledge of the political or newspaper landscape. Not only that, he was also there to do the bidding of His Master's Voice. At least he was to be successful at that.

Naturally, the opposition danced with glee over Montgomery's appointment. It was the best news in a bad year for Kelvin MacKenzie, who had assumed the Maxwell scandal would bring us to our knees. In fact, it did the opposite; it brought renewed enthusiasm from a staff determined to prove the rest of Fleet Street wrong. We, on the other hand, had assumed the Mirror board would be drummed out of the Brownies; any group of men so incompetent as to stand by not noticing that nearly £100 million has disappeared from under their noses in less than six months are hardly adequate stewards of public companies. We were wrong. Of the old board, Clark and Clements – the watchdogs who didn't bark – remained, as did Charlie Wilson, the man on everybody's side, and Roger Eastoe, the advertising chief. Vic Horwood voted against Montgomery's appointment and left the group.

The new *Mirror* editor David Banks was an enormous, roly-poly fellow who had been working as editor of Rupert Murdoch's *Telegraph Mirror* in Sydney. He was due to be sacked on the day Montgomery asked him to London to edit the *Mirror*. In Murdoch's words, 'Banks was a good chief sub, that's all.' But he was Monty's man and he was to preside over the destruction of the *Mirror* staff, circulation and credibility, in the two years he was there.

Alastair Campbell, the political editor, was replaced by David Seymour, a lightweight operator but a Montgomery yes-man. Seymour had previously been on the *Mirror* as a second-string leader writer and had left to join *Today* because he could not stand Maxwell. Seymour was charming, attractive in an exasperating kind of way, and vulnerable. He had an exotic Russian background and a temperament to match. During one of his many emotional crises – his marriage to one of the Labour leader's press officers was breaking up – and emboldened by drink, he threatened to jump out of my office window and had to be coaxed back down again to prevent him making an inconvenient mess of a rush hour New Fetter Lane, thirty feet below. Seymour was no fool and he knew his politics, but he was nowhere near the Haines or Campbell class and Montogomery must have known it. The only reason for ridding the *Mirror* of Campbell was to cut the paper adrift from the Labour leadership and have a political team that answered to Montgomery and did not question his running of the paper and report the horrors back to John Smith, who was clearly worried about what was happening.

Campbell's departure prompted Clive Hollick to get out. He had hoped his appointment as a non-executive director would open the back door to a takeover, but although he professed to be appalled by Montgomery's butchery, he did little about it until Campbell was sacked. This was too hot for Hollick, Campbell was very close to Neil Kinnock – who had sent Hollick to the Lords – as well as Peter Mandelson and Tony Blair. Hollick got out before too much mud stuck to him, although some did. His ineffective tenure at the *Mirror* was ended; he had not covered himself in glory.

The exodus continued. Anne Robinson and Campbell went to *Today*. As did Barry Wigmore, a talented and questioning feature writer who had been the first to expose child abuse 'scandals' as little more than the rioting imaginations of kids fed a diet of video nasties. Paul Foot's resignation was spectacular; he produced his column entirely on the scandal at the *Mirror* and put it forward to Banks for publication. Banks declined and asked Paul for another, which he refused to produce. Paul resigned and Banks suggested he should see a doctor. It was a squalid end to a column that had been unique and one of the finest investigative pages Fleet Street had ever produced. To end it by a third rate Montgomery man suggesting Foot was ill, said just about everything that needed to be said about Montgomery's régime. The bad publicity was unremitting and, as staff streamed out of the building, readers streamed away from the *Mirror*. It wasn't just the journalism that had deteriorated, Montgomery had sacked both Ian McDonald and Ian Herbertson, leaving printing and circulation departments in chaos equalling that of editorial. The destruction of all three meant that editions went to the wrong areas and were often late. Night football, which had proved so successful for us because of our ability to get to the right places on time in colour, was now failing to go to the right areas and turning disappointed readers away in droves.

In their first 12 months, Banks and Montgomery lost on average around 200,000 circulation and, in the second year, the rate of decline was only slightly better. The *Mirror* was in freefall. It looked terrible, it broke few stories, its best columnists had all gone, its editor was hopeless and the chief executive appeared to have no idea how to stop the rot he had started.

Banks was followed into the *Daily* chair by *Sunday Mirror* editor Colin Myler but he was no better; three years into his rule, Montgomery had lost the *Mirror* close on 400,000 in circulation.

Not that the banks cared. As Montgomery threw more and more *Mirror* staff on to the streets, the share price rose, enabling them to reach their precious 170p. They had got their money back with a tidy little earner on the side. Montgomery and Wilson had made a fortune out of share options. On the day he joined, Montgomery had been given an option to buy 1,475,409 Mirror shares at 61p each, about as giant a carrot as it was possible to dangle before men hungry for a big bonanza. Wilson was handed options to buy 842,105 shares at 76p and John Allwood, who came from News International to work with Montgomery as financial director, was awarded 983,606 at 61p. The fourth refugee from Wapping to arrive at the Mirror's new Canary Wharf headquarters seeking his fortune was none other than Kelvin MacKenzie, for years the *Mirror*'s chief rival editor of the *Sun*. MacKenzie reckoned he had finished with newspapers, TV was his new love, but TV did not love him. He had gone to Sky as managing director under the dazzling but dangerous and difficult Sam Chisholm, who had been hired by Murdoch to hoist Sky out of its post-launch pit, when all about the new satellite station seemed to be collapsing. Chisholm had done a spectacular job, so it was unduly optimistic of MacKenzie to try and take him on; there was only going to be one result and Kelvin went, refusing a pay-off after a testy breakfast with Murdoch which had been organised to try and restore peace. So now the Mirror had three former Murdoch editors earning between them more than £1 million a year and they still had three lousy newspapers losing circulation hand over fist.

Montgomery, Wilson and MacKenzie had one thing in common apart from enormous salaries. They had all been waved bye-bye one way or another by Murdoch and were all desperate to show him they could cut the mustard in newspaper management. Nonetheless, they were all prepared to dig their snouts deep into the *Mirror* trough. Montgomery excused his excoriating policy by claiming that the *Mirror* was hugely overstaffed, fat, self-satisfied and peopled by drunks, 'the old *Mirror* culture', as he called it. If this was true once, then it had radically changed since the arrival of Maxwell, in spite of the spectacular Peter Cook – John Penrose incident. With Maxwell living over the shop it was quite impossible, but it was easy for Montgomery to convince media critics who rarely even bothered to read tabloid papers that not much had changed at the group since Maxwell had arrived. All journalists should be made to endure a course of exposure to their colleagues' reporting talents to realise how appallingly bad some of it is. The Maxwell affair gave me some sympathy for politicians who are always moaning about the accuracy of newspapers; much of it was straightforwardly wrong, with subsequent comment ill-informed and inaccurate. Interestingly, the broadsheets were a great deal worse than the tabloids. MacKenzie's *Sun*, for example, could and would be nasty about us but its reporting was frequently more accurate than the *Guardian*.

So what was the new *Mirror* culture? Fill your boots, is the answer. By 1995, Montgomery's pay package was £356,000, boosted by those massive share options. In with both feet Wilson's salary was £261,000 with the options of 842,105 granted at 76p now reinforced with another 64,000 at 125p. If he had sold them when he eventually left the company, they would have realised £950,000. He was allowed to keep the options because, said director Paul Vickers, 'it is a gesture to his excellent service with the company'. As Wilson, in his two jobs as managing director of Mirror Group and editorial director, presided over the disintegration of the papers without appearing to do much to stop the decline, it is difficult to see quite where the excellent service came in. MacKenzie was to earn £320,000 with a £50,000 bonus as chief of L!VE TV, the company's cable station which nobody watched in spite of MacKenzie's best efforts – News Bunny, the weather in Norwegian and stuttering news readers. At least L!VE TV did perform one genuine service – if you could avoid the dross, it gave young people a real chance to learn the business, from reporting news stories to editing their own material, a valuable training ground only found rarely elsewhere, as daughter Hannah found out when she joined the fledgling Newcastle operation. It was to stand her in good stead when she finally landed a job with Sky TV.

When Wilson was finally shoved out, MacKenzie became deputy chief executive to Montgomery, an interesting appointment as he couldn't stand Monty and had once sacked him from the *Sun*. Privately he was scathing about the job Montgomery had done, or failed to do, a view underlined by the fact that within ten days of taking over responsibility for the newspapers, he had dramatically improved the look and content of the *Mirror*, by this stage struggling under the editorship of Piers Morgan, a talented young journalist but clearly at that stage out of his depth until MacKenzie provided him with water wings.

The triumvirate of editors left a new, young, inexperienced editor disastrously exposed. When the *Mirror* was handed a copy of the Tories' 1996 budget – a scoop to dream of – the paper failed to run it, preferring instead the style to the substance, revealing the *Mirror* had been handed a copy but had given it back. The reason for keeping quiet was given as the effect it would have on the money markets, hardly something a left-of-centre newspaper should worry about.

But even this flimsy excuse was blown out of the water the next day by the paper itself when the excuse had changed to the fact that the Budget was so boring. In that case, how could it affect the markets? It was this daft piece of journalism that made me write to Montgomery pointing out that the *Sun* was beginning to take the *Mirror*'s water – it was shortly before Murdoch came out in favour of Tony Blair's New Labour – and that the paper was rapidly becoming irrelevant because its personality, sense of purpose and crusading qualities had disappeared.

Monty suggested 'a quiet lunch'. I had already been told by MacKenzie that the chief executive hadn't a clue what to do with the papers and the lunch made that all too clear. The papers, he said, needed to be 'aspirational', 'modern thinking' and geared towards 'lifestyle', the usual buzzwords which mean absolutely nothing. When I asked him what all that meant, he couldn't explain, another shrug of the shoulders. Not only was he wallowing over the newspapers' content, he clearly had no idea where to take the business next. Investors – the banks had taken and run with their money by this time – were demanding a share price of 250p and he admitted he hadn't a clue how to deliver it. Certainly not by the newspapers' performance – all three circulations continued to dive.

MacKenzie's stewardship of the papers was brief but decisive. Morgan found his feet and the paper was given a new confidence, but MacKenzie was not the man to be in overall control of a paper like the *Mirror*, something he has admitted on several occasions. He asked me to write a column on the *Daily* and *Sunday Mirrors*. But there was no way I could go back while Montgomery remained in charge. It would be a betrayal of all those who had refused to bend to his will and walked out, as well as those who had been culled. Instead, I offered to go back as editor – as long as I could take 20 of the best journalists who had left the paper because of the chief executive. It was an offer MacKenzie found easy to refuse.

Why did David Montgomery destroy the existing *Daily Mirror* when, by his own admission, the paper was working successfully? The answer lies in his own deep-seated insecurity and obsessive control freakery. He believed he had all the answers, both journalistic and business, in spite of all the evidence pointing the other way. In this, he was not unlike Maxwell and, like him, was not motivated entirely by money but by a determination to be accepted by those whom he felt had rejected him.

The sacking of Campbell resulted in more than 170 Labour MPs signing a lack-of-confidence motion in Montgomery. He was attacked by both Neil Kinnock and John Smith, and the adverse publicity for the *Mirror* was terrible. The only reason he could have taken such a calamitous course was because he perceived Campbell to be a threat, with a straight through line to both the Labour leadership and Hollick, who resigned after Campbell left, although he had publicly remained silent up until that moment. By appointing Seymour, he ensured he had someone in charge of politics who would do his bidding, just as he had at *Today*. Placemen were positioned everywhere and, as a result, the Mirror Group became infested with inadequates while the best of the Mirror was forced out. Few of Monty's army believed in what either the *Mirror* or the Labour Party stood for and, in spite of the cynicism of Fleet Street rivals, belief is important to the lifeblood of the *Mirror*. Without the passion and spine of left-wing faith, the paper is nothing more than just another red-top tabloid, something it became increasingly under Montgomery. Worse, for most of his reign it was a pretty poor version of just another tabloid.

MacKenzie didn't last long in his new job, although long enough to sack Bridget 'Death' Rowe – whom he held responsible for the disaster areas of the Sunday papers – and to introduce the City Slickers to the *Mirror*, a potent virus that was to surface nearly two years later and plunge the group into yet another crisis and a second, long-running Department of Trade inquiry. For years, Kelvin had been moaning about making money for others and how he wanted to make a bundle for himself, and now he had the chance, by leading a successful consortium bidding for the ailing Talk Radio. The appointment of the Slickers proved his point that he was not the man to run the *Mirror*; their philosophy was much more akin to that of the MacKenzie *Sun* and the Thatcherite '80s. When Hugh Cudlipp first introduced a City column into the *Mirror* during the mid-'60s, he did it with the specific intention of protecting readers against the get-rich-quick spivvery of slickers looking for every opportunity to fleece them of their hard-earned cash by dodgy share deals. Now iffy City spivs had infiltrated the money pages of the paper by placing share 'tips' with the Slickers in order to make an overnight killing.

Six months after MacKenzie's departure, Montgomery himself was gone, a victim of a merger planned with the regional newspaper group Trinity, because he was considered an obstacle to selling the group by the new chairman Sir Victor Blank. By a splendid irony, he didn't fit in with the new *Mirror* 'culture' personified by Trinity, a highly successful regional newspaper group. His pay-off was generally reckoned to be around £1.4 million, which together with almost three-quarters-of-a-million he made out of previously cashed share options, meant he trousered more than £2 million.

During his reign of terror, which began with the rallying cry that he was going to make the *Mirror* titles great again, the flagship had lost more than 500,000 copies a day. The *Sunday Mirror* had lost 779,891 – more than a quarter of its entire sale, and the *People* 412,315 – just under 20 per cent. Altogether, the three papers had lost a staggering 1,722,420 – 5,000 more than the entire circulation of the *People*. The decline of the *Daily Mirror* accelerated at an alarming rate under Montgomery, particularly in his early years. Between March 1981 and 1991, the circulation dropped 528,149. In the next ten years, it dropped a further 786,296, that's over a quarter of million more than the previous ten years and from a significantly smaller base. So much for Montgomery's new *Mirror* culture. Not much seizing of the initiative from Murdoch either. The banks, which had helped create the Maxwell disaster, got out with cash to spare at the cost of countless *Mirror* jobs in every area of the business. The board paid itself lavishly while employing inexperienced young people on short-term contracts for misery wages and forcing them to work immensely long hours.

But even though Montgomery was gone, his legacy lived on. The City Slickers could not have survived on the *Mirror* at any other time in its history. After Cudlipp's inception of the City page, all reporters who worked on it were given extra pay because they were not allowed to deal in shares. This was rigorously imposed by the first city editor Derek Dale and his successor Robert Head. But the Montgomery culture had fostered a cynicism staggering even by the standards of a cynical profession. It is hardly surprising when people are employed only on a short-term basis for a minimum wage, knowing full well the directors are on lucrative share option deals which depend on maximising profit, minimising pay and increasing hours. The close-to-the-wind activities of the City Slickers James Hipwell and Anil Bhoyrul were found to be very useful by elements in the City. Piers Morgan, the *Mirror*'s editor, became embroiled in the scandal when it was revealed he bought £20,000 worth of shares in Viglen – the Alan Sugar company tipped by the Slickers the morning after the editor bought them. He has always maintained he did not know the company's flotation was to be the subject of an 'exclusive' story in the Slickers column that day. Whatever the truth of it, this situation simply could not have arisen during the time I or any of my predecessors was editor. The *Mirror* held two editorial conferences a day, one in the morning and one in the late afternoon. These were attended by all the heads of department and schedules were produced by the news, pictures, City and sports desks on both occasions. The reason was twofold: first, to let the editor know what stories were about and how they were progressing; and second, to let each other know what the various departments were working on in order to prevent doubling up. Therefore, the Viglen story would have been on at least one of the schedules in front of the editor – unless the Slickers thought the story so hot they kept it off the schedule in order to prevent it leaking, in which case they would have told the editor privately.

The afternoon conference has been abandoned because of the sheer weight of material now being processed, certainly a great deal more than ever before. The position of Trinity *Mirror* seems strangely ambivalent; a board which swiftly dismisses the Slickers in a flurry of moral rectitude is then, several months later, prepared to shell out £16,000 compensation to Bhoyrul in order to avoid a public wrongful dismissal hearing. Whatever the internal hand-wringing, the Viglen affair has made it difficult for the *Mirror* to savage City greed and avarice, at a time when the gap between rich and poor has never been greater. The paper which first coined the phrase Fat Cats to describe the quick buck and rip-off merchants of the City – the lawyers, accountants and bankers making a fortune out of the Maxwell affair – can no longer use the phrase without inviting an obvious critical comparison. A newspaper which prided itself on its willingness, ability and power to take on the forces of privilege on behalf of those sunk in poverty, sickness, unemployment or rotten housing cannot now do so without facing taunts about indulging in the sins it seeks to expose.

Nonetheless, in spite of downward circulation trends, the *Mirror* is a much improved newspaper from the dark days of Montgomery, and many of the opportunists and second-raters he brought in to do his bidding have now gone. Its additional pagination and magazines make it much more value for money than it was when I was there and its news coverage is as good as it ever has been. Morgan, apart from his vulnerability over the Slicker affair, is a good journalist and dedicated to the *Mirror*'s cause, but he is not a natural left-of-centre crusader. However it is largely down to him that after weathering the Slickers scandal, he distinguished himself and his paper with his coverage of the September 11th attack on the Trade Center twin towers and the war in Afghanistan, a sustained quality which was rewarded with the *What the Papers Say* award for Newspaper of the Year in 2001, 20 years after last winning it.

But the hard fact is that the *Mirror* must be more than a good newspaper. It has to be the flag-bearer of the left and of a massive swath, of people who cannot afford to buy huge chunks of shares. That conviction has to run through the whole paper and never more so than when the grassroots are losing faith in their leaders at Westminster, yet only the excellent Brian Reade and the truculent Paul Routledge wear the uncomfortable hair shirt of Labour conscience. As Tony Blair's Labour Party moves further to the right, it is the job of the *Mirror* to remind the party of its roots and its founding principles. It is not there to be a cheerleader for the comfortable and instinctively Conservative middle classes where Montgomery would have taken in it; that's *Daily Mail* country. One legacy of the Montgomery era is that all *Mirror*-trained and home-grown talent was cleansed, leaving the vast majority of the top end of the three papers under Montgomery both managed and edited by former News International staff, who had neither the instinct nor the stomach for left-wing politics. That may have been a relief to Tony Blair, but it was dangerous for the *Mirror*.

Nowadays, the *Sun* is frequently inferior to its great rival but the much derided David Yelland has managed to de-MacKenzie the *Sun* for a new generation without losing significant circulation. It has been achieved, too, without resorting to a price cut, apart from matching the Mirrors 20p policy, which was the final solution in the last days of Kelvin. The *Sun* has managed to adapt to the Blair era, somewhat uncomfortably and disingenuously it is true, but the transformation has been made and by doing so the *Sun* has presented the *Mirror* with a serious problem. What is its job?

Piers Morgan found part of the answer in the days after the World Trade Centre bombing and the subsequent war in Afghanistan. The *Mirror* developed a distinctive voice, questioning the bombing, the prosecution of the war, the casualties and whether the politicians really knew what they were doing, while the *Sun* stuck to its inevitably gung-ho line. The *Mirror*'s path was more rocky and dangerous for a popular newspaper, but it showed it was thinking and providing a brave, distinct alternative to the *Sun*, a considerable change to the earlier years of Montgomery when the received wisdom was to try and out-*Sun* the *Sun*, always a disastrous policy and one long since abandoned, even by Maxwell. Mass circulation newspapers are gradually becoming a feature of the past, as television channels proliferate, 24-hour news services are available to all and reading becomes an ever rarer habit.

The *Mirror*'s role in a modern, right-wing world dominated by a pragmatic Labour Party is to fulfil the task Michael Foot set for Labour politicians during the 1983 election campaign at a time when Thatcherism was rampant and the Labour Party was low on self-esteem and self-belief. His words would raise a guffaw among the New Labour hierarchy today, but remain a pretty good template for Britain's only left-wing popular daily newspaper as it, too, faces the problem of finding a role for itself in an increasingly bland landscape: 'We are not here in this world to find elegant solutions, pregnant with initiative, or to save the ways of profitable progress. No, we are here to provide for all those who are weaker and hungrier, more battered and crippled than ourselves. That is our only certain good and great purpose on earth, and if you ask me about those insoluble economic problems that may arise if the top is deprived of their initiative, I would answer, To hell with them. The top is greedy and mean and will always find a way to take care of themselves. They always do.'

After Maxwell and Montgomery, the *Mirror*, of all papers, knows the truth of that.

17

The nearest I had come to meeting Rupert Murdoch was back in the '60s at the *Mirror*'s pub The Stab in the Back – its real name, but never used, is The White Hart. He turned up at a farewell for Vic Mayhew, the *Mirror* chief sub he had hired for the *Sun* in a spectacular raid on our backbench – the night production team working under the night editor – when he filched three at the same time. None of them knew the others were going until they met up at the *Sun* offices. Neat. That was shortly after he relaunched the *Sun* as the paper we now know and his bravado wrong-footed the *Mirror*, as it was to do intermittently for the next three decades.

This was the only time I had come close to him, and then it was only his back as he and Larry Lamb, the *Sun*'s editor, waited in vain to be served. I had also interviewed his mother in their up-country estate outside Melbourne after the press pack received a tip that John Stonehouse had camped out with her following his discovery in Australia. I was chosen to knock on her door – 'you're on the *Mirror*, you have nothing to lose' – by the assembled hacks, most of whom worked for Murdoch papers. Don't worry, we are all behind you, you just do the talking, I was assured. So when Dame Elisabeth came to the door, I introduced myself and 'all the others'. 'What others?' she asked. I turned round and found they had hidden round the side of the house until they had gauged her reaction. We were served up a fine cup of tea, but sadly no Stonehouse.

The last time I had been in the same room as him, I caused a sharp intake of breath from News International staff with what turned out to be a spectacularly ill-judged joke. It was a dinner to celebrate Kelvin's ten years as editor of the *Sun* and the climax of the evening was a full-scale private *This Is Your Life* production presented by Michael Aspel. This is the same as the real thing, the only difference is that it doesn't go out on air. I was brought on, not only as editor of the *Daily Mirror* but a friend who had known him since the early days in South-East London. Kelvin referred to me 'taking the Maxwell shilling' and as this was at a time when

Murdoch's money problems were being well aired. I replied, 'At least he's still got one.' I thought it was funny and there was some nervous laughter as all eyes switched to Murdoch's table; at least he managed a rather wintry smile. He also had the last laugh. At the time I said this, Maxwell's private companies had piled up debts of £1 billion and he was already beginning to move money out of the *Mirror* and its pension fund. When finally we met, Murdoch had the grace not to remind me of it.

I was to meet him for the first time at News Corp's offices on New York's Sixth Avenue, or Avenue of the Americas as we have to call it now. Andrew Knight, the chairman of News International in London, had asked me to edit *Today*, to replace Martin Dunn who had decided to take up Mort Zuckerman's offer to edit the *New York Daily News*. Andrew assured me my appointment was all his doing, although I detected the hand of Kelvin in there somewhere. He had convinced Murdoch that *Today* would be better off supporting Labour, the Tory supporters' end of the ground was crowded, and only the *Mirror* and *Guardian* were propping up the other end. This made journalistic and business sense. Both Kelvin and Rupert could see only too easily the *Mirror*'s disarray following the arrival of Montgomery and Banks and a rival would put another cat among the already bloodied pigeons. It would also be useful if *Today* could lure key *Mirror* staff across to Wapping.

The first thing that strikes you about Rupert Murdoch is his charm and his genuine interest in and extensive knowledge of newspapers. He is also a good and attentive listener; after Maxwell, it was like a breath of fresh air. Maxwell was impatient with discussion; Murdoch encourages his executives where Maxwell denigrated them. Murdoch is an accomplished newspaperman whereas with Maxwell it was the one thing he desperately wanted to be. Neither have any small talk and the knowledge of the world outside their own business empires was remarkably limited in both men. Murdoch, for example, would be able to tell you who Tony Blair and Gordon Brown are, but after that he would be struggling if asked to put Cabinet names to jobs. For a movie mogul, his knowledge in that field is limited, as I was to find out when I told him that a Tory Arts Minister, when asked if he had seen any Jeanne Moreau films, replied that he had never seen him act. Murdoch looked puzzled. 'So what, I haven't see any of his films either,' he said. Whoops. Make smoke and zig-zag as my old friend and Naval buff Alan Hobday used to say when we faced yet another crisis at the *People*.

Maxwell once managed to oust Michael Jackson from the presidential suite of a Tokyo hotel. 'I had to get rid of somebody called Jackson,' he told me when he rang to say where he was.

'Michael Jackson?' I asked.

'Yes, why, is he famous?' He replied.

'Just a bit, Bob, he's a big star singer.'

'Really,' pondered Maxwell. 'Is he black?'

'Up to a point, Bob, up to a point.'

Both Murdoch and Maxwell had the ability to flatter, and Murdoch was disarmingly generous about the way we had kept the *Mirror* fighting its corner since Maxwell's death. He was also alarmingly frank about other editors in the group in front of me, another disconcerting trait he shared with Maxwell along with the chopping grand gesture.

But, for the moment, it was a question of circling this strange animal from the other camp and seeing if I was up to the job of running *Today* as the only left-of-centre paper in the Murdoch London stable. I suspect even at this early stage of the Major Government – it was only seven months after his surprise 1992 victory over Neil Kinnock – he was already beginning to think of the possibility of withdrawing his support at the next election. He was certainly contemptuous of Major, a sentiment made worse by the débâcle of Black Wednesday and our precipitate exit from the European Exchange Rate Mechanism. In truth, he had time for few politicians, treating them with an ill-concealed disdain as men and women who had no experience of the real world.

Today was born in March 1986 in the triumphant wake of Eddy Shah's epic battle against the National Graphical Association at his free-sheet plant in Warrington. Nobody had heard of him until that time, when he decided to do what Fleet Street had been too cowardly to do for decades – he took on the might of the print unions and, after a war of attrition and intimidation mounted against him, he won. It was the most significant victory in newspaper industrial relations for many years.

Shah decided to build on this success by launching himself on to the national scene with a new colour newspaper. But he had neither the expertise nor the money. From the start he was unclear what *Today* was going to be, apart from a colour paper. But it needed to be more than that, it had to supply a need and it did not do so. Its politics, news coverage, features and sport were all run-of-the-mill and its colour was dreadful – so out of register that it became known as Shahvision. His TV blitz on the launch featured his staff saying, 'We're Ready, Eddy.' but sadly they weren't, and the first circulation figures showed *Today*'s sale at a derisory 340,125. Yet the paper had been effective in other areas, the bits the readers don't see. New technology, satellite printing, distribution by road rather than rail and, most important of all, the drastic reduction in the power of the trades unions, were all part of Fleet Street's future and the message was clear to the big boys: change or take the consequences. The message was not lost on Murdoch, who firmed up his plans to do a midnight flit to Wapping where he was, ostensibly at any rate, planning a new London paper. The launch, like Montgomery's relaunch five years later, was a technical disaster and an editorial non-event, and few newspapers can survive that. Shah could not sustain the losses and sold the paper to Lonrho for £10 million which, in turn, sold it to Maxwell. Or, at least, that was the plan.

In the summer of 1987, Maxwell did a £10 million deal with Lonrho and even had Mike Molloy begin redesigning it. But he couldn't resist a bragging phonecall to Murdoch to tell him he had bought the paper. It was a phonecall too far. Murdoch was being pestered by David Montgomery, then editor the *News of the World* and doing a good job there, to let him be his own business boss. Murdoch also liked the idea of having a mid market paper but, most of all, he relished the thought of delivering another poke in the eye to Maxwell whom he had already decisively defeated over the purchase of the *News of the World* and the *Sun*. He realised from Maxwell's call that the *Today* deal had not been finalised, so he tripled the offer and the paper was his. Maxwell was humiliated, but it was to prove an expensive joke.

As I explained in the previous chapter, after some initial success pandering to the Thatcherite yuppy market – readers bought at an enormous marketing spend – Murdoch had second thoughts about his Montgomery experiment, not least because of the moans coming from MacKenzie, holed up in Wapping, that Montgomery was allowed what appeared to be unlimited pagination and non-stop TV advertising. When Murdoch checked the cost of all this he was appalled and ordered the independent *Today* operation in Vauxhall Bridge Road – its original home – to be shut down and brought into the Wapping compound. At the same time Montgomery decided to relaunch editorially in a last-ditch effort to revive an ailing circulation. He was told, however, that he would have to use the Wapping technology which he was violently against, and not without reason; it was basic and extremely poor. But instead of just getting on with it and making the best out of a bad job, he sulked in his tent and continued to resist. The outcome was both a technical and editorial cockup which resulted in a lower sales figure after the relaunch than before, virtually unheard of, even by Fleet Street's eccentric standards. It was so bad he had to apologise for the launch in the next day's paper.

As a result, Montgomery was on his bike and Martin Dunn, MacKenzie's deputy at the *Sun*, was put in charge of the rescue until he decided to take up an offer he couldn't refuse – the editorship of the *New York Daily News*. When I came to the paper, he had done a fine job in rehabilitating the circulation; by January 1993, it had reached 513,226. But the main problem remained; *Today* was just another right-wing newspaper with no real personality. My mission was to change that by turning it into an iconoclastic, left-of-centre, top-end of the popular market paper with good writers, strong opinions and a vibrant news sense.

We developed all three. There were some fine reporters on *Today* and, augmented by disaffected *Mirror* staff, including Alastair Campbell and Anne Robinson, who fled the Montgomery cleansing, they blended into a terrific team with little of the bickering you might expect from such a hybrid animal. *Today* broke many stories and was frequently the agenda setter, but the finest investigations were done by one man, Alan Watkins, who doubled up as the night news editor. Watkins exposed both the BSE scandal and Gulf War Syndrome in spite of some pretty dirty tricks by both the Ministry of Agriculture and the Ministry of Defence. They branded Watkins as a loony obsessive and, indeed, he did look somewhat eccentric. He was a world expert on bus tickets, train timetables, classical music and, luckily for us, Mad Cow Disease and Gulf War Syndrome. The secret briefings against him by the ministries were all too easily swallowed by the rest of Fleet Street which meant he fought a valiant lone battle. They tried to seduce me, too. This is a typical letter from Armed Forces minister Nicholas Soames after yet another desert fever revelation by Watkins: 'Your newspaper has repeatedly misreported the facts of the alleged syndrome in what I can only describe as an alarmist way, creating unnecessary concern amongst personnel and their families, and creating a highly charged, emotive atmosphere around an issue that requires calm, objective and scientific analysis ... I find this misleading and selective reporting particularly disturbing ... I regret that I have little confidence that the reporters who have been engaged on this story will report objectively and fairly on this issue. Therefore, I would like to offer an invitation to you personally to come to the MoD for a briefing by myself and my officials.'

This is one of the oldest tricks in the book – by-pass the reporters and compromise the editor with a confidential background briefing explaining 'the truth' about the situation. Buckingham Palace does it all the time and editors are still falling for it. When, some months later, the MoD had been condemned by a select committee of MPs for their handling of Gulf War Syndrome, I cornered Soames at the Tory Party Conference and asked whether he might like to apologise for his high-handed and incorrect stance over not only Gulf War Syndrome but BSE as well – he had been at the Min of Ag, too – a rare double even by Fatty Soames's Bunteresque standards.

'Oh, they were only technical cock-ups,' he explained with an airy wave of a pudgy arm. Very reassuring for the 80-odd families with victims who are now technically very dead from the human form of Mad Cow Disease.

Watkins wasn't the only reporter who was brave enough to tread where others dare not. I first met Tina Weaver when she was a young reporter on the *People*. She had enormous talent and when I went back to the *Mirror*, I asked her to come over. But she was unhappy under Banks and, like many *Mirror* staff, joined me at *Today*. Tina beat the world with her exposure of the persistent allegations of child abuse against Michael Jackson. To do this, she had to spend many weeks alone in Los Angeles facing down not only a hostile Jackson camp but a hostile and threatening Hollywood, too, which saw a lucrative cash machine disappearing out of Peter Pan's Never Never land. It is a tribute to her great talent and bravery that she managed to break a series of exclusives about Jackson's alleged abuse, including the evidence that he had paid out millions of dollars to Jordy Chandler. It was an heroic piece of reporting for which she justly won Reporter of the Year and, for me, it demonstrated the difference between Montgomery's *Today* which paid £275,000 for Jackson's cosmetic, anodyne memoirs and ours, which exposed his alleged child abuse through top-class journalistic skills.

Today was a wonderful opportunity for Murdoch to seize the top end of the popular market and squeeze the ailing *Mirror* from both sides. But his mind was elsewhere and his managers failed to take their chances. For years at the *Mirror,* we had envied News International their management, believing the group to be better run than ours, and under Bruce Matthews it was. But when I actually got there, Bruce was long gone and I was amazed to find excesses – the place was a licence to print money for cab firms – inefficiency, overstaffing and editorial production indiscipline long since eradicated at the *Mirror*. The print run of the *Sun*, the Times and *Today* was rarely managed without some form of disaster. Quite often, it was caused by immensely late editorial on one or more of the papers and neither editorial nor production staff had a clue how to master colour efficiently, presumably because they had taken their cue from Murdoch who still insisted it didn't sell newspapers. Chairman Andrew Knight and managing director John Dux were both certain there was something fundamentally wrong with the presses and the Wapping press hall which housed them, but I wasn't convinced. I believed the problem was human and quite likely sabotage was involved, as indeed it proved to be when Ian McDonald was brought in to make a full report on the state of the News International print process.

The unpalatable truth was that, in spite of the flight to Wapping, News International was still overmanned in the printing area and morale was so low that some of the worst Fleet Street practices – including sabotage – had made a comeback. McDonald's report was dynamite and John Dux insisted all copies of it went to him. MacKenzie got wind of this and told Murdoch, who demanded a copy. From that moment on, Dux's days were numbered.

Murdoch had another problem. Because morale was so bad – Wapping, at the best of times, was a pretty hideous and soulless place in which to work – there was a very real danger that trades unions could fight their way back, especially if Labour won the next election and insisted on free votes within companies on trade union representation. With Wapping in this state, many staff would welcome the unions with open arms. That, together with the fact that communications within the company generally had become so bad, is the main reason why Gus Fischer, the chief executive brought in to replace the departing Andrew Knight, and John Dux had to go. It was time for a more human face in order to keep the unions out. Murdoch's problem was that the trauma of the long-running battle at Wapping had created a siege mentality and those who manned the barricades were kept on regardless of talent and their ability to capitalise on the benefits the Wapping victory brought. In many ways that victory had been superseded, particularly by the introduction of colour, and News International was beginning to lag behind. The loyalty of those who had put their faith in Murdoch as opposed to the unions was understandable and laudable, but it was having an adverse affect on the business.

Les Hinton, an old Murdoch hand and former *Sun* reporter, was brought in as executive chairman and his more relaxed, informal and accessible style kept the unions out of Wapping. But for Murdoch, it had been a damned close run thing, too close for comfort.

Meanwhile, *Today* continued to pick up disenchanted *Mirror* readers and, with the introduction of a Saturday magazine, the circulation reached more than 650,000 thanks to a one-off price reduction. It was at this time Murdoch should have put all his energies into promoting the paper, but instead News International blew hot and cold. A reduction in price in Scotland was reversed almost immediately. The Saturday magazine was plagued with appalling reproduction, putting off advertisers and readers alike. Promotion was fitful and underfunded. The brutal truth was that Murdoch was determined to make the *Times* a success and it was costing him a fortune. He was not prepared to spend money on *Today*, particularly when he decided to go for cutting the cover price on both the *Sun* and the *Times*. The paper was a nuisance he could do without.

With the death of John Smith and the advent of Tony Blair, Murdoch moved up a gear. Here was a man with whom he could do business and he invited him to his annual St James's cocktail party. By now, I knew Blair because he had pinched Alastair Campbell from *Today* where he had taken up residence after being usurped by David Seymour as the *Mirror*'s chief political guru. Seymour had moved across from *Today* and I told him before he left that there was no way Campbell would work with him as his boss. But he was under the illusion he could persuade him, which, of course, he could not. Alastair had been close to Blair for some time, a friendship forged through knowing Peter Mandelson, and it was obvious that Blair, like Kinnock before him, wanted Alastair as his press secretary.

From the first moment I met Blair we agreed on one major issue, that only Labour could produce a meaningful reform of the welfare state, including the National Health Service. At that time, it appeared to be his major concern, with education a short step behind. In Labou's first term it was put on the back burner, presumably because Frank Field, having been asked to think the unthinkable, did so, and Blair didn't like what he saw, a huge increase in income tax would have been necessary to fund Field's proposals. The April 2002 Budget, however, has seen the return of the NHS as a priority for Blair's Government – and it is national insurance contributions rather than income tax, which is funding the return to pre-eminence. This was consolidated by Gordon Brown's unprecedented plans announced later in the summer.

I reckon that evening in his flat at St James's, was the first time Murdoch met Blair and he asked me to introduce him, even though it was his own party and there was nothing on earth to stop him introducing himself, except perhaps a natural shyness and awkwardness. 'When are you going to introduce me to your man?' he said.

'Now, if you want,' I replied, which wasn't difficult as Blair was standing next to me. I introduced them and left them to it. I thought I might as well go the whole hog, so I offered to introduce Lady Thatcher to Blair as well, but she wasn't having any of it. 'I don't think now is the time,' she said from behind a large whisky, although she was only too happy to agree when I suggested that New Labour would not have got off the ground if it had not been for her dominance of politics during the 1980s.

Blair and Murdoch clearly got on well because the Labour leader was invited, much to the horror of Murdoch's top executives, as the star speaker at the News Corporation Love-In held in 1995 on the exclusive and seriously rich man's playground, Hayman Island in the Whitsundays, off the Queensland coast. By this time, there was no Andrew Neil and no Kelvin MacKenzie. Neil, for all his outsize, fragile ego and spiky reputation, I always found a likeable man who had done a remarkable job at the *Sunday Times*, making it unchallengeable as the number-one Sunday newspaper. By the time I reached News International, he sounded as if he had had enough of editing and was constantly sniping at both Andrew Knight and Murdoch himself. It seemed obvious to me that he wanted Knight's job and it was equally obvious that he wasn't going to get it. Murdoch hated his editors to become too high-profile and he felt this about both Neil and MacKenzie; he had disapproved of Kelvin's virtuoso performance before a Commons select committee where he routed the MPs who seriously underestimated him. Andrew was winkled out of the *Sunday Times* with a promise of a New York TV career, which he took seriously enough to have his hair straightened. Kelvin, by now heartily sick of editing the *Sun* after an extraordinary 13 years, also left for a truncated TV career as managing director of Sky under Sam Chisholm, although that wasn't quite as he saw it. I was the only one of Murdoch's editors who was not home grown and, maybe as a result, never experienced any of his famous bollockings. In fact, we never had a disagreeable word about journalism, although on politics we remained at arm's length. His knowledge of British politics was not extensive; it didn't need to be in the Thatcher years, as she and Norman Tebbit were about the only people he bothered to speak to.

By 1995 and with only two years to go before the next election, John Major's Government was in deep trouble and his party, so used to power, had become corrupted by it. It was necessary for Murdoch to address some hard realities. The *Sun* of the Thatcher '80s seemed no longer appropriate for the mid-1990s, but editor Stuart Higgins had been Kelvin's deputy and was firmly in his mould. The *Times* was still losing a fortune and *Today* was nowhere near making money, although it might well have been if he had invested more in it. The first sign of his decision to rid NI of *Today* came when Gus Fischer phoned and asked whether I wanted to buy it, or if Lord Hollick might like to take it. At this time – and, certainly now – there are few with stomach enough to invest in newspapers and it was clear that there would be precious little interest in the City to finance the sale of a paper which would have to rely on someone else to print it and would be at the mercy of Murdoch's predatory pricing policy. So instead I turned, albeit reluctantly, to Lord Hollick. The last time I had spoken to him, at a party at Alastair Campbell's home, I told him bluntly that he was one of the men responsible for ruining the *Daily Mirror*, as Montgomery could not possibly have made it to the chief executive's chair without his support. Hollick was interested and, to keep his interest alive, Murdoch offered him £5 million to take *Today* away. At a breakfast meeting at the Savoy, together with John Sharkey, a partner in the advertising agency Bainsfair Sharkey Trott, who had advised me in our attempt to buy out the *Mirror*, I suggested to Hollick that he should take *Today* and whatever money he could get out of Murdoch and buy the Express Group, then put the two titles together with *Today* as the dominant partner. That way, he would have a solid base on which to build – a printing plant, a circulation which would even by the most conservative estimates double overnight and a springboard on which to launch a seriously challenging mid-market paper, the one area of newspapers where there was a chance of growth as more and more people moved out of the old traditional working class and into a more wealthy middle income. He appeared to like the idea, but eventually walked away because he wanted more money than Murdoch was prepared to pay. Both Murdoch and Hollick remained blind to the possibilities. However, I remain convinced that this was a golden opportunity missed, a view reinforced by the trend since *Today*'s closure towards the kind of paper we had pioneered. Instead, Hollick was to get the worst of all worlds, an ailing *Daily Express* without an injection that *Today*'s energy and youth would have brought to it, and the death of a newspaper which had so much life in it.

Hollick turned out to be the worst kind of owner; he loved the idea of newspapers and he revelled in the high political profile ownership brought, but he recoiled at the journalist's world. Like Clive Thornton at the *Mirror*, he was attracted to the idea of the circus but hated the high-wire acts, clowns and wild animals. He was desperate to feast with the tycoons at the top table, but in the end he wasn't big enough to pay the bill.

In his early days as *Express* owner, he asked me to lunch with his senior executives, including the editor of the paper. The conversation, naturally enough, was about how to tackle the *Daily Mail*. If the ideas he came up with that day were the best he could do, no wonder he sold the *Daily Express* to a pornographer.

After Hollick pulled out as a potential white knight, it was only a matter of time before Murdoch struck, and he did so to coincide with the appointment of Les Hinton as NI's new chairman and chief executive. With Hinton by his side, he told me he had decided to close *Today* and an announcement would be made the following day. This was just two days after saying he thought *Today* was a great paper, rather better than the *Sun*. His resolve to go for closure had nothing to do with quality; Murdoch could be surprisingly easily stung and he had been hurt by some parliamentary criticism. His decision seemed, in part at least, a knee-jerk reaction to that.

I was appalled, but even more surprised by his next announcement. As a prelude, he laid on the famous Murdoch flattery with a trowel, which he probably does with all the girls, certainly ones who are not home grown and he wants to woo. It is very seductive. His approach was remarkably similar to the one he adopted with Harold Evans when he offered him the *Times*. 'You are one of the best three editors I have known in my time,' he said, and added that he would like me to edit the *Sun*. I told him I would not edit a paper that supported the Tories and he gobsmacked me even more by saying, 'It doesn't have to be like that, it could support Labour.' I pointed out I had been brought over to edit *Today*, change the politics and raise its profile, all of which I had done. The *Sun* was his paper; together with Larry Lamb and Kelvin, he had made it what it was, it could never be my paper any more than the *Mirror* could be Kelvin's. And by the way, Rupert, who are the other two editors? Larry Lamb, he said immediately, but refused to be drawn on the other one. Kelvin? I ventured. 'Hmmm, he gives the impression that he walks on water,' was his cryptic answer. Only Rupert is allowed to do that at News Corp.

Murdoch seemed to accept my reasons for demurring but he wasn't easily put off. He later came back, insisting that columnists liked Joe Haines and Annie Robinson could easily fit into the *Sun* which, in his view, needed to be taken a notch or two away from the bottom end of the market. In short, he reckoned it needed to be de-Kelvined. I was not as convinced as he appeared to be that a *Mirror*-type gloss on the *Sun* was what it needed and, anyway, I didn't believe that Rupert had suffered a Paul-like conversion on this particular road to Damascus. He was, and always would be, a Thatcherite at heart, but he believed Tony Blair would be better for News International than John Major. In the Tory Party election contest called by Major in order to clear the air over his leadership, Rupert was very much a Portillo man – the unreconstructed Portillo, that is, not the almost-out-of-the-closet, bleeding heart Portillo we know and despise today. I told him that a Portillo victory would be the best result for Labour; it would polarise the Tories and split them apart for the foreseeable future, removing what little doubt remained about who was to form the next government. This was greeted by one of Rupert's lengthy telephone silences. The telephone as psychological weapon was another thing Murdoch had in common with Maxwell.

Why Murdoch called off the closure of the paper as suddenly as he announced it I don't know, except that he was apparently persuaded to do so by Sam Chisholm because he looked as if he was doing so in a fit of pique because of the parliamentary criticism. Once he had pulled back, however, he announced a big new investment in the paper which everyone saw as a vote of confidence, although by this time my own views on the promises of media moguls were severely jaundiced. Justified, too, as it turned out because unknown to me at the time Gus Fischer had commissioned a report on *Today*'s prospects which turned out to be extremely gloomy. However, Doug Flynn brought from Australia by Murdoch to bolster NI'S shaky management reckoned that virtually every supposition on which the report was based was wrong – quite possibily because it was the sort of conclusion News International wanted to hear. On such insurmountable prejudices lay the fortunes of *Today*. The effect of the reprieve was that I was able to go to Hayman Island and witness the three-yearly gathering of the Murdoch empire's top men and women in a no-expense-spared celebration of News Corporation. Every area of the business was represented, so it was entertaining to watch the Fox film executives – easily recognised because they all looked and sounded like Barbra Streisand's hairdresser. It was fun to see them pretending they enjoyed Piers Morgan, then editing the *News of the World*, crowing that he had an exclusive interview with Divine Brown, the hooker who had oral sex with Hugh Grant, just before his next film was to go on release courtesy of Fox.

In the middle of all this was the slight frame of Rupert Murdoch, trying to keep all the strands together when they often seemed in danger of pulling apart. The American film and TV people were openly contemptuous of the newspaper platoons and frequently privately dismissive of Murdoch's ability to run the entertainment arm, although they were quite happy to take both his money and lavish corporate hospitality. For a newspaper group where executives in Britain had complained of the profligacy of the *Mirror*, it was instructive to see a mega junket at work and play. On Hayman Island, everything was provided free, from luxury yacht voyages for the wives with champagne on tap, to chauffeur-driven cabs to the airport in Sydney and the best tickets at the Opera House. There were plenty of lectures and group discussions with group leaders, task forces and suchlike conference junk but, as far as I know, nothing ever came out of it apart from a cemented relationship between Tony Blair and Rupert Murdoch. Blair had been wary of going to Hayman Island, fully aware of the criticism he was likely to attract from the ranks of his own party. But he was right to go and he was careful to adapt his speech to his audience. When he arrived in Sydney he was put up at Kirribilli House, the Sydney residence of the Prime Minister, and Alastair asked me to run through the speech with him and Blair to see if there were any obvious omissions or elephant traps. There weren't, although I did suggest he strengthen a section about the importance of the family. At this time, Blair was much exercised about the possibility of winning support from the *Sun* and I told him I believed Murdoch would swing his support behind Labour at the next election. I told him, too, of the danger I felt *Today* was in and that Rupert had offered me the *Sun* which I had turned down. Tony wasn't worried about *Today* but he was enraged about the *Sun*, as he saw my going there as the chance to swing the paper behind Labour. 'Bloody hell, Richard, I'll kill you if you do that,' he said, mercifully failing to grasp that I had already said 'No'. I was not, and never could be, a *Sun* man, even though the paper was to go through the motions of supporting Labour. It didn't believe in the Labour I believed in, just the parts it could bolt on to its unshakeable belief in the remnants of Thatcherism. That is largely its position today. Its support is one of total self-interest, as is Rupert's. There is nothing wrong with that, it just isn't for me. I have to believe wholeheartedly in what I am doing to edit a paper successfully, and I don't believe in what the *Sun* stands for any more than Tony Blair does.

We had built up the circulation of *Today* slowly and painfully, but at least it was still going up. However, the trend was dealt a fearful blow when News International – once again belying its super-efficiency reputation – managed almost to run out of newsprint. The result was that all the papers were rationed, but in order to protect the *Sun* and the *Times*, *Today*'s print run was severely curtailed, making it unavailable in a substantial part of the country. We relied heavily on 'casual' sales, purchases from newsstands as opposed to home deliveries, and this was a terrible setback for us. It also gave us a pretty firm indication of how far down Murdoch's agenda we were. He could not see that newspaper demographics in Britain were changing and that many red top tabloid readers were aspiring to a more middle-class life and wanted a newspaper to go with it. All the market research showed that *Today* was providing that, which is why we were successful in attracting readers from the *Mirror* and why the *Sun* price cut had little effect on the *Mirror*'s circulation fall. Those who wanted to change had already done so – it was the attraction of *Today* that was taking *Mirror* readers, not the reduced price of the *Sun*. This was confirmed when *Today* eventually closed and the vast majority of readers went to the *Mail*, not the *Sun* or the *Mirror*.

There was a dalliance with Mohamed Al Fayed over the possibility of selling *Today* to him, but Murdoch knocked that on the head on the basis that he would not sell out to someone he considered to be less than honest. So the inevitable came on Wednesday, 15 November 1995, when Les Hinton took me to dinner and told me *Today* was to close. The previous week, Murdoch had been in London and we had talked about future plans for the paper and again he expressed enthusiasm for its punch, energy, look and aggression. Murdoch, in spite of his fierce reputation, does not like confrontation and he was well out of the country by the time Les delivered the news, something I told Les I found tatty, particularly as only a few months earlier he had given such a public display of support. I told him too, that I felt News International had consistently failed to capitalise on what should have been a great asset. Les didn't disagree. 'It has been consistently fucked up,' he said.

The next day, I told a handful of senior executives and Mary Riddell, my deputy, who had been consistently superb both in her executive job as number two and also in her big-name interviews. It is always hard for a woman to come into a top executive newspaper job, and it is doubly so if you are coming from a rival group. Mary managed both, overcame the initial suspicion, and won the grudging but eventually wholehearted support of the staff.

For Lloyd Turner, *Today*'s number three, closure was a particularly hard blow. Lloyd had thrown all his enthusiasm into the paper after being sacked from the *Daily Star* in the wake of Jeffrey Archer winning £500,000 libel damages over the paper's assertion, via a relative of prostitute Monica Coghlan, that Archer did take advantage of her services. The story should never have been run in the form it was; it was an unhappy chain of events on a Friday evening when Lloyd was on his way back home from Manchester to his Kent farm, and there wasn't the sort of control over it there would have been at other times. The trial had destroyed his confidence, which was tragic, because at his best he had been an aggressive editor and the *Star* had fared well under his leadership. He was bitter because he was convinced Archer had not told the truth in court and that the Express Group, owners of the *Star*, should have appealed against the damages, singling out for criticism the judge's notorious summing up in which he described Mary Archer as 'fragrant' and asked the jury if Archer himself was really in need of 'rubber-insulated sex', not quite as open-and-shut a case as the judge implied. It was by any standards, a bizarre summing-up.

We discussed Archer often. I was especially interested because I had experienced my own brushes with him. At the *Mirror*, we had tried to publish a story about him being arrested for shoplifting in Canada but he flatly denied it and, in spite of Paul Foot travelling to Toronto to investigate what happened, we failed to stand it up sufficiently to satisfy the lawyers who were, no doubt, suitably impressed by Archer's £500,000 win. There had indeed been a statement from a man called Jeffrey Archer admitting to stealing three suits from a store called Simpsons, but the statement was unsigned. When Paul questioned Archer about this, he came back with, 'I was not involved in any such incident.' However, in his immensely entertaining biography of him, Michael Crick revisits the story, saying it did happen but Archer mistook the geography of the store and there was no intention to steal. Archer never challenged Crick's version, but obviously both the Crick account and Paul's could not be true. Either he was involved in an incident or he wasn't. The story, as with so many about Archer, remains unresolved, although I think one could take a pretty educated guess now about what really happened.

At the same time as we were struggling with this, we discovered Archer had been warned off Britain's racecourses because of an unpaid £500 bet, (£2500 today). The debt was ten years old when he became deputy chairman of the Conservative Party in 1985 and, in order to avoid embarrassment, Tattersall's, the horseracing watchdog, wrote reminding him he was banned in case he should turn up at the Derby or Ascot and be turfed out. At first, he denied it when I put the story to him, claiming he would sue and that the allegation was an appalling libel. I told him we had it from an impeccable source, there was no doubt the story was true and that I would run it in spite of his denial. Perhaps ... ummm ... the cash demand went to a wrong address, Jeffrey? There was a short silence at the other end of the phone and then he said, 'It may well have gone to a wrong address. That is thoroughly understandable and I may well not have received it ...' The cash, he promised, would be paid immediately. It is a great tragedy that Lloyd Turner is no longer with us, because I used to cheer him up when he got angry and depressed about the Archer saga by telling him that the truth always comes out ... eventually. It can take days or years, but something, somewhere, happens to put the record straight.

National newspaper closures are rare in Britain. It was an emotional time; so many people had put so much into *Today*, it was much more than just a job. Many believed it represented a break with old-fashioned tit and bum popular journalism, and was succeeding in presenting an independent view of the world. Even though we were clearly anti-Conservative, we were also telling Blair he had to come up with some hard-headed policies and present us with a real alternative – he managed to avoid that until well after the 1997 election. It was the first sign of Murdoch's growing detachment from his British newspapers, failing to see that the taste of newspaper readership was drifting upwards, away from the mass circulation red tops. He had been out of Britain for too long and he wasn't particularly fond of it anyway. There was, in his view, no room for *Today* when, in fact, it was the one paper there was room for. The *Express* was a spent force and the predominantly young profile of *Today* and its lack of sacred cows were powerful arguments for keeping it going and investing in a market where there was undoubtedly a gap. If he had done so, I am quite sure the paper would be both viable and editorially successful by now.

I announced the paper's death from the newsroom floor and it was difficult to avoid the tears. Many didn't – it was not a sight for the faint hearted – and I felt not just for those *Today* veterans who had stuck through crisis after crisis, but for the *Mirror* refugees who had come with me in the hope of keeping alive the left-of-centre standard. There were precious few places left for them to go.

I wrote the last leader which was as much an epitaph for my own editorships as for *Today*. I had decided I didn't want to edit newspapers any more, even if someone did ask me. Two proprietors, 12 years and five editorships were long enough and I was never again going to match the excitement and challenge of the months following Maxwell's death. I wrote of *Today*:

In the past three years, Today *has discovered a real identity, a left-of-centre investigative, campaigning newspaper which has won some deserved honours. We were the first to expose the extent of the Michael Jackson child abuse scandal, the first to reveal the horrors of Desert Fever and Mad Cow Disease, the first to expose the greed of our privatised Fat Cats – a phrase that has now entered the language as a description of the second-rate bunch of money-grabbers who run the gas, water and electricity industries.*

We have dared to tread where others have not. We have exposed the bankruptcy and corruption of this government and its party relentlessly. It is a tragedy that we will not be around to see it finally put to flight. Yet the spirit of Today *will live on in its readers, you who have stood by us through thick and thin, and there has been plenty of thin. The spirit of* Today *will live on, too, through its superb editorial staff, the people who have produced the chemistry that has made this paper possible and will now disperse to other newspapers. At times we have felt it has been us against the world. And at times it has. We believed in the right of our readers to know what our rulers were doing. To bring to account those who seek privilege but shirk responsibility. Those whose greed lined their pockets at your expense.*

We made enemies and were glad to face them down. The rich and the powerful could not shut us up. We tried to make the voice of the poor, the oppressed and the weak heard above the clatter and chatter of self-interest and hypocrisy. Now we are forced into silence by the granite and unforgiving face of the balance sheet. But such principles that Today *has tried to live by do not easily die. We are proud to have worked for a paper we believed in. We are proud of our achievements and we are proud of you for standing by us. Our greatest campaign of all has been to stay alive and it's one that we've finally lost. We'll miss you. Goodbye.*

Tony Blair mourned the passing of 'an excellent newspaper' which ran some great campaigns, but was careful not to attack Murdoch's decision and, in an operation which was to become familiar in the succeeding years, put up Peter Mandelson for TV interviews, who said what the leader would like to say but wouldn't do so in public. After all, he had bigger fish to fry and the menu appeared in a special *Sun* pull-out published in the last edition of *Today* in a vain attempt to win readers now cast adrift. After paying lip service to *Today,* Blair went on to spell out his real message under the headline WHY SUN READERS ARE TURNING TO LABOUR: 'They recognise there is a mood for change. They are turning to Labour because we lost touch with the people during parts of the '70s and '80s – we are back in touch now.'

Rupert Murdoch, although he still hadn't spoken to me, praised our forthright style and committed stance as being in the best traditions of journalism. Although he hadn't managed to make time to speak to the staff either, he praised the editorial team as a 'credit' to the company, even as the *News of the World's* managing editor moved in to appropriate their chairs. He said NI had 'no option' but to close the paper because the circulation had remained 'fairly static'. The reason for that was because it had not been promoted sufficiently or with enough imagination, but we could not escape the fact that both its launch and relaunch had been disastrous. Newspapers rarely recover from that. Nonetheless, in the three years since we had revamped *Today* with a left-of-centre independent stance, circulation had increased by more than 12 per cent as opposed to the *Sun*'s price cut-assisted 10 per cent and the *Mirror*'s circulation dive of more than 200,000 copies a day. Over the past six years, I am told Murdoch has privately wondered whether he was right to close the paper and, at one stage, he did consider reviving it. But I doubt whether he has had too many second thoughts. His first and overriding commitment is to the *Sun*, and *Today* would just have got in the way, particularly as the *Sun* now supports New Labour, however patchy and underwhelming that support is. Murdoch's main concentration of interest was then, and remains, in a global TV network, and newspapers, particularly those in Britain, take up less and less of his time. He is no longer in the close touch he was and I firmly believe the Murdoch of 20 years ago would not only have persevered with *Today* but turned it into the successful middle-market paper it could so easily have been. He would have sensed the way of the wind and promoted the tabloid lower-middle-market approach of *Today* rather than the hybrid ramblings of the *Times* around the top end of the middle-market.

The last night was mayhem as the vultures from other papers gathered at Henry's, the Tobacco Dock wine bar, indeed the only sign of life in the derelict Tobacco Dock next to the Wapping plant. The champagne flowed – it always does at newspaper wakes – and the evening became more drunken as more mourners joined in. A bottle was thrown by one drunk – not a journalist – and it hit a photographer on the head, causing a deep gash. That was the detonator for a lot of pent up fury and fights broke out all over the bar. Bottles and fists flew as a police rapid response unit also weighed in with what looked like a suspicious amount of enthusiasm. Ever prepared to answer to the call, journalists battled with police and running fights broke out the length of Tobacco Dock. Barbara Jackson, matriach of the travelling Jacksons, *Today*'s family of travel writers and a former agony aunt of the *People*, had to be prevented from a full-scale frontal assault on the forces of law and order and husband John, the former *Mirror* reporter, was pinioned to the wall in a last-ditch effort to stop his next travel piece describing the charms of Wapping nick. Others were less lucky and were carted off to appear in court the next day.

The following morning, Doug Flynn, News International's managing director, went down to Henry's where what remained of the bar was being cleared up. He made out a cheque for £2,000, no questions asked. Doug was a free spirit, a big supporter of *Today* – an unusual bird at News International – and had been one of the few management voices to speak out against Murdoch's decision. It was right he should have the honour of presiding over the last rites.

It was fitting, too, that a paper which pioneered all the new techniques of a newspaper born into an explosively new electronic world should go out in a time-honoured Fleet Street way. For nearly ten years, it had put up a bloody good fight; it was only right to end with one.

18

There is not a lot you can do as an ex-editor. You can try your hand at management, start a public relations company, become a media commentator or retire gracefully to spend more time with your cuttings book. I didn't fancy any of those and, when *Today* closed, I was at a bit of a loose end. I read a lot, the kind of books I had always wanted to read and never got round to, and sat about wondering what to do. There is nothing so ex as an ex-editor, except possibly an ex-Prime Minister. All the power and the parties disappear overnight along with the chauffeur driven car and the expenses. I didn't care much about any of that, which in itself was an indication that it was time to go. On the other hand, I was only 52, too early to retire and, anyway, I was still getting angry about the way of the world, a sure sign that I should avoid newspaper management and public relations at all costs.

Ex-editors are rarely wanted on board another ship; they are either considered too much of a threat to the incumbent and a natural rallying point for the disaffected, or a source of implied criticism from someone who has been there and done that. I did a few book reviews for the *Times*, but that was it until I received a fax from the *News of the World* asking me to do a diary at the annual Labour conference. A diary wasn't really me; I'm not great on the gossip circuit, but a column, well, that was a different matter. Phil Hall, the *News of the World*'s editor, was one of my old news editors. He had started as a reporter at the *People* and was responsible for the devastating investigation into the behaviour of Martin Edwards, the Manchester United chairman. He was an excellent reporter who became a successful news editor and eventually made it to the editor's chair at the *News of the World*. Phil was a rare bird; he genuinely questioned the ethics and prurience of stories, a difficult trick at the *News of the World*, but he was responsible for some fine exposées. These culminated in the revelation that Jeffrey Archer had fabricated evidence during the preparation of his libel action against the *Daily Star* over the claim that he had had sex with the prostitute Monica Coghlan. Phil ran the story even though he had been advised against it by Les Hinton, News International's chairman. That took guts and his decision was fully justified by subsequent events. These decisions are hair's breadth ones and, no doubt, if he was given his time again, he would have held up the Lawrence Dallaglio revelations for a week while he secured corroborative evidence of some of the matters the then England rugby captain spoke about. Nonetheless, in a high-risk and high-profile job, Phil Hall's record was extremely sound. It would be difficult, for example, to see him creating the muddle, uncertainty and double standards the *News of the World* managed to achieve over what was a perfectly justified investigation into the business affairs of the Countess of Wessex and to what extent she played on her royal connections. Niether would he have caused the outbreak of vigilante violence by the ill-thought-out naming and shaming of paedophiles, in which the *News of the World* set itself the impossible task of unmasking more than 100,000 child molesters in Britain.

The column I was to write for three years began as a fortnightly operation. I alternated with Alan Clark, the randy and wonderfully entertaining Conservative MP and former minister. Alan was a great diarist but, as he was the first to admit, the *News of the World* was not his natural habitat; well, not as a columnist, anyway. He had featured in the news pages over his double affair with the wife and daughter of a South African judge and it was a tribute to both the sense of humour of Clark and Hall that he took on the column. Lurking in the background was the increasingly ancient spectre of Woodrow Wyatt who had been relegated to the 'back of the book', the pages behind the centre spread, sandwiched between the crossword and the sports pages. Successive editors had tried in vain to get rid of Wyatt's increasingly out-of-touch and eccentric column, but he was always saved by Rupert Murdoch. Wyatt had been one of Murdoch's few supporters when he arrived in England in the 1960s and Murdoch never forgot it, he was commendably loyal – a strong Murdoch trait – even if the column did tax editors' ingenuity in their efforts to reduce its prominence without either the proprietor or Wyatt complaining. Wyatt served another purpose for Murdoch who spent little time in England; he had a straight through line to Mrs Thatcher and was useful as Murdoch's representative on earth with her. The problem with all this is that the *News of the World* had too many columns; that's why Alan and I had to share the job, at least until I was offered columns on the *Daily* and *Sunday Mirrors* and Phil decided to axe Alan who, by then, was only too happy to go.

Having your own column is like having your own individual size newspaper – all the fun of editing and writing your own opinions without the worry of having to be in the office all the time and worrying about the circulation and the opposition's front-page stories. You populate it with your own caravan of on-the-make politicians, saints, sinners, conmen, frauds and phonies, all the people who make newspapers go round. And if they respond to you, so much the better. In that respect, it was impossible to make a better enemy than Mohamed Al Fayed.

The allegations against him would fill a book – indeed they have. He has been accused of many things, from corrupting MPs to lying about Diana's last words. The ground has been well raked over and Al Fayed was a columnist's dream because he could never resist biting back, usually with even more abuse than had been heaped on him. I had awarded him Retailer of the Year in my annual awards, marking it with a few well chosen insults. He replied with his usual volley of abuse to match mine – although he didn't deny any of the points I made – and then returned to something that clearly obsesses him, the size of the male organ – little Dick, in my case. Fayed is incapable of opening his mouth without putting his foot in it and one of the first rules of writing to newspaper columnists – if you really feel you have to – is not to afford them the chance of having another go. By the reference to the size of my organ he drew attention to the admission that he made about his own. The tiny nature of 'the sacred part of my body' he said was causing some concern 'because all the girls will keep away from me.' His regular correspondence accused me among other things of being a bully – a tribute indeed from such a formidable proponent of the ancient art – disgraceful, and insulting, rabid and defamatory, slavering. And that was all in one letter. As I say, a columnist's gift.

Less funny is the deep well of hatred and prejudice some stories generate. The *News of the World* is a naturally right-wing newspaper, so it was brave of Phil Hall to take on a columnist with very different views from the paper, even though the coming of Tony Blair was beginning to blur the edges a bit. When Enoch Powell died, I realised I would have to write something which went against the raft of right-wing claptrap lauding him as a great man. I also realised that this would bring out the green ink, lavatory paper and capital letters brigade, which it did in force.

There is a small but significant section of the country which is not only racially intolerant but quite happy to give vent to that intolerance in the most violent and obscene language. These people are usually, but not always, elderly men who establish their credentials by reciting their war record and complaining that their jobs have been usurped by blacks and Asians. On pointing out that the first black immigrants came to Britain because white people would not do the jobs taken on by West Indians, all you get is a volley of further abuse. In the end I took to posting my Powell reply letters in Brixton, and the correspondence soon stopped.

The other story that revealed a gloomy side of human nature was the Tony Martin affair, the farmer convicted of the murder of a gypsy teenager who tried to burgle his house. The extraordinary reaction to this was close to mass hysteria and it spoke volumes about not only the fears most people have of their houses being broken into, particularly at night, but the rabble-rousing, right-wing populism of virtually all our press. It was easy to caricature Martin as the aggrieved party, a martyr to the cause of a man standing up for his rights and freedom against an increasingly lawless world, watched over by authorities which constantly support the criminal rather than the victim. This view of the Martin case is simply not sustainable and the barrage of letters I received when I pointed this out all said I was out of touch with 'ordinary' people. I was typical of the élite who should be hung, drawn and quartered.

But the absurdity of their position was that 'ordinary' people had decided Martin's fate; he had been tried by a jury of his peers who, unlike newspaper readers, had heard all the evidence, not a selected and edited version which all too often was tailored to the newspapers' views. We are in danger of having a serious problem here with our tabloid papers; the agenda has shifted radically to the right. The Richard Littlejohn cab driver school of journalism is rampant.

My years on the *News of the World* were thoroughly enjoyable and, in spite of a few spats with the green ink brigade, the majority of readers were both intelligent and thoughtful critics, not at all the demonised half-wits fondly imagined by the broadsheet press. Indeed, the *News of the World*'s circulation is so large, and its readers so catholic in their tastes, it has as many top-end-of-the-market readers as the *Guardian*.

A column allows you to gnaw away at issues in more detail than editing a paper, even if, on occasions, it leads you to a sharp division of opinion. One such was with Michael Howard at the Tory Party Conference when, as Home Secretary, he had made yet another rabble-rousing speech promising longer jail terms in a cynical bid to win votes. When I pointed this out to him in a somewhat forthright way – 'Another speech full of sound and fury, signifying fuck all' was how I actually described it – he threatened to throw a glass of white wine over me. Ah, the cut and thrust of political debate.

Over the years, a stream of unresolved questions billowed out behind me like weeds on a barnacled boat. What was Jonathan Aitken really doing at the Ritz in Paris that he had to keep so secret, even to the extent of perjuring himself? Why hasn't the British government accepted responsibility for the illnesses of nuclear veterans and their descendants who are suffering indescribable illnesses and deformities because of the atom bomb tests in the 1950s? Why can't Labour come up with a brave and bold reform plan for the NHS? Why, even after so many examples of bribery, can MPs still not be prosecuted for corruption in connection with their parliamentary duties? Why did it take so long for Mohamed Al Fayed to be refused a British passport and so little time for Mr S.P. Hinduja to be granted one? Why does the Labour Party still flirt with rich men when the gap between rich and poor is growing at an unprecedented rate?

A columnist's currency is his indignation and there remains a lot to be indignant about. At the same time as I scribbled away in my pulpit at the *News of the World*, I graduated into cyberspace with a twice-weekly column on the Microsoft Network. At the suggestion of Geoff Sutton, a former *Mirror* reporter and *Today* news editor, who had given up newspapers for the delights of the Net and Bill Gates's electronic evangelism, I joined Microsoft's news network as it got off the ground. Thanks to Geoff and his team, it now manages a phenomenal nine million hits a day. The vast majority of this mind-boggling hit rate is because of the Microsoft home page, but, nonetheless, a new constituency of cyber reader is being formed. I have no idea who they are, but they bear no resemblance to the traditional profile of newspaper readers who are easily identified and defined. It is easy to understand what sort of Net reader replies to columns – they are largely anoraks, in much the same way as regular newspaper letter writers do not tend to be typical of the vast majority of readers. The same is true in cyberspace. But whoever they are, at least another door has opened up for the dissemination and dissection of news and comment.

My tenure at the *News of the World* came to an end when Phil Hall was sacked and replaced by News International's young starlet Rebekah Wade. It is the fate of all editors to get the chop at some stage and it is the fate of columnists to await their successor's pleasure. I should have known when I got the football club chairman 'we have full confidence in the manager' treatment, a Christmas card from Rupert thanking me for 'your continuing and stimulating contributions'. But Murdoch's interest in his London newspaper operation continued to wane, and with it came an uncharacteristic slowness in reacting to good new ideas. *Metro* was a highly successful Swedish free newspaper selling on the Stockholm underground railway system and it was suggested within News International that it would work here. For almost six months, the idea was batted back and forth with Murdoch showing little enthusiasm, but finally he gave the go-ahead to produce a dummy and present a potential deal to London Transport. This Doug Flynn did, and I produced the editorial mock-up. But we might as well not have bothered. Associated, publishers of the *Daily Mail* and London *Evening Standard*, had been much quicker off the mark. They were first in and offered a great deal more money than NI was prepared to put on the table. There was no contest; NI had been well and truly beaten in both speed of reaction to a good idea and the ability to put its money where its mouth was, something that would never have happened a decade earlier. *Metro* went from success to success for Associated, which produced not only a money-spinner but a paper that could attract the young, hardly surprising as it was free on stations. More important, it prevented NI producing a twenty-four hour paper which would have destroyed the sale of the *Evening Standard*. Belatedly, Murdoch realised what had slipped through his fingers and planned to contest the contract when it came up for renewal. If he goes through with the plan, it could mean the resurrection of *Today*.

No rising again for me, however, with the change of editor at the *News of the World*. My column was not wanted on Rebekah's voyage of discovery, something I could hardly complain about, as I had replaced enough columnists in my time. The writing was on the wall in the second week of her editorship when I wrote a column hostile to Prince Charles and Camilla following a *News of the World* pro-Charles and Camilla scoop that had clearly had St James's Palace as its source, a 'present' in her first week of editing. Rebekah refused to use my piece on the grounds that I disagreed with the *News of the World*'s view and that it could annoy her contact. That, unfortunately for editors, is what columnists worth their salt tend to do. We were not destined to last long and we didn't. I was sacked because, she said, she wanted to 'change the politics', although it cannot have escaped her attention that over the years I had been highly critical of Prince Charles's hypocrisy, his freeloading and the attempts to royal Camilla Parker Bowles. After all, she and her husband, the former *EastEnders* star Ross Kemp, have chosen as their holiday companion the ubiquitous Mark Bolland, Prince Charles's former deputy private secretary. I thought this change of politics line meant a right-wing ranter along the lines of Peter Hitchens or Littlejohn. Fair enough, it was her call. I was not, however, prepared for the change of politics to be a New Labour babe (male) who assiduously toed the Downing Street line in the hope – successful as it turned out – of winning selection as a New Labour parliamentary candidate. This is unlikely to make for a red-blooded read every Sunday, and it didn't. I would be lying if I said there was no sense of grim satisfaction in Sion Simon's failure. Columnists no longer put on circulation for newspapers, but they are an essential mix in the cocktail of a successful one, giving a unique flavour and a kick not always available from news stories and features. I made my excuses and left, removed not at Claridge's on this occasion but the American Bar at the Savoy. Not a bad way to go and, judging by the letters of sympathy, the audience was still there even if the director wanted a change of cast.

Time at last to leave the stage; it had been a great run. Curtain down. Spotlights off. Auditorium lights up. Exit doors wide open. End of show. The last goodbye at the stage door. Disappear into the fog.

Unless of course ...

The phone rang. With that exquisite sense of timing journalism can sometimes manage, it was Tina Weaver, newly appointed editor of the *Sunday Mirror*; would I unpack my column and write for her? I most certainly would. Up lights, front-of-house doors open, spotlights on. Overture and beginners please and curtain up on a new show and let's hope it runs and runs. The great thing about this job is you never know where the jungle path may lead. Thank God I was nice about her in the book.

* * *

September 11th changed everything, including the newspaper world. In Britain, the papers were superb; you could find any view you wanted on show. The presentation was excellent; for the first time, the broadsheets adopted tabloid techniques, with huge projections of pictures enhanced by the stunning material available and high-quality colour reproduction. It was all a long way from Murdoch's claim a decade earlier that colour would never sell newspapers. It certainly did after the World Trade Center and Pentagon atrocities.

For old *Mirror* hands who had spent the past five years roundly castigating Piers Morgan and being repaid in kind, there was a change of heart about their old paper. Unlike the typically gung-ho *Sun*, the *Mirror* did not settle for the Government's line and both John Pilger and Paul Foot were rolled out to attack Tony Blair, George Bush and Jack Straw. This was a rerun of the war between the *Sun* and the *Mirror* over the Falklands which the *Sun* supported – Gotcha and Stick it up your Junta – and the *Mirror* which was against. As with that conflict and the Gulf War, it will take years to judge the wisdom of Britain's involvement in the action against the Taliban and Al Qaida. However, there seems little doubt that the Gulf War was one of the many staging posts on the road to the catastrophe of the World Trade Centre and, even now, the United States cannot understand that not everyone wishes to be ruled by the paternal rod of Uncle Sam's God Almighty dollar.

The September 11th atrocities proved that nobody in the world can present a huge story as quickly and with such quality as the British press. The muscularity and diversity of opinion remains second to none and few can match the fine writing available in both broadsheet and tabloid papers. But wars don't last for ever and the great treadmill of the circulation graph, after a month of soaring sales, was soon back to the churning battle for the hard yards, the success of which is measured in years, not months. So how do our dailies stand now at the beginning of a new millennium?

The *Sun* editor David Yelland has taken a lot of stick for producing a boring newspaper, obsessed with the Euro and all things American. Certainly, the paper doesn't have MacKenzie's wit or edge, but neither does it have his reputation for invention, xenophobia, passive racism and lying. Yelland has largely managed an extremely difficult trick, to change the *Sun* to fit into a world beyond Mrs Thatcher's get-rich-quick, sod-you society to Tony Blair's touchy-feely version. Blair is seen as sufficiently Thatcherlike for the *Sun* to be able to alter its stance, with difficulty and uncertainty, but without losing too much circulation and maintaining the huge gap between itself and the *Mirror*. Page Three remains, in spite of Murdoch's fervent desire to be rid of it.

The *Star* – given a new lifeline because of the above, but unlikely to do to the *Sun* what Murdoch did to the *Mirror* – grabs its circulation from the bottom up. Even though he is losing interest, Murdoch's too cute for that...isn't he?

The *Express* – finished, I'm afraid. It has no role and has been neglected for too long by proprietors who wanted to open doors for themselves while closing too many for their paper.

The *Mail* – king of the jungle. Its politics are old-fashioned right wing, its writers old, its agenda out of the ark. But it's coverage – news, features, sport – is astonishingly good and comprehensive and, although its writers may be pushing Zimmers, they are still quick enough to burn the anti-skid rubbers off the legs. Huge investment over three decades has made it unassailable, mostly due to two great *Mail* editors and one great proprietor.

The *Telegraph* – a Saturday package second to none but, as the Tories fall to pieces, the *Telegraph* has become more strident in its approach and its once awesome news coverage tainted by comment and a not-so-hidden agenda. Also still suffers badly from its ill-thought-out policy of cut-price copies. Like the party it supports, there could be long-term problems there.

The *Guardian* – a fine newspaper which knows exactly where its readers are coming from and where they would like to go. Terrific writers, comprehensive news and features and improved immeasurably by Alan Rusbridger when he took over from Peter Preston who had lost the plot.

The *Times* – the plot is constantly being rewritten here. Nobody seems to be quite clear what the *Times* stands for nowadays, a problem spelled out spectacularly in its 1997 election leader when it urged readers to vote for anyone who was against closer ties with Europe, particularly the single currency. That meant the nation's élite were being encouraged to vote for the politics of both Tony Benn and Sir James Goldsmith. Ludicrous. Good writers, patchy news coverage but the biggest problem is that the *Times* remains confused about what kind of paper it wants to be. Circulation has more than doubled in ten years, but that was because of the cut-price policy which cost Murdoch millions. However, the fact remains, in spite of swallowing enormous rivers of cash it has not succeeded in overtaking the *Telegraph* or even denting the *Guardian*. The only paper that policy killed off was its News International stablemate, *Today*. Murdoch once suggested that the *Times* could go tabloid, much to the horror of traditionalists. I think he's got a point.

The *Independent* – the only other paper that really suffered from the *Times* cut-price policy. Now massively underfunded but tries very hard, sometimes with great effect but not often enough to make any impression. Too many columnists, only some of whom are good.

In spite of the doom merchants our national newspapers remain in passably rude health. They are in many respects better than they were 10, 20, 30 years ago. They are much bigger and have sprouted magazines of considerable class. They are as bloody minded, infuriating and contentious as they ever were. The *Mirror* and the *Sun* no longer rely on Bingo for their twice yearly injection of transient circulation and with it has come the slow realisation that the swollen sales figures Bingo brought were little more than fool's gold. For years it masked one incontrovertible fact, the days of massive daily circulations of four million and more are over. Although the new direct input computer technology has meant papers are slicker and better laid out, there are three areas where standards have dropped. The reporting of politics now has more supposition, assumption, speculation and straightforward bad journalism than it did even ten years ago. Spin works both ways, and the politicians are as much spinned against as spinning. City reporting suffers from the same problem, with too many of the square mile reporters, with acres of space to fill and too few facts to fill it, prepared to swallow not only the PR line, but hook and sinker as well. The third area is football reporting where agents rule and truth is the first casualty in the pursuit of ever larger bundles of cash. But in the larger war the battle for the tabloids now is to remain relevant to a society that is shifting, unsurely and sometimes unhappily, its loyalties, traditions, politics and geography.

Which brings me back to the *Mirror*. As it approaches its centenary in 2003, the paper is faced with a realignment, not only of British politics, but of British newspapers. When Maurice Edelman wrote his eulogy to the *Mirror* back in 1966, he said its genius was to align itself with the aspirations of the age, but aspirations of the age are fickle and transient. The *Sun* seized the moment in the late '60s and maintained it through the turbulence and impotence of Labour in the '70s and the Thatcherite revolution of the '80s, reflecting its genuine reform but also its greed and amorality. In the same decade, the *Mirror* was able to rediscover its voice because the country needed an antidote to Thatcher and the introduction of colour gave it a sparkling shop window. Maxwell haters will loathe it, but the second half of the '80s was the only time the circulation of the paper increased in almost 40 years. Much of the '90s was a write-off because of the legacy of Maxwell, bringing on the horrors of Montgomery. It is only with the resumption of reasonably normal service under Trinity Mirror that the paper can once again look forward to a comparatively stable future. However, Tony Blair and New Labour brought new problems for the *Mirror*, because both the party and the country have moved to the right. As John Prescott said, we are all middle-class now.

But, of course, we aren't. The country is more divided now that it has been in half a century and the aspirations of the age vary from get-rich-quick City of London fat cats wondering where the next ten million is coming from to the poverty-stricken and dispossessed ghettos of too many northern cities who are dying from a bad diet in as big a number as they did in the Second World War. So much for New Labour, New Britain. This is a difficult problem for the *Mirror*, which, ever since the *Sun* started to make inroads into its circulation, has been keen to discard its cloth cap image. But what do you replace it with when everybody wears a baseball cap?

Tony Blair, much to Piers Morgan's fury, has embraced both Murdoch and the *Sun* for two reasons. First, because it is seen to be more influential than the *Mirror* with voters who are not dyed-in-the-wool Labour supporters; and second, to avoid it returning to the Tory fold and ganging up with the *Mail* against the Government. The two together would make formidable foes; singly, that is not the case. For the *Mirror*, the danger is that it becomes irrelevant because it has no natural home. At the moment it is a superior journalistic product to the *Sun*, but as I said earlier, a successful newspaper has to be more than that. It has to stand for beliefs and principles that are shared by a substantial number of people and articulate their hopes and fears; it must be the Clarion Van for those whose voices would otherwise not be heard. In Tony Blair's Britain, that remains a sizeable chunk and it is to them that the *Mirror* is a natural home. New Labour's sapling roots may cover much of the country but they are shallow, its principles flimsy, ill-formed and untested except in the proven ability to run the economy. But the vitality of a strong economy needs dynamic social ideas to spring from it and, so far, Tony Blair's Labour hasn't come up with too many. In spite of the massive public spending cash injection, we are still waiting for the radical reforms of the health service and the welfare state Tony Blair promised before he entered Downing Street. Where is the regeneration of Britain's manufacturing industry and, with it, a thriving career structure for working men and women? These are the issues that matter to the deep roots of the Labour party and the *Mirror* and its readers.

Andy Capp may no longer be with us, but his sons and daughters are and the Britain they live in is far removed from the metropolitan life of London, where six Barclays Bank futures traders can blow £44,000 on a dinner. The *Mirror*'s roots are as deep, almost as old and certainly as sorely tested as the Labour Party's, and its roar must be powerful and clear enough to be heard above the pneumatic drill of government and the braying certainty of judges. It must be relentless enough to tear through the heartless red tape and inertia of bureaucracy, committed to a burning and often uncomfortable belief in justice for those broken by the ambitions of powerful men and speak for those who voices cannot be heard.

The sob story of a last newspaper romantic, possibly. But it is, to use the modern plastic jargon, a mission statement that has stood the test of time and the attacks on its integrity from within and without. It is a job description that should apply to any newspaper but it does not. For much of its life, it has applied to the *Mirror* and it is heartening to see that Piers Morgan has, almost a decade after the disastrous arrival of David Montgomery and his legion rejects from Rupert Murdoch, seen the importance of protest and the alternative view. The *Mirror*'s rebranding is still unsure, but that is a problem it shares with New Labour. And like New Labour it has been rewarded with accolades, in the *Mirror*'s case two Newspaper of the Year awards, a feat only five years ago that would have been considered laughable. However the men and women in charge of the *Mirror*'s destiny should beware the siren voice of broadsheet newspaper praise and awards, gratifying though they are. Media pundits – usually failed reporters whose inaccuracy is matched only by an impressive ignorance of newspaper history – judge tabloid papers by their own experiences which rarely involve working on popular papers. Worthy newspapers with a mission to explain might well win prizes; they might even win the occasional reader in the boardroom. But they don't win them on what used to be the shop floor and the canteen. Nor does it cut much ice in the ghettos and the unemployment queues. Saturation coverage of the war between the Taliban and the Northern Alliance will never match saturation coverage of the war between the Wales's. *Mirror* men and women, above all, know that. In the later stages of his career. Hugh Cudlipp tried the worthy way, the primrose path to broadsheet respectability. And the result was Rupert Murdoch's *Sun*. Which, more or less, is where we came in.

EPILOGUE

One of the most enduring of newspaper features is *Where Are They Now?* So it seems only right to catch up with the strange cast that has strutted its stuff across these pages.

There are few survivors from the early days; my mother died in 1995 at the age of 93 but, in reality, the light had gone out years ago. She never knew I had become an editor, which meant more than the last decade of her life was spent in the dark world of dementia. All that was left of her life was a dog eared picture of my father and an empty handbag. Sister Judith has spent the past 20 years battling her own demons, and brother-in-law David, now ex, but as close a friend as he ever was, has retired from TV and embarked on a second career as a painter of considerable talent. He has even allowed his paintings to be exhibited but has always refused to sell. His TV star reputation is secure, and his work remains the inspiration of so many comedians, from French and Saunders to Eddie Izzard. Johnny Thorn lives on, long retired from Winchester but, at the age of 76, still teaching twice a week at Portsmouth Grammar School. Willy Lane has gone to meet his maker, although not before entering his employ, he was ordained as a priest after leaving Clifton.

Dan Ferrari died in the early 1980s and his life was celebrated by one of the great *Daily Mirror* funerals in which the local pub was drunk dry after receiving its monthly delivery from the brewery only the day before. As the landlord surveyed the scene when the last of the mourners crunched his way unsteadily to the door through broken glasses strewn like confetti on the floor, he was heard to wonder disbelievingly, 'If that was a *Daily Mirror* funeral, I would love to see a fuckin' wedding.' Ed Vale went the same way with the same quality send-off.

Of my old friends at the *Bucks Herald,* Julie Lunn married the local baker and runs a riding school, but, sadly, Roger Duckworth who had been in ill-health for some time, died in 2000. Roger pitched up on the *Sun* as the East Midlands, football reporter, a foot soldier of quality and humour that helps to make journalism such a wonderfully rich profession.

Also in the East Midlands the wonderful Frank Palmer, my number two on the Don Revie investigation and one of Fleet Street's great district reporters, died after a heart-attack in the same year. Frank added immeasurably to the gaiety of the *Mirror* and, when he retired, he carved out a second career as a crime novelist. He is sadly missed and irreplaceable. PJ Wilson remains as accident prone as ever, even though he manages to run a holiday complex up in Scotland. Ken Jenour went off to the *Hollywood Reporter*, and Brian Hitchen to edit the *Daily Star* and lecture on the *QEII*, as well as to provide the living proof for anyone who is adamant Mussolini faked his death. John Smith's son Kevin now appears to have taken over America as far as coverage for British newspapers is concerned.

The Maxwell brothers proved the British jury system is alive and kicking, by being found not guilty of fraud, and Michael Stoney never even came to trial. The DTI said he 'failed to act to discharge his duties'. That's one way of putting it. Ernie Burrington and Lawrie Guest were mildly rebuked by the DTI report into the Mirror flotation, but were not so easily forgiven by the *Mirror* staff who had to suffer the consequences of their shortcomings. I last saw Sir Robert Clark early one morning on Waterloo station clutching his DTI report hot off the press. Neither he nor Alan Clements were spared the inspectors criticism: 'Although the board owed a collective duty ... Sir Robert Clark and Mr Clements should have found out much more about MGN before the flotation.' They bear the 'major responsibility' amongst the directors, said the inspectors.

Charlie Wilson has retired to spend more time with his bank balance and third wife, yet another redhead, and David Montgomery tried to launch an Internet news service in pubs and, a former iron supporter of the Protestant cause, relaunched himself as a fundraiser trying to integrate education in Ulster, a healing process he singularly failed to embrace at the *Mirror*. Thankfully for the newspaper trade, nobody has yet found it advantageous to hire his services again. Kelvin MacKenzie is set to make the fortune he set his heart on, floating Talk Radio, even though the share price has taken a tumble, fulfilling his ambition of at last making money for himself instead of Rupert Murdoch, although, as Rupert has a large stake in Kelvin's business, he is still working for him. Alan Watkins from *Today* appears to have little interest in newspapers any more; he never received the credit he should have for exposing both the after effects of the Gulf War and the BSE scandal. Tina Weaver has finally made her way through the executive jungle and emerged as editor of the *Sunday Mirror*, a thoroughly justified success for a superb journalist who has made it the hard way, by solid achievement rather than glitzy networking. Meanwhile, Phil Hall exchanged the exposures of the *News of the World* for a quite different form of exposure as editor-in-chief of *Hello!* before leaving London for the pleasure of the North. Mohamed Al Fayed has triumphed with Fulham Football Club, taking this once unfashionable and broke club into the Premiership while plunging it £24 million into the red. One of the few other clubs of a similar nature was Oxford United, then owned by Robert Maxwell. Joe Haines has retired, a waste, as his political brain is still second to none, but the Maxwell years will forever be a blight on his otherwise brilliant career. He has contented himself by writing a book which blows the lid off the last days of Harold Wilson's Government; somebody ought to be brave enough to publish it. Paul Foot nearly died after a massive aortic aneurysm but has recovered enough to hobble around on a stick, his brain mercifully as incisive and critical as ever.

Then there are the top dogs. Alastair Campbell and Annie Robinson, both rescued from the gutter, at one stage in their lives even the lampposts looked down on them. Both are tributes to the invincibility of the human spirit and proof that anything is possible in a topsy-turvy world, where prime ministers are treated with a contempt usually reserved for PR men and public relations gurus – Bolland, Clifford, Matthew Freud – are accorded a deference editors used to extend to prime ministers. Alastair, probably the second most powerful man in Britain, is one of the four who made New Labour work. And Annie, well, what do you say about Annie Robinson? For a few heady weeks, she was the most famous woman in the United States, dressed in black, insulting contestants in *The Weakest Link* and, with her dearest wish achieved, she is now worth even more than Charlie Wilson, her first husband. Dragged from the gutter of despair to the most popular woman on American television before the ratings inevitably plummeted, she achieved the fame she had always sought although not, perhaps, in the way she had expected. Wonderful, the stuff dreams. Little did we toilers in the dream factory know that Annie and Alastair would actually make them come true and emerge as glittering, star-studded, best-in-show champions. Well, that's showbiz. That's politics. And, thankfully, that's journalism. Dog and lamppost. Gutters and stars.

RICHARD STOTT DIED ON 30 JULY 2007.

APPENDIX

The *Daily Mirror*'s Harry Arnold discovered the Camilla and Charles tape was a record of part of the couple's conversation in the early hours of Monday, 18 December, 1989, only 13 days before Diana's own taped talk with James Gilbey. Charles was on a mobile and speaking from Eaton Hall, Cheshire, the stately home of his great friend the Duke of Westminster, Britain's richest man, where he was staying overnight at Eaton Lodge, one of the cottages on the estate. Camilla was at her home in Corsham, Wiltshire. This very private conversation that finally exploded the truth of a public deception:

Charles: '... he was pretty anxious, actually.'
Camilla: 'Was he?'
Charles: 'Yes, he thought he might have gone a bit far. Anyway, you know, I mean, that's the sort of thing one has to beware of, and one feels one's way along with, if you know what I mean.'
Camilla: 'Umm. You're awfully good at feeling your way along.'
Charles: 'Oh, stop! I want to feel my way along you ...'
Camilla: 'Mmmm ...'
Charles: '... all over you and up and down you and in and out ...'
Camilla: 'Oh Charles!'
Charles: '... Particularly in and out.'
Camilla: 'It's just what I need at the moment.'
Charles: 'Is it?'
Camilla: 'Mmmm. I know it would revive me. I can't bear a Sunday night without you.'
Charles: 'Oh God.'
Camilla: 'It's like that programme ... *Start the Week*. I can't start the week without you.'
Charles: 'I fill up your tank.'
Camilla: 'Yes you do.'
Charles: 'So you can cope.'

Camilla: 'Then I'm all right.'
Charles: 'What about me? The trouble is I need you several times a week.'
Camilla: 'So do I. All the week. All the time.'
Charles: 'Oh God. I'll just live inside your trousers or something. It would be much easier.'
Camilla (laughing): 'What are you going to turn into, a pair of knickers?' (Both laugh) 'Oh, you're going to come back as a pair of knickers.'
Charles: 'Or, God forbid, a Tampax. Just my luck.'
Camilla: 'You are a complete idiot. Oh, what a wonderful idea.'
Charles: 'My luck to be chucked down the lavatory and go on and on for ever, swirling round on the top, never going down.'
Camilla: 'Oh, darling!'
Charles: 'Til the next one comes through.'
Camilla: 'Perhaps you should come back as a box.'
Charles: 'What sort of box?'
Camilla: 'A box of Tampax, so you could just keep going …'
Charles: 'That's true.'
Camilla: 'Repeating yourself. Oh, darling. Oh, I just want you now.'
Charles: 'Do you?'
Camilla: 'Mmm.'
Charles: 'So do I.'
Camilla: 'Desperately, desperately, desperately. I thought of you so much at Yaraby.'
Charles: 'Did you?'
Camilla: 'Mmm. Simply mean we couldn't be there together.'
Charles: 'Desperate. If you could be here. I long to ask Nancy sometimes.'
Camilla: 'Why don't you?'
Charles: 'I daren't.'
Camilla: 'Because I think she's so in love with you. She'd do anything you asked.'
Charles: 'She'd tell all sorts of people.'
Camilla: 'No, she wouldn't because she'd be much too frightened of what you might say to her. I think you've got, I'm afraid it's a terrible thing to say, but I think those sort of people, you know, do feel very strongly about you. You've got such a hold over her.'
Charles: 'Really?'
Camilla: 'I think, as usual, you are underestimating yourself.'
Charles: 'But she might be terribly jealous or something.'
Camilla: 'Oh. Now that's a point, I wonder. She might be, I suppose.'
Charles: 'You never know, do you?'

Camilla: 'No. The little green eyed monster might be lurking inside her. No, but I mean, the thing is you're so good when people are so flattered to be taken into your confidence, but I don't know they'd betray you. You know, real friends.'
Charles: 'Really?'
Camilla: 'I don't ... gone to sleep?'
Charles: 'No, I'm here.'
Camilla: 'Darling listen. I talked to David tonight again. It might not be any good.'
Charles: 'Oh no!'
Camilla: 'I'll tell you why. He's got these children of one of those Crawley girls and their nanny staying. He's going ... I'm going to ring him again tomorrow, he's going to try and put them off until Friday. But I thought as an alternative perhaps I might ring up Charlie and see if we can do it there. I know he's back on Thursday.'
Charles: 'It's quite a lot further away.'
Camilla: 'Oh, is it?'
Charles: 'Well I'm trying to think. Coming from Newmarket ...'
Camilla: 'Coming from Newmarket to me at that time of night you could probably do it in two-and-three-quarters.'
Charles: 'Really?'
Camilla: 'Well, it takes me three.'
Charles: 'What, to go to, um, Bowood?'
Camilla: 'Northmore.'
Charles: 'To go to Bowood?'
Camilla: 'To go to Bowood would be the same as me really, wouldn't it?'
Charles: 'I mean to say, you would suggest going to Bowood.'
Camilla: 'No, not at all.'
Charles: 'Which Charlie then?'
Camilla: 'What Charlie did you think I was talking about?'
Charles: 'I didn't know, because I thought you meant ...'
Camilla: 'I've got lots of friends called Charlie.'
Charles: 'The other one. Patty's.'
Camilla: 'Ooh, oh there! Oh that is further away. They're not ...'
Charles: 'They've gone.'
Camilla: 'I don't know. It's just, you know, just a thought I had, if it fell through, the other place.'
Charles: 'Oh right. What do you do, go on the M25 and down the M4 is it?'
Camilla: 'Yes, you go, um, and sort of Royston, or M11, at that time of night.'

Charles: 'And then the M25.'

Camilla: 'M25 and then M4.'

Charles: 'Yes. Well, that'll be just after, it will be after shooting anyway.'

Camilla: 'So it would be, um, you'd miss the worst of the traffic. You see the problem is I've got to be in London tomorrow night …'

Charles: 'Yes …'

Camilla: '… And Tuesday night A's coming home.'

Charles: 'No.'

Camilla: 'Would you believe it? Because … I don't know what he's doing, he's shooting down here or something. But, darling, you wouldn't be able to ring me anyway, would you?'

Charles: 'I might just. I mean, tomorrow night I could have done.'

Camilla: 'Oh, darling, I can't bear it. How could you have done tomorrow night?'

Charles: 'Because I will be (yawns) working on the next speech, a business in the community one, rebuilding communities.'

Camilla: 'Oh no, when's that for?'

Charles: 'A rather important one for Wednesday.'

Camilla: 'Oh God.'

Charles: 'I know.'

Camilla: 'Well at least I will be behind you.'

Charles: 'I know.'

Camilla: 'Can I have a copy of the one you've just done?'

Charles: 'Yes.'

Camilla: 'Can I, I would like it.'

Charles: 'I'll try and organise it, but, oh God, when am I going to speak to you, I can't bear it. Wednesday night?'

Camilla: 'Certainly Wednesday night. I'll be along Wednesday, you know, the evening, or Tuesday. While you are rushing around doing things, I'll, y'know, be alone 'til IT reappears. I mean, he'll be leaving at half-past eight, quarter-past-eight.'

Charles: 'Oh will he? Mmm … on Thursday?'

Camilla: 'On Wednesday.'

Charles: 'Right.'

Camilla: 'He won't be here Thursday, pray God. Um, that ambulance strike, it's a terrible thing to say this, I suppose won't come to an end by Thursday?'

Charles: 'It will have done?'

Camilla: 'Well, I mean, I hope for everybody's sake it will have done, but I hope for our sake it's still going on.'

Charles: 'Why?'
Camilla: 'Well, because if it stops he will come down here on Thursday night.'
Charles: 'Oh no!'
Camilla: 'Yes, but I don't think it will stop, do you?'
Charles: 'No neither do I. Umm ... just our luck.'
Camilla: 'It would be just our luck.'
Charles: 'It's bound to.'
Camilla: 'No it won't. You mustn't think like that. Think positive, mustn't we?'
Charles: 'I'm not very good at that.'
Camilla: 'Well, I'm going to because if I don't, I'll despair. Gone to sleep?'
Charles: 'No. How maddening.'
Camilla: 'I know. Anyway he's doing his best to change it – David – but I just thought, you know, I might just ask Charlie.'
Charles: 'Did he say anything. Did Charlie say anything?'
Camilla: 'No. I haven't talked to him.'
Charles: 'You haven't?'
Camilla: 'Well, I just talked to him briefly, but, you know, I just thought I, I just don't know whether he's got any children at home, that's the worry.'
Charles: 'Right.'
Camilla: 'Oh ... darling, I think I'll ...'
Charles: 'Pray, just pray.'
Camilla: 'It's so wonderful to have one night to set us on our way, wouldn't it?'
Charles: 'Wouldn't it. To wish you a happy Christmas.'
Camilla: 'Happy. Oh don't let's think about Christmas. I can't bear it. (Pause.) Going to go to sleep? I think you'd better, don't you? Darling?'
Charles: (sleepily) 'Yes, darling?'
Camilla: 'Will you ring me when you wake up?'
Charles: 'Yes I will.'
Camilla: 'Before I have these rampaging children around. It's Tom's birthday tomorrow. (Pause.) You all right?'
Charles: 'Mmmm. I'm all right.'
Camilla: 'Can I talk to you before, I hope, before those rampaging children?'
Charles: 'What time do they come in?'
Camilla: 'Well, usually Tom never wakes up at all, but as it's his birthday tomorrow he might just stagger out of bed. It won't be before half-past-eight. (Pause.) Night, night, my darling.'

Charles: 'Darling.'
Camilla: 'I do love you.'
Charles: (Sleepy) 'Before …'
Camilla: 'Before about half-past-eight.'
Charles: 'Try and ring?'
Camilla: 'Yes, if you can. Night, darling, love you.'
Charles: 'Love you, too, don't want to say goodbye.'
Camilla: 'Well done for doing that. You're a clever old thing. An awfully good brain lurking there, isn't there? Darling, I think you ought to give the brain a rest now, night night.'
Charles: 'Night darling, God bless.'
Camilla: 'I do love you, and I'm so proud of you.'
Charles: 'Oh, so proud of you.'
Camilla: 'Don't be so silly, I've never achieved anything.'
Charles: 'Yes you have.'
Camilla: 'No I haven't.'
Charles: 'Yes you have.'
Camilla: 'Don't want to have an argument now.'
Charles: 'Your great achievement is to love me.'
Camilla: 'Oh, darling, easier than falling off a chair.'
Charles: 'You suffer all these indignities, tortures and calumnies.'
Camilla: 'Oh darling, don't be so silly. I'd suffer anything for you. That's love, it's the strength of love. Night-night.'
Charles: 'Night, darling. Sounds as though you're dragging an enormous piece of string behind you, with hundreds of, um, tin pots and cans attached to it.'
Camilla: 'Really, I'm sorry, I think it must be your telephone. Night night before the battery goes. (Blows kiss.) Night, love you.'
Charles: 'Don't want to say goodbye.'
Camilla: 'Neither do I, but you must get some sleep.'

There are then a lot of goodbyes and 'I love you' with both of them reluctant to end the call. Eventually, Charles takes the initiative.

Charles: 'Going, going, g'bye. I'm going to press the tit.'
Camilla: 'All right, darling. I wish you were pressing mine.'
Charles: 'God, I wish I was.'

The call then finishes with more 'love you's', 'adore you's' and 'good nights' as Charles drifts off into sleep.

INDEX

Acland, Henry 83, 85
Acland, Sir Richard 85–6
Afghanistan war (2001) 39, 334, 335
Aitken, Ian 308
Aitken, Jonathan 361
Al Fayed, Mohamed 144, 350, 359, 361, 371
Al Qaida 364
Alexander QC, Robert 156
Alexandra, Princess 142
Allason, Rupert 285–6
Allen, Dave 101–2, 269
Amin, Idi 134–5, 165
Andrew, Prince 17, 22
Anne, Princess 20, 22
Appleyard, Christena 190–1, 205, 257
Archer, Jeffrey 133, 156, 239, 350–2, 357
Archer, Mary 351
Archer, Sir Peter 318
Arnold, Harry 17, 19, 373
Ashcroft, Michael 43
Ashcroft, Peggy 70, 85
Asher, Jane 102
Aspel, Michael 337
Assad, Hafez Al, President of Syria 39
Associated Newspapers 117

Baddeley, Jean 245–6
Ball, Alan 174–5, 178, 179
Bankers Trust 306, 311
Banks, David 190, 325–8, 338
Banks, John 217, 241–2
Barron, Jim 173–4
Batson, John 91
Bauwens, Mona 53, 263
BBC 252
Beale, Simon Russell 81
Beatles 101, 108, 118–19
Beavan John 127
Beaverbrook, Lord 91, 239
Beckett, Margaret 126
Beeching, Lord 94
Beevor, Anthony 323
Benn, Tony 50, 365
Berry, Wendy 24–5
Bevan, Nye 41
Biggs, Ronald 125
Birk, Ellis 157, 158
Birt, John 41
Bishopsgate Investment Management (BIM) 291, 315

Black, Conrad 30
Black, Guy 28
Blair, Tony xi, xii, xiii, 33–40, 41, 42, 43, 44–9, 50, 51, 56, 145, 156, 188, 198, 199, 327, 330, 334, 338, 344–5, 348, 349, 352–3, 359, 364, 366–7
Blake, John 220, 239, 261, 280
Blank, Sir Victor 332
Blunkett, David 40
Bolland, Mark xii, 28, 362, 371
Boothby, Lord 131
Bourgeois, Joska 42
Bower, Tom 42, 240
Boxall, Pat 280
Boyle, Edward 146
Bhoyrul, Anil 333
BPPC 261
Brady, Ian 222
Bramall, Field Marshal Lord 250
Bremner, Billy 173–4, 176, 181
British Printing Corporation (BPC) x, 253
Brockington, John 251–2
Brown, Gordon 34, 35, 40, 41, 48, 51, 338, 344
Brown, Divine 348
Bryan, John 16, 22, 23, 24, 27, 315
Bryant, Tommy 106, 113
BSE ('Mad Cow Disease') 341–2, 353, 370
Buckingham Palace 16, 18, 19, 22, 23, 25, 27, 29, 30
Buckley, Sheila 161, 162–3, 165
Bucks Herald 89–103, 204, 369
Burrington, Ernie 204–5, 261, 280–1, 285, 289–95, 298, 304–5, 307–8, 310–13, 315–16, 322, 370
Bush, George 272, 318
Bush, George W. 188, 364
Butler, Richard Austen ('Rab') 147
Butler, Tommy 97, 98–9, 110

Callaghan, James 148, 158
Callan, Paul 184, 185–6, 191, 221
Campbell, Alastair 16, 34, 35, 36, 37, 40, 42, 43–9, 56, 198–9, 292, 293, 327, 331, 341, 344, 346, 349, 371
Campbell, Naomi 27
Carman QC, George 54, 266
Carpenter, Humphrey 69–70
Carpenter, Les 201, 209, 210, 213, 318

Carter, President Jimmy 318
Ceasescu, Elena 257, 284
Ceausescu, Nicolae 257, 284
Chamberlain, Neville 48
Champion, Ralph 125
Channon, Paul 48
Charles, Prince of Wales 15–20, 21, 23, 24, 25, 27–9, 34, 45, 210, 362, 368, 373–9
Chase Manhattan Bank 306
Cher 265–6
Chicago Tribune Group 271
Chisholm, Sam 328–9, 345, 348
Christ Church 83
Christ Church Cathedral Choir School 73–4
Christiansen, Arthur 91, 183
Christiansen, Mike 131, 183
CIA (Central Intelligence Agency) 162, 163, 164
Citibank 301
City Slickers 332–4 *see also* Bhoyrul, Anil and Hipwell, James
Clapham train crash 236–7
Clark, Alan 358
Clark, Sir Robert 213, 278, 293–5, 311–14, 317, 324, 326, 370
Cleese, John 81
Clements Alan 278, 293–5, 311, 317, 326, 370
Clifford, Max xii, 55, 371
Clifton College 75–84, 86, 232
CNN 284
Cobb QC, John 154–5, 156, 159
Cobb-Taylor report 156–8
Coghlan, Monica 350, 357
Cole, Bob 272, 274
Collier-Wright Charles 266
Confait, Maxwell 138–9
Conservative Party 43, 51, 86, 94, 103, 107, 143, 146, 147, 148, 153, 167, 232, 264, 330, 342, 347–8, 351, 360
Cook, Peter 20, 245–6, 329
Cook, Trevor 315–16
Cooper Lybrand 279, 281
Cooper, Leo 159–60, 164
Corbett, Gerald 114
Cordle, John 152–3, 155, 159
Corrie, Hugh 189, 232
Cousins, Maurice 93–4, 96, 104
Coventry Evening Telegraph 89
Cowdrey, Colin 124–5
Cox, Steve 90, 94
Crick, Michael 351
Crofton, Sir Malby 168
Croker, Ted 179

Crossman, Richard 107
Crother, Rachel 74
Cudlipp, Hugh xi, xiii, 117–20, 125, 127, 128, 129, 130, 131, 132, 157, 183, 187, 203, 205, 213, 217–18, 220, 223, 247, 332–3, 368
Cummings, John 110
Cunningham, Andrew 152
Cunningham, Jack 152

Daily Express 91, 108, 117, 135, 151, 195, 243, 299, 346–7, 352, 364
Daily Herald 119, 203
Daily Mail xii, 29, 43, 177, 187, 191, 193, 287, 334, 347, 350, 362, 364–5, 367
Daily Mirror ix, x, xi, xii, xiii, 15, 16, 17, 19, 20, 22, 23, 24, 27, 28, 30, 43, 47, 48, 51, 52, 105, 106, 115, 117–20, 124, 126, 127–31, 133, 152, 155–8, 161–4, 174, 176, 178–81, 183, 186–92, 194–8, 200–1, 203, 205, 206, 208–10, 214–26, 230–41, 244–51, 253–5, 257–9, 261–3, 266, 268–71, 274, 276–7, 279, 281, 283–6, 288, 291–3, 296–300, 302, 304–18, 321, 323–5, 337–9, 341–4, 346, 347, 349–52, 354, 355, 358, 361, 363–8, 369, 370, 373
Daily Record 209, 281, 296, 309, 313
Daily Sketch 117
Daily Star 126, 204, 224, 350–1, 364, 370
Daily Telegraph 44, 92, 238, 248, 261, 365
Dallaglio, Lawrence 358
Daniels, Danny 126
Davies, Nick 123, 282, 285–9, 294, 296
Day, Sir Robin 148
Dendy, Reverend David 74
Denning, Lord 26, 145, 156, 170–1
Department of Trade and Industry (DTI) ix, x, 34, 154, 157, 264, 282, 295, 310, 317–18, 332, 370
Desmond, Richard 216, 347
Diana, Princess of Wales 15–19, 21–5, 27–30, 45, 210, 235, 359, 368
Dimont, Madelon 128
Dinkins, David 303

Dobson, Frank 40
Douglas Home, Sir Alec 147
Douglas, Michael 26
Downing Street ('Number Ten') xi, 33, 36, 37, 39, 43, 44, 45, 48, 49, 54, 141, 151, 156, 165, 363, 367
Duckworth, Roger 91, 92, 94, 103, 369
Duncan Sandys, Lord 142
Duncan Smith, Iain 51
Dunkley, Frank 105–6, 107–8, 113, 114
Dunn, Martin 273, 338, 341

Eastoe, Roger 285, 295, 309, 314, 324, 326
Ecclestone, Bernie 41, 42–3
Edelman, Maurice xiii, 366
Edward, Prince 28, 29
Edwards, Bob 197–8, 203, 209, 213–14, 218–220, 223, 225, 226
Edwards, John 186, 187
Edwards, Martin 263, 357
El Vino ix, 185
Elizabeth II, Queen 19, 20, 21, 24, 27, 28, 29, 239
Epstein, Brian 108, 118
Ernst and Young 310–12
European Human Rights Act 24, 26
Evans, Harold 193, 347
Evans, Matthew 288
Evening News 106, 111, 113
Evening Standard 44, 106, 112, 113, 191, 362
Express Group 346, 351

Ferguson, Alex 47
Ferrari Press Agency 105–6, 112, 113
Ferrari, Dan 105–6, 115–16, 120, 121, 124, 127, 369
Field, Frank 344
Filkin, Elizabeth 145–6
Financial Times 299, 301
Finney, Albert 70, 85, 101
Fischer, Gus 343, 346, 348
Fisher, Keith 259, 316
Fitzwalter, Ray 149, 155
Fleet Street ('Street of Shame') ix, x, xiv, 20, 21, 23, 96, 97, 99, 104, 105, 112, 113, 122, 129, 137, 191, 198, 200, 219, 221, 222, 226, 233, 234, 259, 270–1, 272, 318–19, 324, 326, 328, 331, 339, 341, 355, 370
Fleet Street News Agency 106

Flynn, Doug 348, 355, 362
Foot, Michael 335
Foot, Paul 52, 188–90, 255, 268, 318, 327–8, 351, 364, 371
Football Assocation (FA) 178–80
Foreign Office 43, 165
Foster, Albert 169–70
Fountain, Phil 90, 92, 94, 95, 103
de Fraine, Brian 89
Fraser, Frank 109, 110–11
Fraser, Lady Antonia 65
Freud, Matthew 371
Frolik, Josef 160–4
Frost, David 20, 41

Galloway, Andrew 292–4, 306–8, 310–11
Galloway, George 285
Gates, Bill 361
Gavin, Kent 135, 174, 201, 221
George, Eddie 301
Gielgud, John 70, 71–2, 85
Gilbey, James 17, 373
Golden Jubilee of Queen Elizabeth II 19
Goldman Sachs 301
Goldsmith, Sir James 365
Goody, Gordon 97–8
Gorbachev, Mikhail 282–4, 303
Gorbachev, Raisa 267
Grant, Hugh 348
Great Train Robbery 96–8, 108
Green, Felicity 127, 192
Greenslade, Roy 258, 267–8, 283, 285
Gregory, Albro B 136–7
Grey 216–17
Griffin, Charles 255, 308
Grobelaar, Bruce 54, 179
Groves, Wendy 90, 95
Guardian 210, 305, 308, 329, 338, 360, 365
Guest, Lawrie 208, 281–2, 289–95, 304, 307–8, 310–12, 316, 370
Gulf War 264, 272, 364, 370
Gulf War Syndrome 341–2

Hagerty, Bill 267, 309, 313, 324
Hague, William 43
Haines, Joe 142, 164, 199, 200, 220, 232, 234, 240, 241, 250, 258, 259, 262, 267–8, 280–1, 287, 292, 293, 295–6, 299, 304, 309, 317, 323, 327, 347, 371

Hall, Margaret 126
Hall, Phil 357–9, 361, 371
Hambro 299, 317, 323
Hamilton, Neil 144
Hammond inquiry 38, 39
Harmsworth, St John 111–12
Harris of Peckham, Lord 281
Harrison, Fred 221–2
Harry, Gareth 89–90, 93, 94, 96, 103–4
Harry, Prince 28
Hartley QC, Richard 54
Hastings, Stephen 164–5
Hatton, Derek 50
Havers, Michael 164, 318
Hazell, Gordon 79–81, 229
Head, Robert 201, 206, 221, 333
Headington Hill Hall 216, 252–3, 255
Healey, Denis 221
Heath, Edward 134, 142, 147, 148, 151, 167, 318
Hemburrow, Gill xiv, 225, 298
Hendry, Tom 238
Henry, Wendy 258, 261–2
Herbertson, Ian 309, 316, 328
Hersh, Seymour 285–6, 288–9
Herzog, Chaim 304
Higgins, Stuart 345
Hill Samuel 213, 278
Hillsborough disaster 236–8
Hindley, Myra 222
Hinduja passport affair 33, 35, 36, 37, 45
Hinduja brothers 36
Hinduja, S.P. 361
Hinton, Les 343, 347, 350, 358
Hipwell, James 333
Hitchen, Brian 126, 370
Hither Green train crash 114
Hobday, Alan 280, 338
Hockey, Jeff 91, 99
Hoffman, Jerome 143, 146, 148–9
Holgate, Ellen Eliza 59
Holland, Jackie 112
Hollick, Lord 231, 299, 316, 321, 323, 327, 331, 346–7
Holloran, John 261
Horne, Alistair 167
Horwood, Vic 281, 289–91, 294–5, 298, 304, 310–13, 326
House of Commons 48–9, 141, 145, 146, 149, 153, 154, 158, 162, 163, 164, 180, 211, 265, 285, 345
House of Lords 42, 46, 51, 127, 133, 167

Howard, Lee 117, 128, 130
Howard, Michael 360
Howard, Trevor 81
Humperdinck, Engelbert 26, 200
Hunt, Sir John 162, 164
Husak, Captain Robert 160, 163
Hussein, Saddam 53, 54

Independent 30, 35, 326, 365
Independent on Sunday 297
Ingham, Sir Bernard 30
International Publishing Corporation (IPC) 119, 129, 148, 203, 213
Irvine QC (later Lord Chancellor), Alexander ('Derry') 156–7, 159

Jackson, Jesse 317
Jackson, John 123, 174, 297, 355
Jackson, Michael 266, 322, 338–9, 342, 353
Jacobson, Sydney 127
James, Paula 20
Jameson, Derek 214, 252, 321
Janvrin, Robin 22
Jarratt, Alex 129, 205, 209, 213, 215, 318
Jay, Peter 243, 250, 252, 258
Jenkins, Hugh 170
Jenkins, Roy 50
Jenkinson, John 118, 151, 285
Jenour, Kenelm 124, 370
John, Elton 239
Johnson, Frank 238
Jones, Chief Superintendent Alan 138–9
Jones, Elwyn 318
Jones, Lydia 65–6
Jones, Tom 200
Jones, Vince 65–6
Josef 274–6
Junor, John 113
Junor, Penny 16, 17

Kagan, Lord 141
Keays, Sarah 232, 264–5
Keble College 69, 83–4
Keeler, Christine 167
Keen, Barry 93, 96
Kegworth disaster 236–7
Kennedy, President John Fitzgerald 101
Khashoggi, Adnan 270
King, Cecil x, 119–20, 131, 148, 151, 203, 206
Kinnock, Glenys 50, 56, 244

Kinnock, Neil xi, 34, 45, 47, 50–1, 199, 210, 244, 292, 300, 327, 331, 338, 344
Knight, Andrew 338, 343, 345
Kray brothers 110, 111
Kray, Ronnie 131

Labour Party xi, xiii, 34, 50, 51, 52, 94, 107–8, 119, 126, 127, 147, 196, 201, 205, 210, 220, 221, 222, 232, 244, 270, 291, 299–300, 318, 327, 331, 334–5, 338, 366
see also New Labour
Lady Ghislaine 270–1, 272, 296, 300, 302
Lamb, Larry xi, 131, 151, 337, 347
Lamont, Norman 318
Lancaster, Terence 162, 215
Lane, Caroline 81, 85, 232
Lane, Michael ('Willy') 81–2, 83, 84–5, 86, 369
Langdon, Julia 216
Leeds United 173–8, 180–1
Lehmans (Lehman Brothers) 301
Lennon, John 101
Lennox, Ken 266
Liberal Party 142, 149
Liverpool Echo 194
L!VE TV 330
Lloyd Webber, Andrew 184
Lloyd, Nick 200, 204, 321–2
Lockerbie disaster 48, 236
Long, Douglas 201, 205, 209, 213–14
Longford, Lord 110
Lonrho 142, 340
Lunn, Julie 91–2, 93, 94, 103, 369

MacArthur, Brian xiii
McCartney, Paul 102
McDonald, Ian 269–70, 272, 309, 316, 328, 343
McGowan, Frankie 263
McGregor, Lord 18
McIntosh, Ian 292, 294, 311
MacKenzie, Kelvin xi, xiii, 55, 112–13, 117, 190, 219, 224, 234, 238–9, 267, 326, 328–32, 334, 337–8, 340–1, 343, 345, 347, 364, 370
Macleod, Iain 147
Macmillan, Harold 101, 147, 166–7
McQueen, Alastair 246–8, 321
Mail on Sunday xii, 44, 191, 262, 298
Maitland, Lady Olga 113

Major, John 27, 41, 54, 145, 155, 339, 345, 348
Manchester United 240, 263, 357
Mandelson, Peter 28, 33–40, 42, 45, 46, 47, 48, 49, 51, 52, 199, 327, 344, 353
Manifold, Laurie 204
Margaret, Princess 117
Marples, Ernest xii, 166–71, 183
Marshall, Bill 184–5, 191
Martin, Andrea 282, 288, 296
Martin, Tony 360
Matthews, Bruce 234, 342
Maudling, Martin 150
Maudling, Reginald xii, 143–59, 210
Maxwell Communications Corporation (MCC) 278, 298, 299, 301, 304, 310, 318
Maxwell, Betty 297, 300
Maxwell, Ian 281, 297, 299, 305–6, 370
Maxwell, Kevin 289, 297–9, 301–2, 309–10, 370
Maxwell, Robert ix–xi, xiii, 19, 47, 54, 94–5, 103, 119, 141, 142–3, 188–9, 198, 205, 209–11, 213–27, 229–36, 239–59, 262–3, 266–318, 323, 326, 327, 329, 331, 332, 334, 335, 337–40, 352, 366, 371
Mayhew, Vic 127, 337
Mellor, David 27, 53–5, 264
Mellor, Phil 242–3
Mencken, H.L. xiii–xiv, 141
Merritt, John 47, 198–9
Metro 362
MGN (Mirror Group Newspapers) *see* Mirror Group
MI5 56
MI6 160, 163–5
Microsoft 361
Miles, Tony 130–1, 183, 185, 186, 190, 194, 200, 201, 204, 205, 209–210, 213–14, 218, 220
Milhench, Ronald 138
Millar, Fiona 45, 47, 199
Millennium Dome 34, 36, 38
Miller, Eric 141–2, 143, 150, 151
Mills, Jack 96, 97
Ministry of Agriculture 341–2
Ministry of Defence (MoD) 341–2
Mirror Group Newspapers (MGN) ix–x, 186, 190, 197, 203–5, 209, 210, 213, 217, 231, 234, 253, 258–9, 261, 267, 269, 281, 289, 294, 298, 301, 304–7, 311–12, 317, 329, 331, 370
Mirror plc x
Mitterand, François 24
Molloy, Mike 127, 129–30, 131, 181, 183–4, 188, 189, 194, 200, 204, 209–210, 213–15, 218–20, 223–4, 226, 241, 245–6, 267, 340
Montgomery, David ix–x, xiii, 19, 190, 204, 253, 268, 317, 319, 321–35, 338, 340–2, 346, 366, 368, 370
Moore, Bobby 174
Moore, Sally 123
Morgan, Jean 268
Morgan, Piers 189, 330–31, 333–5, 348, 363, 367–8
Morris, William (later Lord Nuffield) 61–2
Morton, Andrew 15, 16, 18, 23
Mossad 285–7, 289, 292, 299
Mountbatten, Lord 120
Mowlam, Mo 35
Mugabe, Robert 286
Murdoch, Dame Elisabeth 337
Murdoch, Rupert xi, 29, 41, 107, 119, 128, 213, 233–4, 244, 252, 253, 254, 258, 262, 267, 270, 281, 282, 297, 301, 317, 321–5, 327, 328–30, 332, 337–40, 342–50, 355, 358, 361–2, 364–5, 367–8, 370
Murray, Braham 81, 85

National Graphical Association 207, 271, 339
National Health Service (NHS) 40, 51, 344, 361
National Heart Hospital 120
National Union of Journalists (NUJ) 113, 123, 133, 255, 279–80, 324
NatWest Bank x, 41, 156, 213, 281, 289, 309, 315
Neil, Andrew 18, 289, 345
New Labour xi, xii–xiii, 33, 34, 38, 39, 40, 41, 42, 43, 46, 49, 50, 330, 334, 345, 349, 354, 361, 363, 366–8, 371
New Statesman 41, 42
New York Daily News 269–71, 273, 281, 291, 299, 338, 341
News Corporation xiii, 338, 347–8
News International (NI) 234, 270, 277, 323, 328, 337, 338, 342–4, 345–50, 354–5, 358, 362, 365

News of the World 28, 35, 222, 239, 258, 261, 262, 322, 325, 340, 348, 353, 357–62, 371
Newson, Leslie 139–40
Nicholson, Harold 146–7
Nixon, President Richard 166
Northcliffe, Lord 120, 137
Nottingham Forest 173–4
Nureyev, Rudolf 96
Nyerere, Julius 134

O'Brien, Mike 37
O'Toole, Peter 196, 236
Oborne, Peter 43
Obote, Milton 134
Observer xiv, 36, 38, 152, 155, 198, 210, 214–15, 262, 267
Odhams 119, 203
Ogilvy, Angus 142
Onassis, Christina 242–3
Otton, Mr Justice 55, 56
Owen, Will 160, 163
Oxford 57, 61–70, 73
Oxford United 173, 223, 371

Page, Dick and Penny 225
Paige, Elaine 184–5
Palestinian Liberation Organisation (PLO) 53, 54, 264
Palmer, Frank 126, 180, 370
Palmer, Jill 51
Panorama 284–5
Parker Bowles, Andrew 17
Parker Bowles, Camilla 15, 17, 18, 19–20, 27, 28, 34, 45, 362, 373–9
Parker, Sir Peter 309
Parkinson, Anne 264
Parkinson, Cecil 232, 264
Peacock, Lilian Mary ('Lily P') 64, 75, 76, 85
Penrose, John 186, 192–4, 195–6, 197–8, 242–7, 253, 261, 329
People 30, 53, 55, 125, 176, 197, 198, 200, 203–7, 209, 210, 214–16, 221–3, 225–6, 239, 253, 258, 259, 261–4, 265, 267, 269, 274, 280–1, 283, 309, 313, 321–2, 324–5, 332, 338, 342
Pergamon Press 142–3, 216, 244, 252, 255, 281
Philip, Prince, Duke of Edinburgh 17, 20, 21, 22, 29, 30
Pickford, Bertha see Stott, Bertha
Pickford, John Joseph 58–9
Piggott, Lester 221

Pilger, John 184, 186–9, 364
Pincher, Chapman 164
Pinnington, Geoff 128, 203, 204, 322
Pole, John 255, 308
Pollard, Eve 322
Portillo, Michael 348
Poulson, John 143, 144, 146, 148, 149–55
Powell, Enoch 147, 148, 359–60
Prendergast, Peter 124–5
Prendergast, Teddy 130
Prescott, John 33, 366
Press Complaints Commission (PCC) 18, 28, 29, 44
Preston, Peter 365
Priestland, Gerald xiv
Private Eye 52, 118, 149, 189, 244–5, 265
Profumo affair 101, 170
Proops, Marje (Marjorie) 127, 130, 151, 184, 191–2, 194–5, 221, 279, 321

Queen Mother 43, 45, 104

Rachman, Peter 101, 168
Racing Times 291
Radio One 234
Ramsey, Sir Alf 180
Rantzen, Esther 55
Raphael, Adam 152
Reade, Brian 334
Reagan, President Ronald 286, 318
Redgrave, Michael 81
Reed/Reed International x, 129, 148, 200, 201, 208–9, 213, 214, 271, 278, 281, 314
Reveille 190
Revie, Don 173–81, 183, 200, 370
Reynolds, Brice 98, 99
Richardson, Charlie 98–9, 108–9, 110, 111
Richardson, Eddie 99, 108–110, 111
Richman, Alfred 122–3
Ricketts, Ron 123, 181
Riddell, Mary 191, 265, 350
Robert Maxwell Estates 294
Robert Maxwell Group 290, 306
Robert Maxwell Holdings 281
Roberts, Albert 152–3, 155, 159
Roberts, Taff 90
Robinson, Anne 186, 192–6, 199, 244, 267, 341, 347, 371
Robinson, Dr Ann 139–40
Robinson, Geoffrey 34–5, 41–2

Rogers, John 106, 196
Rothermere, Viscount 29
Routledge, Paul 334
Rowe, Bridget 309, 332
Rowland, Tiny 142
Royal Family 16, 18, 20, 21, 27, 29, 30, 45
Rudman, Michael 85
Rusbridger, Alan 365

Samuel Montagu 277–9, 281, 292, 307, 310–11
Scargill, Arthur 256, 263
Scotland Yard 15, 18, 23, 151, 154, 204, 301, 310, 318
Scott, Norman 142
Scragg, Air Vice-Marshal Sir Colin 102, 248–9
Scragg, Penny 102 *see also* Stott, Penny
SDP (Social Democratic Party) 220
September 11th 334, 363
Seymour, David 327, 331, 344
Shaffer, Peter 101
Shah, Eddie 235, 322, 339–40
Shamir, Yitzhak 303
Shapiro, Helen 101
Sharkey, John 346
Sherwin-White (later Sherwin), David 68, 69
Simpson, Charlie 59
Simpson, Dr Keith 139–40
Singleton, Valerie 20
Sky xiv, 263, 328, 330, 345
Slater, Richard 134–5
Smith, Chris 36
Smith, Delia 127
Smith, John (journalist) 125, 204, 370
Smith, John (leader of Labour Party) xi, 51, 327, 331, 344
Smith, Kevin 370
Smith, T. Dan 149, 152
Soames, Nicholas 16, 341–2
SOGAT (Society of Grpahical and Allied Trades) 271
South East London Mercury 111, 113
Sparrow, John 88, 127
Spectator 43, 44, 187
Sporting Life 203, 206, 281
Sprake, Gary 173, 175–7
Stab in the Back (The White Hart pub) ix, 125, 186, 197–8, 337
Stephens, Alan 311
Stephens, Peter 242–3
Stevens, Lord 231
Stoddart, Michael 261, 267,
269, 273–4, 309
Stokoe, Bob 177–8
Stonehouse, Barbara 161, 163, 165
Stonehouse, John xii, 124, 160–6, 337
Stoney, Michael 281–2, 290–1, 293–5, 304, 306, 311, 370
Stott, Amelia (paternal grandmother of Richard) 58
Stott, Bertha (mother of Richard) 58–65, 70, 72–3, 75–6, 89–90, 369
Stott, Christopher (son of Richard) xiv, 55–6, 132, 225, 273, 283
Stott, Emily (daughter of Richard) xiv, 132, 225, 256
Stott, Fred Brooks (father of Richard) 57–9, 60–4, 70–1, 73, 75
Stott, Hannah (daughter of Richard) xiv, 132, 225, 283, 330
Stott, John (elder brother of Richard) 61, 75, 76, 82–3, 87–8, 90, 252
Stott, John (paternal grandfather of Richard) 58
Stott, Judith (elder sister of Richard) 61, 65, 70–2, 82, 101, 102, 369
Stott, Patricia (elder sister of Richard) 61
Stott, Penny (née Scragg, wife of Richard) xiv, 102, 132, 225, 248–9, 251, 283, 292
Stott, Richard
  as reporter on *Daily Mirror* ix, xiv; as columnist on *Daily Mirror* xiv; as editor of *Daily Mirror* ix, xiv; as features editor of *Daily Mirror* ix, xiv; as editor of *Today* xiv, 25; sacked as editor of *Daily Mirror* 19, 34; as editor of *People* 30, 53–5; conversations with Mrs Thatcher 52; David Mellor affair 53–5; Esther Rantzen court case 55–6; birth 63; childhood and adolescence 63–86; at Christ Church Cathedral Choir School 73–5; at Clifton College 75–84; interview at Keble College 83–4; joins Ferrari Press Agency 105; joins *Bucks Herald* 90; joins *Daily Mirror* as reporter 119; marries Penny 132; sent to